Pro Windows Server
AppFabric

Stephen Kaufman
Danny Garber

Pro Windows Server AppFabric

Copyright © 2010 by Stephen Kaufman and Danny Garber

ISBN-13 (pbk): 978-1-4302-2817-2

ISBN-13 (electronic): 978-1-4302-2818-9

Printed and bound in the United States of America 9 8 7 6 5 4 3 2 1

President and Publisher: Paul Manning
Lead Editor: Jonathan Gennick
Technical Reviewers: Ewan Fairweather and Scott Zimmerman
Editorial Board: Clay Andres, Steve Anglin, Mark Beckner, Ewan Buckingham, Gary Cornell, Jonathan Gennick, Jonathan Hassell, Michelle Lowman, Matthew Moodie, Duncan Parkes, Jeffrey Pepper, Frank Pohlmann, Douglas Pundick, Ben Renow-Clarke, Dominic Shakeshaft, Matt Wade, Tom Welsh
Coordinating Editor: Debra Kelly
Copy Editor: Patrick Meader
Compositor: Bytheway Publishing Services
Indexer: Julie Grady
Artist: April Milne
Cover Designer: Anna Ishchenko

Distributed to the book trade worldwide by Springer-Verlag New York, Inc., 233 Spring Street, 6th Floor, New York, NY 10013. Phone 1-800-SPRINGER, fax 201-348-4505, e-mail orders-ny@springer-sbm.com, or visit http://www.springeronline.com.

For information on translations, please e-mail rights@apress.com, or visit http://www.apress.com.

Apress and friends of ED books may be purchased in bulk for academic, corporate, or promotional use. eBook versions and licenses are also available for most titles. For more information, reference our Special Bulk Sales–eBook Licensing web page at http://www.apress.com/info/bulksales.

The source code for this book is available to readers at http://www.apress.com.

I dedicate this book to my wife, Cathy, and to Jared and Alyssaa—thank you for all your help and support.
—Stephen Kaufman

I dedicate this book to my family: Inna, my dearest friend and wife; and my lovely daughters, Bella and Letal—for their love, support, and faith in me.
—Danny Garber

Contents at a Glance

Contents

About the Authors

■ **Stephen Kaufman** is an Architect with Microsoft Consulting Services who focuses on middle-tier technologies and has worked with BizTalk since the original BizTalk CTP in 1999. He is also an author, trainer, and speaker. He has written a many articles, including Microsoft Knowledge Base articles; a BizTalk tools whitepaper; an article in the Microsoft Architecture Journal; and several others. He was a contributing author for the BizTalk Certification Exam 74-135. Stephen also writes a blog focused on integration technologies at `http://blogs.msdn.com/skaufman` and is a co-author on the popular Pro BizTalk 2009 book. He also speaks internationally at events such as TechEd North America, TechEd Europe, Microsoft's SOA & BPM Conference, Microsoft's Developer Days, as well as many other conferences and events.

■ **Danny Garber** is an US Azure Community Lead Architect and SOA Integration Solution Architect with the Microsoft Services North America CTO Team. He joined Microsoft in July 2006 as an SOA and BizTalk Server Integration SME. From November 2007 to June 2009, Danny was an East Region Integration Community Lead Architect. During his more than 22 years of IT experience, 14 of them in a role of a software architect, Danny has been engaged on various consulting engagements assisting customers to plan and implement .NET, BizTalk Server, and SOA solutions, helping them address various best practices and technologies. Danny is an active member of Microsoft Azure, SOA, and BizTalk Product Team Insiders groups helping to shape the current and future of Microsoft Azure and BizTalk Server product, SOA Service Offerings, and Software + Services (S+S) strategy.

Prior to joining Microsoft, Danny was a Delivery Excellence Leader of Microsoft Practice in IBM Global Services, where he served as a member of SOA Competency Architect Team practicing and enhancing IBM SOA methodology and IBM SOA reference architecture on the Microsoft platform.

Danny often speaks at technology events, including the Microsoft SOA & BP Conference, TechEd, TechReady, and IBM SHARE. He has also written many whitepaper and magazine articles, which were published in *Microsoft Systems Journal* and for the MSDN Online Library.

Danny is a Microsoft Certified Architect (MCA), IBM Certified Architect, Microsoft Certified Solution Developer (MCSD), and Certified Technical Specialist (MCTS) in BizTalk Server 2006.

He can be reached at dannyg@microsoft.com or through his blog at: http://blogs.msdn.com/dannyg/.

About the Technical Reviewers

Ewan Fairweather is a Program Manager in the Business Platform Division (BPD) at Microsoft, where he works on the Customer Advisory Team (CAT), focusing on BizTalk, other application tier technologies, and SQL Server.

Prior to this, Ewan spent three years working for Microsoft UK in the Premier Field Engineering team. In this role, he worked with enterprise customers, helping them to maintain and optimize their BizTalk applications. Ewan has also worked in a dedicated capacity on some of the world's largest BizTalk deployments, predominantly within financial services.

Ewan co-authored the successful Professional BizTalk Server 2006 book, and he has written many whitepapers for Microsoft, including the "Microsoft BizTalk Server Performance Optimization" guide, which is available on Microsoft's MSDN website. Prior to joining Microsoft, Ewan worked as a Cisco Certified Academy Instructor (CCAI) for a regional training organization, delivering advanced routing and networking courses. Ewan holds a first class honors Bachelor of Science degree in Computing with Management from the University of Leeds. Ewan's hobbies include reading, taking part in as many sports as possible, and regularly going to the gym.

Scott Zimmerman (MCSD, MCTS BizTalk Server, MCTS ADO.NET 3.5, and MCTS WinForms 3.5) is a Solutions Architect with Microsoft. He has authored several books and articles, and he has won two awards for web service design. He enjoys jogging, biking, and tennis with his wife Vera in Washington, D.C., where they try to keep a low carbon footprint.

Acknowledgments

First off, I want to thank my co-author on this book, without whom this book would not have been possible. I have learned a ton in my years working with Danny, and we continued learning together during the process of putting this book together. I am looking forward to many more years of learning from each other.

I would also like to thank Jonathan Gennick at Apress for working with us as we shaped the thoughts and ideas that became the foundation for this book and for helping us navigate through all the little things that came up through the process of writing this book. I would also like to the rest of the team at Apress, especially Debra Kelly and Patrick Meader for all their work organizing, arranging, and editing.

Next, I would like to thank the exceptional technical reviewers for all their help and insight. The book is of much better quality as a result of their efforts. Scott and Ewan worked tirelessly and their comments, insights, and suggestions were right on.

In addition, I would like to thank everyone on the AppFabric team at Microsoft for all their hard work, answering our questions and working with us through the beta process to ensure we had all the material we needed to write the content.

Finally, I would like to thank my family members for all their support and understanding.

Stephen Kaufman

The idea of writing a book about the Windows Server AppFabric belongs to Stephen and dates back to the late spring of 2009, when Stephen and I were both presenting on various sessions at the TechEd 2009 conference in Los Angeles. At that time, Stephen approached me with his idea of writing a book about a Microsoft initiative codenamed *Dublin*, which both of us had been vaguely familiar with through a series of internal meetings in Redmond. Of course, I didn't know what I signing up for. Nor did I know how much effort and creativity it would take from both of us to make this book a reality.

That said, this book is the result of a collaborative effort that involved a great number of bright people at both Microsoft and Apress.

We would like to thank our technical reviewers, Scott Zimmerman and Ewan Fairweather at Microsoft. They took the time to read through the draft material and provided us much needed feedback and criticism, while ensuring the correctness of the technical content. It is a pleasure for me to acknowledge their contributions and express my deepest appreciation for their efforts.

Jonathan Gennick at Apress deserves special mention for helping to lay the foundation for this book. His input has greatly influenced the final form and content of the book.

Special thanks go to Tony Meleg and Mark Berman from the AppFabric product team at Microsoft for providing substantial assistance with the book material, helping to get us the latest bids of the AppFabric previews and beta source code, and helping us to address various technical issues related to the writing of the sample business scenario code for this book.

We owe a great deal to the production and editing team at Apress, led by Debra Kelly and Patrick Meader, who helped us stay on a publishing schedule and ensured that this book conformed to accepted grammatical conventions.

Finally, this book might have never been written were it not for our families, who have supported us all the way through the process of writing this book.

Danny Garber

Introduction

Through the years, Microsoft has released various middle-tier technologies to help architects and developers design and implement n-tier solutions. And through the years, we have utilized these technologies to build our applications. Some of the technologies, such as COM+, have fallen out of favor, such as COM+; however, others, such as BizTalk, remain both popular and powerful.

When new tools are released, it's always natural to look at them and try to determine where they fit. It's important for you to determine whether they are replacement or complementary technologies. As you perform your analysis and make your comparisons, remember that Alan Kay once said that perspective is worth 80 IQ points. We, the authors, hope that reading this book will give you a solid understanding of where you can utilize AppFabric in the middle tier. We also hope it will help you understand when you should utilize AppFabric rather than other technologies.

It is the need for perspective that led us to undertake writing this book. As we looked to gain perspective on AppFabric ourselves, there were two areas that stood out to us. First, after working with middle-tier technologies for the past 15 years, we have seen how important and necessary it is to have information available on new technologies as they are released. This book has been published alongside the release of Windows Server AppFabric, and it is our hope that it will guide you along your path of designing, developing, and deploying your AppFabric applications. Second, when .NET was introduced, developers who used Microsoft tools began to move away from COM components and away from using COM+ as a hosting model. This move away from COM+ left a vacuum that so far has gone unfilled—a hosting vacuum that AppFabric promises to fill. In this book, we will walk you through how to utilize and take full advantage of this new technology.

We targeted architects and developers when we put this book together. These are the two groups that will be designing and implementing the solutions outlined in this book. It is our hope that this book will give you the know-how and tools needed to successfully implement an AppFabric solution.

This book begins by covering an overview of AppFabric. Next, it covers decision points for when to select AppFabric or BizTalk. As you move through the chapters, you will learn about developing an AppFabric application in the context of a practical business scenario, as well as by looking at the architecture of AppFabric and the services that it provides. The latter part of the book walks you through advanced concepts, as well as how to deploy, track, and monitor applications.

Chapter Descriptions

The following list describes the contents of each of this book's chapters:

Chapter 1: Introduction. This chapter defines AppFabric and outlines why you need it. It also looks at scenarios that you can address by using AppFabric.

Chapter 2: Choosing AppFabric. This chapter talks about who would benefit from AppFabric and when you should choose to use AppFabric. This comparison also looks at when you should use AppFabric and when you should use BizTalk.

Chapter 3: Laying the Foundation. This chapter examines the underlying foundation of AppFabric by taking a close look at IIS and Windows Process Activation Services (WAS) and how they relate to AppFabric. It also explores what the .NET Framework 4.0 will provide to help you build AppFabric applications.

Chapter 4: Understanding the Architecture. This chapter focuses directly on the architecture of AppFabric and its core services. It looks at monitoring and persistence, as well as AppFabric's core hosting services. It also looks at AppFabric's caching services. Finally, this chapter explains how all these parts fit together.

Chapter 5: Configuring AppFabric. This chapter drills down into how you install and configure AppFabric.

Chapter 6: Developing WCF Applications. This chapter looks at the new features contained in WCF, including how you can use these new features in your AppFabric application.

Chapter 7: Developing WF Applications. This chapter looks at the new features contained in WF, including how you can use these new features in your AppFabric application.

Chapter 8: Running AppFabric as a Host. This chapter explains how to configure AppFabric as a host to your application. It also covers the steps required to host a sample business scenario in AppFabric and introduces the AppFabric Dashboard.

Chapter 9: Deploying AppFabric Applications. This chapter focuses on how to deploy your AppFabric application through both the UI and PowerShell cmdlets.

Chapter 10: Advanced Concepts. This chapter explains how to incorporate advanced concepts into your application, including such topics such as content based routing, correlation, and long-running transactions.

Chapter 11: Montoring and Tracking. This chapter dives deeply into the monitoring and tracking services, explaining how you can manipulate them and incorporate them into your applications.

Chapter 12: Implementing High Availability. This chapter explores methods for implementing high availability in your AppFabric middle-tier architecture.

Chapter 13: Upgrading to AppFabric. This chapter walks you through accepted best practices for migrating your current applications to the .NET Framework 4.0; specifically, you will learn how to host them within an AppFabric host.

Source Code

The source code for this book is available to readers on the book's page at www.apress.com. Please feel free to visit the Apress site and download all the code at this site.

CHAPTER 1

■ ■ ■

Introduction

Implementing distributed systems, let alone systems that provide real business value, has been challenging to accomplish over the years. Non-distributed systems have always been the first type of application that developers start creating. As such, when developers start to enter the realm of distributed systems, they often take many issues for granted that pose significant challenges. These challenges might be obvious to veteran developers that have had to create hosts for these distributed processes, but they still seem to rear their ugly heads. The biggest challenge consistently has been that of tightly coupled systems. It becomes prohibitively expensive to make changes as needed to meet the demands of the business when systems contain tightly coupled components.

Distributed systems that implement large-scale business processes almost always run on a wide spectrum of technologies, both inside and outside the organization. Consider the number of technologies used in any of the large-scale applications you have been involved with. These applications typically include a RDBMS system, as well as a presentation-tier technology that can range from Windows Forms to Web forms to Silverlight rich Internet applications (RIAs). If these large-scale applications need to scale to support many users, they typically include a middle tier to host business components. This middle tier might utilize off-the-shelf software, but typically it utilizes a customized host created in .NET that you might host in IIS or implement as a Windows Service (these are background processes that run without a user interface).

You often create these custom middle-tier solutions with the idea that they are cheaper than purchasing an existing software package. However, you might find, , if you were to do the analysis, that within a year or two the cost of maintaining and enhancing the custom solution might easily exceed the cost of the off-the-shelf system and does not offer the loosely coupled, scalable system that your business needs to meet its ever-changing business scenarios.

Developers often take for granted how easy it is to create a two-tier environment. In that scenario, you only need to take care of the database tier and the presentation tier. While n-tier architectures have been implemented for years, the problems of how to host middle-tier components have existed from the beginning. Writing plumbing code and tightly integrated systems is not productive and provides no business value; developers have also learned that writing host code is hard to do and becomes complex quickly.

Introducing Windows Server AppFabric

At the Professional Developers Conference (PDC) in 2008, Microsoft announced a new product code named Dublin. Dublin, now called "Windows Server AppFabric" will provide a middle-tier hosting environment built on top of a proven platform of Windows Server and IIS. In AppFabric, Microsoft does what it does best. It provides plumbing that enables you to focus directly on implementing your business requirements. This allows you to get your application to production faster and provide the features that you expect from a middle-tier hosting system.

What is AppFabric? The simple answer is that it is an application server, but there is more to it than that, which you'll learn about momentarily. An easier question to answer is this: "Why do we need AppFabric?" Answering that question helps you frame what AppFabric is.

Evolution of Distributed Applications

So, why do you need AppFabric? You can answer that question by taking a trip in the WABAC Machine[1] (pronounced Wayback) to the days before .NET, to the days of COM and COM+. In those days, when you had to scale out your object-oriented and object-based applications, you created middle-tier code libraries and *hosted* them in COM+.

For those who have forgotten—or never had the opportunity to know, COM was a language-neutral implementation for software components that you could use in different environments—even across machine boundaries. COM also allowed you to reuse objects (components) without needing to know their internal implementation. It accomplished this by enforcing well-defined interfaces that were kept separate from the implementation code.

Difference Between Components and Services

You might wonder whether you can host a component and/or a service in AppFabric; the answer is yes. In any case, it's important to understand the difference between a component and a service. This topic has received attention for many years as various technologies have blurred the distinctions between the two.

When you look at the differences, you need to look first at reusability. Reusability is one of the foundations in a distributed environment. Components use an object-oriented paradigm that relies on a combination of encapsulation (state data) and exposed behavior (functions) in a class.

A component is a unit of compiled code that you can aggregate with other components to build applications. You can reuse a component in the same application, as well as with other applications. The basic concept is this: once a component is fully functional, it can help you reduce costs because you can leverage it as many times as makes sense, without having to rewrite the code that provides its functionality.

A service is implemented by one or more components, and it operates at a higher level of aggregation than a component. You use components to build services. The aggregation of components into a service provides a means to extend the concept of reuse to heterogeneous environments. This is difficult to accomplish with components because you typically relegate them to homogeneous environments. A service allows a component, or set of components, to accept and pass messages using open standards. A service, for the scope of this book, will follow the definition used with Service Oriented Architecture, and will adhere to the four tenets of service orientation. Services are independently versioned, deployed, operated, and secured in a message-oriented manner.

Service Hosting Environment

COM+ enhanced COM and included a hosting environment built into the operating system. COM+ made it easier to create large, distributed applications from the COM components it hosted. The COM+ host provided instance management (just-in-time activation), role-based security, and automated

---

[1] The WABAC Machine is a reference from Peabody's Improbable History from The Rocky and Bullwinkle cartoon. Mr. Peabody and Sherman used this machine to go back in time.

transaction management. It also provided better memory and processor management, distributed transactions, resource pooling, event publication, and subscription services (called COM+ events), as well as Queued Components.

You can build COM components to take advantage of the services just described in the hosting environment. However, COM, and thus COM components, was originally built to enable applications to interact with other applications and to promote code reuse locally. COM was not designed to work with remote computers. To support the need to perform remote method invocation, Microsoft created DCOM (Distributed COM). DCOM added a network protocol to COM that allows a developer to locate and invoke a component on a remote computer as if it were a local component. This provided the ability to distribute your component across different locations, according to the application requirements.

These COM and DCOM components that ran under the control of COM+ were called COM+ applications. COM+ has two types of applications: server and library applications. The components hosted in a library application executed in the process space of the client and were not hosted. The components deployed in a server application were executed in the surrogate process hosted by COM+, so they were in-process and ran under the control of the COM+ host. As a COM+ administrator you had the option to set the COM+ application mode. It is this server application within COM+ that most closely aligns with the hosting concept in AppFabric.

All of the functionality included in COM+ remains important today when developing enterprise .NET applications. However, when .NET was introduced, business developers began moving away from creating COM components, and especially from using COM+ as a hosting model. As .NET gained popularity, developers created middle-tier components, but they didn't want to have the overhead of wrapping these components in a COM Callable Wrapper (CCW). A CCW is a proxy that enables you to call .NET objects through COM. It might still be possible to take .NET code written for COM+ and host it in AppFabric, but you should be aware that there were many issues with the COM and DCOM model that prompted developers to look for alternatives in the first place.

Problems to Be Solved

Let's review some of the issues that existed with DCOM. This review will provide a view of why COM+ didn't survive as the component host.

In DCOM, the location of a component was not supposed to vary from one place to another. This scenario worked within an organization, but it fell apart as soon you crossed organizational boundaries.

DCOM was created so that calling a remote method would be as simple as calling a local method. Unfortunately, this led to bad programming practices and resulted in increased network traffic. Developers didn't take into account that, from a design perspective, you needed to ensure that your components didn't keep state between calls. This issue is as important today as it ever was.

DCOM was created before the Internet boom, and it was never created with the Internet in mind. To use DCOM across locations, it typically meant you had to sacrifice security by opening ports in the firewall. Compounding this problem, the ports that needed to be opened were picked at random, and this meant that you had to open all the ports with a specific range. It would be hard to imagine any network administrator allowing this to happen in this day and age.

As you can see, there were definite reasons to move away from COM/DCOM and COM+. However, the move away from COM+ left a hosting vacuum that has gone unfilled until now

AppFabric is the product that will fill this vacuum.

Getting to AppFabric

You need to cover a lot more ground before you're ready to get on with the rest of the chapters in this book. Those chapters will take you on a much deeper journey, describing what AppFabric is and how to utilize its functionality.

Before jumping into those chapters, let's look a deeper at why AppFabric is necessary. What has happened since .NET was introduced in 2000? Developers did what developers do best. They wrote code! In an attempt to fill the hosting vacuum, they created their own hosts, which typically took the form of custom Windows Services. Unfortunately, these Windows Services typically didn't include multithreading, scale-out capabilities, tracking, or monitoring—all the functionality that developers were accustomed to getting with COM+.

It so happens that the same functionality that developers were missing when they created their own hosts has long been available through BizTalk. (You'll learn more about BizTalk, including when to use BizTalk and when to use AppFabric in Chapter 3). When Microsoft looked at BizTalk, as well as at the .NET Framework, it determined that BizTalk had many great features that could help application developers fill the vacuum and address gaps in the framework. Many of those features were scaled appropriately for composite applications that developers wrote using an object-based methodology (and not a message-based methodology).

Consider again what developers do best. The question might still remain: "Why is it a problem to create your own hosts?" Besides the fact that implementing multithreading solutions remains difficult, it is also time-consuming to build in the crosscutting features that are the staples of successful hosting environments. These crosscutting features include items such as tracking, monitoring, scale-out functionality, security, adapters for back-end systems, exception handling and error recovery, and transaction support. When you finish the custom software, you will likely end up with a highly customized, hand-coded application. While this could meet your current needs, it would require a development team to stay on to maintain and upgrade it. Within a short period of time, the cost of maintaining and enhancing this custom solution would easily exceed the cost of the application built on top of this custom host. Finally, you must consider the issue of time-to-market: how long will management (and the business groups) wait to get their requirements fulfilled while you work on plumbing code that doesn't get them closer to a solution?

Enough Already! What is AppFabric?

For .NET developers writing applications using WCF and WF, AppFabric will be the middle-tier application server host. It will also provide scalability and support for long-running transactions. It will simplify deployment, configuration, management and scalability of composite applications. The goal of AppFabric is to provide a server infrastructure, through the Windows Application Server, where the business logic you develop in WF can be executed and exposed through WCF endpoints—all without needing to design, develop, and support the infrastructure's code.

You will use the Visual Studio, .NET Framework, and IIS skills you already have to build applications to host in AppFabric. In fact, after installing AppFabric, you will see eight new AppFabric services within IIS Manager:

- Application export
- Application import
- Database configuration
- Diagnostics

- Persisted instances

- Services

- Tracking configuration

- Tracking profiles

Who Is the Target Customer?

You now know what AppFabric is; the next step is to consider who should consider utilizing its functionality. AppFabric benefits both enterprise developers and IT professionals. For developers, it provides integration with Visual Studio that makes it easy to create a WF service, run and debug it using AppFabric, and then package it for deployment onto the production server.

For IT professionals, AppFabric makes it simpler to deploy, configure, manage, and scale out the .NET 4.0 WCF/WF services. It also provides an upgrade for the existing .NET 3.0/3.5 WCF/WF services. Finally, it provides a similar administration experience and tools for WCF/WF services as for Web applications.

This quick summary reveals the following target customers for AppFabric:

- Enterprise developers who create service-oriented, middle-tier applications using .NET

- Independent software vendor (ISV) developers who build commercial SOA software products using .NET

- IT professionals who deploy and manage these applications and services.

Let's walk through the list of target customers and assess who will benefit most from hosting their WCF and WF workflow applications on AppFabric. The main beneficiaries, of course, are developers, particularly developers who write code using WCF and WF.

The second group that will benefit from AppFabric consists of the people often referred to as IT professionals, or application owners and operators. These people take control of the applications and/or services developers write, then deploy them and make them run in more scalable and distributed environments, such as web farms and server groups, to serve the purpose of enterprise-quality business applications.

Finally, you have the group of people and companies called ISVs. This group will acquire AppFabric components and services in an *a la carte* fashion as it builds its own composite, complex commercial products.

It is important to remember all these target groups of AppFabric users as you explore the architecture details of AppFabric components, including how they work. You'll explore this subject in detail in Chapter 4.

AppFabric Component Architecture

Experienced developers are now familiar with n-tier application architectures in which the application is broken out into tiers. These tiers include at least the three classic layers: the user interface, the business-logic layer, and the data layer. Of course, you can break these layers down further to provide for additional scalability and flexibility. Figure 1-1 depicts a common application architecture taken from the Microsoft Patterns and Practices (P&P) Application Architecture Guide.

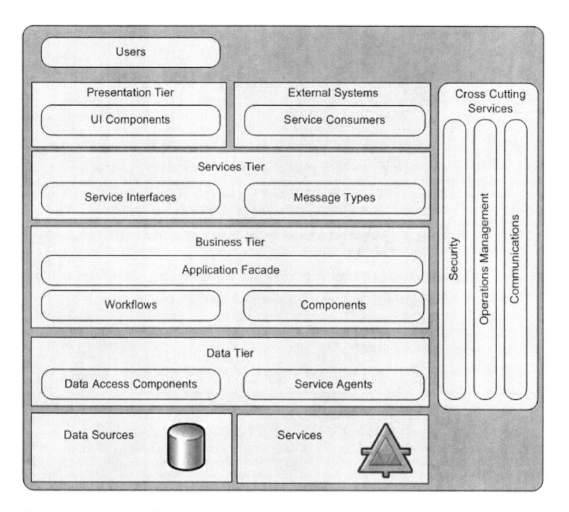

Figure 1-1. Common Application Architecture

Figure 1-1 shows a classic business tier. However, the middle tier can also be scaled out to incorporate the Data and Services block. The diagram also shows the inclusion of the crosscutting functionality that is crucial for a successful application.

AppFabric provides a host for all the components that make up the entire middle tier of this architecture. In this case, the entire middle tier includes the Data and Services blocks, as well as the Business blocks. What makes this diagram interesting is what you see between the .NET framework functionality in ADO.NET for the data components, WCF for the service endpoints, and WF for the business workflows: you can create an entire application's middle tier in that space. All of the components that make up this middle tier fit into AppFabric.

Drilling into Figure 1-1's middle tier brings you to Figure 1-2, which shows AppFabric's technology stack. AppFabric will be brought together through components in the operating system, the .NET framework, and additional components that you will acquire in an online download for the initial release.

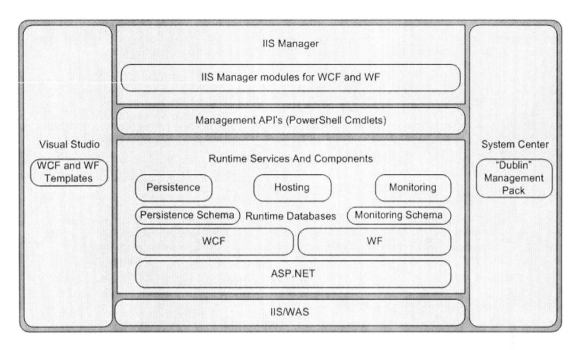

Figure 1-2. AppFabric Technology Stack

Take a look at the technology stack in Figure 1-2. You can see that IIS, WAS, and the IIS Manager are components that are part of the Windows operating System. Everyone is familiar with IIS and the IIS Manager; however, far fewer people are probably familiar with WAS (Windows Process Activation Service). WAS is a new service in IIS 7.0 that provides a process activation mechanism to support protocols such as TCP, Named Pipes, and MSMQ. Before version 7 in IIS, the activation mechanism only supported HTTP. Microsoft created WAS to manage the activation and lifetime of the processes that contain applications hosting WCF services. You will learn more about WAS and how it relates to AppFabric in more detail in Chapter 2. One thing to keep in mind is that WAS is not the same as AppFabric because AppFabric builds on WAS and provides the missing pieces.

Figure 1-2 shows enhancements that will be surfaced in the .NET 4.0 Framework. These enhancements include a persistence schema (along with the persistence provider), tracking and tracking participants and WCF and WF Visual Studio templates. To address the new requirements in AppFabric, Microsoft is enhancing the Windows Server platform to include new components for the second generation of Windows Communication Framework (WCF) and Windows Workflow Foundation (WF). If you look at the new features of the .NET 4.0 Framework on top of IIS, you can see that the framework will extend IIS to be a standard host for applications that utilized either WCF and/or WF. These enhancements to the Windows Server Application Server will simplify the deployment, configuration, management, and scalability of composite applications.

The remaining boxes show the functionality that is provided by installing the online download. This download installs the root functionality of AppFabric. Previously, you learned that AppFabric will be the standard host for WCF and WCF applications; however, AppFabric is much more than that. AppFabric also provides prebuilt developer services that include Visual Studio templates, content-based message forwarding, and message-based correlation. AppFabric also provides scalability through the scaling out of stateful workflows and deployment features. It also includes persistence, tracking stores, and enhanced management and monitoring. In addition, you can find an entire set of management APIs implemented through PowerShell commandlets. Finally, this is a server-based role, so there will be a separately available management pack for System Center Operations Manager (SCOM).

Key Scenarios Addressed by AppFabric

AppFabric is a versatile system. It can support many different architectures and styles of applications. The two most common that you'll learn about in this book are composite applications and integration applications.

Composite Applications

Composite applications are those you build by combining multiple existing functions into a new application. These existing functions are typically drawn from several sources; however, they can be individually selected components from within other applications. They can also be entire systems, where the output has been assembled as business functions, .NET assemblies, or web services.

Defining a Composite Application

When putting together a composite application, you need to follow the application-separation rules dictated by an SOA architecture. A thorough description of SOA and SOA architectures are outside the scope of this book. However, a composite application, even one that utilizes services, does not make a SOA based application. You can build composite applications using any number of architectures and technologies.

Finally, the scope of composite applications typically encompasses local application logic. These applications typically do not interact with cross-organizational components, leaving that aspect to applications that utilize Enterprise Application Integration solutions.

Why Deploy Composite Applications?

You now know what composite applications are; next, let's look at why you might want to use this architecture with an AppFabric-based solution.

As companies look for ways to achieve code reuse and create services, they often turn to services and components, which can be used to quickly and easily create new applications. As companies create these new applications and increasingly use them across their business, new requirements arise to scale out the middle-tier services layer. These new requirements always include solutions to deal with the challenges around scalability, performance, and reliability. The standard strategies for optimizing traditional applications do not garner the same results in the more complex composite-application environments. More often than not, composite applications are more complex and require more effort to deploy, manage, and upgrade. This often prompts developers to write more complex infrastructure code, including code to handle sophisticated operations, as well as additional code to handle deployment, management and monitoring.

To address these new requirements, composite application must contain functionality that includes management of highly asynchronous transactions, automation of long-running durable workflows, coordinating processes across tiers, and communications using the latest standards. Managing this complexity requires a new set of tools and techniques. The tools and server components that are part of

AppFabric make the creation of composite applications more streamlined and maintainable. This gives developers a hosting environment that allows them to focus on the business logic and reduce the amount of custom code.

Integration Applications

Integration applications focus on connecting existing applications and systems. Custom integration applications are mainly server-based and don't necessarily need a GUI interface (or any interface at all). Until now, integration applications have been the purview of BizTalk. There are scenarios in which customers will utilize both AppFabric and BizTalk to handle different workloads within their enterprise. Customers that don't need the enterprise level line-of-business or business-to-business connectivity provided by BizTalk can deploy AppFabric to host and manage the middle-tier applications. Customers that need both middle-tier applications and cross-enterprise heterogeneous systems can deploy both AppFabric and BizTalk and be assured they will work nicely together. You can find more detailed discussion on when and why to use AppFabric and/or BizTalk Server in Chapter 3.

When focusing on integration applications, it's important to realize that integration-server and application-server workloads are complementary, but still distinct. You will find a lot of blog entries and hype around using AppFabric for integration applications. You will hear this feature trumpeted most loudly, but AppFabric is good for much more than that. The biggest take away here is that integration-application design has become more mature, which makes it easier for people to understand its use within AppFabric.

Take care that you don't confuse application servers and integration servers; they are not the same thing. Applications servers should provide common services to application developers, which will make it easier for them to build applications and focus on the business logic. Application servers are servers focusing on services for a single application. Integration servers are focused on enterprise-class applications that span multiple applications and can span across business boundaries, as well.

The Roadmap for AppFabric

The best part of putting a roadmap together for a first-generation product is that you know it will have a long future to map out. The difficult part is that there will always be unforeseen variations. AppFabric is not a typical first-generation product. AppFabric benefits from strong cross-pollination between the AppFabric and BizTalk teams within Microsoft. The AppFabric team has learned much from its days working on BizTalk, and it has been able to take that knowledge and incorporate it into the planning and design of AppFabric. If you have developed applications previously in BizTalk, be sure to take a look at the screen shots as you read this book: you will recognize many similarities.

Of course, discussing the roadmap for AppFabric requires taking a minute to discuss the roadmap for BizTalk, as well. You might have heard some of the many rumors that BizTalk is dying or will be subsumed by AppFabric. This is not the case. BizTalk has a long future ahead of it. The development of BizTalk Server 2009 represented a large investment by Microsoft, and planning for the next two versions of BizTalk is under way.

The first bits of AppFabric will be available for download for customers that have a Windows Server license. In the future, AppFabric will be included directly as part of the Windows Server OS installation. AppFabric will be made available after the .NET 4.0 Framework and Visual Studio 2010 ship. Updates to AppFabric are currently slated to coincide with the .NET Framework releases.

But let's begin by focusing on what you can do with AppFabric today, including the benefits it provides now. One of the biggest benefits: Applications that you build (or have already built) using WCF and/or WF on both Windows Server 2008 and the .NET 3.5 Framework can be hosted in AppFabric.

Business Scenario

Now that you have a better idea of what AppFabric is and what it includes, it's time to explore a business scenario that will serve as a common thread throughout the chapters. The business scenario is centered on an insurance company, and the sample application will incorporate all of the aspects that come into play when creating AppFabric-based applications.

Contoso is a mid-size insurance company that provides auto, boat, home, and life insurance services. Like many other insurance companies, Contoso has expanded its insurance business over the last eight years by acquiring smaller insurance companies. As it has grown through merger and acquisitions, Contoso has managed to integrate most of the acquired IT systems that are necessary for supporting it various lines of insurance businesses.

However, the integration exercises haven't always been perfect, and duplicate IT functions reside within the company. Over time, the redundant functions have made it harder for Contoso to introduce new product bundles. For example, the company now has many applications that are slow and unable to scale to meet the new business load. Furthermore, multiple claims-processing systems with overlapping functions exist for the auto-insurance practice alone. As a result, Contoso has experienced delays in launching products due to application complexity and overlapping functions between its systems.

In the last year, Contoso launched an initiative to identify and implement core IT capabilities required for supporting its insurance business. Increasing business agility is the key business driver behind the initiative, and reducing ongoing operational cost and management complexity are expected to be important by-products of the initiative.

The company's business-IT group has analyzed several business function categories in its efforts to improve the company's business processes. One business function category that has been targeted for upgrading is the insurance-claim process. This process is a critical business process that cries out to be automated and integrated. At a high level, the claims process is a fairly standard procedure across insurance business practices; it consists of the following key steps:

1. *Filing claims*: The insured party or its insurance agent/broker can submit a claim for an incident. For example, it can file a claim for auto repair due to an accident. Supporting documentation and evidence for the incident should be submitted along with the claim.

2. *Soliciting bids*: After receiving the claim documents, Contoso will send out a bid request to its network of appraisal agents. Contoso has a broad network of contract-appraisal agencies.

3. *Assigning cases*: After reviewing the bid responses from appraisal agents, Contoso will assign the customer case to the appraisal agent who wins the bid. The appraisal agent will work with the customer to review the incident and conduct further assessments with approved repair contractors. The appraisal agency recommends a remedy to the Contoso at the end of the research.

4. *Rental car coordination*: The Contoso agent will work with a rental car agency to coordinate a substitute car rental for a period of the repair assessed by the appraisal agent.

5. *Billing*: After completing coordination between the customer and the repair contractors and the customer and the rental agency, Contoso will submit the claim to its billing application. When all repair paper work is completed and signed off, the client and the contractors are compensated and reimbursed accordingly.

You can see the current claims processing business-use case in Figure 1-3.

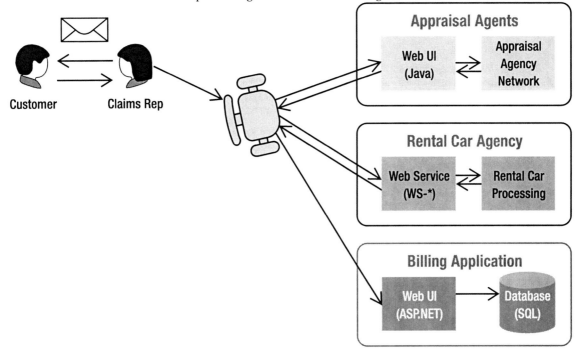

Figure 1-3. The Current Claims-Processing System

The existing claims processing system requires significant human interaction and significant coordination between various Contoso systems and partners. Such architecture is prone to errors and response delays, and it is not scalable. A more scalable approach will need to support the business's increased number of customers and business transactions. Specifically, it should be able to support a five- to ten-fold increase in both connected agents and a similar increase in additional throughput.

Based on the preceding observation, Contoso's IT architects were able to design a multi-phased iterative solution for processing insurance claims for a number of Contoso's insurance practices. The company's new extensible architecture will allow various auto, boat, and life insurance modules with customized business logic, workflow, and business data to be plugged into the solution.

The new solution should also provide the non-functional requirements that include tracking, monitoring, and the ability to view middle-tier messages that result in errors. It must also simplify deployment, configuration, and management. The final goal is to provide a SOA architecture foundation and reference architecture for future applications.

In the following chapters, we will walk you through each phase of implementation of this solution using AppFabric and other latest Microsoft technologies. As you progress through each iteration of building this solution, you will learn some cool development techniques for incorporating services in AppFabric. You will also learn about some powerful tools that will assist you in achieving the goals and objectives outlined in the requirements for this business scenario.

Summary

This chapter introduced you to the reasons that you need an application-server hosting environment. You also learned about the history of what was available in COM+, why COM+ isn't used today, and how the vacuum left by the absence of a replacement to COM+ will be filled.

This chapter also looked at the scenarios that can be covered with AppFabric and the differences between composite applications and integration applications.

Finally, this chapter shared the roadmap for AppFabric, explaining how you can take advantage of AppFabric today, as well as what you will be able to do in the future.

CHAPTER 2

■ ■ ■

Choosing AppFabric

When Microsoft first introduced developers to Microsoft Server AppFabric in the early months of 2008, many of those developers who tried out the AppFabric Community Technology Preview (CTP) bits noted a striking resemblance between aspects of the AppFabric UI and core capabilities of Microsoft BizTalk Server. The reason for this: Microsoft looked at BizTalk Server and the Windows Application Server 2008 platform, and it determined that BizTalk Server, if built into an Application Server platform, would help to address some gaps in Microsoft's application platform. Microsoft Server AppFabric will provide business-application developers with new capabilities directly out-of-the-box—and without having to invest in either building complex custom solutions or buying third-party products.

We, the authors, imagine at least two groups of people will read this book. One group will be those who have BizTalk experience, whether in implementing it on projects, learning it, or investing in it, and now are wondering about this new thing called Windows Server AppFabric. For example, if you're part of this group, you might wonder how AppFabric Server changes the picture, and especially, how it behaves relative to BizTalk. We also anticipate a second group of totally *fresh* people will be interested in this book. If you're part of this group, you've always wanted to learn BizTalk and/or WCF and WF, and now, with yet another new technology knocking at the door, you want to understand which of these new technologies makes more sense in your projects.

If you're coming from the BizTalk world, it is easy to see the introduction of AppFabric as a clash of the Titans: BizTalk is a heavily built and powerful giant versus a light but fast creature (in Chapter 10, you will see the low latency that Windows Application Server will be known for). You might be wondering which tool will win this clash, but the fact is there should be no clash at all. The context of this chapter will illustrate how, for any group of readers, and you won't have to worry about such conflicts when you decide which technology to use for any particular project.

As you read this chapter, you will be presented with the different scenarios in which BizTalk and Windows Application Server work side-by-side, together, or individually, each providing solutions for different business problems and business scenarios. After reading the chapter, you should be able to provide an answer the question, "When should I choose which?" You should also be able to discuss that question with your boss and co-workers when you need to make a decision on technology selection as you begin a new project.

This chapter will provide you with the information you need to understand the function and use of these two technologies from both a business and a technical perspective. You will receive an overview of the unique characteristics of each technology, including guidance on specific scenarios in which one technology is better than the other. You will also receive guidance for cases where you can use both technologies together. Following that, you will see a comparison of the technical capabilities provided by each of these technologies. After you review this chapter, you will find yourself in a better position to make a more informed decision on the use of these two technologies for the specific scenarios these technologies address.

Before you start exploring and comparing the capabilities of AppFabric and BizTalk Server, you might find it helpful to take a quick glance at what the BizTalk Server is, especially if you have no previous experience with BizTalk. Obviously, you'll perform this review while also keeping BizTalk's relationship to Windows Application Server in mind.

BizTalk as an Integration Server

Enterprise integration is the task of making disparate applications work together to produce a unified set of functionality. You can custom develop these applications in house or purchase them from third-party vendors. They typically run on multiple computers and frequently on multiple platforms; they can also be geographically dispersed. Some of the applications might run outside of the enterprise, operated by business partners or customers. Other applications might not have been designed with integration in mind and might be difficult to change (you might not even have the source code). These issues (and others like them) make application integration complicated.

So, what makes good enterprise integration? If integration needs were always the same, you would only need one integration path. Yet, as with any complex technological effort, enterprise integration involves a range of considerations and consequences that you need to take into account for any integration opportunity. BizTalk Server is Microsoft's integration and connectivity server for enterprise integration. BizTalk is currently in its sixth release, and it provides a solution that allows organizations to connect more easily with disparate systems. BizTalk Server provides connectivity between core systems both inside and outside your organization, including connectivity to more than 25 multiplatform adapters and a robust messaging infrastructure. BizTalk Server has built-in support for load balancing, message durability and guaranteed delivery, throttling, high availability and message tracking, archiving, and automatic retry logic.

In addition to integration functionality, BizTalk also provides strong, durable messaging, a business-rules engine, a Visual Studio-graphical message transformation editor (Mapper), an Enterprise Service Bus Toolkit for SOA-based solutions, Single Sign On authentication, EDI connectivity, a Flat File Schema Wizard, Business Activity Monitoring (BAM), RFID capabilities, and IBM Host/Mainframe connectivity.

Having a broad grasp of the problems BizTalk addresses is the first step in understanding BizTalk Server's architecture. Going deeper means looking into the mechanics of how this technology actually works. The best place to start is with the basics of message flow (see Figure 2-1).

BizTalk Server architecture implements a pub-sub (publishing and subscribing) integration pattern that is fully described in an infamous book by Gregor Hohpe and Bobby Woolf called *Enterprise Integration Patterns* (Addison-Wesley, 2003).

As Figure 2-1 illustrates, all messages that flow through BizTalk get stored or persisted in the SQL Server database called *MessageBox*. MessageBox plays the role of central mail box for all messages delivered by publishers (receive ports, orchestrations, and two-way send ports) and picked up by subscribers (send ports, orchestrations, and two-ways receive ports).

An incoming message is received by a receive port, a logical BizTalk component that includes at least one physical receiving location that knows how to communicate with a message's source system through one of more than 50 available receive adapters that ship with BizTalk out-of-the-box. You can attach the receive pipeline component to a receiving location to help decode encrypted messages, convert (disassembling) messages from its native format to XML, and perform some initial message validations and party resolution tasks. You can also transform an incoming message into a canonical message format using one of the BizTalk maps (that use XSLT transformation) configured on a receive port.

Once a message reaches the MessageBox, it can be then picked up by a subscribing to its message type component, such as an orchestration or a send port.

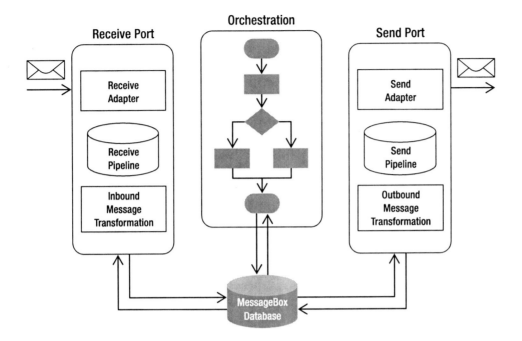

Figure 2-1. BizTalk Server Architecture

Developers create orchestrations in the Visual Studio environment using a graphical tool called BizTalk Orchestration Designer. This designer leverages a toolbox group of various shapes that express various tasks in a business workflow: message receive and send shapes, conditional decisions, message transformations, loops, delays, and other workflow behaviors. Orchestration can also use custom build .NET components that developers can write specifically to provide additional extensibility to the BizTalk orchestration shapes. Moreover, orchestrations can optionally evaluate complex sets of rules by calling the BizTalk Business Rule Engine.

Once an orchestration processes a message, it can either send it back to the MessageBox for another subscriber to pick it up for processing—this subscriber can be another orchestration, send port, or a receive port. This subscriber can return an ACK message to an original caller or send it directly to a specified send port for outbound-message processing.

A send port is a physical port that acts as an antipod to a receive port—it could first (optionally) transform an outbound message using the attached XSLT maps, then process it through its send pipeline, which typically assembles messages in the specified native format, such as flat file (with or without message encryption). As a receive port, the send port communicates with the destination system through a send port adapter that you can configure to use with one of many available transport and messaging protocols supported by BizTalk.

In a nutshell, Microsoft BizTalk Server provides customers with a set of capabilities that enable the integration of various systems within an organization and between organizations. It also provides a scalable platform upon which business processes that span these heterogeneous systems can be designed and automated.

AppFabric as an Application Server

Now let's take a look at this new thing called *AppFabric*, which is a powerful and scalable platform for developing and managing Web and composite applications. This platform enables developers to focus on building mission-critical business applications using familiar .NET programming models.

Today, developers are provided with an out-of-the-box host through Windows Process Activation Services (WAS). Or, developers can roll their own service and workflow hosts, but there are many capabilities that customers must round out to provide a host with server-like behaviors and functionality. WF developers are forced to make all sorts of decisions and trade-offs when choosing a host for their workflow. This area has seen some progress in recent years, but there is no clear, easy choice.

AppFabric addresses this issue by providing an application server infrastructure through a set of extensions to the Windows Server. You can then execute or otherwise expose business logic developed in WF and/or WCF through WCF endpoints, all without needing to design, develop, or support the application infrastructure from scratch.

AppFabric offers a consistent WF host that provides automatic support for important WF concepts such as persistence and messaging. AppFabric also supplies administrators with a coherent way to view and interact with running and suspended workflows. Administration is where AppFabric solves a problem with current WCF and WF hosting options. Today, you have no straightforward way to iterate all WCF services on a web site, nor do you have a way to get a consolidated view of a service's status. AppFabric's IIS and WAS extensions give you a new way to monitor services and interact with WF workflows.

Figure 2-2 illustrates a scenario that combines several technologies—AppFabric, WCF, and WF—to accomplish a common task. Before the introduction of AppFabric, you could accomplish such a task using only BizTalk Server. Frankly, BizTalk Server wasn't built for the scenario described in Figure 2-2. The scenario asks you to build a Web service that coordinates the activity of multiple constituent Web services, which in turn requires you to implement web service aggregation through service abstraction in the service oriented architecture (SOA) Service Aggregation pattern. Figure 2-2 depicts granular or service data web services on the right, which are orchestrated and abstracted by a business-oriented web service shown on the left. You can achieve and build this scenario using BizTalk Server; however, if all you want to do is aggregate some services is, then the BizTalk Server solution, with its MessageBox message persistence, service message publishing, and subscription functionality, will probably be overkill. In Figure 2-2's scenario, a solution that relies on WCF, WF, and AppFabric would be serve you better.

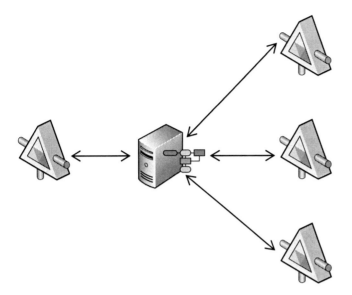

Figure 2-2. An AppFabric-Based Web Services Aggregation Scenario

AppFabric and BizTalk: Friends or Enemies?

AppFabric is being positioned as a core Windows Application Server, while. BizTalk Server is positioned as an Integration Server. Despite the fact that each organization is unique, these tools can address some common scenarios relating to custom application development, Enterprise Application Integration (EAI), human workflow, and business process management (BPM). Tables 2-1, 2-2, and 2-3 provide guidance on when you should choose to use either AppFabric or BizTalk Server, or both.

When to Choose AppFabric

Table 2-1 lists some project characteristics, or a solution approach, where you should think about applying AppFabric to the problem at hand. The table also elaborates on the technical reasoning behind each of the choices.

Table 2-1. Reasons to Choose AppFabric

Solution Approach	Technical Reason
Your solution development is driven primarily on a *Code First* basis	Code First developers start designing an application using a domain model that represents business objects. Creation of and interaction with these objects is then generally achieved by writing or producing code. This is a different approach to the *Schema First* approach used in BizTalk Server. The Code First approach is the same approach used by the WF and WCF programming models; it's also the one that AppFabric provides additional capabilities for.
You need an enterprise-ready platform to host and execute WF and/or WCF applications.	AppFabric provides a number of scalability and manageability features required by enterprise-wide applications. It also enhances IIS and WAS to provide an application-server infrastructure for applications that use workflow or communications. Traditionally, these server host features would be custom developed; their existence in AppFabric will shorten the time required to implement this traditional development approach.
You need to integrate a web site with back-end line-of-business (LOB) applications and/or data, and you need the web site to provide immediate feedback to the user.	An order-entry system can provide a good example of this solution approach. You might have a site user entering orders, and that site user might require immediate confirmation from the financial system that an order has been accepted. AppFabric's architecture is more optimized towards lower-latency communication than is BizTalk Server's architecture. This, combined with the communication functionality of WCF, enables an application to access LOB systems and display responses in the application with potentially less latency.[1] This communication, however, is limited to LOB systems built with WF that you can communicate with through WCF.

[1] *This information is based on the current feature set of AppFabric at the time this book was published.*

When to Choose BizTalk Server

Just as there are good reasons for preferring AppFabric for some given scenario, there are also good and valid reasons to apply BizTalk Server to other scenarios. Remember, the two products share some features, but that does not mean that they are interchangeable. Table 2-2 lists some of the characteristics of a solution approach that should lead you to choose BizTalk Server.

Table 2-2. Reasons for Choosing BizTalk Server

Solution Approach	Technical Reason
Your solution development is driven primarily on a *Schema First* basis.	When developing a message-driven solution, XML schemas serve as the cornerstone of the solution's design and are used as the domain model representing business data and events. Within BizTalk, you typically implement interaction with a message (an instance of an XML schema) using various modeling tools and, where necessary, by writing code.
You need to integrate back-end line of business (LOB) and legacy systems across a variety of platforms, technologies, and communication protocols.	BizTalk Server is an enterprise-integration platform, the architecture of which is geared towards managing the specifics of communication with a wide range of systems by using its out-of-the-box adapters to connect to a range of technologies. BizTalk Server provides a messaging and transformation infrastructure to normalize the data contents and data structures of different service schemas and/or different LOB applications. BizTalk Server also provides a range of tools to assist with the integration effort, including a Schema Editor, Mapper, Flat File Wizard, pre- and post-processing pipelines, and the Enterprise Service Bus (ESB) Toolkit.
You need to ensure that your integration solution can scale on an enterprise level as volume grows and/or the number of integration projects increase.	BizTalk Server provides high availability and easy scale-out functionality. It also gives you the ability to separate and balance integration functionality across many servers. AppFabric won't provide a distributed management experience.[2] The PowerShell cmdlets and IIS Manager extensions are designed to configure only the local server, and each server in the farm must be managed individually. However, AppFabric will leverage the remoting capabilities in both IIS Manager and PowerShell to allow the Administrator to configure multiple machines from a single console.
You want to provide your organization and/or your partners with the ability to interact with your business services in a way that isolates them from changes made to the systems and processes that affect these services.	Point-to-point integrations changes made to the provider system can have a profound impact on the consuming application. BizTalk Server natively provides a hub-based integration model that eases this burden. It also allows organizations to provide business services that are isolated from the impact of changes made to the systems and processes on which these services are based. You achieve this by using separate schemas; the associate ability lets you easily develop message-transformation logic using BizTalk's Mapper tool.

You need to integrate a number of systems and/or services in a manner that will enable you to make agile and dynamic changes in the way messages are received and sent between the various systems.	BizTalk Server provides a robust publish-subscribe engine that makes use of a flexible-content and property-based message-routing engine.
You need a mechanism through which your integration with internal and external systems can be implemented on a reliable and robust basis.	BizTalk's MessageBox database architecture provides you with a store-and-forward pattern to ensure that, in the event of errors in communication, robust retry functionality is available.
You want to be able to automate a variety of business processes that interact with a number of external or internal systems.	BizTalk's orchestration and messaging engine provide you with the tools required to automate business process and integrate these business processes with other systems within or outside of your organization. The orchestration engine also provides advanced correlation semantics that allow you to implement sequential and/or parallel message convoy patterns. It also provides an architecture that ensures that correlations on long-running transactions can be performed across multiple heterogeneous systems through out-of-the-box adapters.
You have a scenario in which a message must be routed through a series of components in a pre-defined order; this order might not be known at the design time.	This scenario is also known as a Routing Slip integration pattern. The implementation of this pattern is provided by the BizTalk ESB Toolkit.
You have specific business-to-business (B2B) requirements built around integration with your partners or external systems. For example, you might want to integrate these systems using various industry standard protocols: EDI, SWIFT, RosettaNet, AS2, HIPAA, and/or HL7.	BizTalk Server provides out-of-the-box functionality through its various adapters and accelerators that can assist you in implementing solutions based on various industry standard protocols: EDI, SWIFT, RosettaNet, AS2, HIPAA and/or HL7.
You need a platform to assist you with batch processing of data between different systems, such as retrieving a batch of data from SQL Server, and then calling other services or LOB applications for each item in the batch.	The de-batching and batching capabilities of BizTalk Server's pipeline architecture and its ability to process batches within an orchestration enable you to perform batch processing with relative ease.
You have specific RFID requirements in your organization and/or project.	BizTalk's RFID architecture is provided when you license BizTalk Server. You can integrate its RFID architecture to take advantage of RFID events in the automation of business processes.

You want to achieve easy interoperability with multiple LOB applications (such as SAP, Siebel, or Oracle Applications) simultaneously.	Customers can achieve easy interoperability with multiple LOB applications (such as SAP, Siebel, or Oracle Applications) simultaneously with the BizTalk Adapter Pack. These adapters require no code for point-to-point connections from BizTalk Server, SQL Server, and custom .NET applications to key LOB systems, such as SAP R/3, Siebel, and Oracle.
You have legacy systems or back-end LOB applications that you want to expose as business services for use by other applications in your organization. However, you *cannot* communicate with these systems using XML via web services (WCF).	If you cannot communicate with legacy systems or back-end LOB applications using XML via WCF, then you should use BizTalk Server and out-of-the-box adapters to assist you with legacy proprietary-communication protocols and data formats.
You have legacy systems or back-end LOB applications that you want to expose as business services for use by other applications in your organization. Also, you *must* provide transactional support, reliable message delivery, and/or in-ordered delivery.	When the back-end systems do not take advantage of WS* protocols that provide atomic transactional support, reliable message delivery, or exactly one in-ordered delivery, you should use a BizTalk adapter within the BizTalk Server to provide these capabilities.

[2] *Use of BizTalk Adapter Pack in AppFabric requires purchasing a separate license, while a license for the BizTalk Adapter Pack is included in the purchase of a BizTalk Server license.*

Key Differentiating Points

While Table 2-1 and Table 2-2 have a clear 1:1 match between the solution approach or business scenario and the specific technology you should use. However, you might encounter other scenarios in which the guidance given in the tables is not so easy to apply. For example, you might be faced with a mixture of requirements that span both technologies. Figure 2-3 provides a view on the capabilities uniquely included in the two technologies, as well as an indication of the capabilities that are common to both technologies.

■ **Note** Figure 2-3 is not intended to present a complete list of each technology's capabilities, but a set of the core capabilities of each technology.

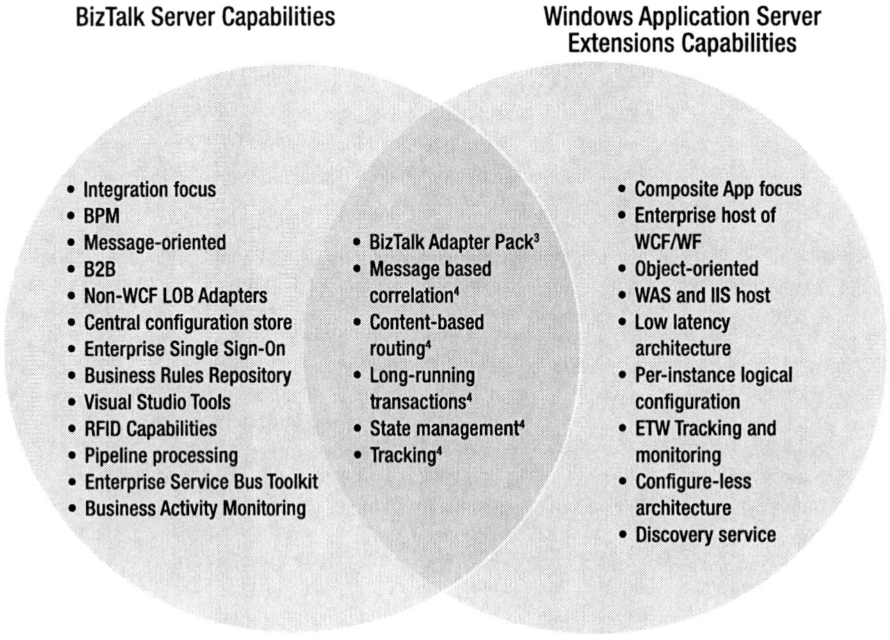

BizTalk Server Capabilities
Windows Application Server Extensions Capabilities

- Integration focus
- BPM
- Message-oriented
- B2B
- Non-WCF LOB Adapters
- Central configuration store
- Enterprise Single Sign-On
- Business Rules Repository
- Visual Studio Tools
- RFID Capabilities
- Pipeline processing
- Enterprise Service Bus Toolkit
- Business Activity Monitoring

- BizTalk Adapter Pack[3]
- Message based correlation[4]
- Content-based routing[4]
- Long-running transactions[4]
- State management[4]
- Tracking[4]

- Composite App focus
- Enterprise host of WCF/WF
- Object-oriented
- WAS and IIS host
- Low latency architecture
- Per-instance logical configuration
- ETW Tracking and monitoring
- Configure-less architecture
- Discovery service

Figure 2-3. *The Unique and Overlapping Capabilities of AppFabric and BizTalk Server*

[3] *Using the BizTalk Adapter Pack in AppFabric requires that you purchase a separate license, while a license for the BizTalk Adapter Pack is included in the purchase of the BizTalk Server license.*

[4] *These features in AppFabric present a subset of the features that exist today in BizTalk Server; therefore, they do not provide a 1:1 match in functionality.*

Let's review what makes BizTalk Server unique and useful. The first differentiating point is BizTalk's focus on integration and broad connectivity. The fact that BizTalk Server has LOB adapters such as for SAP and JD Edwards, host integration adapters (including adapters for HIS and JMS), connectivity-protocol adapters (including adapters for FTP, AS2, and EDI), and accelerators (including accelerators for HIPPA, HL7, SWIFT, and RosettaNet) sets BizTalk Server apart in direct feature comparisons to AppFabric.

The first release of AppFabric won't come anywhere close to equaling all the features currently built into BizTalk, not least because AppFabric focuses mostly on web service interfaces and workflow hosting. Broad transport connectivity and back-end applications interoperability requirements will drive the technology choice towards BizTalk Server in those cases.

Other features of BizTalk Server set it apart from AppFabric. These include features such as enterprise readiness, unified tooling experience, and high availability and scalability. If these are among the check marks on your technology comparison spreadsheet, they will swing your decision towards BizTalk Server and away from AppFabric.

On the other hand, the differentiating features of AppFabric are its lightweight implementation and low latency. Describing AppFabric's implementation as lightweight does not mean it provides merely a subset or limited set of functionality compared to what you find in the set of features in the Enterprise Edition of BizTalk. Instead, calling it lightweight refers to the way it allows practically any developer with prior .NET and WCF/WF experience to install, deploy, and learn how to operate AppFabric in matter of few days. BizTalk Server is a different story. Suffice it to say that BizTalk Server takes minutes to install, hours to configure all its features, and days and weeks to learn about every aspect of its design, development, deployment, and operation.

Low latency in BizTalk can be measured by the rate at which received messages are being persisted to the MessageBox for processing or delivery. To deliver message guaranteed delivery and fault tolerance enterprise capabilities, the distributed BizTalk Server agents communicates asynchronously with BizTalk MessageBox checking for message state updates to pick up new messages for processing. This polling process introduces the inherent latency of BizTalk applications. This means that AppFabric has the advantage over BizTalk in scenarios where the overall environment is experiencing high loads under less than 100 ms for end-to-end business transaction-processing speed requirements.

Points of Difference in the Overlap

Even in the areas where BizTalk Server and AppFabric overlap with each other, you can see some key essential between the technologies. The following subsections discuss different capabilities found in common between the two platforms. Each subsection contrasts the implementation of a common feature between AppFabric and BizTalk server, helping you to make the right choice for your own needs.

BizTalk Server Adapters

The license for BizTalk Server includes about 20 adapters that you cannot purchase separately for AppFabric. These adapters include File, FTP, MSMQ, WCF, SOAP adaptors, among others. You can also find BizTalk Adapter Pack 2.0, which includes adapters for SQL Server, Oracle E-Business Suite, Oracle Database, mySAP, and Siebel eBusiness applications.

You can only purchase BizTalk Adapter Pack 2.0 separately from BizTalk Server. Customers can host an adapter from that pack in-process within a custom WCF service hosted within AppFabric or host it out-of-process by hosting the adapter service in IIS or WAS. Neither choice will lead to the sort of seamless experience you get today with the built-in BizTalk Server adapters.

Message-Based Correlation

BizTalk Server implements advanced correlation functionality to correlate messages sent and/or received. This functionality includes the following characteristics:

- It's not limited to request-response patterns.

- You can perform correlation on message content and on message-context properties.

- It allows for sequential and parallel convoy-message patterns.

AppFabric, on the other hand, provides only limited correlation functionality to correlate multiple response messages to a single request message. You can perform correlation only on message content.

Content-Based Routing

BizTalk Server implements advanced content-based routing functionality that is characterized by the following features:

- Its routing is performed based on message content and context properties.

- Its context properties can be extended to contain properties unrelated to the message content.

Routing rules are maintained in a BizTalk Administration Management Console, and you can change these without requiring redeployment.

AppFabric implements limited correlation functionality to correlate messages between SOAP request and a response; it has the following characteristics:

- It's limited to SOAP request routing.

- Filters are defined using XPath statements on SOAP messages.

- It provides no context properties for routing.

You store routing rules in the web.config file. The router uses these rules dynamically; AppFabric's router represents an evolution of the WSE SOAP router.

Long-Running Transaction Support

BizTalk Server provides the following rich functionality to support long-running transactions:

- Business processes are automatically persisted at numerous stages of their execution.

- Specific transaction control allows for atomic (relying on a *compensation* block to execute logic for roll back) and long-running transactions.

- Compensation functionality is built into the business process plan, with capabilities for nested compensations across different transactions.

BizTalk Server also performs hydration and dehydration of processes automatically.

AppFabric does not provide the same rich support found in BizTalk. Instead, it gives you limited support for long-running transactions, with only the following characteristics:

- Process flows are persisted *manually* only when the developer adds the relevant activity.

- Long-running transactions support the compensation model.

- No nested compensation is available.

Like BizTalk Server, AppFabric provides for the automatic hydration and dehydration of process flow.

State Management

State Management support is native to BizTalk Server. It derives from BizTalk Server's publish-subscribe architecture, with the MessageBox database playing the role of the message-storage database. The state of message processing and business process execution is stored in the BizTalk Server database automatically.

Communication state management functionality is also available in BizTalk Server. This ensures that failed message communication is automatically retried, using a backup transportation protocol, if necessary.

In contrast, the developer must configure state management support in AppFabric during design time. Here are the core state management capabilities of AppFabric:

- You can configure the state of message processing so it stores in SQL.

- As the developer, you control the saving of the state.

State management for communication is the developer's responsibility in AppFabric. The tool does not provide support for state management on the level of what you see in BizTalk Server.

Tracking

BizTalk Server provides rich tracking functionality, including the following features:

- Tracking of messages

- Tracking of pipeline processing, communication, and orchestration steps

- Recording of tracking information in the BizTalk Server Tracking database

You can set and query tracking configuration using the BizTalk Administration Console. By contrast, the tracking tools in AppFabric are not as feature rich as those in BizTalk Server. AppFabric supports only tracking of WF steps, which you can record in the AppFabric tracking database (SQL Server).

Using AppFabric and BizTalk Server Together

In the event that the requirements in a given business scenario cannot clearly drive the decision between one technology or the other, it becomes necessary to consider using BizTalk Server and AppFabric together. You might be skeptical, but it makes sense to combine the two technologies in several scenarios.

Consider a scenario in which you might need to receive EDI flat files from one of your trading partners, and you need to processes these EDI files through several internal business processes that you have previously created with WF. In this scenario, BizTalk receives the EDI files, parses them, and maps them to your internal XML format. BizTalk could then route the data through WCF adapters that will call back-end WF services hosted in AppFabric.

Or, you might have some internal applications programmed with WF/WCF that needs to expose some EDI functionality to external systems. In this case, AppFabric hosted WF services can call BizTalk Server orchestrations or a send port directly—again, using WCF—to transfer those messages in EDI format for the external system's consumption. You can see several of these types of scenarios illustrated in Figure 2-4.

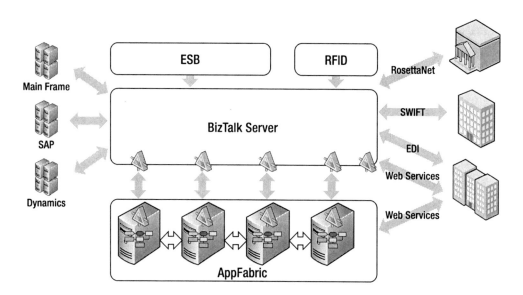

Figure 2-4. BizTalk Server and AppFabric Complementing Each Other

Figure 2-4 shows how AppFabric and BizTalk Server avoid clashing with each other in an enterprise application. Rather, they complement each other.

The following sections illustrate some basic business scenarios in which you could think about using AppFabric and BizTalk Server together. You'll see four examples that show clear benefits from combining both technologies. Please don't consider our four examples as representing the only four cases in which combining the technologies makes sense; you will encounter many other scenarios in which it might make good business sense to build a solution that leverages both AppFabric and BizTalk Server.

Example 1: BizTalk Server with ESB and AppFabric

Assume you're already using BizTalk Server in your organization to integrate heterogeneous systems, and that it is providing a number of services to your organization, in line with your organization's SOA strategy. However, some of these services aren't meeting your low-latency SLA requirements due to the latency overhead introduced as a result of BizTalk Server's publish-and-subscribe approach.

You should move services that require low latency (less than 500ms) to WF and hosted them with the AppFabric server host, provided that you can connect the relevant legacy systems and/or back-end LOB applications through WCF and without message transformation. When the services in BizTalk Server need to be able to utilize these WCF services, you can use BizTalk Server to integrate then integrate using the WCF adapter.

Some services might provide access to legacy systems and/or back-end LOB applications that you cannot access via WCF without message transformation. You can choose to retain these services in BizTalk Server, applying the relevant BizTalk Server performance tweaks for low latency to try and improve their performance. Alternatively, you can move those services to WF, host them in the AppFabric server, and allow the transformation logic to be handled by the low latency message transformation service implemented with the Enterprise Service Bus (ESB) Toolkit.

Example 2: BizTalk Server and AppFabric

Now assume you're already using WF, but you have a requirement to integrate to a number of heterogeneous LOB systems. This is another case in which it can make sound business sense to mingle the two technologies.

In this scenario, AppFabric can provide the improved hosting infrastructure for WF applications. AppFabric can also facilitate WCF communication to BizTalk Server WCF services. At the same time, you can use BizTalk Server to integrate with the LOB systems, perform necessary transformations, and provide a set of normalized or canonical services for consumption by your WF applications.

Example 3: BizTalk Server and AppFabric

Next, assume you want to be able to automate business processes that integrate with a variety of systems. People also need to interact with these processes during their execution.

You can use AppFabric to host the WF-based, people-driven processes and expose these processes as services using WCF. Next, you use BizTalk Server to execute the business processes and to integrate with heterogeneous systems. When a business processes needs to invoke a people-driven process, BizTalk Server can then use WCF to call the AppFabric services that you have created.

BizTalk Server or AppFabric

The next scenario assumes you have legacy systems or back-end LOB applications that you want to expose as business services for use by other applications in your organization. You can communicate with these systems using XML through web services (WCF).

In this case, you can use either technology to implement this broadly stated scenario. The key in this scenario is that you use XML (through WCF) to communicate with the legacy or back-end systems. In this case, your choice of technology might depend more on a combination of your existing skill set, tooling available for the technology, your organization's SOA strategy, and manageability and the scalability of the technology you're using.

Cost Considerations

Certain situations allow you to use either technology to achieve the same core objectives. Now consider the fact that using WF, WCF, and AppFabric doesn't require an additional licensing fee to those of Windows Server. At the same time, using BizTalk Server does incur an additional licensing fee. This leads to an obvious question: "If I can do the same thing in WF, WCF, and AppFabric that I can do in BizTalk Server, why should I invest in BizTalk and purchase a BizTalk Server license?"

■ **Note** The pricing for AppFabric has not been finalized at the time of writing. The final licensing fees associated with the AppFabric extensions to Windows Server, if any, will be available on or before Microsoft officially releases AppFabric.

The main reason to invest in BizTalk Server is because of the way it simplifies integration of disparate systems across many heterogeneous environments. BizTalk Server gives you a broad set of core capabilities to make all that integration happen. You also need a development experience that masks much of the inherent complexity of integration, which enables you to build your application quickly.

Capabilities that you will need include the various BizTalk Server core architecture features and tools (such as the Schema Editor, BizTalk Mapper, BizTalk Administration Console, Business Rules Engine, BizTalk Server Groups, and so on). BizTalk Server's development platform for integration is flexible, reliable, and scalable. BizTalk Server provides these capabilities and simplifies the development experience through the existence of more than three million lines of .NET code. Also, it lets you leverage and integrate the tooling that Microsoft development teams have written, extensively tested, refined, improved, and optimized in the nine years since BizTalk Server was originally released. All of these factors combine to makes BizTalk Server a robust and stable platform. Saving an organization this hidden cost of development is the ROI value, which some estimate can add up to hundreds of thousands of dollars per year for medium- and large-size organizations.

On the other hand, your solution and business requirements might fall into one of the smaller-scale categories described earlier, in which it makes sense to favor AppFabric. Your solution might not have the degree of complexity for which BizTalk is designed, and you might never plan to get to that point. In that case, AppFabric might prove a more cost-effective choice.

Planning for BizTalk Server vNext and AppFabric

Microsoft knows that its enterprise customers need to make longer-term plans about their infrastructure investments, often more than five years into the future. In response to this need, Microsoft is providing customers with greater visibility into products release cycles.

Microsoft's goal is to release a new version of BizTalk Server approximately every two years, plus additional interim releases of service packs as appropriate. Each full BizTalk Server release will integrate the previous major release with the latest service pack(s) and new functionality. BizTalk Server vNext (the release after BizTalk Server 2009) will continue to provide support for solutions built using existing BizTalk Server artifacts. It is also possible that you might sometime see both BizTalk and AppFabric benefit from a common workflow engine, the new modeling platform called SQL Server Modeling Services, and future releases of .NET Framework.

While there has been a logical move to take some of BizTalk's strongest ideas and make them accessible outside of the product, you should not expect Microsoft to cannibalize BizTalk until all that remains is a flat-file parser. The Microsoft integration server (as BizTalk Server is categorized) is about more than connecting disparate applications and/or services. Rather, it addresses a full set of non-functional requirements around fault handling, reliability, single sign-on, event publishing, and robust orchestration. BizTalk Server is a no-brainer for EAI and B2B scenarios, but it also continues to have a home as an ESB that enables an extensive set of use cases within your organization. If you already have a number of BizTalk Server applications deployed, and you're wondering whether you should start planning on moving your BizTalk Server applications to AppFabric, our recommendation is simple: use the guidance in this chapter to help you in making the right decision about which technology to use.

For example, if your deployed applications do not need to take advantage of AppFabric's low–latency architecture, you will need to focus on upgrading your existing BizTalk Server applications. In that case, BizTalk Server will guide you through upgrade process for BizTalk Server vNext. This upgrade process will let you use wizards to ease the pain that typically accompanies upgrading, and at this time it appears that you won't need to make any changes to existing BizTalk Server artifacts. Additionally, exposing the interfaces of your BizTalk Server applications as WCF endpoints—using the out-of-the-box WCF adapters—will help you ensure seamless WF connectivity in the future.

Summary

In this chapter, you learned about scenarios where it makes more sense to use AppFabric, BizTalk, or both. Will all scenarios fit into AppFabric? Not a chance.

Which you should use often comes down to a cost to a buy vs. cost-to-build analysis. On an individual project basis, the decision sometimes becomes a difficult one. When you think about enterprise-wide solutions, typically the cost to buy a supportable product with a core set of features is the better answer. With BizTalk, you get adapters, high availability, robust development tools, EDI, RFID, flat-file parsing, administration, BAM, and more. While some of these items are being moved further down into the stack, not all of them will be.

The buy vs. build analysis will become more difficult going forward. We think that is a good thing. The end goal in development (as in many endeavors) is to do more with less and to lower the cost for consistently delivering supportable and maintainable code that meets your requirements. We think AppFabric (and .Net 4.0) helps you with that down that road. But there will always be a need for BizTalk as a core component in the enterprise when it makes sense, and while we do not foresee a world without BizTalk, we are excited about a world with options that include BizTalk and AppFabric.

CHAPTER 3

■ ■ ■

Laying the Foundation

Let's start this chapter in a simple, straightforward way. A Windows Workflow Foundation (WF) or Windows Communication Foundation (WCF) service cannot be used until is it hosted.

Every WF or WCF service must be hosted in a process known as a host process (roughly speaking, you can think of this as a Windows executable program). The important point is that WF and WCF services cannot run by themselves. A single host process can host multiple services, and the same service can reside in multiple hosts.

Reviewing the Methods for Hosting a Service

There are four methods you can use to host a WF or WCF service. You should be familiar with all of them, so that you can choose the method best-suited for your application. The four methods include the following:

Self Hosting: This method requires that the developer provide the host process. This host process can be a Windows Forms application, a console application, or even a WPF rich client application. This host process must be running before the service can receive messages. For the service to start receiving messages, you will need to place the code for the service inside the managed application code, define an endpoint for the service either in code or through a configuration file, and then create an instance of ServiceHost. At this point, you will need to call the open method on the ServiceHost object to create and open a listener for the service. After the service finishes receiving messages, you close the service session by calling `System.ServiceModel.Channels.CommuncationObject.Close` on the ServiceHost. In most cases, this will occur when the application closes.

Two kinds of self hosting occur more frequently than others: hosting a service within a console application and within a rich client application. Hosting a service within a console application is useful when debugging, trying to get trace information, and stepping through a round-trip service call. This proves useful during the development phase, enabling you to make modifications easily, as well as insert additional error checking and handling. This scenario also allows you to move the application around quickly to test different deployment scenarios.

The second common type of self-hosting occurs in rich client applications. These applications can host services that allow the application to communicate with other services to exchange information. This kind of service also allows other applications to communicate with it by providing a means for other clients to connect to and share information with it.

Managed Windows Service: This method of hosting a service is similar to self hosting; however, in this case, you host the service in a managed Windows Service (previously known as a NT Service). Note that the developer must also write the host code when using this method. The advantage of a Windows Service over other self-hosting scenarios is that you can start a Windows Service and listen automatically. The Windows Service becomes both a Windows Service and a WCF service once the implementation code inherits from the **ServiceBase** class and a WCF service contract interface. As when using the self-hosting method, you create and open the ServiceHost; the difference here is that you do so inside the Windows Services **OnStart** overridden method, and you close the ServiceHost within the **OnStop** overridden method. As with all Windows Services, an installer class that inherits from the Installer class must also be implemented to allow the Windows Service to be installed by the **InstallUtil.exe** tool and controlled by the service control manager (SCM) for Windows Services.

This method of hosting, which is available in all versions of Windows, provides the option of hosting a long-running WCF service, outside of IIS, but without the automatic message activation. The operating system manages the lifetime of a Windows Service, so it isn't tied to the lifetime of the applications that use the Windows Service. Also, these Windows Services don't have the services that come with hosting in IIS, as you'll see in the next section.

IIS Hosting: IIS hosting is integrated with ASP.NET and thus uses the features that ASP.NET provides. First, you don't need to write any hosting code to take advantage of this approach. Second, you can find several services already provided. These services include process recycling, idle shutdown, process health monitoring, and message-based activation; however, you should keep in mind that the message-based activation included with IIS hosting works only with the **HTTP** protocol.

All of the services provided by IIS have made it the preferred host for web service applications that require high availability and scalability. IIS has been available for many years, has matured over the course of many versions, and is included in all Windows operating systems. Unfortunately, people often forget that different versions of IIS come installed on the different versions of the operating system. These differences can lead to different behavior and different functionality. One such example revolves around message-based activation. When working with IIS 5.1 on Windows XP, IIS blocks self-hosted WCF services on the same computer from using port 80 to communicate. When working with IIS 6, IIS provides the ability for hosted services to run in the same worker process (implemented as an Application Pool) as other applications. In this case, WCF and IIS 6 (and IIS 7) use the **HTTP.sys** component. This means they can now share port 80 with other self-hosted services running on the same machine. The **HTTP.sys** component was eventually separated from IIS, and it is now a standalone component that is used by IIS, but which can also be used by your application.

Windows Process Activation Services (WAS): This is a new process-activation method that Microsoft released with Windows 2008; it is also available with Windows Vista and Windows 7. WAS has a similar activation method to what is available through IIS hosting. Unlike IIS, WAS hosting has no dependency on the **HTTP** protocol. WAS provides message-based activation over other protocols supported by WCF, including TCP, MSMQ, and named pipes.

IIS 7 uses WAS to accomplish several things. First, it enables message-based activation over **HTTP**. Second, WCF components can plug into WAS to provide activation for the other protocols that WCF supports.

In looking at the four methods of hosting, the added functionality from WAS provides the best of all hosting options because it allows applications that use communication protocols to use all of IIS's features (listed under IIS hosting) that were only available to HTTP-based systems. Also, hosting in WAS doesn't require you to write any hosting code as part of your application.

Table 3-1 recaps the information listed above and shows what is available from a hosting environment. It shows the hosting methods are available on which platform, available transports, and the benefits and limitations that come with each hosting method.

Table 3-1. *Hosting Methods Available by Platform*

Hosting Environment	Platform	Transports	Scenarios	Benefits/ Limitations
Self Hosted	Windows Vista Window Server 2003 Windows Vista Windows Server 2008	HTTP Net.tcp Net.pipe Net.msmq	Console App Winform/WPF App	-Easy Deployment -Flexibility -Not enterprise ready
Windows Service	Windows XP Windows Server 2003 Windows Vista Windows Server 2008	HTTP Net.tcp Net.pipe Net.msmq	Long-running WCF service	-Controlled process lifetime -Application scope -Supported on all versions of Windows
IIS (5.1, 6.0)	Windows XP (5.1) Windows Server 2003 (6.0)	HTTP	Services running alongside ASP.NET in IIS	-HTTP only -Process Recycling -Idle Shutdown -Health Monitoring -Message-Based Activation
Windows Process Activation Services	Windows Vista Windows Server 2008	HTTP Net.tcp Net.pipe Net.msmq	Services running without needing to have IIS installed	-IIS is not required -Message Activation with all WCF supported protocols -All benefits of IIS listed previously

WF and WCF have been around since the release of the .NET 3.0 Framework, so people should be familiar with the first three hosting models. WAS was released more recently, with Windows Server 2008, so it hasn't been something most people have worked with. As such, the sections that follow will focus on what WAS is and how it can be utilized to host services. It is important to gain a deeper understanding of what WAS is, as well as how you can take advantage of it. This is important because AppFabric is based on both IIS and WAS.

So, let's begin by looking at the new functionality in IIS, and then dig a little deeper into WAS hosting.

Understanding IIS Architectural Changes

One strength of WCF is that you can host WCF-based services in any Windows process, including from within a console application. Previously, you learned about the fact that you can host services in IIS, and that by default, those services must utilize the **HTTP** protocol. WAS lets you use protocols other than **HTTP**. You might wonder what changed, that Microsoft can now provide this ability to utilize other protocols and activation services. In order to answer that question, and show why IIS 7.0 is better, we need to review the architecture of IIS 6.

IIS 6 Architecture

When a request message is sent across the wire and arrives at the server, it is first processed by the **HTTP** stack (**http.sys**). The **HTTP** stack used to be tightly coupled with IIS in previous versions, but it has now been separated and lives at the kernel level. Once the **HTTP** stack processes the message, it is delivered to a listener process.

The IIS 6 architecture (see Figure 3-1) is divided between a listener process and a set of worker processes. The listener process is implemented through the **w3svc** service. The listener process *listens* for messages to arrive across **HTTP**. When one does, the w3svc process looks at the request URI and maps it to a specific IIS application running inside a specific application pool. This mapping is based on configuration information stored in the IIS metabase. The metabase in IIS 6 has been upgraded from the previous binary format and is now based on the metabase.xml file in the **%windir%\system32\inetsrv** folder.

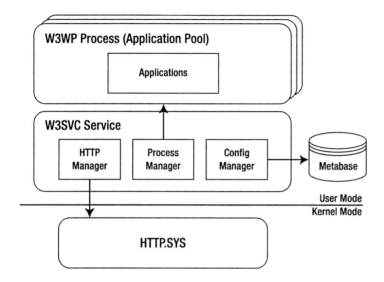

Figure 3-1. IIS 6 Architecture

Once this mapping occurs, the **w3svc** process sends the message to the appropriate worker process. The worker processes are hosted in application domains in the **w3wp.exe**. These worker processes contain the code that processes the request instance.

Before the request can be sent to the worker process, a couple of things need to happen. First, the **w3svc** service must determine whether the worker process and application pool are already running (they might already be running from a previous request). If they are already instantiated, then the message is forwarded.

However, if the worker process and the application pool haven't been instantiated, then that must occur before the request can be sent to the new instance of the **w3wp** process. The activation part comes into play at this point. When the new instance of the w3wp process is instantiated, an activation request will start it. At startup, the **w3wp** process will load the w3wphost.dll, which also loads the aspnet_isapi.dll that contains the managed components of ASP.NET. The **aspnet_isapi.dll** loads the common language runtime into the worker process and creates the default domain. By default, there is one application domain for each IIS application.

When looking at the architecture shown in Figure 3-1, you can see that the **w3svc** service performs multiple tasks. It functions as the **HTTP** listener and manages the communications with the **http.sys**. It is also initiates the process of receiving the incoming **HTTP** request. Finally, **w3svc** includes the functionality that implements process activation for starting new instances of the **w3wp** process and forwarding those requests to the newly created process. As you learn more about IIS 7, you will see that it is these tasks that have been refactored.

IIS 7 Architecture

The architecture of IIS 7 (see Figure 3-2) is similar to the architecture of IIS 6. For example, all of the components (application pools, application managers, listener process, and the worker processes) are present in IIS 7. The primary difference is that IIS 7 activation supports non-**HTTP** protocols. All of the services that IIS provided, such as message activation, health monitoring, manageability, and rapid failure protection, are now available to services that utilize the other protocols that WCF supports.

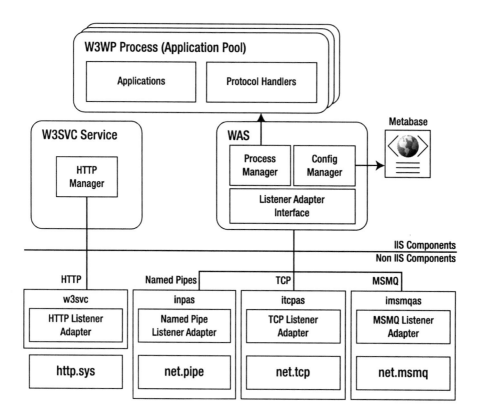

Figure 3-2. *IIS 7 Architecture*

In IIS 7, however, the responsibilities of the listener process and the activation process of starting new **w3wp** process instances and routing request messages have been split into separate Windows services.

The **w3svc** process still acts as the **HTTP** listener; however, the configuration-management and process-activation functions have been separated from the IIS core and merged into the new service called Windows Process Activation Services (WAS). This means that you can't understand the architecture of IIS 7 without also learning about WAS. Even if you receive only **HTTP** traffic, you will still be utilizing the services in WAS. The WAS architecture consists of the following services:

The configuration manager. This service reads application and application-pool configuration information from the new metabase. The metabase, as it was, no longer exists. It is now contained in the `applicationhost.config` file.

The process manager. This service provides the mapping function to map application pools to existing worker processes. It is also the component that creates new instances of the `w3wp` process. This is the process that will host the new application pool instances that respond to activation requests.

The listener adapter interface. This service lays out the contract that defines how external listeners will communicate the activation requests received back to the WAS services for a specific protocol. The WWW Service provides the `HTTP` listener, while IIS provides Windows services for the other protocols. IIS 7 pairs the listener adapter and the protocol listener.

The protocol listeners. These services receive the requests for the specific protocol. The `HTTP` listener is implemented in `http.sys`. The listeners for the other supported protocols are provided by the following listeners: `inpas` for Named Pipes, `imsmqas` for MSMQ, and `itcpas` for TCP.

The protocol handlers. These services function as the conduit for the request. WCF currently provides managed handlers for `HTTP`, named pipes, TCP, and MSMQ. This architecture also provides the foundation to support additional protocols in the future.

Earlier, you learned that the `w3svc` process is still the `HTTP` listener. That process communicates directly with the kernel level `http.sys` component and passes on the activation request to WAS through the listener adapter interface. For non-http traffic (TCP, Named Pipes and MSMQ), the WCF libraries use the listener adapter interface to forward the activation requests.

`SMSvcHost.exe` contains the protocol listeners WCF provides. Although all four services reside in the same binary, they are separate Windows services, and you can stop and start them individually.

Because WAS controls and manages the processes for both `HTTP` and non-`HTTP` protocols, you can run applications with different protocols in the same application pool. This allows you to create an application and expose it over both `HTTP` and `net.tcp`.

WAS is more than a fundamental part of the IIS 7 architecture; it also provides the ability to host WCF services listening to additional protocols outside of `HTTP`. One of the benefits of the IIS 7 architecture is that you can install the WAS components without the need to install the `HTTP` stack, if so desired.

Installing WAS

A good understanding of WAS is important if you want to utilize AppFabric to its best effect. AppFabric is built on the top of and extends the functionality of WAS. Understanding how to use WAS—and understanding where WAS's functionality ends and AppFabric's functionality begins—will help you understand your application needs better. It will also help you architect better solutions.

The rest of this chapter will show you how to install and configure WAS, create a WCF service, and host it in WAS. Finally, you will learn how to create a client to call your service. The techniques you learn in the sections that follow will provide an important foundation for future chapters, enabling you to extend your service and begin to take advantage of the services of AppFabric.

▨ **Note** WAS currently runs on Windows Vista, Windows 7, and Windows Server 2008.

Installing WAS on Windows Vista requires two steps. First, you need to install the WCF non-HTTP activation components. Second, you need to add the site bindings to the WAS configuration.

Installing Activation Components

To install the activation components on Windows Vista, open the Control Panel and double-click on **Programs and Features**. When the dialog box opens, click **Turn Windows Components On or Off** in the left pane. When the Windows Features dialog box appears, expand the **Microsoft .NET Framework 3.X** tree node and make sure that the **Windows Communication Foundation Non-HTTP Activation** item is checked. Also, expand the **Windows Process Activation Service** tree node and select the underlying checkboxes (see Figure 3-3).

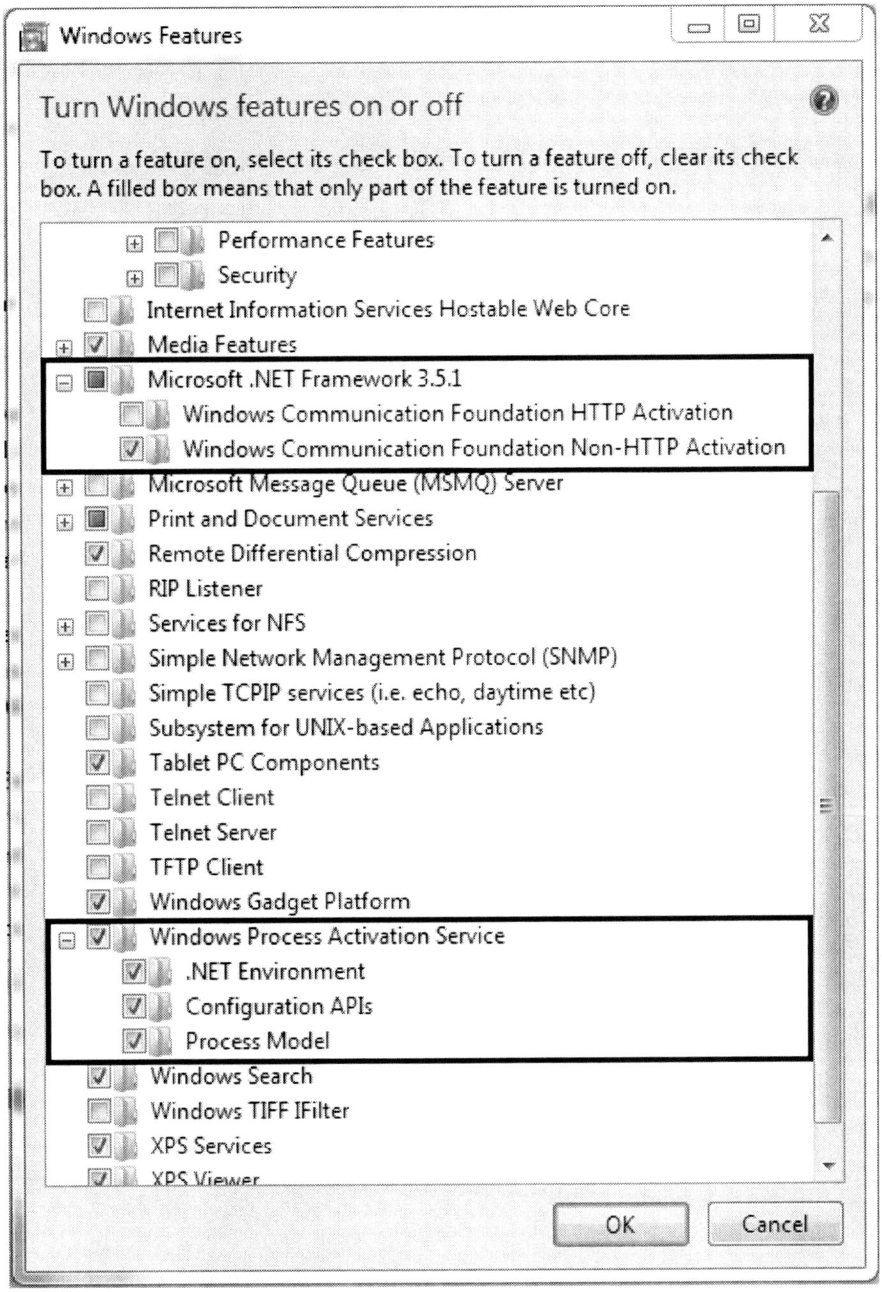

Figure 3-3. WAS installation Settings

To install the activation components on Windows Server 2008, open the **Server Manager**, which you can find under **Administrative Tools**. Once the **Server Manager** dialog box opens, scroll to the bottom and click **Add Roles**. This brings up the **Add Roles wizard**; click **Next** to move to the page that lists the roles, and then select **Application Server (Installed)** (see Figure 3-4).

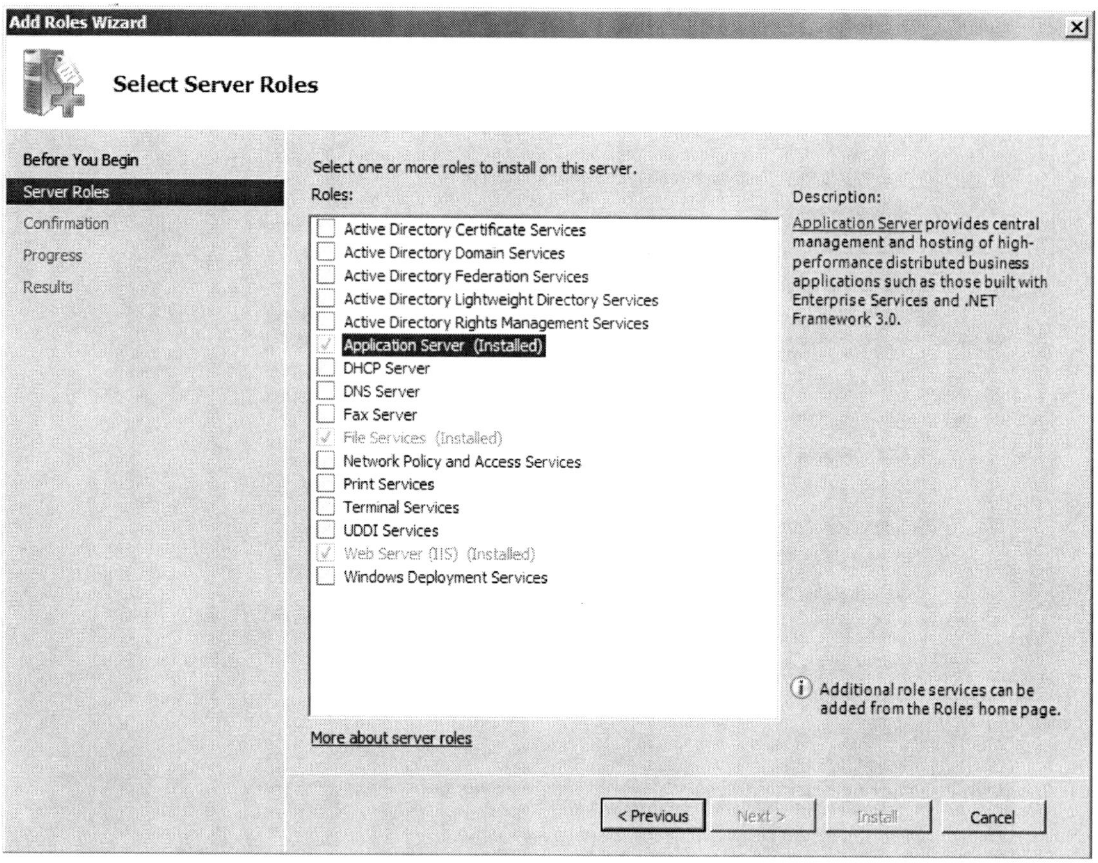

Figure 3-4. Server Role Settings

Click **Next** until you get to the **Role Services** section. Select the services that you wish to include, but make sure that you select the **Windows Process Activation Service Support** node (see Figure 3-5).

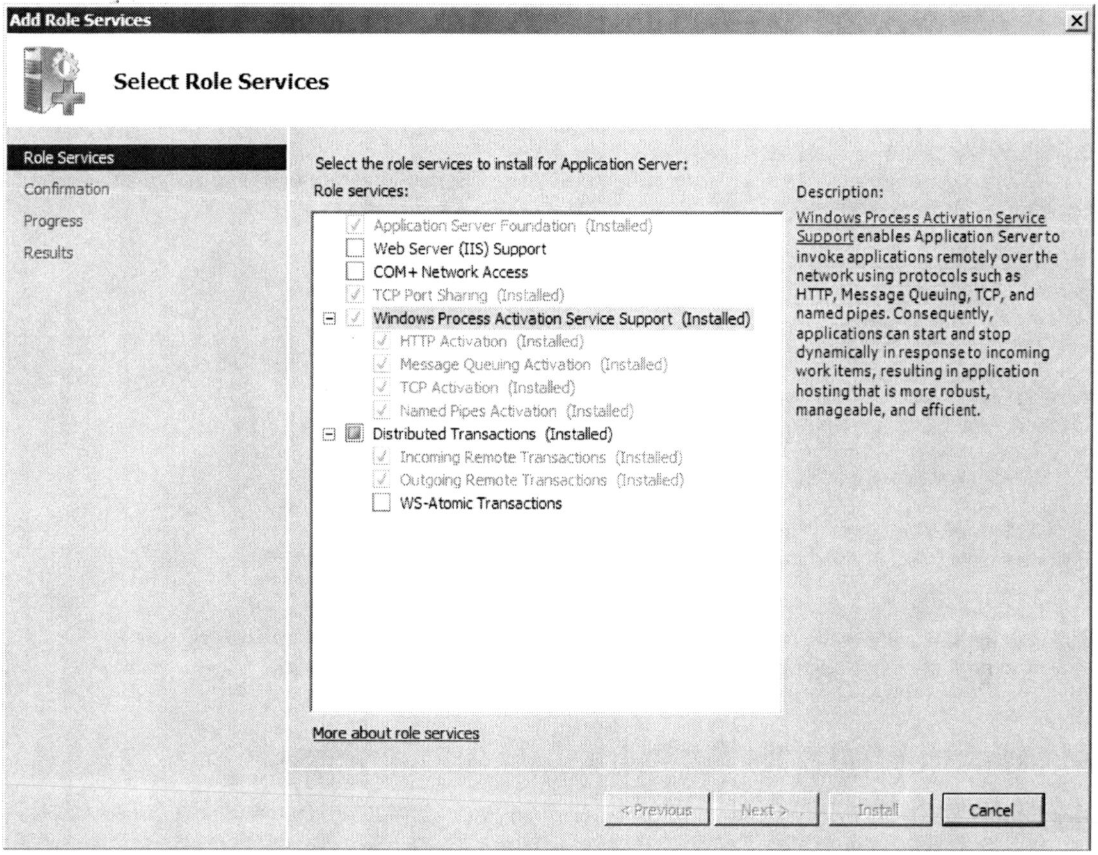

Figure 3-5. *WAS Role Services*

If you also wish to install the Web Server role, you can select that option at this time. If you want to run WAS without installing the Web Server, then don't select that option. Click **Next** until the **Install** button is enabled. Click the **Install** button.

I would also recommend installing the IIS management console, whether you intend to run the Web Server or only WAS. This console is not technically required, but it will undoubtedly make your job much easier. You can install it by clicking **Add Roles**, just as you did previously. This time, you want to select the **Web Server (IIS)** role. Again, you can select the services that you want to install. The main reason you're using this dialog box is to install the management console, so scroll down until you see the **Management Tools** node. Select the **IIS Management Console** node and click the **Next** button until the Install button is enabled. Finally, click the **Install** button.

Configuring Site Bindings

Once you install WAS, you need to set up the site bindings. The site bindings will match and configure protocols to the IIS site. To set up the site bindings to the WAS configuration, start a command prompt by right-clicking and selecting the **Run as administrator** option. When the command prompt appears, you need to type three different commands for each of the protocols you want to enable, using the **appcmd.exe** to configure the protocols. The **HTTP** protocol is supported and installed by default. You can choose to install and configure everything, or you can select only the protocols you intend to utilize. If you use Windows 2008, check your config file before you run these commands because these entries might already be entered as part of adding the role.

Run any or all of the following commands to perform the configuration you require (for this book, you can get by using only TCP). Use this code to configure named pipes:

```
%windir%\system32\inetsrv\appcmd.exe set site
"Default Web Site" -+bindings.[protocol='net.pipe',bindingInformation='*']
```

You can use this code for TCP:

```
%windir%\system32\inetsrv\appcmd.exe set site
"Default Web Site" -+bindings.[protocol='net.tcp',bindingInformation='*']
```

Finally, you can use this code to configure MSMQ:

```
%windir%\system32\inetsrv\appcmd.exe set site
"Default Web Site" -+bindings.[protocol='net.msmq',bindingInformation='*']
```

Running these commands updates the **applicationhost.config** file. Remember that the **applicationhost.config** file is located in the **<driveletter>\Windows\system32\inetsrv\config** directory or in the **<driveletter>\Windows\SysWOW64\inetsrv\config** directory.

Managing Protocols for Individual Applications

After binding the default web site to the specific protocol, you will still need to enable the protocols for the individual web applications. And at some later date, you might also want to review the protocols for an application, or you might want to remove one or more protocols.

■ **Note** You haven't created an application yet, so let's do that now. You can create an application in Visual Studio or by using the IIS 7 management console. Once you create your application, you can proceed to the next step.

Creating an IIS 7 Application

You can create an IIS 7 application by opening IIS manager and following these steps:

1. Expand the **Sites** node in the Connection pane.

2. Right-click the site you want to create as an application.

3. In the **Alias** text box, enter a value for the application URL.

4. Click **Select** to choose a different application pool, if needed. When the **Select Application Pool** dialog box appears, select the application pool you want from the list and hit OK.

5. Type the physical path of the applications folder in the Physical path text box.

6. If you want to specify credentials, then click **Connect**. If you do not use specific credentials, then select the Application user on the **Connect As** dialog box.

7. Click **Test Settings** to verify all the information you entered and then click **OK**.

It is also possible to create the application using the command line. Use the following syntax to create an application:

```
appcmd add app /site.name: string /path: string /physicalPath: string
```

The **site.name** string is the name of the web site that you want to add the application to. The **path string** is the virtual path of the application and the **physicalPath** string is the physical path of containing the application code on the file system.

Adding Protocols for an Application

After creating the application, you can run the following command to enable support for the individual applications and select which protocols you wish to have enabled. Reference the protocols as **HTTP**, **net.tcp**, **net.pipe**, and **net.msmq**. The command that follows enables the **net.tcp protocol**:

```
%windir%\system32\inetsrv\appcmd.exe set app
"Default Web Site/AppFabricBook/WASHost" /enabledProtocols:net.tcp
```

In addition to running the command manually for each application you want to enable, we can create code that is part of your automated install and deployment routine. The C# code that follows enables the protocols you designate for the application you designate. The code that follows requires both a virtual path and a physical path. The virtual path is in the format of **<site>/<application>/<vdir name>**, while the physical path is the physical location on the disk:

```csharp
private static void EnableWasAndProtocols(string virtualPath,
  string physicalPath, string enabledProtocols)
{
  using (ServerManager sm = new ServerManager())
  {
    // create the application
    sm.Sites[0].Applications.Add(virtualPath, physicalPath);
    sm.CommitChanges();
    // set up and configure the enabled protocols
    Application app = sm.Sites[0].Applications[virtualPath];
    app.EnabledProtocols = enabledProtocols;
    sm.CommitChanges();
  }
}
```

Listing the Protocols for an Application

So far you have learned how to manually enable your protocols through the **appcmd.exe**, as well as how to enable your protocols through code. However, what do you do if you don't know what protocols have been enabled for an application? How would you know what protocols have been set? You can paste the following code into a simple Windows Console application in Visual Studio. This code loops through the applications and lists the protocols that have been enabled for that application:

```
using System;
using System.Collections.Generic;
using System.Linq;
using System.Text;
using Microsoft.Web.Administration;
using Microsoft.Web.Management;

namespace WASProtocolListing
{
    class Program
    {
        static void Main(string[] args)
        {
            //Lists the applications and the enabled protocols
            using (ServerManager manager = new ServerManager())
            {
                Site defaultWebSite = manager.Sites["Default Web Site"];

                foreach (Application app in defaultWebSite.Applications)
                {
                    Console.WriteLine(
                        "{0} has the following protocols enabled: '{1}'",
                        app.Path, app.EnabledProtocols);
                }
            }
                Console.ReadLine();
        }
    }
}
```

Removing Application Protocols

Now that you know what protocols have been enabled, what happens if you want to remove an enabled protocol? You can remove the protocol from the list of enabled protocols for the application, or you can remove the protocol binding from the machine.

The following snippet shows you how to remove an enabled protocol from the application:

```
%windir%\system32\inetsrv\appcmd.exe set app " Default Web
Site/AppFabricBook/WASHost" /enabledProtocols:http
```

If you compare this to the command listed previously, where you were enabling the protocols, you will see that they are almost identical. The only difference is that this command specifies only the protocol that you want to install; that is why it lists only the **HTTP** protocol.

If you want to remove the protocol binding from the machine, then you can run this line of code:

```
%windir%\system32\inetsrv\appcmd.exe set site "Default Web Site"
-bindings.[protocol='net.tcp',bindingInformation='808:*']
```

When running this command, use the same binding information that you used to register the binding. If you ran this command with more than one port, then specify the specific port you want to disable in the **bindingInformation** parameter.

Access and Processing Considerations

At this point, you have the site and application enabled. However, if you intend to utilize the MSMQ protocol, then you need to keep a couple things in mind and implement a couple more steps.

When you set up your queue, you need to set the access control list credentials on the queue to allow the worker process to read from and peek at the queue. If you have not changed the credentials for the worker process, then you need to add the **NETWORK SERVICE** credentials to the queue security.

Finally—and this is important—the MSMQ activation only works if the queue has the same name as the **.svc** file. This means that if your service endpoint is **/<ServerName>/<ApplicationName>/<ServiceName>.svc**, then you need to make the queue name **<ApplicationName>/<ServiceName>.svc**. The service configuration entry for the endpoint entity looks like this:

```
<endpoint address="net.msmq://localhost/private/AppFabricbook/wasservice.svc"
  binding="netMsmqBinding" bindingNamespace="urn:AppFabricbook"
  contract="IMsmqWASService" />
```

Note that all non-**HTTP** endpoints do *not* flow through the IIS processing pipeline. Instead they will be routed to the WCF runtime. This also means that you will not be able to utilize an **HttpModule** to provide pre or post processing. It also means that the **Application_Start** and **Application_End** methods of the **HttpApplication** class will not be fired. You might be used to putting clean up code in these methods, but now you will need to place that clean up code in the **Opening** and **Closing** event code in the class derived from the ServiceHost. To utilize the code placed in these two methods, you will need to wire up the handlers for these events after the ServiceHost instance has been created and call the Open method. Unfortunately, this is not possible when using the ServiceHost directive in the .svc file. Instead, you will need to create a customer service host factory because this gives you the ability to interact with the **Opening** and **Closing** events. When specifying the attributes in the **.svc** file, you should use an attribute—named **Factory**, aptly enough—to specify the custom host factory to use.

If you find yourself in the situation of needing to listen to the Opening and Closing events, and you need to create your own factory object, you can do something like the following:

```
public class CustomHostFactory : ServiceHostFactoryBase
{
  public override ServiceHostBase CreateServiceHost(
    string constructorString, Uri[] baseAddresses)
  {
    Type service = Type.GetType(constructorString);
```

```
        ServiceHost host = new ServiceHost(service, baseAddresses);
        //wire up the event handlers
        host.Opening += OnOpening;
        host.Closing += OnClosing;
        return host;
    }
}
```

You're now finished setting up WAS; next, you will learn how to create a service.

Creating and Connecting to a Service

When creating a service and publishing it to the virtual directory, you must include three items; the compiled service code in the **/bin** directory or the source code in the **/App_Code** folder; a **.svc** file (which is the service endpoint); and a configuration file. If you're already up to speed on WCF development, you will recognize these as standard items for a service.

Understanding the .svc File

If you are relatively new to WCF, the .svc file connects the URI to the service implementation. A .svc file includes the following line:

```
<% @ServiceHost Service="WASService" %>
```

In this case, the ServiceHost directive associates the internal plumbing code required to host the service to the service type specified in the Service attribute. If you create your own HostFactory to use that plumbing code, then your **.svc** file will look like this:

```
<% @ServiceHost Service="WASService" Factory="CustomHostFactory" %>
```

The **Factory** attribute specifies the type name of the factory that you will use to instantiate the service host. If you don't include **Factory** attribute, then the default **ServiceHostFactory service host** will be used.

The configuration information for WAS is stored in the two locations. The first location is in the **web.config** file, while the second is in the **app.config** file. If you peruse the **web.config** file, you will see entries that look like this:

```
<add path="*.svc" verb="*" type="System.ServiceModel.Activation.HttpHandler,
System.ServiceModel,...../>
```

You will also see entries like this in the protocols section:

```
<add name="net.tcp"
processHandlerType="System.ServiceModel.WasHosting.TcpProcessProtocolHandler,
System.ServiceModel.WasHosting, Version=3.0.0.0, Culture=neutral,
PublicKeyToken=b77a5c561934e089" appDomainHandlerType=
"System.ServiceModel.WasHosting.TcpAppDomainProtocolHandler,
System.ServiceModel.WasHosting, Version=3.0.0.0, Culture=neutral,
PublicKeyToken=b77a5c561934e089" validate="false"/>
```

You will also see the **<bindings>** element for the web site. These elements are nested inside the **<system.applicationHost>** element.

You can see that there will be an entry for each of the protocols that you registered with the preceding commands:

```
<system.applicationHost>
  <sites>
   <site name="Default Web Site" id="1">
     <bindings>
       <binding protocol="http" bindingInformation="*:80:" />
       <binding protocol="net.pipe" bindingInformation="*" />
       <binding protocol="net.tcp" bindingInformation="*" />
       <binding protocol="net.msmq"  bindingInformation="*" />
     </bindings>
   </site>
  </sites>
</system.applicationHost>
```

This section defines what protocols WCF and the web site will support. If you don't see a binding element for a protocol that you want to utilize then you will need to run the appcmd.exe command again to register the specific protocol.

You've learned how to use the **appcmd.exe** command to configure these settings; however, you can also configure them using a GUI available in IIS 7. The Site Bindings link will allow you to add, edit or remove any of the protocol bindings. This GUI allows you to set the port and IP address for each of the protocols. This book covered the command prompt approach as well because it's important that you could understand what is happening beneath the hood and so you could appreciate better the differences between the versions of WAS in Windows Vista and the one in Windows 2008. In Windows Vista, the bindings are not pre-configured. Also, you cannot add them using the GUI. In Windows 2008, the bindings are configured by default.

The second configuration location is in the **app.config** file, which holds the required information for the services hosted as part of your application. The information used by WAS and WCF is contained entirely in the **system.serviceModel** element. When dealing with a service hosted in WAS, you don't need to include a base address; WAS determines the address using the web site address and virtual directory.

Creating a Service

Let's write some code. Start by opening Visual Studio and creating a service project named **WASService**. Create a **.svc** file and insert the following code:

```
<%@ ServiceHost Language="C#"
  Debug="true" Service="WASService"
  CodeBehind="~/App_Code/WASService.cs" %>
```

Next, change the **.cs** file's name to **WASService.cs** and insert this code:

```
using System;
using System.ServiceModel;
```

```
[ServiceContract(Name = "WASServiceContract", Namespace =
"urn:AppFabricbook")]
public interface IWASService
{
    [OperationContract]
    string Echo(string inputvalue);
}

public class WASService : IWASService
{
    public string Echo(string inputvalue)
    {
        return "Echo: " + inputvalue;
    }
}
```

If you're not familiar with WCF , this code uses the [ServiceContract] attribute to let the WCF runtime know that this interface will contain the service operation definitions. The class implementation uses the [OperationContract] attribute to expose the individual methods as service operations.

You now have two of the three required items to create a working service. The only item missing is the config file. Open the app.config file in the solution and insert the following XML code:

```
<?xml version="1.0"?>
<configuration
  xmlns="http://schemas.microsoft.com/.NetConfiguration/v2.0">
  <system.serviceModel>
    <services>
      <service name="WASService"
        behaviorConfiguration="WASServiceBehavior">
       <endpoint binding="netTcpBinding"
          bindingConfiguration="PortSharingBinding"
         contract="IWASService" />
         <endpoint address="mex" binding="mexTcpBinding"
            contract="IMetadataExchange" />
      </service>
    </services>
    <bindings>
      <netTcpBinding>
        <binding name="PortSharingBinding"
          portSharingEnabled="true">
          <security mode="None" />
        </binding>
      </netTcpBinding>
    </bindings>
    <behaviors>
      <serviceBehaviors>
        <behavior name="WASServiceBehavior">
          <serviceMetadata />
            <serviceDebug
               includeExceptionDetailInFaults="False"/>
        </behavior>
```

```
        </serviceBehaviors>
      </behaviors>
    </system.serviceModel>
</configuration>
```

In this configuration file, you specify the service name, the binding, and the contract. Your service will use the TCP binding.

Creating a Client

To utilize the **WASService** service, begin by creating a new C# Windows Forms application and name it **WASServiceClient**. You will need to create a proxy for the WCF service. A proxy is a local representation of an object that exists in a different address space. The client thinks that it is talking with the server object, but instead communicates through the proxy to translate the client's call to a remote call. The proxy also receives the response and forwards it to the client object. You can create the proxy either directly through Visual Studio by selecting Service Reference, or you can accomplish this using the **svcutil.exe** command. These two methods will read the service metadata exposed either by a WSDL file or a MEX endpoint. You can use this syntax if you decide that you would like to use the **svcutil.exe** command:

```
svcutil.exe net.tcp://localhost/AppFabricBook/WASHost/WASService.svc/mex
```

Your service is exposed over TCP; this means you will point to the MEX endpoint because only the **HTTP** protocol based endpoints will have a WSDL file. In addition to creating the proxy, the svcutil.exe will also create a configuration file. The configuration will contain all the information required to connect to the service, and it will be populated with the information from the service's metadata.

You now have two files that you need to add to your Visual Studio solution. Add the WCF proxy and add the **output.config** file. After you add the **output.config**, make sure you to rename it to **app.config**. You should see the following in the **app.config** file you just added:

```
<?xml version="1.0" encoding="utf-8"?>
<configuration>
  <system.serviceModel>
    <bindings>
      <netTcpBinding>
        <binding name="NetTcpBinding_IWASService"
          <................../>
        </binding>
      </netTcpBinding>
    </bindings>
    <client>
      <endpoint address=
        "net.tcp://localhost/AppFabricBook/WASHost/WASService.svc"
        binding="netTcpBinding"
        bindingConfiguration="NetTcpBinding_IWASService"
        contract="IWASService"
        name="NetTcpBinding_IWASService" />
    </client>
  </system.serviceModel>
</configuration>
```

Now you're ready to write the code that uses the proxy to access the service. Begin by adding a **command** button to the form and name it **btnWASServicePing**. You can create a **click** event by double-clicking the button in the Visual Studio form designer to create the event automatically, and then inserting this code:

```
private void btnWASServicePing_Click(object sender, EventArgs e)
{
    WASServiceClient proxy = new WASServiceClient();
    MessageBox.Show(proxy.Echo("Just Called From Client Code"));
}
```

After you compile this code, it will invoke the **Ping** method of the **WASService** through the proxy class, and you should see the message appear in the message box.

At this point, you have learned how to create and access a service using TCP. You will also recall that you learned about MSMQ earlier. But what changes must you make if you want to use named pipes?

Incorporating Additional Protocols

Previously you used the **appcmd.exe** command to register the activation protocols. If you used the example above that included all of the protocols, then you won't need to register the following lines of code. However, if you didn't register all of the protocols, then you need to run the following command to register the named pipes binding:

```
<DriveName>\Windows\system32\inetsrv\appcmd.exe set site
    "Default Web Site" -+bindings.[protocol='net.pipe', bindingInformation='*']
```

You also need to run this command to register the protocol for the site:

```
%windir%\system32\inetsrv\appcmd.exe set app
    "Default Web Site/AppFabricBook/WASHost" /enabledProtocols:http, net.pipe
```

Next, you need to modify your service's **app.config** file. The **app.config** should look like the following snippet if you want to include the named pipe configuration and binding:

```
<system.serviceModel>
  <services>
   <service name="WASService"
     behaviorConfiguration="WASServiceBehavior">
     <endpoint binding="netNamedPipeBinding"
       bindingConfiguration="Binding1" contract="IWASService" />
     <endpoint address="mex" binding="mexNamedPipeBinding"
       contract="IMetadataExchange" />
   </service>
  </services>
  <netNamedPipeBinding>
    <binding name="Binding1" >
      <security mode = "None">
```

```
      </security>
    </binding >
  </netNamedPipeBinding>
 <behaviors>
 <serviceBehaviors>
  <behavior name="WASServiceBehavior">
    <serviceMetadata />
    <serviceDebug includeExceptionDetailInFaults="False" />
  </behavior>
 </behaviors>
 </serviceBehaviors>
</system.serviceModel>
```

When you implement or incorporate this **app.config** code, you will have all that you need to support **named.pipes** within your service.

To consume the named pipe configured service you create a proxy and config file, just as you did previously. And, as before, you can either use Visual Studio and the Set Service Reference functionality, or you can use the **svcutil.exe**. If you decide to use the **svcutil.exe** command, then you need to run this command:

```
svcutil.exe net.pipe://localhost/AppFabricBook/WASHost/WASService.svc?WSDL
```

This command creates the proxy and the config file. Add those two files to your client project, then open the **output.config** file, copy the **<netNamedPipeBinding>** and **<endpoint>** sections, and place them in your **app.config** file.

Once you do this, you can write code to access the service. You write this code taking exactly the same approach that you used in the Creating a Client section of this chapter. The proxy will handle everything related to the protocol; all that you need to do is instantiate the proxy object and call the methods it contains.

Is WAS the Be All End All?

If you can host your components in WAS, why not just end the book here? The answer is that WAS has some shortcomings. Its chief shortcoming is its message-based activation. And we know what you are thinking: we were just touting the benefits of message-based activiation!

When a service is hosted in WAS, a service instance doesn't get created until the first message is received. Therefore, when a message arrives addressed to that service, it must first initialize a new instance. Part of initializing the new instance includes allocating memory, loading libraries, and creating any required objects. All of this takes additional time and causes delays in starting the service.

In future chapters, you will learn how to use the functionality that AppFabric provides, not only to deal with this limitation, but also to incorporate additional functionality that will make AppFabric the full-featured host that you require for your applications.

Summary

This chapter outlined your options for hosting components. Specifically, it helped you acquire a deeper understanding of what WAS is and how you can take advantage of it. This understanding included learning how to install, configure, and add protocols to WAS. In addition, you created a sample service and client so you could see how you can utilize these additional protocols.

This deeper understanding of IIS and (especially) WAS will prove important because AppFabric is based on both of these technologies, in addition to providing additional services. In future chapters, you will learn more about all the services and functionality provided by AppFabric.

CHAPTER 4

■ ■ ■

Understanding the Architecture

This chapter will take you on a journey that walks you through how Microsoft created AppFabric, covering both its architecture and how you use it. We take this approach because using AppFabric successfully is correlated directly to a thorough understanding of its components and services, as well as how they work together.

The chapter will begin with an overview of the AppFabric software stack, including all of those parts that make up AppFabric and where they fit. Then, the chapter will explore what's under AppFabric's hood, explaining how it was built and how it works.

It is critical that you understand the components and services that specifically comprise the AppFabric software stack. You need to know what its constituent parts are and how those components and features can relieve some of your current pain when building and configuring application environments. You also need to understand the value-proposition Microsoft is offering you with this new technology.

AppFabric Architecture in a Nutshell

First came Windows Server 2008. Windows Server includes a variety of installation roles administrators can assign to servers by using the Server Manager, a role-based management tool for Windows Server 2008. One of the expanded server roles that you can assigned within the Server Manager is the Application Server role. The Application Server role provides an integrated environment for deploying and running custom, server-based business applications (see Figure 4-1). Based on.NET Framework 3.5, today's Windows Application Server (WAS) offers runtime support for deploying and managing high-performance, server-based business applications. These applications can service requests from remote client systems, including Web browsers connecting from the public Internet or from a corporate network or intranet. These applications can also service remote computer systems that might send requests as messages. Windows Server 2008 also installs a group of technologies called Application Server Foundation, which includes Windows Communication Foundation (WCF), Windows Workflow Foundation (WF), and Windows Presentation Foundation (WPF). These technologies are commonly used for developing server-based and client-based applications.

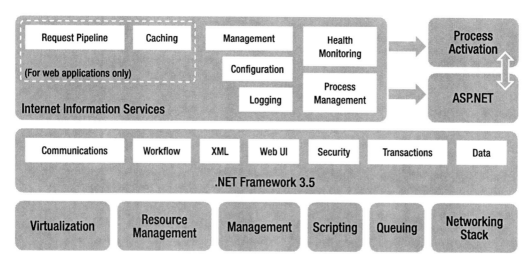

Figure 4-1. Windows Application Server 2008 Architecture

New Requirements

Windows Application Server Foundation provides a great platform that supports hosting highly-available business applications and services written in .NET, WCF and WF; however, some companies seek more automated, tool-based solutions that support adoption of service-oriented architecture principles and embrace composite applications. Many organizations have tried to achieve that goal by developing their own hosting solutions that use the full spectrum of web services as part of their applications. These range from simple RESTful services to advanced web services utilizing WS-* standards. When companies try to reuse services and compose new applications quickly and easily, however, they encounter new requirements arise for the application server. These new requirements often come about because composite applications are more complex for IT departments to develop, deploy, manage, and change.

To address these new requirements, Microsoft has enhanced both the .NET Framework and Windows Server. The company has added significant functionality to the new version of WCF and WF as part of the .NET Framework 4.0 release; it has also introduced a set of enhanced Windows Server capabilities called AppFabric. The enhanced capabilities offer greater scalability and easier manageability, and they extend IIS to provide a standard host for applications that use workflow or communications (see Figure 4-2).

Taken together, the enhancements to the Windows Application Server simplify the deployment, configuration, management, and scalability of composite applications, while allowing developers to use their existing skills with Visual Studio, the .NET Framework, and IIS.

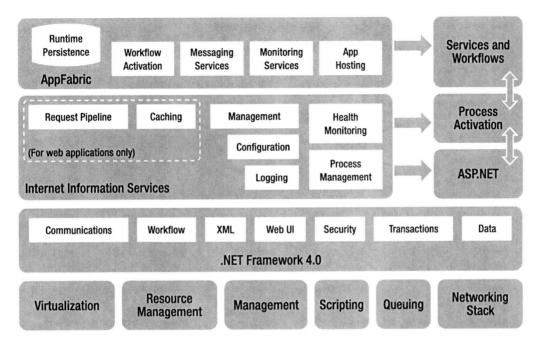

Figure 4-2. *Windows Application Server with AppFabric Extensions and .NET Framework 4.0*

Foundation and Core Services

Now let's drill down into the AppFabric architecture (see Figure 4-3). AppFabric is built on top of IIS and WAS, and it leverages the .NET Framework 4.0's broad set of frameworks (including WCF and WF) and services. The ASP.NET layer also provides a hierarchical configuration model that allows AppFabric to provide seamless configuration mechanics for both WCF and WF services and applications hosted in AppFabric. Also, Microsoft integrated the distributed caching model (previously known by the codename, *Velocity*) into AppFabric; this version offers significant improvements in performance and scalability for WCF services and WF activities hosted in AppFabric.

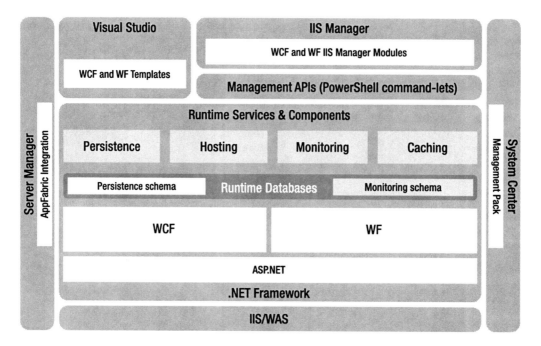

Figure 4-3. *AppFabric Architecture*

Runtime Components

The two AppFabric runtime databases are *Persistence schema* and *Monitoring schema.* These databases do what their names suggest: the Persistence schema offers persistence capabilities to save the state of your WCF and WF services, and the Monitoring schema offers monitoring capabilities to monitor the activity of your WF workflows and WCF services.

To enable persistence and monitoring capabilities, Microsoft built the runtime database services and components on top of the runtime databases. Components incorporated into the AppFabric software stack include a SQL persistence provider in a SQL Server database and a system service called *Workflow Management Service* (WMS). WMS gives you the ability to manage and control the lifecycle of your WF workflow activities hosted in AppFabric by allowing you to monitor, suspend, resume, terminate, or gracefully shutdown your workflows or WCF services through either AppFabric management extensions UI built into IIS or through PowerShell scripting commands.

The *Hosting* system component (see Figure 4-3 under the Runtime Services and Components) serves as a hosting environment for WAS activated services; it also enables you to activate XAML-based[1] services.

The Hosting system component also has a feature called *Auto-Start*, which essentially provides the capability of pre-warming activation of your services. This proves useful in some low-latency scenarios you'll learn about later in this chapter.

---

[1] XAML-based services or Declarative services are one of the new features included in the .NET Framework 4.0. In a nutshell, declarative services are WCF services modeled and implemented entirely in XAML.

The Hosting system component is also accountable for other AppFabric runtime services, such as the *Routing Service*, which provides a message-based routing capability. You'll also learn about the details of Routing Service and other services and features of AppFabric later in this book.

The third runtime system component shown in Figure 4-3 is called *Monitoring*. It consists of the *Event Collector Service*, which tracks the event-based information[2] on each running WF workflow or WCF service, and stores this information in the Monitoring database in a similar fashion to the BizTalk Tracking Database feature. The Monitoring system component also supports the Event Tracking for Windows (ETW),[3] WCF analytics, and message-logging capabilities.

Human Interface Layers

The top two layers in the architecture are what make AppFabric usable by humans. These layers include a management API layer that makes the various capabilities scriptable through Windows PowerShell cmdlets. On top of that, you get an IIS Manager experience that should feel familiar to today's IIS administrators because it builds on the Windows PowerShell cmdlets. Everything you can do in IIS Manager, you can also do in Windows PowerShell.

These PowerShell cmdlets are fully extensible, which makes them a good source of material for an independent software vendor (ISV) or an IT developer who wants to start building tools and services that run on top of the AppFabric extensions. The *IIS Management Modules* give you a rich graphical user interface (GUI) experience and provide visibility to all your configurable services and workflow activity settings, displaying all the monitoring data for you in the IIS Management Console's rich dashboard. Microsoft has added numerous UI extensions to the IIS Manager for performing the various hosting and management tasks described in this chapter. For example, you can find extensions for deploying and configuring applications, managing applications, and monitoring applications. These extensions also provide a runtime dashboard of your system that show information such as running, suspended, and persisted workflow instances.

Visual Studio Support and Oslo

.NET Framework 4.0 enhances the Visual Studio Templates so you can configure your WCF services and WF workflow activities from the ground up, thus making the Visual Studio Integrated Development Environment (IDE) your essential tool for designing and developing your applications for AppFabric. AppFabric also leverages Oslo's modeling capabilities.

Visual Studio

As you learned in Chapter 1, the role of WAS has been extended to integrate with the AppFabric extensions. This allows you to manage the AppFabric configuration, configuration of the AppFabric system services such as WMS, and the Event Collector Service within WMS's UI.

---

[2] The level or amount of information that is collected by Event Collector Service is fully configurable through the verbose semantic used in the AppFabric configuration UI.

[3] Event Tracing for Windows® (ETW) is a general-purpose, high-speed tracing facility provided by the operating system. Using a buffering and logging mechanism implemented in the kernel, ETW provides a tracing mechanism for events raised by both user-mode applications and kernel-mode device drivers.

Oslo

You might be familiar with the project code-named *Oslo* (see the top left corner in Figure 4-3). If so, you might be wondering how AppFabric relates to that Microsoft initiative. First, Oslo is a new modeling platform being developed by Microsoft to simplify the way you design, build, and manage distributed applications. The modeling platform consists of three main components: the Oslo modeling language (also known as *M*), the Oslo repository, and the Oslo modeling tool (also known as *Quadrant*). Oslo is a platform that other applications and technologies can leverage to simplify the user experience using a model-driven approach.

AppFabric is one of the first technologies to leverage the Oslo modeling platform. With Oslo, you will be able to export models in Oslo WCF, as well as WF applications and services from the repository. From there, you can deploy them easily to AppFabric, where they can benefit from the various hosting and management features discussed in this chapter. Using models to describe and automate application deployments sounds like a win for complex IT environments.

As AppFabric and Oslo continue to mature, it's likely that the integration between the two technologies will continue to grow. Microsoft has stated that the two technologies will be complementary to each other.

System Center Operational Management

Microsoft also provides AppFabric integration with the *System Center Operational Management* (SCOM) in the form of the *AppFabric Management Pack*. The AppFabric Management Pack will let you monitor AppFabric WCF and WF services[4] from the SCOM operational dashboard, allowing you to schedule operational activities and subscribe to the system alerts that are fired by the events generated within the AppFabric environment.

In a nutshell: Most of the components and services illustrated in Figure 4-3 are either not available in .NET Framework 4.0 today or would require significant development effort to achieve functional parity to what AppFabric offers.

AppFabric is complemented by the existing application server capabilities of Windows Server 2008, .NET Framework 4.0, WCF, and WF. Consequently, it will simplify the deployment, configuration, management, and scalability of composite applications, allowing developers to use their existing skills with Visual Studio, the .NET Framework, and IIS.

Persistence Services

So far you've learned about the AppFabric architecture from a high-level point of view. The next step is to drill down to reach some of the core components of the AppFabric architecture described so far. Doing this will help you better understand the mechanics of these core components, as well as how you use them. You'll begin this section with a look at *Persistence Services*, the first core component within the Runtime Services and Components layer—arguably providing the most value of all the layers—that you saw in Figure 4-3. You'll look at Persistence Services first and Hosting Services and Monitoring Services in subsequent sections.

At this point, you should be familiar with the core Persistence Component's functionality and the position it occupies in the overall architecture of AppFabric. The next step is to examine the system

---

[4] The functionality of the AppFabric Management Pack in the first release will be limited to very basic monitoring capabilities, with the intent that more rich operational functionality of AppFabric integration with SCOM will evolve in future AppFabric releases.

services that constitute the Persistence Component and belong to AppFabric's infrastructure. It's also useful to learn which system services are features of.NET Framework 4.0.

Review of Persistence: WF 3.5 vs. WF 4.0

But first, let's step back and review what persistence is. For example, you might wonder what persistence means for your long-running WF workflow activities. Or, you might wonder how the persistence feature in .NET 4.0 differs from that of .NET 3.5? Let's look at these questions and their answers.

One of the main reasons that developers use WF today is that they need to code long-running business logic programmatically. For example, WF provides a mechanism that lets you use regular .NET objects that can execute over long periods of time. WF persists the .NET object state into a persistence store (SQL Server database) automatically whenever the workflow instance becomes idle. The WF instance goes into an idle state each time it is not actively waiting (read: idling) for a new message request. WF developers typically use the persistence service to allow workflows to persist the workflow-activity state (if the workflow were to crash or be shut down, the state is still preserved) or balance work across multiple processes or servers—the service lets you do both of these things without having to do extensive programming.

The ideas behind workflow persistence have not changed in WF 4.0, but the implementation differs significantly from that of WF 3.5.The changes mean you can say goodbye to classes such as *WorkflowRuntime*, *WorkflowRuntimeService*, *WorkflowQueue*, *ActivityExecutionStatus*, *IEventActivity*, and a number of other familiar classes and interfaces; the new API looks quite different.

Workflows in WF 4.0 are now, by default, authored declaratively in XAML, as are custom activities. In fact, the activity model also looks quite different. An activity is now the base unit of creating a workflow, rather than the *SequentialWorkflowActivity* or *StatemachineWorkflowActivity* classes. The *WorkflowElement* class provides the base abstraction of workflow behavior. You construct new activities as composite activities, which ultimately derive from *WorkflowElement*. However, neither of these types of activities is actually executed. Instead, a *WorkflowInstance* is created from a tree of activities referred to as a workflow program.

Because the steps in a workflow are defined as a hierarchy of activities, the topmost activity in the hierarchy defines the workflow itself. The executing host now uses *WorkflowInstance* to persist and unload the workflow, then reload and reactivate the workflow in response to the resumption of any other pending work (*Bookmark* objects, for instance) in a particular workflow. You can attach *WorkflowInstance*'s arbitrary state to an executing activity in the form of variables. An activity can only bind its own state (modeled explicitly in the form of arguments) to variables declared on its parent or other ancestors. This is a different model than the one used in WF 3.5, where capturing the state of an executing workflow required that you serialize the entire activity tree, including those activities that had finished executing and those that had yet to start executing. You can see this in Figure 4-4, which illustrates the old approach to workflow persistence.

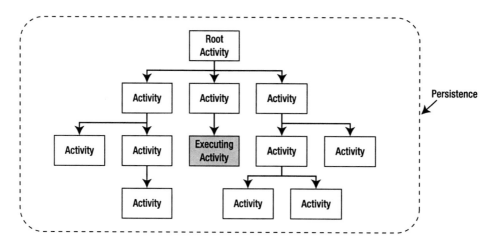

Figure 4-4. Persistence in WF 3.5

The WF 4.0 model requires only that you serialize the currently executing set of activities because they cannot bind state outside of their parental relationships (see Figure 4-5). This makes persistence much faster and more compact.

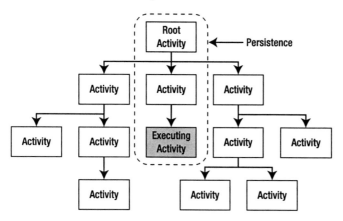

Figure 4-5. Persistence in WF 4.0

Some of the real power of the workflow infrastructure in WF 4.0 only becomes apparent when you plug in persistence services, or so-called *Persistence Providers*. One such provider is the SQL Server Persistence provider, which is available out-of-box with the .NET 4.0 Framework.

Persistence Components in AppFabric

Returning to the present, it's time to review the Persistence Component services of AppFabric.

In Figure 4-6, the dark background boxes show the Persistence architecture components that are part of the AppFabric infrastructure, and the light grey background boxes show the Persistence architecture components that are part of the .NET Framework 4.0 infrastructure.

Figure 4-6. Persistence Services

Persistence Components from .NET Framework 4.0

Let's start with the .NET Framework 4.0 components that found their way into the AppFabric Persistence Services and review each service component in the order they appear in Figure 4-6 (from the bottom left corner):

- *SQL Persistence Provider.* .NET Framework 4.0 provides an extensible provider, which anyone (such as an ISV) can build or extend to achieve specific needs. The AppFabric team itself used this provider to build a SQL Server Persistence provider to capture and store WCF and WF activity instances states in the SQL Server database.

- *Instance Control Endpoint.* .NET Framework 4.0 provides a workflow management service with the capability to start, terminate, pause, and resume workflow instances, which has been integrated into the AppFabric Instance Control Endpoint service. Figure 4-7 shows how you can persist any arbitrary message in the AppFabric Persistence database every time the workflow instance that processes this message hits the *Persist* activity in the executed workflow.

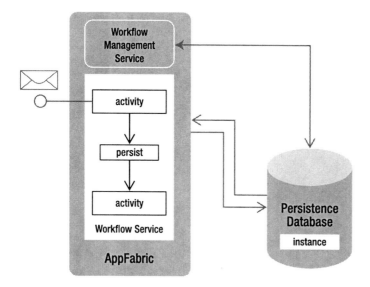

Figure 4-7. *Instance Control Endpoint*

Now, if something goes wrong—perhaps the whole host crashes and the service instance goes away—the Workflow Management service will pick up the "crashed" instance from the Persistence database and resume its activity flow from the last persistence point.

The *Durable Timer Service* is a new .NET Framework 4.0 feature that allows services to go into an **Idle** or dehydration state, where they can wait without consuming any memory resources. You can then reactivate these services later, as required. This service is a part of the .NET Framework, so you can go and use it out-of-the-box. However, you are still required to implement a data store and host and wire it all together. AppFabric, on the other hand, presents it all for you through its configuration UI—you don't need to write any code. The moment the workflow instance executes the **Delay** activity using the AppFabric Durable Timer Service, however, the current service workflow state is persisted in the AppFabric Persistence Database (see Figure 4-8). The Workflow Management service begins a countdown of the time specified in that **Delay** activity.

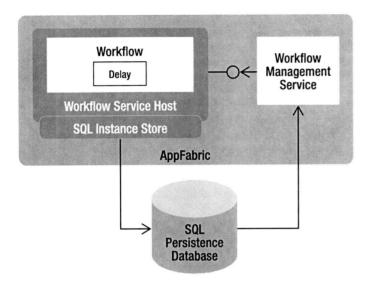

Figure 4-8. Durable Timer Service

When the time elapses, the Workflow Management Service wakes the "sleeping" workflow instance from its persisted state in the Persistence Database and resumes the workflow's activities.

AppFabric also knows how to take advantage of the new IIS/WAS auto-start feature. This feature enables you to start services when the machine starts up, rather than waiting for the first message. The AppFabric auto-start function allows one or more services to be automatically loaded as soon as the service is configured. This is useful for services that use non-activating channels. Examples of such channels include WCF communication mechanisms that do not automatically start a service, such as FTP or SMTP. Auto-start can also improve response time for services that must carry out initialization tasks before handling their first request.

Persistence Components Specific to AppFabric

AppFabric provides several enterprise-ready services that offer reliability, scalability, and error handling functionality On top of the services that are based on the existing components of the .NET Framework 4.0 (see Figure 4-6 from the top left corner to the right):

- *The Instance Recovery Service*: This service is constantly monitoring the AppFabric Persistence database, searching for "orphan" instances that might be left there by incomplete WF workflow activities when, for instance, your server crashes or network connectivity is lost. The Instance Recovery Service's job is to resume orphan workflow instances and their activities on the same server (after it has been recovered) or on another available and running server. This service effectively guarantees that any incomplete workflow instances will continue to work from the last known persistence point that was saved to the Persistence database at the moment before the machine or network crashed.

- *Error Handling Behavior.* AppFabric makes error/exception handling much easier for developers by providing the error-handling functionality through the configurable options in the IIS AppFabric UI. This service puts all "trouble-making" workflow instances into a **suspended** state every time an exception is thrown by the executed code of your activity. This makes it easy for developers to troubleshoot their faulted instances and to be able to retry execution of any suspended instance from its last persisted state in the AppFabric Persistence database.

- *Lock Retry Behavior.* This service is useful in multi-server, scale-out, farm AppFabric deployment scenarios. In such scenarios, messages that participate in a long-running transaction might be sent to a different AppFabric server each time (see Figure 4-9). The load balancer does not know the current state of the workflow instance these messages were supposed to be sent to, so this can result in misrouting behavior by the load balancer.

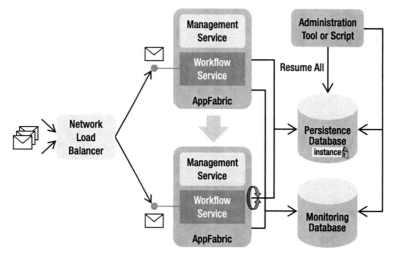

Figure 4-9. *Lock Retry Behavior*

This means some messages might reappear on a server machine that doesn't currently own the workflow instance that these messages belong to, and these messages become temporarily "lost" or invisible for that workflow instance.

You can avoid the deadlock just described by using the Lock Retry Behavior implemented in the Persistence Services of AppFabric. Every time a new workflow instance is activated, the server on which this instance is initialized obtains the lock on that service instance. That lock is then stored in the Persistence Database (see Figure 4-9). When the message arrives to the second "foreign" server, the AppFabric Workflow Management Service attempts to regain the lock from the first server (the original "owner" of that lock) so it can resume processing that particular message on the second server.

Hosting Services

This section dives into AppFabric's core architecture components, exploring the details of hosting of a workflow service. Hosting Services are responsible for managing a workflow service lifecycle; these services control workflow service configuration, activation, stop and resume operations, and so forth. Figure 4-10 depicts the main Hosting services components. Similar to the components that comprise Persistence Services in Figure 4-6, these components can be divided into those that are based on the provided functionality available with the .NET Framework 4.0 (shown in the lighter background boxes) and those that are completely brand new to AppFabric.

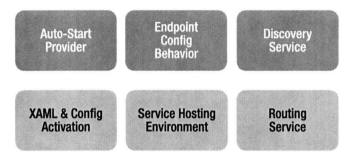

Figure 4-10. Hosting Services

Hosting Components from .NET 4.0

In the .NET Framework 4.0, you get assets such as *XAML & Config Activation* and *Service Hosting Environment* components. Let's review each of these components in deeper detail, with an emphasis on what functionality from these components has been adopted in the AppFabric Hosting Services.

The *XAML & Config Activation* components are essentially based on the build providers for XAML-based and config-based declarative workflow services. The XAML-based provider component activates workflows based on their descriptive configurations found in the corresponding XAML documents (files). The config-based build provider allows you to activate a particular WCF service directly in the runtime by reading information about that service from the configuration file. This makes it possible to activate services even without a `.SVC` file; we refer to that process in this book as *Config activation*. Today, developers can use .NET Framework 4.0 to define config activation of their services in a *fileless* fashion using the configuration settings in the corresponding *web.config* file. The following example shows how to configure an activation endpoint within your *web.config* file:

```
<configuration>
  <system.serviceModel>
    <serviceHostingEnvironment>
      <serviceActivations>
        <add relativeAddress="/PO" service="POService"/>
      </serviceActivations>
    </serviceHostingEnvironment>
  </system.serviceModel>
</configuration>
```

Config activation in .NET Framework 4.0 makes it possible to activate a POService using a relative path of "/PO" (as shown in the preceding sample), but the AppFabric Hosting Services Config Activation component makes this task even easier by providing the Service configuration GUI. You can use this GUI to configure all aspects of a workflow service through configuration *on-the-fly*—and all without writing a line of code (see Figure 4-11).

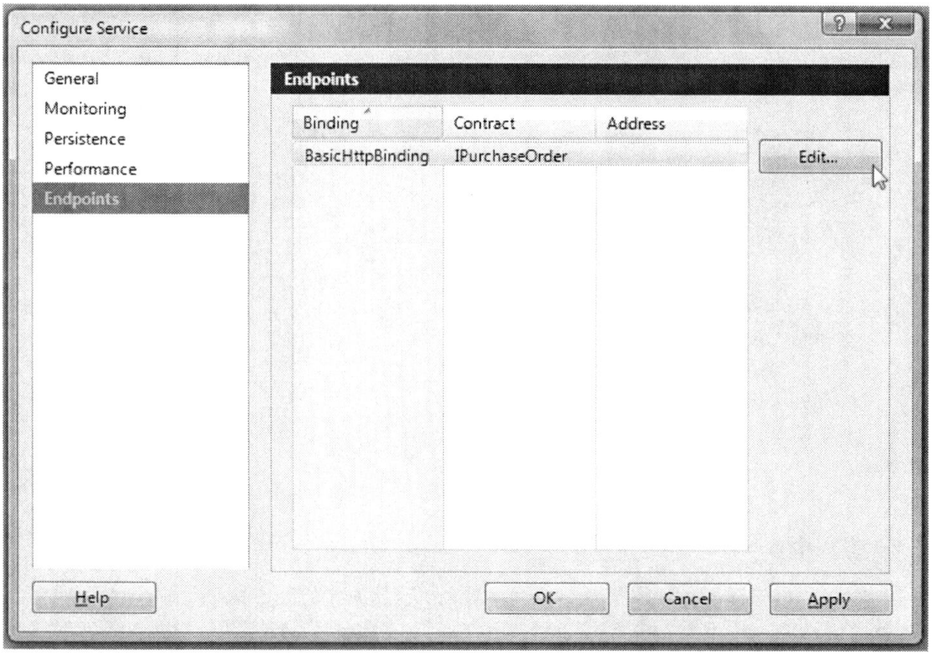

Figure 4-11. Service Configuration in AppFabric

Once you deploy an application successfully, you can begin configuring your services through the other extensions provided by AppFabric. For example, in some situations, the system administrator might need to reconfigure the runtime configuration manually for the persistence and tracking databases. These extensions allow you to change the persistence, tracking, and other settings related to security and throttling WCF settings easily—without having to touch a WCF configuration file:

- *Service Hosting Environment*: To become active, a workflow service must be hosted within a run-time environment that creates it and controls its context and lifetime. Within the AppFabric environment, WCF and WF services are hosted in the *Service Hosting Environment* component, which performs the following major tasks:

  - Receives activation requests from the Windows Process Activation Service (WAS)[5]

---

[5] Windows Process Activation Service (WAS) is the new process activation mechanism for the Windows Server 2008 that is also available on Windows Vista and Windows 7. It retains the familiar IIS 6.0 process model (application pools

- Creates service hosts based on the workflow service configuration

- Dispatches messages to the service host

- *Routing Service*: In some service-oriented environments, it is useful to take advantage of centralized routing services that act as brokers or gateways to the actual business services scattered around the organization. This effectively decouples consumers from the real business services and makes it possible to perform a variety of different types of intermediate processing within the routing logic.

For example, some environments use routing to implement a centralized security boundary that all incoming messages must pass through. Some use content-based routing techniques to determine which target service to use based on the content of a particular incoming message. Others use routing to implement protocol bridging, which enables consumers to use one set of protocols to communicate and the router to use a different set of protocols to communicate with the target service. It is also not uncommon to use routing for various load-balancing or even service-versioning techniques.

Whatever the reason, the *intermediate routing* pattern is a common requirement when building large-scale SOA solutions today. The .NET Framework 3.x did not include official support for routing, although the Framework did provide the necessary APIs to implement your own routing services; the catch was that it required a lot of work to implement these properly.

Routing is a common requirement these days, so the .NET Framework 4 comes with the official routing service that was used to build the Routing Service component in the AppFabric Hosting Services. The whole purpose of the Routing Service is to receive incoming messages from consumers and to route them to an appropriate downstream target service. The Routing Service component determines which target service to use by evaluating each incoming message against a set of message filters. As a developer, you control the routing behavior by defining and configuring the message filters through the AppFabric Service Configuration interface.

Hosting Components Specific to AppFabric

On top of the new .NET Framework 4.0 features implemented in Hosting Services, AppFabric Core Hosting Services provide additional hosting functionality through the following components:

Auto Start Provider: Some Web applications require a large amount of initialization processing time before serving the first request. In some cases, you might also need to load a large amount of data in first request. In earlier versions of web development with ASP.NET, developers often wrote custom code in the `Application_Load` method in the `Global.asax` file to handle the preceding scenarios.

AppFabric's Auto Start Provider component addresses these scenarios. This component is based on the new feature of IIS 7.5 that enables you to start a web application when the application pool is started (when the machine boots up, in most cases), rather than waiting for a web application to start upon the arrival of the first message request.

AppFabric's Auto Start Provider component also enhances this IIS feature by allowing you to configure which WCF and WF services need to be auto-started at boot time. When you enable auto-start for a WCF or WF service, the Auto Start Provider component sends a request to AppFabric Service Hosting Environment component to start all the services that were marked for use with

---

and message-based process activation) and hosting features (such as rapid failure protection, health monitoring, and recycling), but it removes the dependency on HTTP from the activation architecture.

auto-start feature. In this state, these services temporarily might not be able to accept requests. After the initialization process, the WCF or WF services can process the requests.

Endpoint Config Behavior. You must be able to add WCF endpoint behavior through configuration to enable some of the AppFabric Runtime service components, including the Instance Control Endpoint, the Durable Timer Service, the Error Handling Behavior, and others. If you were doing this yourself in a normal scenario, you would find this process quite challenging because it requires that you write some code to create a custom endpoint behavior class that derives from the .NET Framework's *System.ServiceModel.Configuration.BehaviorExtensionElement* class.

Fortunately, Microsoft has already done this custom work for you, by implementing the *Endpoint Config Behavior* into AppFabric. Your only task is to associate your workflow or service with the Manageable service, which exposes all the endpoints for you in an easy-to-manage-and-secure fashion.

Discovery Service. The next major feature the AppFabric Hosting Services inherited from the .NET Framework 4.0 is a service discovery. In some specialized, service-oriented environments, you can find services where the runtime location is dynamic and constantly changing. For example, consider environments where different types of service-enabled devices are constantly joining and leaving the network as part of the overall solution. Dealing with this requires you're your clients dynamically discover the runtime location of service endpoints.

This service is based on the new feature available in .NET Framework 4.0, that enabled WS-Discovery (defined by OASIS[6] as a SOAP-based protocol for dynamically discovering the location of service endpoints at runtime). The Discovery Service enumerates all services deployed on a particular AppFabric machine using the PowerShell `Get-Services` commandlet to check which services are discoverable. The service also lets you check for responses to *Probe* requests to those services; doing this enables clients to probe for service endpoints that match certain criteria, allowing them to retrieve a list of suitable candidates. A client can then choose a specific endpoint from the discovered list and use its current runtime endpoint address. This means you don't need any service to be activated at the point of discovery; services that match the probe respond directly to the client.

This is quite useful in multi-server AppFabric deployments, when services' endpoints could be spread out on various servers or be frequently moved during their operational lifecycle. Services "announce" themselves directly to the discovery proxy, and you can even make this happen across network boundaries when needed. It is the job of the Discovery Service to save the list of known service endpoints and to respond to client-discovery requests.

Monitoring Services

Businesses also need the ability to monitor running applications. This enables them to see how a business is functioning and what changes might be necessary. Prior to AppFabric, it was difficult to troubleshoot a distributed application across multiple services and computers. You had to enable tracing for each service, run activities, turn off tracing and collect all the trace files, and then view them in the Service Trace Viewer. AppFabric provides new options and tools for you to monitor and troubleshoot the health of your deployed WCF and WF services.

---

[6] OASIS (Organization for the Advancement of Structured Information Standards) is a not-for-profit consortium that drives the development, convergence and adoption of open standards for the global information society.

The WCF and WF runtimes in .NET Framework 4.0 already come with a built-in tracking infrastructure that the AppFabric extensions leverage further, making it easy to enable monitoring within your WCF and WF applications. The WF tracking infrastructure instruments a workflow to emit records reflecting key events during the execution. For example, tracking records are emitted when a workflow instance starts or completes. Tracking can also extract business-relevant data associated with the workflow variables. For example, if the workflow represents an order-processing system, the **order id** can be extracted, along with the tracking record. In general, enabling WF tracking facilitates diagnostics or business analytics over a workflow execution. For people familiar with WF tracking in .NET Framework 3.x, the tracking components in .NET Framework 4.0 are equivalent to the tracking service in WF 3.x. In AppFabric Monitoring Services, Microsoft has improved the performance of this tracking. It has also simplified the programming model for the WF tracking feature.

There are two main players in the AppFabric Monitoring Services tracking architecture: *tracking profiles* and *tracking participants*. Developers define tracking profiles that tell the runtime what events to track and then tracking participants can subscribe to those events. The AppFabric Monitoring Services infrastructure follows the observer pattern. The workflow instance is the publisher of tracking records, and subscribers of the tracking records are registered as tracking participants to the workflow. You use a tracking profile to apply a filter.

Tracking Profiles

The WF Tracking Provider (see Figure 4-12) uses the information in the tracking profile to determine what events and data must be sent. The tracking profile acts as a filter for tracking events. It describes what events and data must be tracked and what data doesn't. After a profile is associated with the workflow instance, only those events requested in the profile are sent to the WF Tracking Provider.

Figure 4-12. Monitoring Services

AppFabric comes with some built-in tracking profiles that make it easy to track a common set of useful events. You can easily enable tracking for your application by navigating to one of your AppFabric services in IIS Manager and selecting **Configure** from the **Actions** panel on the right.

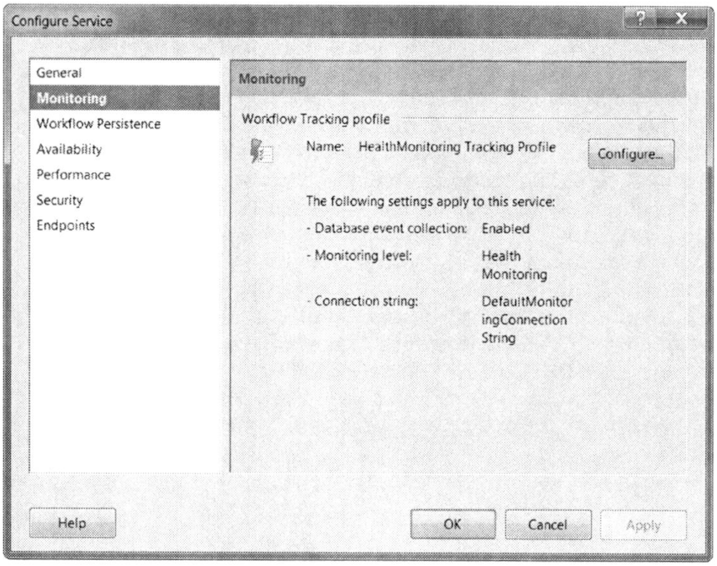

Figure 4-13. Enabling Tracking for Your Service

Clicking the **Configure** button brings up the dialog shown in Figure 4-14; this dialog allows you to select either one of the out-of-box tracking profiles or add your own custom profile for your workflows and services. After you configure this dialog, AppFabric makes the appropriate updates to your configuration, and the WCF/WF tracking infrastructure kicks in.

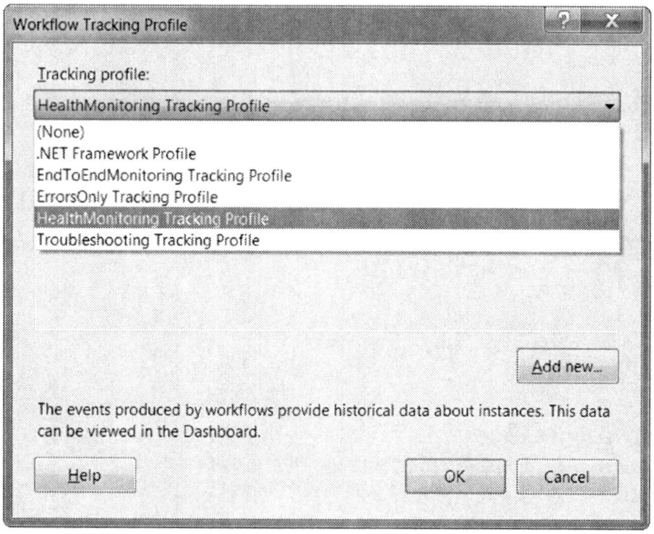

Figure 4-14. Tracking Profile Settings

Tracking Participants

The tracking profiles describe the events and data you want to track, while the tracking participants contain the logic to process the payload from the tracking records. For example, they could choose to write to a SQL database, Oracle database, file, and so forth. The *ETW Tracking Participant* in AppFabric Monitoring Services is an extensibility point that allows an AppFabric developer to consume tracking events from a workflow and put them into the Event Tracing for Windows (ETW). The ETW Tracking Participant writes the tracking records to an ETW session. You configure the participant on a workflow service by adding a tracking-specific behavior in a config file. This code configures the ETW Tracking Participant in the **web.config** file:

```
<configuration>
  <system.web>
    <compilation targetFrameworkMoniker=".NETFramework,Version=v4.0"/>
  </system.web>
  <system.serviceModel>
    <diagnostics etwProviderId="52A3165D-4AD9-405C-B1E8-7D9A257EAC9F" />
    <tracking>
      <participants>
        <add name="EtwTrackingParticipant"
             type="System.Activities.Tracking.EtwTrackingParticipant, ⏎
System.Activities, Version=4.0.0.0, Culture=neutral, ⏎
PublicKeyToken=31bf3856ad364e35"
             profileName="Dublin_Tracking_Profile"/>
      </participants>
    </tracking>
    <behaviors>
      <serviceBehaviors>
        <behavior name="DublinTracking.SampleWFBehavior">
          <trackingComponents>
            <add name="EtwTrackingParticipant"/>
          </trackingComponents>
        </behavior>
      </serviceBehaviors>
    </behaviors>
  </system.serviceModel>
</configuration>
```

Enabling the ETW Tracking Participant allows you to view tracking records in the event viewer, alongside your application and system logs. In the ETW, events are written to the ETW session through a **Provider Id**. You define the Provider Id that the ETW Tracking Participant uses for writing the Tracking Records to ETW in the diagnostics section of the **web.config** (under `<system.serviceModel><diagnostics>`):

```
<system.serviceModel>
  <diagnostics etwProviderId="52A3165D-4AD9-405C-B1E8-7D9A257EAC9F" />
...
```

The ETW Tracking Participant uses a default Provider ID if you don't specify one.

You declare tracking participants in the **<system.serviceModel><tracking><participants>** section. You can associate an ETW Tracking Participant with a profile to specify the tracking records it is subscribed to:

```
<system.serviceModel>

   ...

   <tracking>
     <participants>
       <add name="EtwTrackingParticipant"
             type="System.Activities.Tracking.EtwTrackingParticipant, ↵
System.Activities, Version=4.0.0.0, Culture=neutral, ↵
PublicKeyToken=31bf3856ad364e35"
             profileName="Dublin_Tracking_Profile"/>
     </participants>
   </tracking>
   ...
```

Once you declare them, you can add ETW Tracking Participants to the service behavior. This will add the ETW Tracking Participants to the workflow instance's extensions, so that they begin to receive the tracking events. For this, you simply use the same name you used to declare the ETW Tracking Participant in the previous step:

```
<behaviors>
   <serviceBehaviors>
     <behavior name="DublinTracking.SampleWFBehavior">
       <trackingComponents>
         <add name="EtwTrackingParticipant"/>
       </trackingComponents>
     </behavior>
   </serviceBehaviors>
</behaviors>
```

Consumption of Tracking Data

Once the tracking data reaches the ETW Session, it can be consumed in a number of ways. One of the most useful ways to consume these events is through the Event Viewer, a common Windows tool used for viewing logs and traces from applications and services. This tool allows you to view the Tracking Records that have been emitted by the workflow.

You can follow these steps to enable viewing the Tracking Records in Event Viewer:

1. Open Event Viewer (**eventvwr.exe**).

2. Navigate to **Application and Services Logs > Microsoft > WCF - WF**.

3. Right-click and enable **View > Show Analytic and Debug logs** (see Figure 4-15).

4. Enable the log.

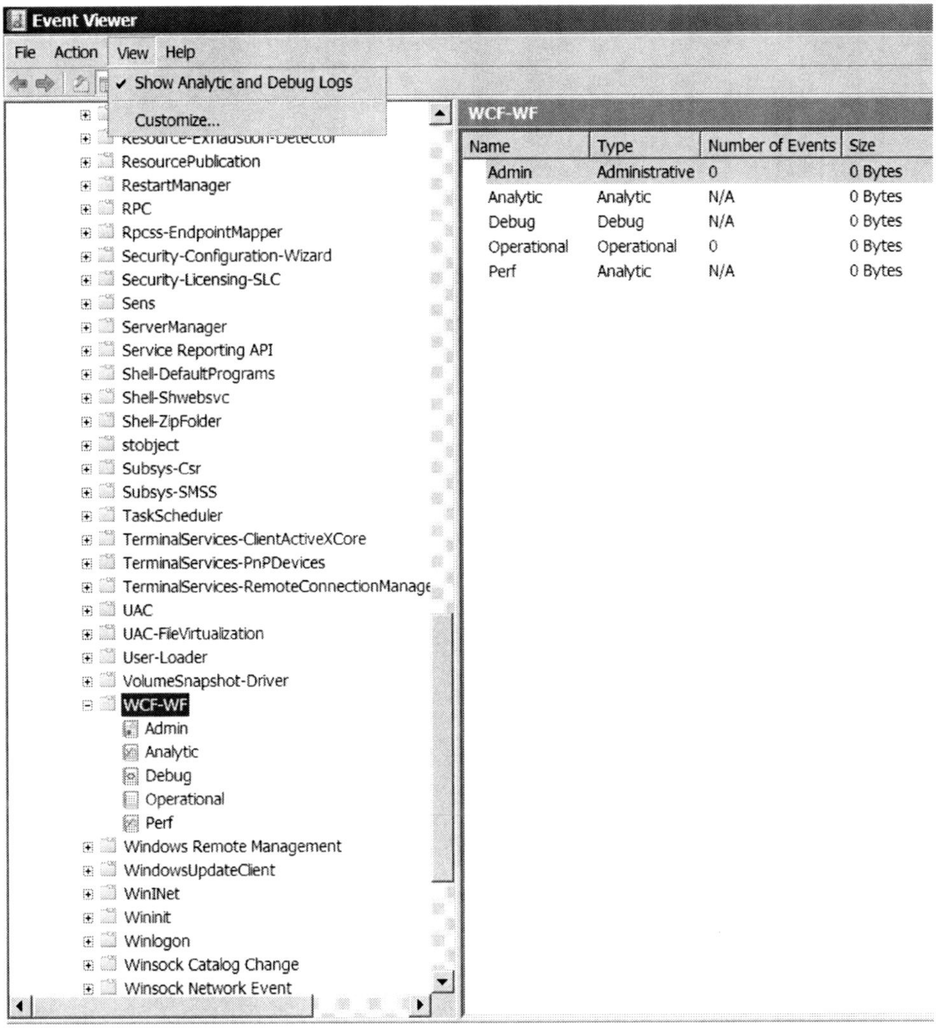

Figure 4-15. *Enabling Workflow Tracking Events in the Windows Event Viewer*

You can see a sample of tracking events displayed in the Event Viewer in Figure 4-16.

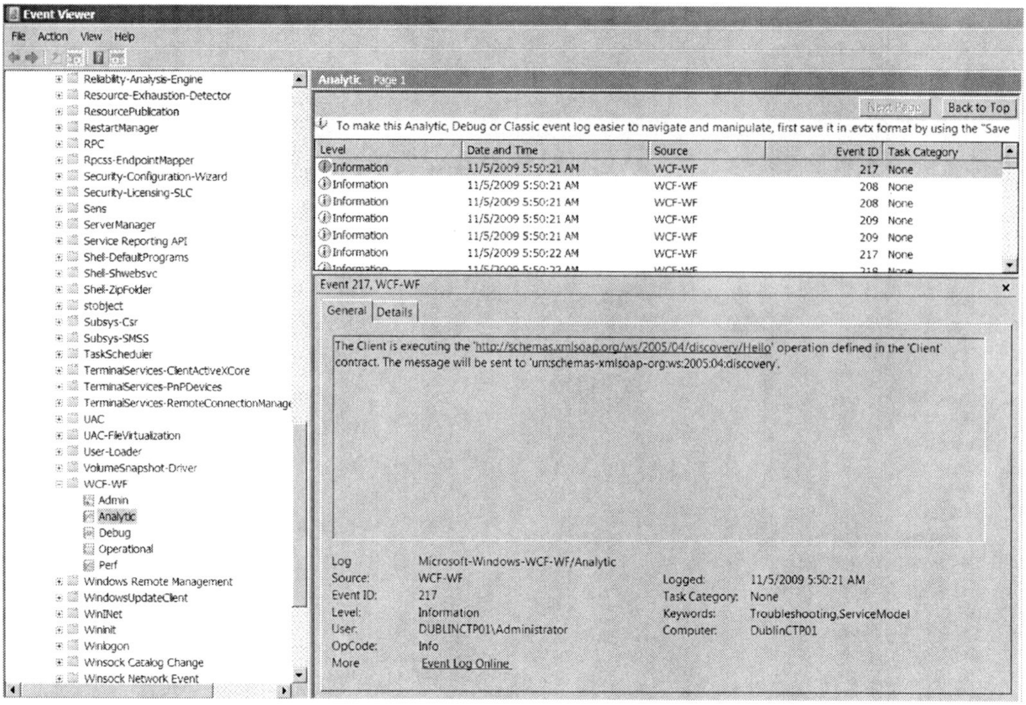

Figure 4-16. Viewing workflow Tracking Events in the Windows Event Viewer

Tracking Records emitted through the ETW Tracking Participant also appear with the appropriate severity level in Event Viewer. This makes it easy to identify any warnings or errors with the execution of the workflow.

If you like, you can also view tracking data through the AppFabric extensions. You can select View Tracking Data while inspecting persisted service instances, which will run a SQL query against the monitoring store to produce a list of tracking events for you to view. When you want to track custom events, you can define custom tracking profiles and configure them through the Tracking Profiles option on the main IIS Manager view.

Other Tracking and Monitoring Features

AppFabric also implements an event-tracing feature called *WCF Analytic Trace*. WCF Analytic Trace unifies WF event tracking with WCF message tracing into one channel that correlates workflow activities and messages grouped in one type. This is designed for expert-level support professionals or detailed diagnosis and troubleshooting tools. This enables you to use WCF Analytic Trace to view and analyze events intended for the same workflow hosted in AppFabric with a single set of APIs or troubleshooting tools.

The AppFabric team has also enhanced another .NET 4.0 Monitoring feature called *WCF Message Logger*. This enhancement enables AppFabric developers to take any WCF message tracked into the WCF

Message Logger and drill down all the way through its workflow instance execution, viewing all types of events emitted for this message—something that was never possible before.

The WCF Analytic Trace correlates a message to its workflow activity where the message was being processed and the WCF Message Logger. Developers can now use WCF Analytic Trace to get a full picture of all workflow activities associated with the message and vice versa.

Event Collector in AppFabric refers to the features that collect instrumentation events and store them in a monitoring database. Emitting and collecting data can be expensive, but enhancements made in .NET Framework 4.0 for ETW use fewer resources than alternatives such as *System.Diagnostics*.

You can also use the Monitoring database in conjunction with one or more instances of the Event Collector service to simplify troubleshooting an application. All of the WCF and WF service events are saved to a SQL Server database. You can store tracking data for multiple WCF and WF services in one Monitoring database, or you can make each service can use a separate database.

The tracking data stored in the Monitoring database includes the following information:

- *WCF run-time trace events*: These help you monitor, troubleshoot, and tune WCF applications. This category includes trace events (transfers) that allow you to reconstruct a message flow between services.

- *Events from WF tracking records*: These events are correlated by instance ID.

- *Service host events*: This category includes any events emitted by the WCF or WF service host

The Monitoring database has been designed so it is open for developers. This means you can run SQL queries directly against the Monitoring database, and you can view objects and code in SQL Server Management Studio. You can also add objects to the database that host the monitoring schema, so long as those objects have only a passive relationship to the objects in the monitoring schema. For example, you can add a new view or stored procedure that depends on data or stored procedures in the monitoring schema, but you cannot create a new index on a monitoring table, extend an existing view with additional columns, or modify object security.

▪ **Note** An instance of the Event Collector runs on every computer that hosts the AppFabric WF and WCF services you want to monitor. Multiple instances of the Event Collector service can run on a single host, but you face a hard limit of ten Event Collector instances per AppFabric host.

When configuring your application or service for monitoring using the AppFabric Management UI, you must enable database-event collection to enable AppFabric Event Collector service monitoring. Event Collector service monitoring and diagnostic tracing and message logging are independent, which means you don't have to enable database-event collection to use diagnostic tracing and message logging, and vice-versa.

Caching Services

Distributed caching is becoming the key application platform component for providing scalability and high availability. Traditionally, in-memory caching has been used primarily for meeting the high performance requirements of applications. By merging caches on multiple nodes into a single unified cache however, distributed caching offers not only high performance, but also scalability. Maintaining copies of data on multiple cache nodes (in a mutually consistent manner) means that distributed caching can also offer high availability to applications. Distributed caching is especially ideal for applications with the following characteristics:

- Web applications with a considerable number of data requests that are mostly read (such as product catalogs)

- Web applications that can tolerate some staleness of data

- Web applications that can work with highly partitioned data (such as session data or a shopping cart)

- Applications that can work well with *eventual consistency*

Distributed caching in AppFabric is not a new concept. During the last couple of years, several caching products have emerged to address the performance and scalability needs of applications. Most of these products are point products, primarily supporting key-based access. Apart from *memcached*, which is an open source technology, most of these products target enterprises and enterprise workloads and scale, but come up short for web workloads requirements. We, the authors, believe that web workloads in large clusters require better scalability and performance than these products can provide. Such applications should also make it easy to manage large clusters or provide the ability for such clusters to manage themselves.

Microsoft began to invest in distributed caching approximately two years ago, when it first introduced a project code named *Velocity*. That project allows any type of data (CLR object, XML document, or binary data) to be cached. Velocity fuses large numbers of cache nodes in a cluster into a single unified cache and provides transparent access to cache items from any client connected to the cluster. As Velocity became more widely deployed and praised by the .NET developer community, Microsoft made the decision to make Velocity an integral part of the AppFabric core services stack, targeting both enterprise and web workloads.

Using Caching Services in AppFabric enables you to improve workflow and web services performance significantly by avoiding unnecessary calls to the data source. AppFabric Caching Services use a cache cluster that automatically manages the complexities of load balancing. It also enables you to achieve better scalability by adding more computers on demand. You can achieve even higher availability by allowing Caching Services to store copies of the data across the cluster. You can run AppFabric Caching Services with any distributed application on the same server, or you can access the services over a network on a remote server.

Figure 4-17 shows the typical architecture model for applications that use AppFabric Caching.

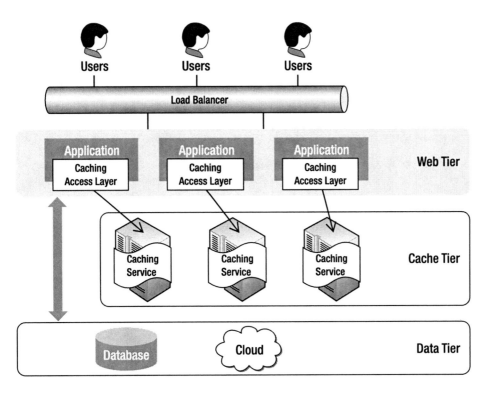

Figure 4-17. AppFabric Caching architecture

AppFabric Caching Services are not tightly coupled to ASP.NET, and you can use them at any layer of an application architecture, including clients, workflows, and services. However, in the context of web applications, AppFabric caching provides ASP.NET developers with a seamless upgrade path (including an out-of-the-box ASP.NET caching provider) to a distributed in-memory caching option when their application requirements exceed the capabilities of the default ASP.NET caching system. Specifically, AppFabric provides an in-memory caching solution that accomplishes the following:

- It supports greater scale-out by offloading caching to a dedicated cache tier.

- It offers high availability of cached data.

- It doesn't require sticky routing.

The performance, scalability, and availability of AppFabric caching services, in conjunction with AppFabric's rich data services, will greatly facilitate rich web and enterprise applications development and deployment.

AppFabric Cache API

The AppFabric Caching Services API is fairly simple. You must first create an instance of the **Cache Factory** object, which under the hood reads the configuration settings from **app.config** of your WF or

WCF service. You need this **Cache Factory** object to retrieve a named data cache object. These will be the least required steps each time you want to access the cached objects (data) from the AppFabric Caching Services. The following code excerpt shows off this technique:

```
//Create instance of CacheFactory
DataCacheFactory fac = new DataCacheFactory();

//Get a named cache from the factory
DataCache catalog = fac.GetCache("YourNamedCache");
```

From here, you can use simple **Get** and **Put** commands to read or write data from or to the AppFabric caching storage. This snippet uses these two commands to write and then read custom data from the AppFabric Cache:

```
//Put data into a cache
catalog.Put("item01", new Item("HD Zune", "$199.00", "..."));

...

//Get the data from the same or a different client
Item orderItem = (Item)catalog.Get("item01");

// If not present in the cache
if (orderItem == null)
{
//Read from the backend layer
        orderItem = ReadFromDatabase();
        //Populate the Cache
catalog.Put("item01", new Item("HD Zune", "$199.00", "..."));

return orderItem;
        }
```

AppFabric Caching Services Session Store Provider

AppFabric Caching Services allow you to share application session state among multiple applications. You can achieve this by using a custom Session State provider that ships with the Windows Server AppFabric. The AppFabric Session State provider uses distributed caching to spread **session** objects across the cluster; this enables it to provide scalability for your web applications.

You can use **SessionStoreProvider** in your web apps by adding the **<sessionState>** element to your app's **web.config** file:

```
<sessionState  mode="Custom" customProvider="SessionStoreProvider">
   <providers>
      <add name="SessionStoreProvider"
           type="System.Data.Caching.SessionStoreProvider,
                 ClientLibrary"/>
   </providers>
</sessionState>
```

This code instructs your application to use AppFabric's SessionStoreProvider instead of ASP.NET's default provider. You will use this provider to read/write session states for your application.

If you want to store your session objects in a different named cache other than **default**, then you will need to modify the **<sessionState>** element in the **web.config** file so it looks like this:

```
<sessionState  mode="Custom" customProvider="SessionStoreProvider">
   <providers>
      <add name="SessionStoreProvider"
            type="System.Data.Caching.SessionStoreProvider,
                  ClientLibrary"
            cacheName="YourNamedCache"/>
   </providers>
</sessionState>
```

Now all the session objects for this web app will be stored in the cache named **<YourNamedCache>**.

■ **Note** Before you can use **<YourNamedCache>**, it will have to be created using Administration Tool [AdminTool.exe].

Similarly, you can configure to store all the **session** objects in one region:

```
<providers>
      <add name="SessionStoreProvider"
            type="System.Data.Caching.SessionStoreProvider,
                  ClientLibrary"
            cacheName="YourNamedCache"
            regionName="<YourRegion>"/>
   </providers>
</sessionState>
```

Now all the **session** objects will be stored in *<YourRegion>* of the named cache *<YourNamedCache>*.

■ **Note** Objects in a region are limited to one cache host only, which means they cannot use a cache cluster. This is *not* a recommended configuration, and you should take this approach only when you need to locate all **session** objects on a single node.

You can also enable AppFabric Cache Logging on the client side. To enable that, you need to add the following section to the **web.config** file:

```
<section name="fabric" type="System.Fabric.Common.ConfigFile,
FabricCommon"allowLocation="true" allowDefinition="Everywhere"/>
```

...

```xml
<fabric>
        <section name="logging" path="">
      <collection name="sinks" collectionType="list">
      <customType
        className="System.Fabric.Common.EventLogger,FabricCommon"
        sinkName="System.Fabric.Common.ConsoleSink,FabricCommon"
        sinkParam="" defaultLevel="-1"/>
      <customType
        className="System.Fabric.Common.EventLogger,FabricCommon"
    sinkName="System.Fabric.Common.FileEventSink,FabricCommon"
        sinkParam="<CacheClientLog>" defaultLevel="1"/>
      <customType
        className="System.Fabric.Common.EventLogger,FabricCommon"
        sinkName="System.Data.Caching.ETWSink, CacheBaseLibrary"
        sinkParam="" defaultLevel="-1" />
    </collection>
    </section>
</fabric>
```

<CacheClientLog> is the name of the file where your logs will be created. Your application should have privileges to write in the location that you specify.

Now let's look at an example that illustrates putting all this information together. The **web.config** file will look like this for an application that uses a cache service running on a local host on port 22233 with logging enabled:

```xml
<?xml version="1.0"?>
<configuration>
  <configSections>
    <section name="dcacheClient" type="
        System.Configuration.IgnoreSectionHandler"
      allowLocation="true" allowDefinition="Everywhere"/>
    <section name="fabric" type="System.Fabric.Common.ConfigFile,
        FabricCommon"
      allowLocation="true" allowDefinition="Everywhere"/>
  </configSections>
  <dcacheClient deployment="simple" localCache="false">
    <hosts>
      <!--List of services -->
      <host name="localhost" cachePort="22233"
                cacheHostName="DistributedCacheService"/>
    </hosts>
  </dcacheClient>

  <fabric>
    <section name="logging" path="">
      <collection name="sinks" collectionType="list">
        <customType
          className="System.Fabric.Common.EventLogger,FabricCommon"
          sinkName="System.Fabric.Common.ConsoleSink,FabricCommon"
```

```
            sinkParam="" defaultLevel="-1"/>
        <customType
          className="System.Fabric.Common.EventLogger,FabricCommon"
          sinkName="System.Fabric.Common.FileEventSink,FabricCommon"
          sinkParam="CacheClientLog" defaultLevel="1"/>
        <customType
          className="System.Fabric.Common.EventLogger,FabricCommon"
          sinkName="System.Data.Caching.ETWSink, CacheBaseLibrary"
          sinkParam="" defaultLevel="-1" />
      </collection>
    </section>
  </fabric>

  <system.web>
    <sessionState mode="Custom" customProvider="SessionStoreProvider">
      <providers>
       <add name="SessionStoreProvider"
            type="System.Data.Caching.SessionStoreProvider,
                 ClientLibrary"
            cacheName="default"/>
    </providers>
    </sessionState>
  </system.web>
</configuration>
```

Stitching It All Together

Now you're ready to begin connecting all the pieces together, including all those AppFabric runtime components that you have learned so far. Doing so will help you see how they all interact with each other under the hood of the one big "mechanical" system called AppFabric. For this exercise, you will use a WF service activation process (see Figure 4-18).

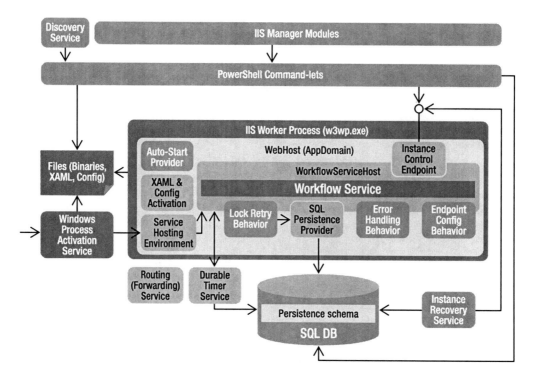

Figure 4-18. *AppFabric Services in Action*

New Service Activation

A new service activation request might come from one of the following sources: WAS, an Auto Start Provider, or an IIS Worker Process handler that responds to a new message arrival. As a new message arrives through an HTTP or REST protocol, the activation request is generated and sent to the AppFabric integration entry point: Service Hosting Environment. You can see this process at work in Figure 4-17.

The Service Hosting Environment first enumerates through the list of build providers, where it learns how this service should be built. For example, the list might indicate that it should be activated from XAML, a config file, or from the .SVC service file that you want to parse. Once the service activation type is identified, the Service Hosting Environment creates a new workflow service host that will activate and host the requested workflow service. At this time, the local machine on which the workflow service host activated the particular workflow instance locks this instance to that machine.

Before this new workflow service is activated, however, the number of WCF service behaviors that were previously configured by the user through AppFabric UI configuration management screens is executed inside the new workflow service host. For example, Endpoint Config Behavior configures your workflow service endpoint using Instance Control Endpoint, Durable Timer Service, Lock Retry Behavior, and the Error Handling Behavior. At this point, all configurable behaviors that you added previously added to your workflow service configuration are kicked off and ready to start. It is here that the workflow service is actually activated and begins to process the requested message and workflow activities associated with that message.

For sake of this exercise, let's assume that the workflow you have just activated has a Delay activity in it that requires the workflow to "sleep" for the next 30 minutes and then come back later to take care of the remaining activities left in that workflow. At this point, the Delay activity sends a message request to the Durable Timer Service, asking it to hold off any following activities in this workflow until the Delay activity's timeout is elapsed.

The Durable Timer Service records the current state of the workflow into the AppFabric Persistence Schema. It essentially says: There is a workflow X, and its instance Y should be re-activated 30 minutes later. At the same time, the workflow stops processing any new messages or activities that are positioned after the current Delay activity until it gets a callback call from the Durable Timer Service. It then changes its status to `Idle`. This is similar to the dehydration process of BizTalk orchestrations in BizTalk Server. In AppFabric, idling workflows are persisted to the persistence database. The workflow state, all the messages, the workflow activity variables, and other serializable workflow elements (such as the message current interim values) are stored in the configured persistence database (such as the SQL Persistence Store, for example). Later, you can query these persisted values—for troubleshooting purposes, for instance. At this stage, the workflow is unloaded from the memory until it is *awakened* from its `Idle` state by the Durable Timer Service.

The Durable Timer Service continuously monitors all the records saved in the Persistence Schema for every workflow instance being currently idled. When the delay timeout is expired, the Durable Timer Service sends the callback message request back to the Service Hosting Environment, asking it to reactivate the unloaded workflow instance Y for the workflow X. With this request, the Durable Timer Service provides all the required data associated with the workflow to be reactivated. The Service Hosting Environment reactivates the workflow service host on the machine that initially locked the workflow. From this moment on, the workflow continues to run from the last point it was persisted.

Integrity

Now let's imagine that the machine on which your workflow instance is executing suddenly crashes. Should you worry about the integrity of our workflow instance? Well, maybe just a little. However, you also know that you can recover from the last point the workflow instance was persisted. Let's take a closer look at how AppFabric does that.

You might recall that all workflow instances are recorded in the Persistence Schema. For each workflow instance that is persisted in the Persistence Database, you can find a persistence lock owned by the workflow service host stored in the Persistence Schema. This lock has a temporary license issued by the workflow service host each time the workflow instance is activated in the context of that workflow service host. Every time the workflow service host persists a workflow instance, it renews its license for the next period of time (you can set this up in the AppFabric Instance Recovery Service configuration).

■ **Note** At the initial AppFabric release, the Instance Recovery Service and Lock Retry Behavior configuration settings such as the number of retries to release the lock, the exponential expiration time, and other settings are limited to the global-machine configuration only.

But what happens when the lock's lease is expired? This is exactly when the Instance Recovery Service kicks in. The Instance Recovery Service cleans up the expired lock and allows the Instance Control Endpoint to reactivate the "orphaned" workflow instance on any available AppFabric server machine from the last persisted point of that workflow.

Exception Handling

If your workflow throws an exception, the Error Handling Behavior is kicked off. This is like embracing your workflow with a big **TRY-CATCH** exception handling block. However, instead of just propagating an exception up and deleting the workflow service instance, the Error Handling Behavior suspends the faulted workflow instance by marking it as **suspended**, and then unloads that workflow instance from memory. Here's the interesting part: you can now go to the Windows PowerShell command shell and execute various scriptable cmdlets to enumerate, resume, or terminate your running, suspended, and/or persisted workflow instances.

For instance, you can execute the following PowerShell cmdlet if you want to enumerate all running workflow service instances for a given application using Windows PowerShell commands:

```
Get-ASAppService -Uri /MyDir/MyApp/POService.svc -Status Running
```

Suspension

Suspending a service instance stops the execution of the instance and prevents it from receiving new messages. You can resume suspended instances later, at which point the instances will begin receiving messages again. Terminating a service instance stops the execution of the instance and removes it from the persistence store, which means it cannot be resumed. Finally, aborting a service instance clears the in-memory state pertaining to the given instance and reverts it back to the last persistent point (which is stored in the persistence store). The Windows PowerShell **Get-ServiceInstance** and **Stop-ServiceInstance** cmdlets provide numerous command-line options for identifying specific service instances from the command-line.

Diagnostics

As the messages push through the WF workflow activities and WCF services, it is important to understand how AppFabric makes it easier to monitor and troubleshoot each step of the message footprint (this is configurable, of course). Figure 4-19 shows you the big picture, illustrating how the AppFabric Monitoring Service components interact with each other.

First, you can see that the **System.Diagnostics** trace didn't go away after all. Yes, it is still there. You can also see how four new AppFabric monitoring and tracking components provide a new way of managing your WF and WCF services and activities (at least, in terms of WF/WCF custom development).

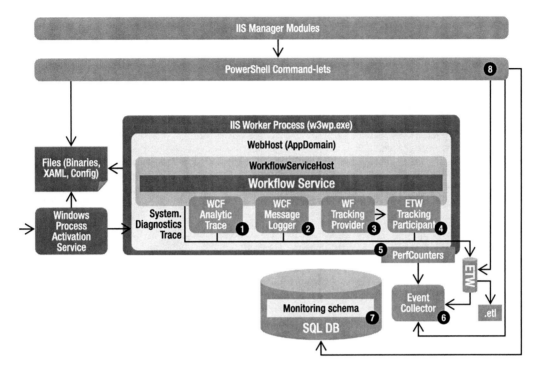

Figure 4-19. *AppFabric Monitoring Services in Action*

System.Diagnostics Trace remains an important debugging API tool that many of us have used hundreds times (along with the .NET tracing feature for .NET custom code troubleshooting), but the `System.Diagnostics` output is sometimes cumbersome to use (due to its unstructured format), especially when the trouble resides deep into the logic of a WCF service or WF workflow activity. This prompted Microsoft, based on customer feedback and requests, to invest significant effort in improving the developer experience related to WCF or WF service workflow monitoring, troubleshooting, and analytics.

For instance, the WCF Analytic Trace component emits numerous helpful message lifecycle events, such as when a message is received, when the service can't be instantiated due to a configuration problem, when a coding exception is thrown, when a fault message was sent to a client, when the throttling threshold was exceeded, and other highly structured and useful events. These events are then available for both displaying various service health checks through the AppFabric Monitoring dashboard and SQL queries on the AppFabric Monitoring database.

Note that events and the log messages generated by the WCF Analytic Trace and WCF Message Logger are not made available for you by default. This is by design; otherwise, all your machine's memory and storage resources would have been tapped when AppFabric gathered all the possible events for each message, workflow activity, or service in its Monitoring Schema. Instead, all generated events are accumulated by the ETW event pipeline, and they become accessible for you only when you explicitly say that you want to start collecting the events for a given application. This means these events won't be collected until you tell the AppFabric Event Collector to start monitoring them.

At that point, the WF Tracking Provider will call the out-of-the-box ETW Tracking Participant discussed earlier. This provider captures a workflow instance's events based on the configuration settings in your service's tracking profile. These events will be also piped into the ETW and become available when you make your request through the Event Collector. The AppFabric Monitoring schemas for WCF and WF events have a lot in common; for example, they make it possible to correlate between the events emitted for the WCF service messages and the WF workflow activities those messages were processed through, and vice versa.

Note that the AppFabric Event Collector component can do more than write events it collects from ETW to the AppFabric Monitoring database; it can also flush out these events to files. You might then use these files to write your own event logging applications or let them be consumed by various operational management systems, such as SCOM.

Also, the Event Collector is a service. This means you can configure it to use PowerShell cmdlets, which you might use to start monitoring a given application, retrieve statistical or operational information about a service or services, or even script some more sophisticated commands based on the particular events that occur in your application. For example, you might tell it to stop an application when the number of errors exceeds 50 in the past 24 hours.

Visual Tools and Performance Counters

Microsoft has built all the features you've learned about so far into AppFabric's visual tools. These tools also support many other helpful features and commands. The visual tools supporting AppFabric work together to make the user experience of monitoring, operating, and troubleshooting WCF and WF services or activities a much more pleasant experience than before.

No AppFabric Monitoring Services overview would be complete without saying a few words about performance counters. In the past, using performance counters with WCF services often meant carrying a heavy performance overhead—in some cases, the penalty ranges has high as 50%. In AppFabric, you no longer suffer a performance penalty when using performance counters. Microsoft eliminated this penalty by refactoring the way the performance counters work in AppFabric. Specifically, AppFabric leverages unmanaged performance counters in the form of on-demand collections. This enables AppFabric to offer developers a set of predefined performance counters by default, without using any switches, because the performance penalty is no longer an issue. This mirrors ASP.NET, where you can also use performance counters. The take away in this case is this: you no longer need to make config file changes to take advantage of performance counters.

Summary

In this chapter, you ventured deep into AppFabric's architecture. Knowing the architecture is important, and it gives you a huge leg up when it comes to using and applying AppFabric. As with any tool, knowing this application's architecture is one of the characteristics that defines a true expert.

However, there's nothing like a bit of experience to give you a feel for how a tool or technology works, including the best way to use it. A good way to get a sense of how you can use AppFabric is to walk through a representative example. The built-in AppFabric support for creating scalable WF-based applications is an important part of what this technology provides. The upcoming in this book will give you a strong sense of how to develop a WCF or WF-based application for AppFabric.

CHAPTER 5

■ ■ ■

Configuring AppFabric

This chapter will walk you through the process for installing and configuring AppFabric on your local machine.[1] The installation process is straightforward, but you should also be aware that no two deployments of AppFabric are the same. This is because AppFabric connects many disparate components both internal and external to your enterprise, so information can flow smoothly and securely in many directions. Before you begin the installation process, gather information on the needs of your enterprise and discuss the scope of your deployment with the IT professionals, system administrators, and developers who will use AppFabric. While even the most basic single-server deployment relies on many variables, most real-world deployment scenarios extend much further to include multiple servers and (eventually) clusters of both physical and virtual computers. Carefully analyzing the specific needs of your enterprise, studying this book, and the Release Notes of AppFabric—which contains important, late breaking information about the AppFabric release—will teach you how to create your own deployment roadmap.

The installation process for AppFabric is the same as for most Windows-based OS features add-ons. However, before you rush to install AppFabric, you must first review the hardware and software requirements, install all software prerequisites, and make sure you have all required server roles and features pre-installed and configured if you are going to install AppFabric on your Windows Server 2008 machine. This chapter will cover all of these required and important steps for installing AppFabric into three broadly defined tasks:

1. Prepare your computer.

2. Install AppFabric software prerequisites such as Windows critical updates, IIS 7.0 Administration Pack, Microsoft SQL Server 2008, and so on.

3. Install and configure AppFabric.

Note that each step contains many variables that might be particular to your enterprise.

Task 1: Preparing Your Computer for Installation

Before you start installing any parts of AppFabric on your server, you must verify that your server meets the minimum hardware and software requirements. This will help you ensure that all AppFabric components will function properly. The next section lists the detailed hardware requirements for AppFabric. These are current at the time of writing, but please remember that we wrote this book against pre-release versions of AppFabric, so it's possible that Microsoft changed the final requirements before

---

[1] Installing and configuring AppFabric on a Server Farm is beyond the scope of this book because the installation and configuration process varies from organization to organization.

the product was officially released. To ensure proper operation of AppFabric, please verify your machine meets the requirements described in Step 1 and Step 2.

Step 1: Verify Hardware Requirements

Table 5-1 shows the minimum recommended hardware requirements for your AppFabric server.

Table 5-1. Hardware Requirements

Hardware Component	Minimum Requirements
Computer CPU	An Intel Pentium-compatible processor that is: 1 GHz or higher for a single processor 900 MHz or higher for dual processors 700 MHz or higher for quad processors Hyper-threading and multi-core processors
Windows OS	Windows 7, Windows Server 2008 R2, Windows Server 2008 SP2, or Windows Vista SP2 The 64-bit versions of AppFabric require a 64-bit operating system running on an x64-based system. Computers based on CPUs that are compatible with the AMD64 (x86-64) and Extended Memory 64-bit Technology (EM64T) processor architecture are considered x64-based systems.
Memory	2 GB of RAM
Hard disk	2 GB of minimum available hard disk space; the hard disk must use NTFS format
Drive	CD-ROM or DVD-ROM drive
Display	VGA or higher-resolution monitor set to 1024 × 768 pixels or higher resolution
Other	Network adapter card and Microsoft mouse or compatible pointing device

■ **Note** In a production environment, the volume of traffic might dictate even greater hardware requirements for your servers than you see listed in Table 5-1.

Step 2: Verify Software Requirements

Table 5-2 lists the prerequisite software you must install on the server that will run AppFabric. The next section of this chapter guides you through installing the software prerequisites listed in this table.

Table 5-2. Software Requirements

Product	Requirements Description
Microsoft Windows OS	Microsoft Windows Server 2008 R2 or Microsoft Windows Server 2008 (32-bit or 64-bit) with Service Pack 2 are required.
IIS 7.0	IIS 7.0 enables Windows Application Server to host internal or external Web sites and Web services that communicate over HTTP. It also includes support for ASP.NET applications that you can access using a Web browser such as Internet Explorer, as well as Web services built using WCF.
IIS 7.0 Administration Pack (not required for Windows 7 and Windows Server 2008 R2 users)	IIS 7.0 Administration Pack adds the following to the set of management features that ship with IIS 7.0: administration UI support for ASP.NET authorization, custom errors, FastCGI configuration, Request Filtering, and more. The Administration Pack also provides a generic configuration editor capable of setting any IIS 7.0 configuration setting and automatically generating scripts to make a task easily repeatable.
Microsoft .NET Framework 4.0	.NET Framework 4.0 contains the latest updates to the managed code-programming model for Windows. Used with AppFabric, .NET Framework 4.0 extends IIS to be a "standard host" for applications that use either WF or WCF.
Windows PowerShell v2.0 (not required for Windows 7 and Windows Server 2008 users)	Windows PowerShell provides a consolidated management interface in which AppFabric cmdlets perform the application, database, and system service management operations. You can access the functionality in AppFabric cmdlets in three ways: through the UI, interactively through the command-line shell console, or by creating and running scripts that contain one or more of AppFabric cmdlets.
Microsoft SQL Server 2008 or Microsoft SQL Express 2008	Microsoft SQL Server or SQL Express houses the AppFabric Persistence and Monitoring databases. You can use the administration component to manage database roles.
Microsoft Visual Studio 2010 (required for development purposes only)	Microsoft Visual Studio 2010 serves as the foundation for all AppFabric development work. This version of Visual Studio includes application templates for both WF and WCF. These templates support the new .NET Framework 4.0 features used in AppFabric. These features include the Base Activity Library and Flowchart Activity Designer (for WF), as well as System Endpoints, WS-Discovery, and Workflow Services (for WCF).
IIS Web Deployment Tool 1.0	Also known as MSDeploy, the Web Deployment Tool can be used for large-scale application deployments, such as deployments to a server farm. MSDeploy is available both as a command-line tool and as a Windows PowerShell interface. You can use it to copy or synchronize an application from one virtual directory or even an entire Web site to another.

Microsoft Hotfix 970772 (not required for Windows Server 2008 users)	FIX: IIS Manager does not display the user interface in the language of the remote server when you connect to a remote Internet Information Services (IIS) 7.0 server.
Microsoft Hotfix 970773 (not required for Windows Server 2008 R2 users)	FIX: The MWA API cannot determine whether an element is present in an IIS 7.0 configuration file if the element has no child elements and has no attributes defined.

The matrix in Figure 5-1 indicates the server roles and features based on the server roles that you must install on your server computer before you install AppFabric.

Windows Server Roles and Features	.NET Framework 4.0 Features				Windows Process Activation Service			Message Queuing		Remote Server Administration Tools	
	.NET Framework 4.0	WCF Activation	HTTP Activation	Non-HTTP Activation	Process Model	Configuration APIs	.NET Environmnet	Message Queuing Services	Message Queuing Server	Role Administration Tools	Web Server (IIS) Tools
Server Roles											
Application Server	●	●	●	●	●	●	●	●	●		
File Server											
Web Server (IIS)	●	●	●	●						●	●

Figure 5-1. Required Windows Server Roles and Features for AppFabric

Step 3: Understanding the Impact

You need to be aware of (and possibly prepare for) several key issues when installing AppFabric. Understanding AppFabric's core capabilities is a good way to get a handle on these issues.

AppFabric has three core capabilities: caching, workflow management, and service management. For web applications, AppFabric includes caching capabilities that provide high-speed access, scalability, and high availability to application data. For composite applications, AppFabric extends the Windows Process Activation Service and IIS Manager to make it easier to build and manage .NET 4 WCF and WF services.

These core capabilities have ramifications with respect to security, remote databases, and remote management. The following sections on these topics describe key points you must consider when installing AppFabric.

Security

Microsoft integrated AppFabric security with Windows, IIS, and SQL Server security models. AppFabric uses Windows security accounts, SQL Server logins, and database roles to determine how much access a user has to system resources such as persistence databases, timer data, monitoring data, and configuration files. The SQL Server setup creates several new Windows security groups and then creates SQL Server logins based on them. These Windows security groups provide the physical implementation for security roles defined by the AppFabric system.

Two security groups are created when you install AppFabric: `COMPUTERNAME\AS_Administrators` and `COMPUTERNAME\AS_Observers`. The Windows built-in groups `NT AUTHORITY\Local Service` and `BUILTIN\IIS_IUSRS` provide NT Service logon and application user security, respectively. System administrator tasks such as deploying applications and configuring file-system security require membership in the local `Administrators` group.

When the monitoring and persistence stores are initialized, database roles are created and mapped to the SQL Server logins. AppFabric uses SQL Server logins and roles, which enables you to manage access to assets such as the persistence and monitoring stores and stored procedures. You apply AppFabric's security policies through permissions on tables and stored procedures; these permissions determine who can read, write, and perform administrative operations to the persistence and monitoring schema. You secure each schema with its own set of security policies.

Table 5-3 lists the SQL Server Logins, Windows Accounts, and database roles that are created when you install AppFabric.

Table 5-3. Logins, accounts, roles

SQL Login Name	Windows Account	Database Role Membership
AS_Administrators	`COMPUTERNAME\AS_Administrators`	public
		MonitoringStoreAdministrator
		MonitoringStoreReader
		MonitoringStoreWriter
		Microsoft.ProcessServer.DurableServices.Control Admins
		System.Activities.Persistence.PersistenceAdmins
AS_Observers	`COMPUTERNAME\AS_Observers`	public
		MonitoringStoreReader
		System.Activities.Persistence.PersistenceReaders
IIS_IUSRS	`BUILTIN\IIS_IUSRS`	public
		MonitoringStoreWriter
		System.Activities.Persistence.PersistenceUsers

LOCAL_SERVICE	NT AUTHORITY\LOCAL_SERVICE	public
		MonitoringStoreAdministrator
		MonitoringStoreReader
		MonitoringStoreWriter
		Microsoft.ProcessServer.DurableServices.Control Admins
		System.Activities.Persistence.PersistenceAdmins
		System.Activities.Persistence.PersistenceReaders
		System.Activities.Persistence.PersistenceUsers

Remote Databases

AppFabric supports both local and remote databases. Using a remote database is as simple as choosing your database in the Advanced Configuration stage of the AppFabric setup.

Remote Management

The Remote Management Tool (RMT) is a remote client that allows remote management of server roles. In its initial release, AppFabric does not support remote access to its homepage through RMT. However, you can access the homepage remotely by visiting the homepage on the local computer, opening IIS Manager, and then connecting from the local computer to the remote computer. You can configure AppFabric remotely once you make this connection.

Task 2: Install Software Prerequisites

In this task, you install the software prerequisites that will be used as the base platform for AppFabric. These prerequisites include Windows updates and hotfixes, administration packs, a database, and the other components that AppFabric depends on.

Step 1: Install Critical Windows Updates

It requires three steps to install critical Windows updates:

1. Click Start ➤ All Programs ➤ Windows Update.
2. Follow the directions on the Windows Update site.
3. Restart your computer (if prompted to do so).

Step 2: Install the Required Hotfixes

You might need to install a few hotfixes for IIS 7.0 before installing AppFabric on your computer (see Table 5-2 to determine whether you need to install these hotfixes). The first hotfix addresses a globalization issue in the user interface when remotely managing an IIS 7.0 server. In this case, the language of the local computer is displayed rather than the language of the remote IIS 7.0 server. Microsoft has issued `Hotfix 970772` for this issue, which is available as a free download.

The second hotfix addresses a bug in the current release of IIS 7.0. This bug means that the Microsoft Web Administration (MWA) API cannot determine whether the non-collection element is present in a given IIS configuration file. Microsoft has issued `Hotfix 970773` to address this; it is available as a free download.

Follow these steps to install Microsoft supported `Hotfix 970772`:

1. Open Internet Explorer browser and navigate to the following URL: `http://support.microsoft.com/kb/970772`.

2. At the top part of the screen, click the highlighted hyperlink with the following text: `View and request hotfix downloads`.

3. After the page reloads, find the `Agreement for Microsoft Services` legal document, read it through, and then click the `I Accept` button to accept the provided terms and conditions.

4. Follow the steps indicated in the next screen to request a hotfix download.

5. Provide your email address, type the verification characters you see in the provided picture, and then click the `Request hotfix` button.

6. Within a few hours, you should get an invitation from Microsoft with a link to where you can download the hotfix. Follow that link to download the hotfix.

7. Download the hotfix and save it on your computer.

8. Run the file you just downloaded to install the hotfix on your computer.

Follow these steps to install Microsoft supported `Hotfix 970773`:

1. Open Internet Explorer browser and navigate to the following URL: `http://support.microsoft.com/kb/970773`.

2. At the top part of the screen, click the highlighted hyperlink with the following text: View and request hotfix downloads.

3. When the page reloads, find the `Agreement for Microsoft Services` legal document, read it through, and then click the `I Accept` button to accept the provided terms and conditions.

4. Follow the steps indicated in the next screen to request a hotfix download.

5. Provide your email address, type the verification characters you see in the provided picture, and then click the `Request hotfix` button.

6. Within a few hours, you should get an invitation from Microsoft with a link to where you can download the hotfix. Follow that link to get to the download area from where you can download that hotfix.

7. Download the hotfix and save it on your computer.

8. Run the file you just downloaded to install the hotfix on your computer.

Step 3: Install the IIS 7.0 Administration Pack

The IIS 7.0 Administration Pack provides a generic configuration editor that AppFabric can use. The Administration Pack can adjust any IIS 7.0 configuration setting and automatically generate scripts to make the task easily repeatable.

Follow these steps to install IIS 7.0 Administration Pack on your computer:

1. Download the IIS 7.0 Administration Pack from the following URL: **www.iis.net/extensions/AdministrationPack**. Note that this utility includes options for the x86 or x64 bit versions of the Administration Pack. You must select the correct one for your version of Microsoft Windows Server.

2. Execute the file you have downloaded to start the installation process for IIS 7.0 Administration Pack (see Figure 5-2).

Figure 5-2. IIS 7.0 Administration Pack Setup Wizard

3. Review the content, and then click **Next**.

4. On the **End-User License Agreement**, read through the Microsoft Software Supplemental License Terms, check the **I accept the terms in the License Agreement** box, and click **Next**.

5. On the **Choose Setup Type** window, click **Custom** to be able to choose the specific program features required for AppFabric.

6. On the **Custom Setup** window (see Figure 5-3), make sure all features are selected except **Authorization** and **Error Pages** under the **ASP.Net Features**.

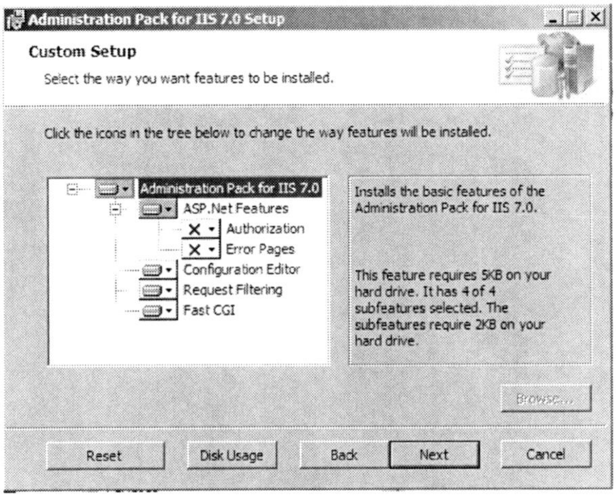

Figure 5-3. IIS 7.0 Administration Pack Selected Features

7. Click **Next** and then click `Install`.

8. Click `Finish` when the installation process completes.

Step 4: Install Windows PowerShell v2.0

Windows PowerShell cmdlets perform many management tasks in AppFabric, and Microsoft embedded the runtime for Windows PowerShell within AppFabric's tools. Windows PowerShell provides a consolidated management interface across all components of AppFabric.

Follow these steps to install Windows PowerShell v2.0:

1. Go to the Microsoft Download Center to download the Windows PowerShell v2.0.

2. Review the information on the web page, then find the appropriate file for your platform (called `PowerShell_Setup_x86.msi` or `PowerShell_Setup_amd64.msi`) and click `Download`.

3. Click `Run`, then click `Run` again. The `Windows PowerShell Setup Wizard` will open (see Figure 5-4).

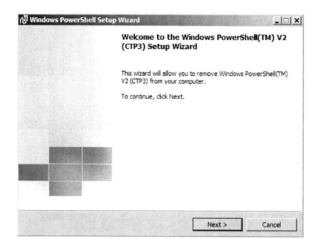

Figure 5-4. *Windows PowerShell v2.0 Setup Wizard*

4. Review the content and then click **Next**.

5. On the **License Agreement** screen, accept the terms and then click **Next**.

6. On the **Start Installation** screen, click **Install**.

7. When **Setup** completes, click **Finish**.

Step 5: Install Microsoft SQL Server 2008 Express

AppFabric provides a rich set of persistence features and the ability to monitor the health of your application or troubleshoot problems by leveraging of Microsoft SQL Server databases. This means Microsoft SQL Server 2008 is required to host databases used by the AppFabric Persistence and Monitoring services. You can install it either as a component of Microsoft Visual Studio 2010 or by using the following procedure:

1. Go to the following website: **www.microsoft.com/express/sql/download/**. You can see the web install page in Figure 5-5.

2. Next, click **Install It Now!** You should see the platform installer page shown in Figure 5-6.

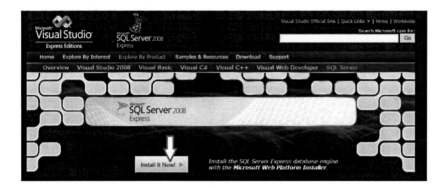

Figure 5-5. SQL Server 2008 Express Web Installation Page

3. If prompted to install the **Microsoft Web Platform Installer**, follow the steps given.

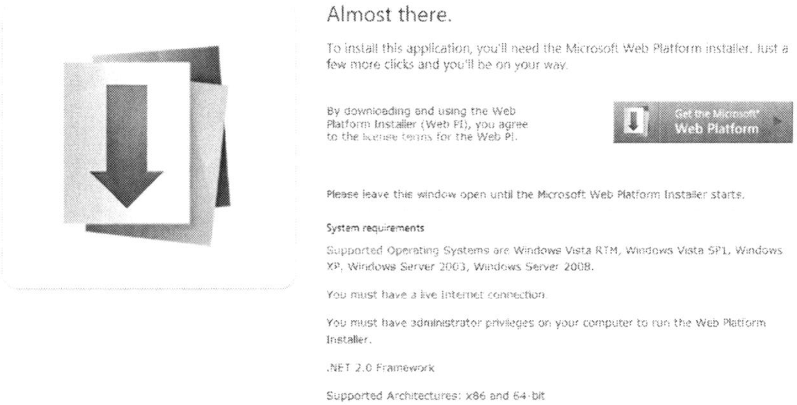

Figure 5-6. Microsoft Web Platform Installer Web Page

4. When the Web Platform Installer launches the SQL Server Express 2008 installer (see Figure 5-7), review the products selected to make sure everything you need is selected, and then click **Install**.

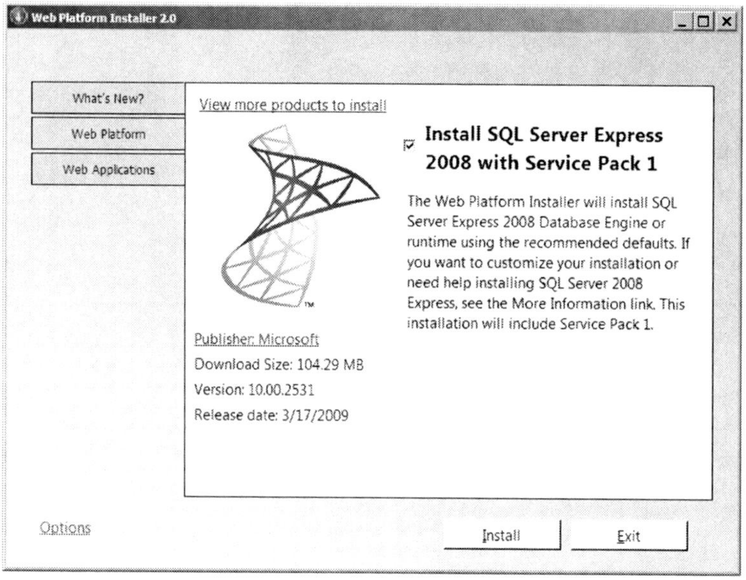

Figure 5-7. Microsoft SQL Server Express 2008 Installer Wizard

5. When prompted, review the **License Terms** and then click **I Accept**.

6. When prompted, enter a **Username** and **Password**, and then click **Continue**.

7. When the product finishes installing, it might prompt you to restart your computer. Close any open programs and then click **Yes**.

Step 6: Install Microsoft Visual Studio 2010

If you do any development work with AppFabric, you will need to install Microsoft Visual Studio 2010. The AppFabric development tools are based on Visual Studio 2010, and AppFabric itself requires the .NET Framework 4.0, which is included with Visual Studio 2010.

Follow these steps to install Microsoft Visual Studio 2010:

1. Insert the **Visual Studio 2010** installation disk into the DVD-ROM drive.

2. Click **Install Visual Studio 2010**.

3. After the installation loads, click **Next**.

4. On the **Start** page, accept the **License terms**, input your **Product Key**, type in any other necessary information, and click **Next**.

5. On the **Options** page, select **Custom**, and then click **Next**.

6. Leave most of the defaults under **Select features to install**. Under **Language Tools**, you can speed up the installation and save disk space if you unselect any languages you don't plan to use in your development tasks. Next, click **Install** (see Figure 5-8).

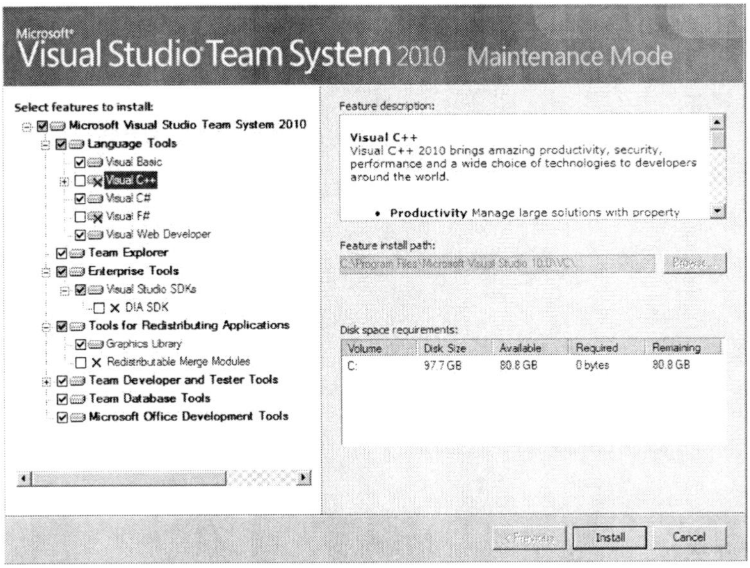

Figure 5-8. Visual Studio Team System 2010 Features Selection

7. On the **Finish** page, click **Finish**.

8. On the **Visual Studio Setup** screen, click **Exit**.

Step 7: Install the Web Deployment Tool

The Web Deployment Tool simplifies the migration, management, and deployment of AppFabric applications. AppFabric leverages the Web Deployment Tool to deploy applications into its hosting environment. The Web Deployment Tool is integrated with both the IIS and Visual Studio environments, so you can easily package and deploy applications directly from within Visual Studio or deploy pre-packaged applications directly from the IIS Manager.

Follow these steps to install the Web Deployment Tool:

1. Go to the following download site: **www.iis.net/extensions/WebDeploymentTool**. Next, download the installation package appropriate to your platform, whether it's x86 or x64.

2. Run the downloaded executable file to launch the **Web Deployment Tool Installation Wizard** shown in Figure 5-9.

Figure 5-9. The Web Deployment Tool Installation Wizard

3. Review the information and then click **Next**.

4. On the **End-User License Agreement** screen, accept the terms and then click **Next**.

5. On the **Choose Setup Type** screen, click **Typical**.

6. On the **Ready to install Web Deployment Tool** screen, click **Install**.

7. When your installation is complete, click **Finish**.

Step 8: Install AppFabric Caching Services

Installing the AppFabric Caching Services requires that you undertake three primary tasks:

1. *Prepare the AppFabric Cache cluster configuration storage location:* Create a shared network folder or SQL Server *database* to store the AppFabric Cache cluster configuration settings. You'll learn more about this later in this section.

2. *Install the AppFabric Caching Services on a Windows Server computer:* Install the Distributed Cache service, the PowerShell-based Distributed Cache administration tool, and then configure the Distributed Cache *cluster* configuration settings in the cluster configuration storage location. You perform this step with the AppFabric installation program; you'll learn how to do this later in this chapter.

3. *Prepare the AppFabric Caching Services client on the Distributed Cache-enabled Windows server computer or development workstation:* Copy the necessary AppFabric Caching Services assemblies and set application assembly references, as needed. You'll learn how to accomplish this step later in this chapter.

■ **Note** You should use SQL Server to store the cluster configuration settings; this will help you minimize contention issues on the Distributed Cache cluster configuration storage location during parallel Distributed Cache server installations.

You also need to prepare a SQL Server Database so that you can use it to store cluster configuration settings. Follow these steps to do so:

1. *Configure the SQL Server instance:* You need to configure this instance so that it can receive connections in a way consistent with your corporate guidelines. Doing this is outside the scope of this book. For more information, see **Microsoft SQL Server Books Online**.

2. *Create the SQL Server database:* A small, distributed cache system might only need a database a few MB in size. Installing the database in a location with 50MB of space available should be more than sufficient for even a 100-server cache cluster. For more information about how to do this, see **Microsoft SQL Server Books Online**.

3. *Create a SQL Server login security identity:* You will use this login for the security identity that performs the cache server installations. Be sure to grant this security identity **db_owner** permissions on the cache cluster configuration database. To create the cache server accounts, this security identity also needs **sysadmin** permissions on the instance of SQL Server. Doing this is also outside the scope of this book. For more information, see **Microsoft SQL Server Books Online**.

4. *Create a SQL Server login to run the cache server(s):* This SQL Server login will be used this by the cache server(s) to run the cache host Windows service. The AppFabric installation program does this for you automatically for each of the cache servers. By default, AppFabric uses the Network Service identity, which means that you must create a logon for each of the domain computer accounts of the cache servers. Each of the cache host SQL Server logins must have the following permissions on the cache cluster configuration database: **db_datareader**, **db_datawriter**, and **EXECUTE**.

Task 3: Install and Configure AppFabric

In this task, you install AppFabric and confirm that the installation succeeded. Next, you configure the Persistence and Monitoring databases.

Step 1: Install AppFabric

Follow these steps to install AppFabric:

1. Close any programs you have open.

2. Download to your Windows operating system the appropriate AppFabric setup program from the official Microsoft AppFabric web site at `http://msdn.microsoft.com/en-us/windowsserver/ee695849.aspx`. For example, if you run a 64-bit operating system, you should download the setup package that begins with **AseSetup_amd64**. I you intend to install AppFabric on a 32-bit OS, you need to download the setup package that begins with **AseSetup_x86**.

3. It's also important to know the Windows Server edition of your system. For example, if you intend to install AppFabric on a computer that runs Windows 7 or Windows Server 2008 R2 with 64 bit, you should download the setup package with the name of **AseSetup_amd64_6.1.exe**. For Windows 7 32 bit, you need the **AseSetup_x86_6.1.exe** installation package. Any previous 64-bit versions of Windows, such as Windows Vista SP2 or Windows Server 2008 SP2, will require **AseSetup_amd64_6.0.exe**. Computers that run 32-bit Windows Vista SP2 or Windows Server 2008 SP2 need **AseSetup_x86_6.0.exe**.

4. Launch the appropriate installation package.

5. On the **Accept License Terms** page, accept the terms and then click **Next**.

6. On the **Customer Experience Improvement Program** page, choose if you want to participate in the program to help Microsoft improve Windows Server AppFabric, and then click **Next**.

7. On the **Feature Selection** page (see Figure 5-10), select the application server components that you want to install for hosting and managing WF and WCF applications, and then click **Next**.

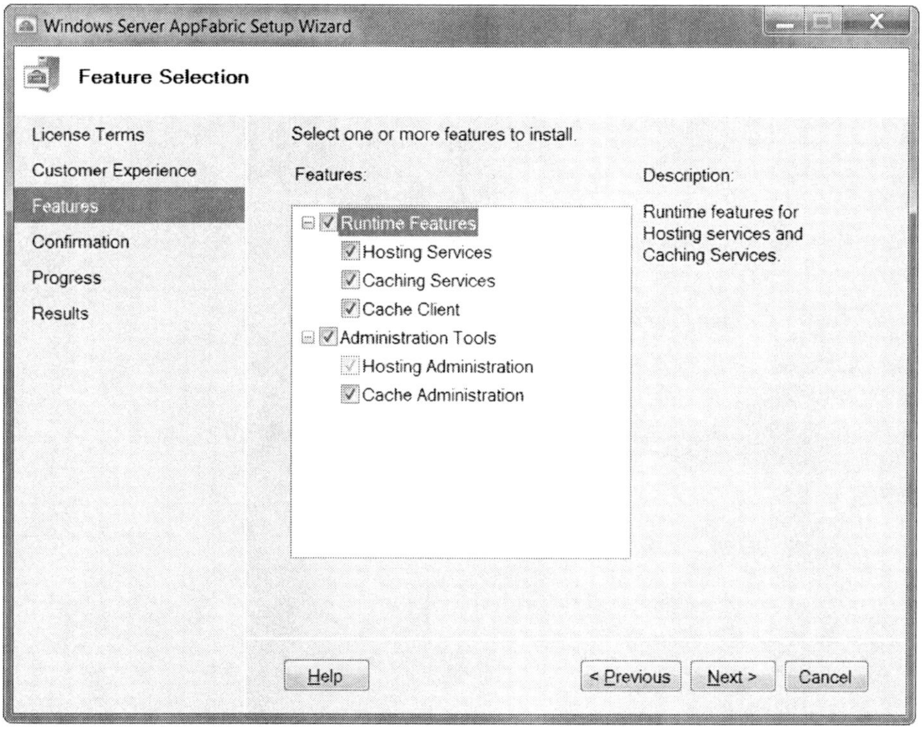

Figure 5-10. AppFabric Feature Selection

8. The following features list provides a brief description of each AppFabric component listed in the **Feature Selection** page:

- Runtime Features:

    - *Hosting Services:* This component installs AppFabric host and management services. When this component is selected, the Hosting Administration feature will automatically be selected.
    - *Caching Services:* This component turns a server host into the node of a distributed cache cluster. You can create a new cluster or join this host to an existing cluster of AppFabric Caching Services.
    - *Cache Client:* This component installs the client libraries that enable you to use cache functionality in your applications during development or runtime.

- Administration Tools:

    - *Hosting Administration:* This component installs the IIS Manager, the AppFabric configuration wizard, and the hosting features PowerShell modules that enable you to administer the Hosting Services.

- *Distributed Cache Admin:* This component installs the components that enable you to administer a cache cluster.

9. On the **Confirm Installation Selections** page, review the list of the features that were selected in the **Feature Selection** page. It displays a list of the required Windows components and the AppFabric features that will be installed. Verify that the list is correct, and then click **Install** to begin installation.

10. On the **Installation Progress** page, you can monitor the progress of the installation.

11. On the **Installation Results** page (see Figure 5-11), verify that the installation has succeeded. To run the configuration wizard, check the **Launch Configuration tool** check box, and then click **Finish** to complete the installation wizard.

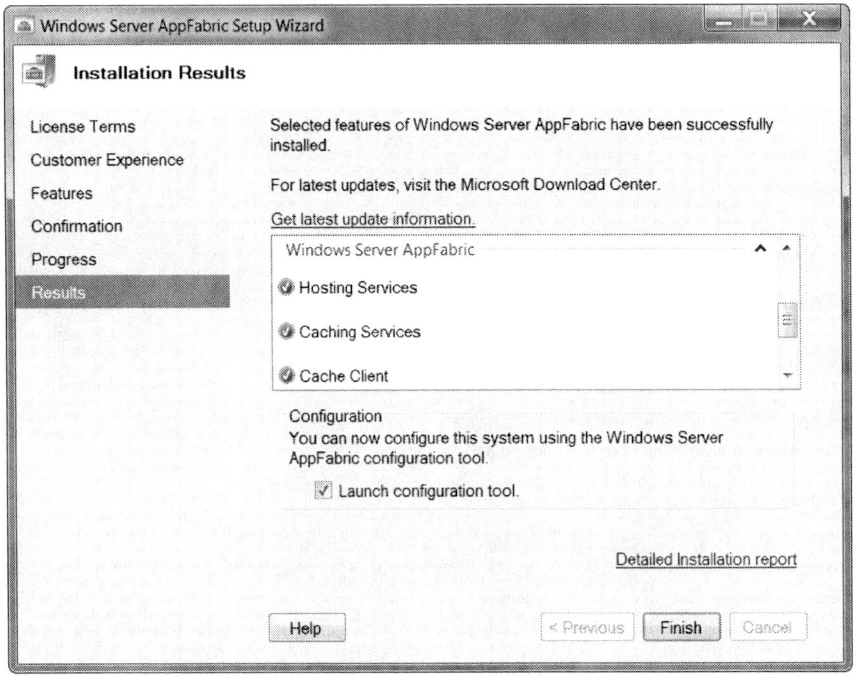

Figure 5-11. Windows Server AppFabric Installation Results

Step 2: Configure AppFabric

If you selected the **Launch Configuration tool** check box on the **AppFabric Installation Results** page during the installation process, the Windows Server AppFabric configuration wizard application will be launched as step 2 of the install process (see Figure 5-12) to give you a chance to configure AppFabric. You can also configure Windows Server AppFabric at a later time by executing the configuration wizard from the Start menu after initial installation. The configuration wizard overwrites existing configuration values with any new values that you enter in the wizard. Many of the steps that are performed in the configuration wizard can be performed manually by executing AppFabric configuration cmdlets.

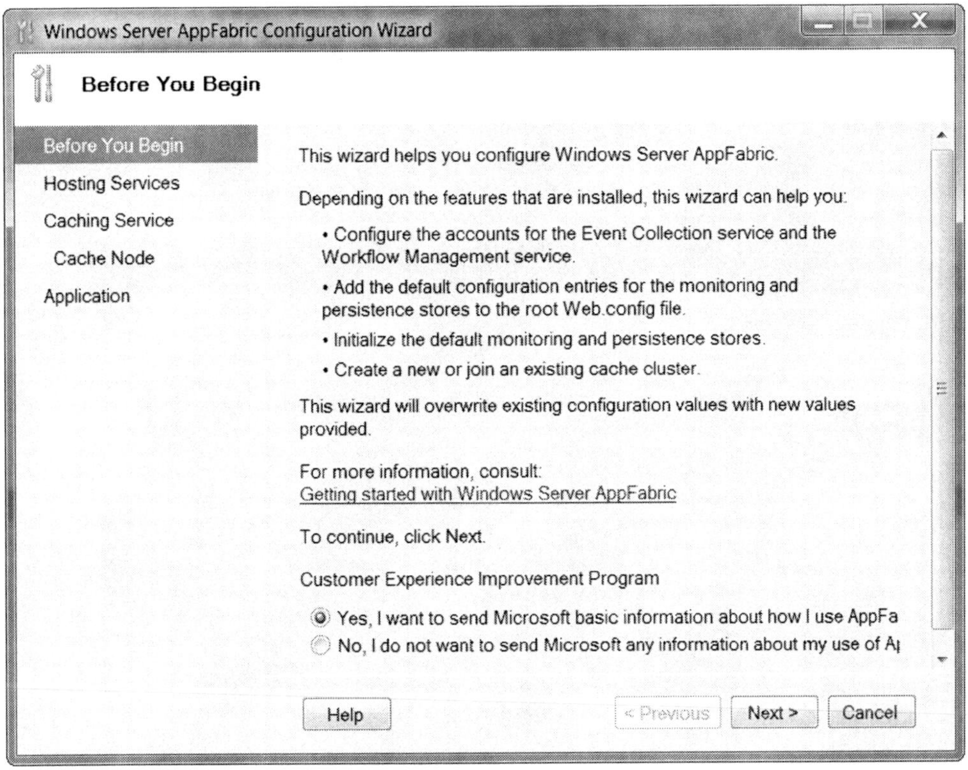

Figure 5-12. Windows Server AppFabric Configuration Wizard

Follow these steps to configure AppFabric through its configuration wizard:

1. On the **Before You Begin** page, select **Yes** to participate in the Customer Experience Improvement program, or **No** not to participate, and then click **Next**. The **Configure Hosting Services** page will be displayed.

2.   On the **Configure Hosting Services** page, you can configure AppFabric monitoring and persistence services. First, you can edit the **Event Collector** service account, which is a member of the **Administrators** group and has administrative access to the **Monitoring** database. By default, the **Event Collector** service account is **NT Authority\LocalService** (see Figure 5-13). By clicking the **Change...** button you can select a built-in account or enter a custom user name and password. You can also select the monitoring provider that will give access to the monitoring database. All valid data providers registered on the local **machine.config** file will be displayed in this list. Furthermore, by clicking the **Configure...** button, you can specify settings to initialize and register an AppFabric monitoring store with the Microsoft SQL Server Monitoring Provider.

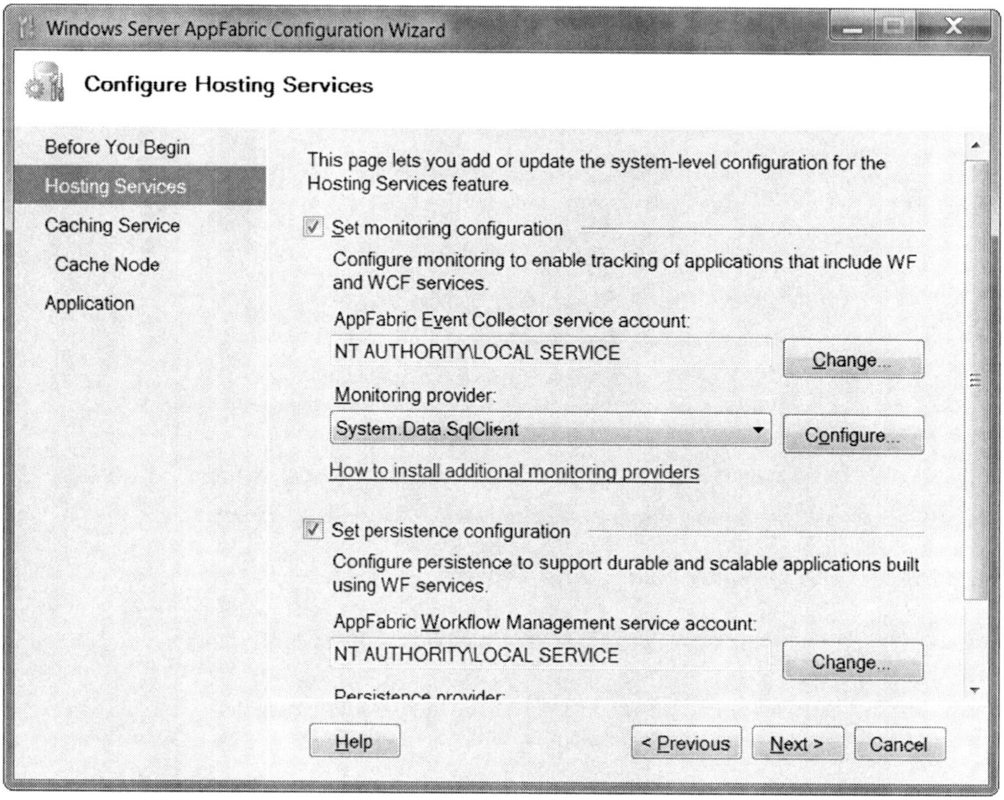

Figure 5-13. AppFabric Monitoring Settings

3. If you clicked **Configure for the SQL monitoring provider** on the Configure Hosting Services page, the Configure SQL Monitoring Store dialog box will be displayed (see Figure 5-14). Select the Register AppFabric monitoring store in the root web.config check box to register the monitoring store identified by the connection string, by adding its configuration to the root web.config file. This includes the ApplicationServerMonitoringConnectionString and its related monitoring behavior. This registration makes the connection string and behavior available at all scopes on the computer.

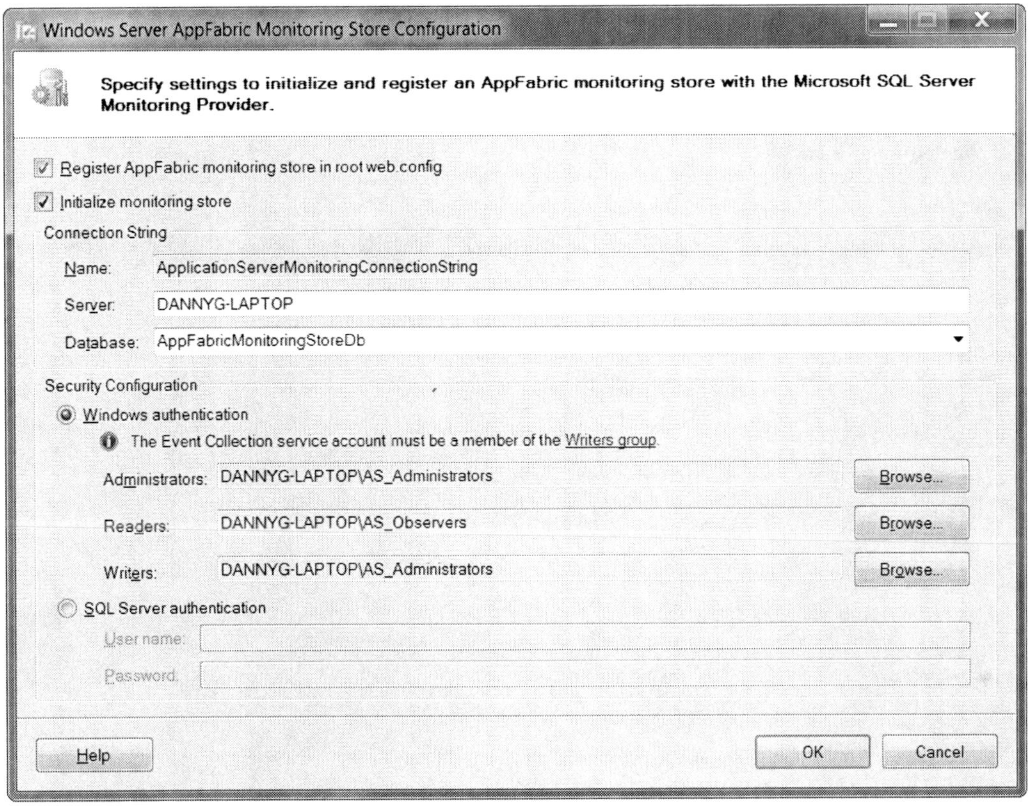

Figure 5-14. AppFabric Monitoring Store Configuration

4. You can also check the **Initialize the Monitoring Store** check box to initialize the monitoring database identified in the connection string, as required before it can be used. Initialization creates the database schema and the structure based upon that schema. If the database does not exist, it will be created and then initialized.

107

5. You can change the value for administrators, readers, or writers in the Security Configuration section on the **AppFabric Monitoring Store Configuration** page.

6. Click **OK** to apply the selected settings for the AppFabric Monitoring Store. Click **Yes** in the confirmation dialog box. After verifying that Monitoring Store was initialized and registered successfully, the **Monitoring Store Configuration** page will be closed, and you will be returned back to the **Configure Hosting Services** page.

7. On the **Configure Hosting Services** page you can also set AppFabric persistence configuration by selecting the **Set persistence configuration** check box. Under the list of all available persistence providers choose the persistence provider you would like to configure; for example, sqlStoreProvider. Then click **Configure...** to specify settings to initialize and register an AppFabric persistence store with the Microsoft SQL Server Persistence Provider (see Figure 5-15).

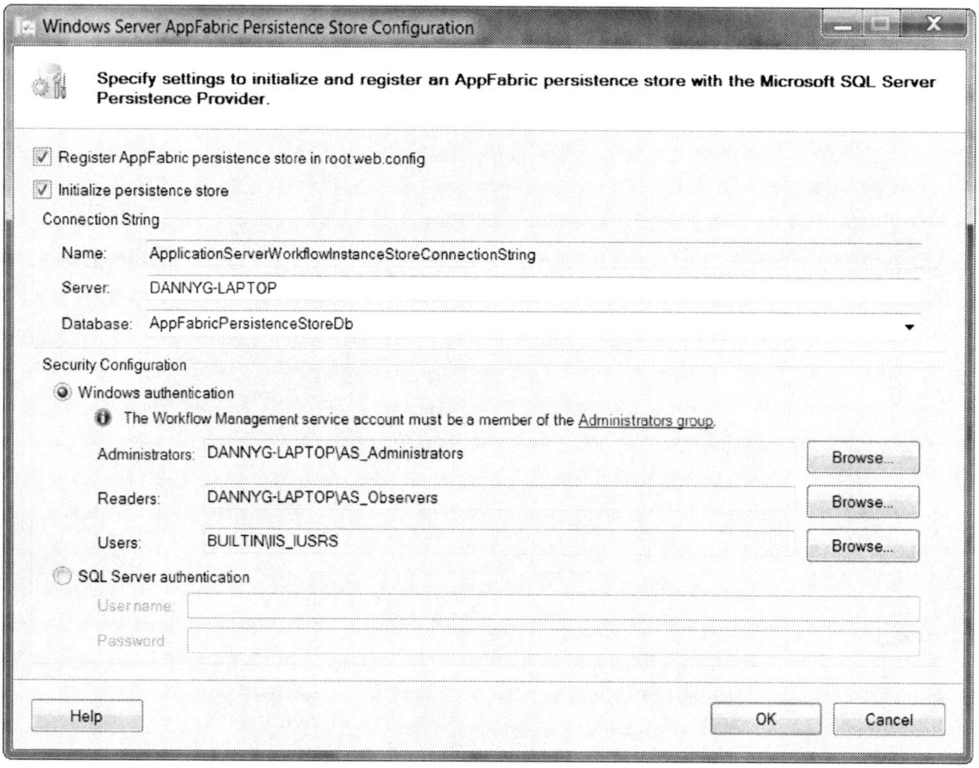

Figure 5-15. *AppFabric Persistence Store Configuration*

8. Check the **Register AppFabric persistence store** in the **root web.config** check box to register the persistence store identified by the connection string, by adding or updating its configuration in the root **web.config** file. This includes the ApplicationServerWorkflowInstanceStoreConnectionString and its related persistence behavior. This registration makes the connection string and behavior available at all scopes on the computer.

9. Type in or select existing SQL database to configure the AppFabric Persistence connection string and to initialize the persistence database. Initialization creates the database schema and the structure based upon that schema. If the database does not exist, it will be created and then initialized.

10. Select **Windows authentication** or **SQL Server authentication**. Windows Integrated Security is selected by default, and the groups are populated with the default built-in groups.

11. Click **OK** to apply the selected settings for the AppFabric persistence store. Click **Yes** in the **confirmation** dialog box. After verifying that persistence store was initialized and registered successfully, the **Persistence Store Configuration** page will be closed, and you will be returned back to the **Configure Hosting Services** page. Click **Next**. At this time, the AppFabric configuration wizard will start the Event Collection service and Workflow Management service, if they are configured, and then display the **Configure Caching Service** page.

12. On the **Configure Caching Service** page (see Figure 5-16), select the **Set Caching Service configuration** check box to add or update system-level configuration of the Caching Service feature. When specifying the Caching Service configuration provider, you have two choices available to you:

XML: Caching Service configuration information is stored in an XML file on a network file share. If you have chosen to store cache configuration information in an XML file, enter or browse to the network file share that will contain the XML configuration file.

■ **Note** You must manually create a network file share that is accessible to all cache servers in the cache cluster.

SQL Server AppFabric Caching Service Configuration : Caching Service configuration information is stored in a SQL Server database.

If you chose SQL Server AppFabric Caching Service Configuration Store Provider as the configuration provider, click Configure to create a Caching Service configuration database (see Figure 5-16).

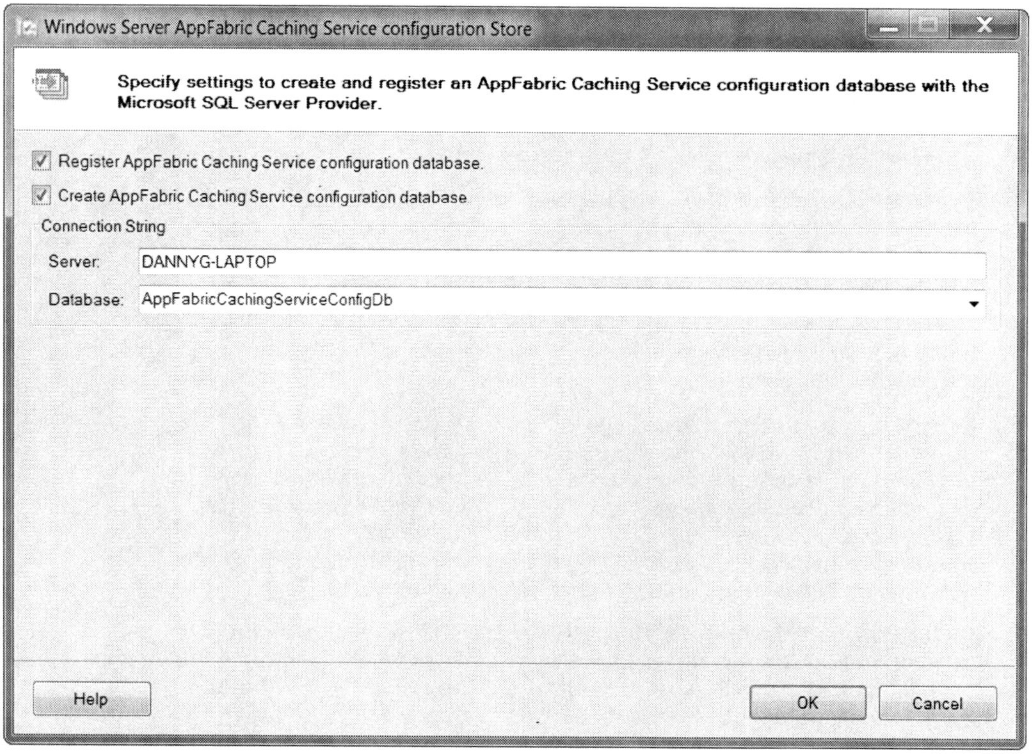

Figure 5-16. AppFabric Caching Service configuration Store

13. On the **Windows Server AppFabric Caching Service configuration Store** page, check the Register AppFabric Caching Service configuration database check box to register the configuration database identified by the connection string by adding its configuration to the root web.config file, and to set the security configuration. This registration makes the connection string and behavior available at all scopes on the computer.

14. Check the Create AppFabric Caching Service configuration database check box to create the configuration database and to specify the connection string or the database name.

15. Click OK to apply the selected settings for the AppFabric Caching Service configuration. Click Yes in the confirmation dialog box. After verifying that the Caching Service configuration database was created and registered successfully, the **AppFabric Caching Service Configuration** page will be closed, and you will be returned back to the **Configure Caching Service** page.

16. Select **New Cluster** if this is the first computer in the cluster. When you run Setup on subsequent computers in the cluster, select **Join Cluster**. The default is New Cluster. To create or join a cluster, you need to specify the location of the configuration data (either in a database or an XML file), and then on the next page (the Configure AppFabric Cache Node page) enter the ports, and set the firewall settings to unblock the services listed. When creating a cluster, you need to indicate the cluster size (the number of computers in the cluster). This enables the system to optimize memory allocation.

17. Your next step is to optimize performance based on your cluster size. When you click Next with the Configure Caching Service page displayed, the Configure AppFabric Cache Node page will be displayed. Note that this setting is available only if you selected at least one of the Caching Services features on the Feature Selection page.

18. Enter or select a unique value for each port, or leave the default settings for the Node ports.

19. In order for the AppFabric Caching Service features to function, you must configure the Windows Firewall Rules to allow access for the Cache Service. After you click Next on the Configure AppFabric Cache Node page, the Windows Server AppFabric configuration wizard will ask you if you want to apply the selected AppFabric Caching Service configuration. Click Yes.

20. On the Configure Application page, select Start Internet Information Services (IIS) Manager to configure an application in the IIS Manager. Click **Finish** to close the configuration wizard.

Step 3: Start Cache Host Services

After the AppFabric configuration wizard has successfully configured the Caching Service, you will need to start the cache cluster.

Follow these steps to start a new cluster in a single-node cluster environment:

1. Open the PowerShell command window.
2. Execute the following cmdlet:
   Import-Module DistributedCacheAdministration
3. Execute the following cmdlet:
   Import-Module DistributedCacheConfiguration
4. Execute the following cmdlet:
   Use-CacheCluster
5. Execute the following cmdlet:
   Start-CacheCluster
6. The resulting PowerShell screen should look like it is shown in Figure 5-17.

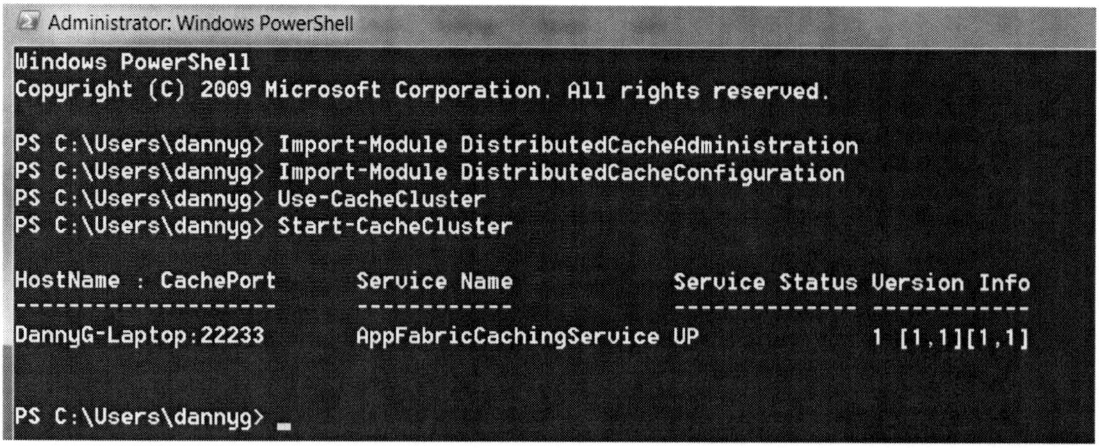

Figure 5-17. Starting a new cluster

Step 4: Verifying Successful Installation of AppFabric

After you configure AppFabric's **Persistence** and **Monitoring** databases, you might want to examine the objects in the database. AppFabric does not provide tools to view the contents of a database, so you will need to use SQL Server Management Studio. If you have used SQL Server Express for your SQL Server database, you might need to download a separate and free Microsoft SQL Server 2008 Management Studio Express from the Microsoft download center.

Follow these steps to verify AppFabric database schemas:

1. Open SQL Server Management Studio and connect to the server that hosts the **Monitoring** or **Persistence** database you want to examine.

2. In the **Object Explorer**, expand the **Databases** node (see Figure 5-18). Double-click the name of the **Monitoring, Persistence Cache Configuration** database to expand the node and view the objects within.

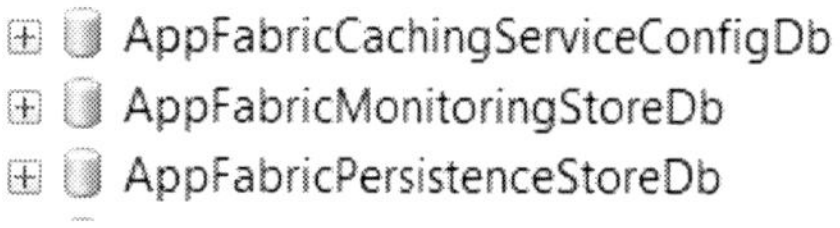

Figure 5-18. AppFabric Databases

Next, you will verify the AppFabric IIS Manager extensions. Follow these steps to verify that the IIS Manager extensions installed correctly:

1. Click **Start**, click **Administrative Tools**, and then click **Internet Information Services (IIS) Manager**.

2. From the left pane, click the desired server node.

3. From the center pane, click **Features View** from the bottom of the pane. The AppFabric IIS Manager extensions are listed in the **IIS Features View** (see Figure 5-19). Most of the extensions are also available at the web site level and the web application level.

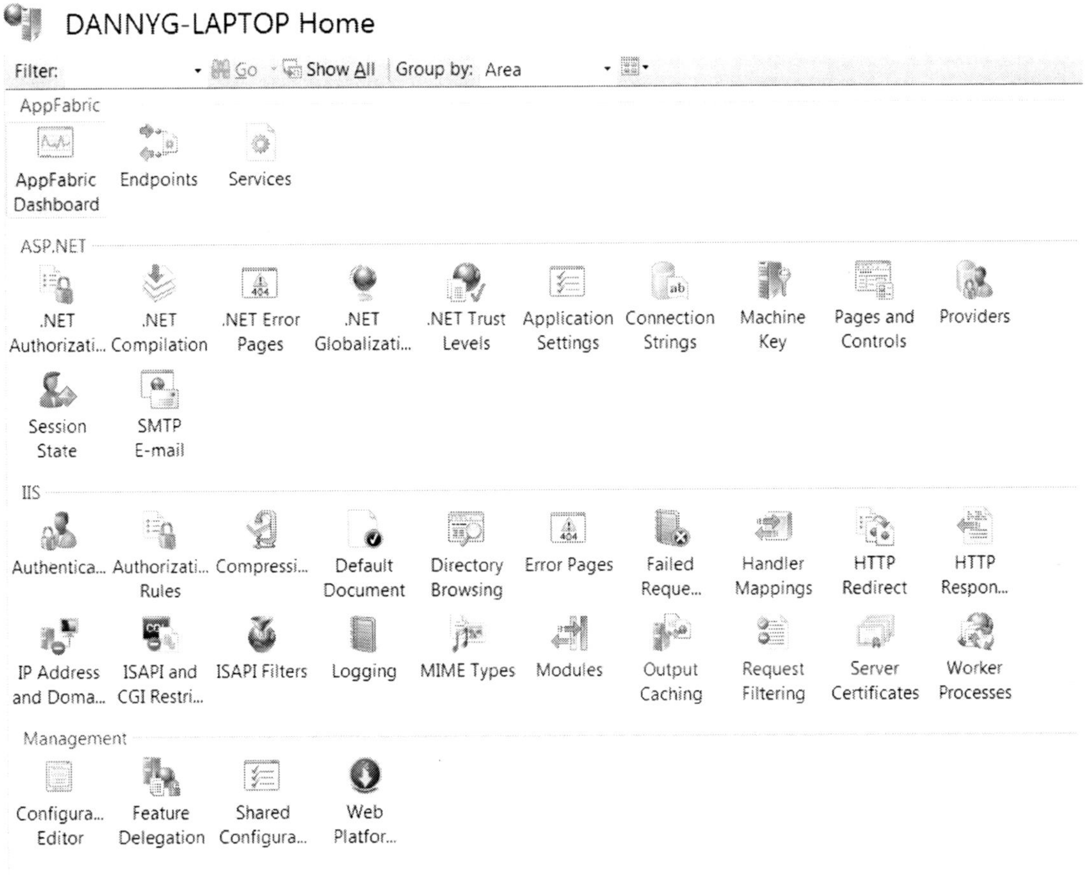

Figure 5-19. AppFabric IIS extensions

Summary: What Did I Just Do?

OK, if you actually followed all these steps on your local computer (not just in your mind), then you now know how to install AppFabric and how to verify the proper configuration of all its components.

For those of you who preferred to read this chapter instead of using it as a manual when performing the installation of AppFabric yourself, we hope this chapter has provided sufficient information for planning the steps required to install AppFabric in your environment when the time comes.

CHAPTER 6

■ ■ ■

Developing WCF Applications with AppFabric

Even if you are a seasoned WCF developer with significant hands-on experience designing and developing web services with WCF 3.0+, the number of compelling new features and improvements in WCF 4.0 will probably please you. These WCF enhancements focus primarily on simplifying the developer experience, enabling more communication scenarios, and providing rich integration with WF 4.0 by making *workflow services* a first-class citizen in distributed, service-oriented applications development

This chapter introduces you to each of the new WCF feature areas in the .NET Framework 4.0 and demonstrates how they work. This example relies on the auto claim insurance business scenario, which you saw first in Chapter 1. This example provides the most efficient way to illustrate the applicability and usage of many of WCF 4.0's new features.

While WCF 4.0 ships with a wide range of features, this chapter focuses only on the main feature areas, summarizing most of what is new in WCF 4.0. By the time you finish this chapter, you will understand how WCF is easier-to-use and provides better built-in support for some of today's most common scenarios and development styles than alternative frameworks.

Incorporating the Business Scenario

In Chapter 1, you learned about a business scenario where Contoso IT is considering ways to optimize its auto insurance claims processing. Currently, customers can only submit their auto insurance claims over the phone, while supplying all additional, required documentation (such as the accident report and policy number) through various communication channels (phone, email, fax, mail, and so on).

In the process of designing the solution for a new Contoso claims processing system, Contoso IT has chosen to develop a new software system incrementally. This allows the developer to take advantage of what he learned during the development of earlier versions of the system. During each iteration, the developer makes design modifications and adds new functional capabilities.

In Phase I of the solution, a new ASP.NET MVC-based web application replaces existing two-tier client server interfaces, which is essential for connecting with various sub-systems in the claims processing business process. The design and development of this new ASP.NET Web site uses a Model-View-Controller (MVC) pattern, which you won't learn about in this chapter because it's beyond the scope of this book (you can learn more about ASP.NET MVC pattern by checking out this site: www.asp.net/mvc.

This iteration places new WCF web services in front of the `Appraisal Agents` and `Billing` applications (see Figure 6-1). It also creates a new WCF service that calls `Appraisal Agents`, `Rental`

Agency, and **Billing** services, returning an email to the customer. The goal of the Phase I milestone is to implement a single web front end to cover all three applications.

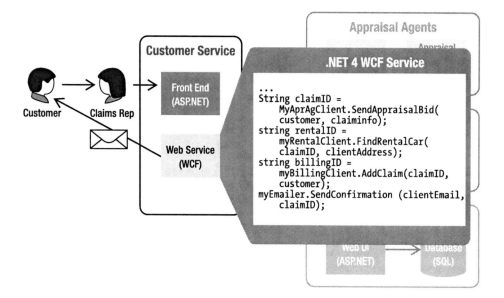

Figure 6-1. *Phase I Contoso Insurance Claim Processing Architecture*

The claim processing workflow includes three major parts:

1. It reviews *pending* or submitted claims on the main web page.

2. It obtains the appraisal summary with the attached map of the accident (here you use the **Microsoft Bing Maps** service to obtain and draw the map).

3. It processes or submits the claim for processing; this includes invoking Billing and CarRental web services.

Figure 6-2 shows the main web site page all users will see when they get access (through the login screen) to the Contoso Claims Processing application.

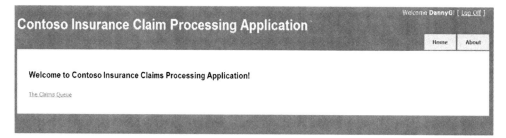

Figure 6-2. *Contoso Insurance Claim Processing Application Main Page*

If the user clicks **The Claims Queue** hyperlink, the application invokes the **Claim Appraisal** WCF service. This service retrieves all the claims received for processing thus far, as well as the claims processed previously. You can see the results in Figure 6-3.

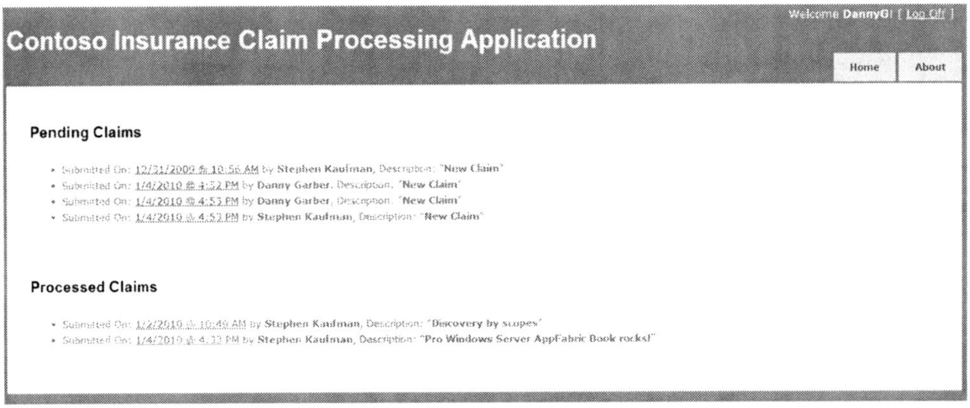

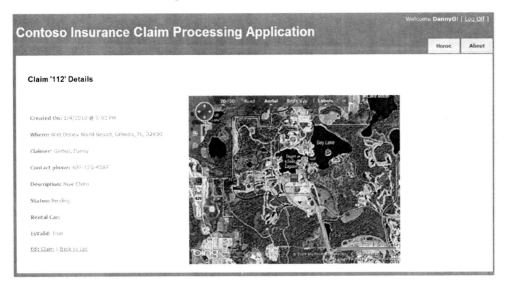

Figure 6-3. *Contoso Insurance Claim Processing Application Claims Queue*

On the screen in Figure 6-3, the user can click one of the newly submitted (*pending*) claims to obtain more information about the claim. For example, the app's user might want to learn more about the place (Bing Map) and time of the accident, the claimant's phone number, the current rental car booking status, and other details (see Figure 6-4).

Figure 6-4. *Claim Details*

The screen in Figure 6-4 illustrates how the user can edit some of the details of the claim, check the map of the accident's location, and finally, submit the claim for processing.

During the processing of the claim, the Claims application invokes two other web services: one for the billing application and the other for the rental car reservation. Both services return the status message, which appears on the details of the claim after it has been processed (see Figure 6-5).

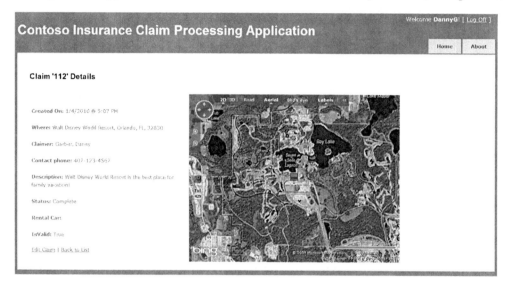

Figure 6-5. Processed Claim Details

Note that the status of the claim changes to **Complete**, while that the status of the Rental Car service remains blank. You will learn more about the implementation of the rental car service later in this chapter.

Architectural Challenges of a Phase I Approach

One of the most difficult challenges Contoso IT developers faced in building new web services with WCF 3.x was dealing with the various configuration options WCF provides. The unified programming model offered by WCF simplifies writing service logic for a variety of different communication scenarios; however, it also increases the complexity on the configuration side of things because it provides so many different underlying communications options independent of the service logic. You need to understand these options before you can get started.

The reality—before AppFabric—is that WCF configuration usually becomes the most costly aspect of using WCF, and much of that complexity lands on IT/operations groups who are usually unprepared to deal with it. Given this, when you consider the net complexity of using WCF 3.x, you might reasonably conclude that WCF is harder to use than its predecessor, ASP.NET Web services (ASMX). With ASMX, you were able to define a `[WebMethod]` operation, and the runtime automatically provided a default configuration for the underlying communications. When moving to WCF 3.x, a developer must know enough about the various WCF configuration options to define at least one endpoint.

The good news for Contoso is that Microsoft recently released its new .NET Framework 4.0, which makes implementing the most common scenarios easier and seamless in terms of migration. To implement new Web services in Phase I with WCF 4.0, Contoso IT developers can now simply decide which new WCF features they want to take advantage of moving forward. You will learn about several of these new WCF 4.0 features in the rest of this chapter.

WCF 4.0's New Default Features

In an effort to make the overall WCF experience as easy as the experience of using ASMX, WCF 4.0 includes a new default configuration model that completely removes the need for any WCF configuration. If you do not provide any WCF configuration for a particular service, the WCF runtime automatically configures your service with some standard endpoints and default binding and behavior configurations. This makes it much easier to get a WCF service up and running, especially for those who aren't familiar with the various WCF configuration options and are happy to accept the defaults. Of course, you are always free to change the values, even if you use simplified default configuration model.

Default Endpoints

If you try to host a service without any configured endpoints with WCF in .NET 3.x, the ServiceHost will throw an exception, informing you that you need to configure at least one endpoint. This is no longer the case with WCF in .NET 4.0 because the runtime automatically adds one or more default endpoints for you, thereby making the service usable even without any configuration.

Creating a Default Endpoint

Now let's take a look at how Contoso's IT developers built their new **Appraisal** Web service using WCF 4.0. You'll begin your Appraisal Web service creation by selecting the **File** → **New Project** menu item within Visual Studio 2010. This brings up the **New Project** dialog. To create a new WCF Service library, you select the **WCF** node on the left-hand side of the dialog and then choose the **WCF Service Library** project template on the right. Make sure that the default project, **.NET Framework 4**, is selected at the top of the window (see Figure 6-6).

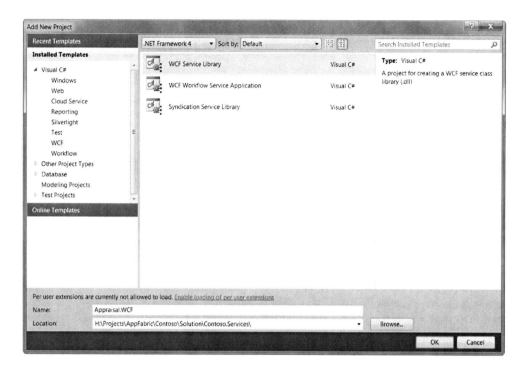

Figure 6-6. Creating a New WCF 4.0 Service Library in Visual Studio 2010

Name the new project **Appraisal.WCF** and click the **OK** button to create it.

The code to implement the preceding WCF service so it provides the necessary application functionality is provided to you by the authors of this book; you can download it from this book's page at **www.apress.com**. In this chapter, you'll focus on the new .NET Framework WCF 4.0 behaviors that can help you build your WCF services efficiently and get them up and running quickly.

With WCF 4.0, you can now use ServiceHost to host the web service you just built without any application configuration whatsoever. What follows shows you how to host the **Appraisal.WCF** web service in a console application. Again, you can assume there's no **app.config** file associated with this program. Before you can test it, however, you must add a new Console Application host project to your solution.

To do this, begin by right-clicking the solution's **Claims** folder within your solution explorer. Next, select the **Add → Existing Project...** menu command. This brings up the **Add Existing Project** browse window, from which you can navigate to the **Assets** subfolder under the **Source Code** directory and load the existing **Appraisal.ConsoleHost** project.

When you add the provided **Appraisal.ConsoleHost** project to your solution, you will see this project has several files (see Figure 6-7).

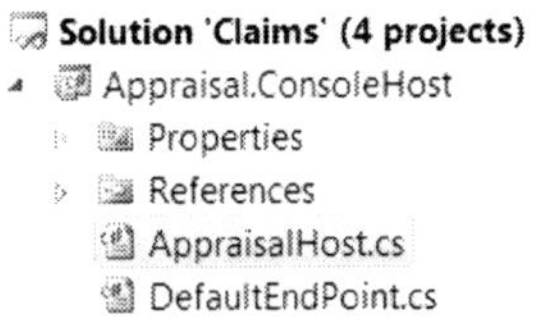

⟲ **Solution 'Claims' (4 projects)**
⊿ 🔲 Appraisal.ConsoleHost
  ▷ 🔲 Properties
  ▷ 🔲 References
    📄 AppraisalHost.cs
    📄 DefaultEndPoint.cs

Figure 6-7. File Structure of the Appraisal.ConsoleHost Project

The WCF 4.0 Web service project doesn't require this structure. These files enable you to test various WCF 4.0 Hosting options described in the rest of this chapter. In fact, developers working on large applications will typically partition the application across multiple projects and solutions to make it more manageable.

When you open the **AppraisalHost.cs** class, you'll find that this is the entry point to the Console application, which, depending on the option you choose to test, calls the appropriate host implementation class, such as the **DefaultEndPoint.cs** class that implements the WCF Default Endpoint host.

When you run this program, you will see two endpoints printed to the console window (see Figure 6-8). You will get one endpoint for the **HTTP** base address and one for the **TCP** base address.

Figure 6-8. Console Output After Running the Service Host Without Endpoint Configuration

---

■ **Note** The **BasicHttpBinding** for **HTTP** base address and the **NetTcpBinding** for **TCP** base address are the default bindings in WCF 4.0.

Remember: This default endpoint behavior only kicks in when the service has not been configured with any endpoints. If you change the console application to configure the service with at least one endpoint, you will no longer see any of these default endpoints in the output. To validate this, add the following line of code, which calls **AddServiceEndpoint** after constructing the **ServiceHost** instance in the **Host()** method:

```
ServiceHost host = new ServiceHost(typeof(AppraisalService),
baseAddresses.ToArray<Uri>());

//NEW: To enforce the explicit WCF binding
host.AddServiceEndpoint(typeof(IClaimInfo), new WSHttpBinding(), "");

...
```

If you run the console application with this line of code inserted, you will notice that only a single endpoint now appears in the output—the one you configured manually in the preceding code (see Figure 6-9).

```
C:\Windows\system32\cmd.exe
Address: http://localhost:9000/AppraisalService
Binding Name: WSHttpBinding
Contract Name: IClaimInfo


Press <Enter> to stop the service.
```

Figure 6-9. Console Output After Configuring the Host with a Single Endpoint

How Does It Work?

When the host application calls **Open** on the ServiceHost instance, it builds the internal service description from the application configuration file, along with anything the host application might have configured explicitly. If the number of configured endpoints remains zero, it calls **AddDefaultEndpoints**, a new public method found on **ServiceHost** that adds one or more default endpoints to the service description. This method is public, so you can call it directly in custom-hosting scenarios.

The implementation of **AddDefaultEndpoints** adds one default endpoint per base address for each service contract implemented by the service. For example, if the service implements two service contracts, and you configure the host with a single base address, **AddDefaultEndpoints** configures the service with two default endpoints (one for each service contract). However, if the service implements two service contracts and the host is configured with two base addresses (one for **HTTP** and one for **TCP**), **AddDefaultEndpoints** configures the service with four default endpoints.

Now that you understand the algorithm and mechanics for adding default endpoints to services at runtime, you might wonder how WCF decides which binding to use for a particular base address. WCF defines a default protocol mapping between transport protocol schemes (such as **http**, **net.tcp**, **net.pipe**, and so on) and WCF bindings. You can find the default protocol mapping in the .NET 4.0 **machine.config** file, which looks like this:

```
<system.serviceModel>
    <protocolMapping>
        <add scheme="http" binding="basicHttpBinding"/>
        <add scheme="net.tcp" binding="netTcpBinding"/>
        <add scheme="net.pipe" binding="netNamedPipeBinding"/>
        <add scheme="net.msmq" binding="netMsmqBinding"/>
```

```
</protocolMapping>
...
```

You can override this default mapping at the machine level by modifying the `machine.config` file. If you would like to override it only within the scope of an application, you can override this section within your application configuration file and change the mapping for particular protocol schemes. Once WCF determines which binding to use through the protocol mapping table, it uses the default binding configuration to configure the default endpoint. If you are not happy with the built-in binding defaults, you can always override the default configuration for a particular binding.

Default Bindings

Every WCF binding comes with a default configuration that is used unless explicitly overridden by the host application for a particular endpoint.

In WCF 3.x, you do this by defining a named binding configuration that you can apply to endpoint definitions through the `bindingConfiguration` attribute. Unfortunately, the mechanics of doing this properly are cumbersome and error-prone.

Let's assume the Contoso network experiences some connectivity and bandwidth problems that correlate to the volume of data and time of day that the service calls are made. To increase the service sustainability during these peak times, Contoso developers decided to implement a special binding configuration to allow more time for service host opening, closing, receiving, and sending operations. This requires adding a new binding profile into both the service and client XML configuration files, as shown in this example:

```
<configuration>
  <system.serviceModel>
    <bindings>
      <basicHttpBinding>
        <binding name="ExtendedTimeout" closeTimeout="00:02:00" ~CCC
openTimeout="00:02:00"
receiveTimeout="00:10:00" sendTimeout="00:10:00" />
      </basicHttpBinding>
    </bindings>
    <services>
      <service name="Appraisal.WCF">
        <endpoint address="" binding="basicHttpBinding" ~CCC
bindingConfiguration="ExtendedTimeout" contract=" IClaimInfo" />
      </service>
    </services>
  </system.serviceModel>
</configuration>
```

In the preceding example, the `ExtendedTimeout` binding configuration overrides the defaults for `basicHttpBinding` by changing the default timeout durations to specified intervals. However, this binding configuration only takes effect when you apply it to a specific endpoint through the `bindingConfiguration` attribute.

WCF 4.0 enables you to define default binding configurations by omitting the binding configuration name. This prompts WCF to use that default configuration for any endpoints that use that binding, but don't have an explicit binding configuration set on them.

In this example, adding the following **app.config** file to the console application shown earlier causes the default HTTP endpoint to pick up this default **basicHttpBinding** configuration, which modifies the default timeout parameters:

```
<configuration>
  <system.serviceModel>
    <bindings>
      <basicHttpBinding>
        <binding closeTimeout="00:02:00" openTimeout="00:02:00"
receiveTimeout="00:10:00"
sendTimeout="00:10:00" />
      </basicHttpBinding>
    </bindings>
  </system.serviceModel>
</configuration>
```

You can add these default binding configurations to the **machine.config** file if you want them to take effect across all services running on the machine. Alternatively, you can define them on an application-by-application basis by adding the default binding configurations to the application configuration file.

This feature gives you a simple mechanism to define a standard set of binding defaults that you can use across all of your services without imposing the complexities of binding configurations onto other developers or the IT/operations staff. These people can choose the appropriate binding and be confident that the hosting environment will provide the proper default configuration.

In addition to default binding configurations, you must also consider what the default behavior configuration for default endpoints should be.

Default Behaviors

WCF 4.0 also makes it possible to define default behavior configurations for services and endpoints. This can simplify things when you want to share a standard default behavior configuration across all services or endpoints running within a solution. This is similar to how default binding configurations work.

In WCF 3.x, you have to define named behavior configurations that you apply to services and endpoints through the **behaviorConfiguration** attribute. With WCF 4.0, you can define default behavior configurations by omitting the behavior configuration name (just as you can in the default binding configurations). If you update the Contoso console application's **app.config** file with the new service behavior, it will look like this:

```
<configuration>
  <system.serviceModel>
    <bindings>
      <basicHttpBinding>
        <binding closeTimeout="00:02:00" openTimeout="00:02:00"
          receiveTimeout="00:10:00"
          sendTimeout="00:10:00" />
      </basicHttpBinding>
    </bindings>
    <behaviors>
      <serviceBehaviors>
        <behavior>
          <serviceMetadata httpGetEnabled="true"/>
```

```
      </behavior>
    </serviceBehaviors>
  </behaviors>
</system.serviceModel>
</configuration>
```

▪ **Note** The `behavior` element contains no `name` attribute.

The preceding example turns on service metadata for any service that doesn't come with an explicit behavior configuration. If you run **Appraisal.ConsoleHost** service host console application again, you can browse to the base **HTTP** address to retrieve the service help page and the service's WSDL definition (see Figure 6-10).

Figure 6-10. Viewing the Service Metadata for the Appraisal.WCF WCF Service in the Browser

Standard Endpoints

Another new feature related to default endpoints concerns *standard endpoints*. You can think of a standard endpoint as a preconfigured endpoint definition built into the WCF framework that you can reuse. Standard endpoints are built in to WCF 4.0 to define endpoint configurations that you do not typically change. For example, in the case of a MEX endpoint, the endpoint definition must always specify **IMetadataExchange** for the service contract. Instead of forcing you to do that in every case, WCF provides a standard endpoint definition for metadata exchange called **mexEndpoint**.

You can leverage any of these standard endpoints in your own service configurations by referencing them by name. The **<endpoint>** element now comes with a **kind** attribute that you can use to specify the name of a standard endpoint. For instance, if Contoso developers want to configure their web services with a MEX endpoint, they can now do it by leveraging the standard `mexEndpoint` definition:

```
<configuration>
  <system.serviceModel>

    <services>
      <service name="Appraisal.WCF.AppraisalService">
        <endpoint address="" binding="wsHttpBinding"
         contract="Appraisal.WCF.IClaimInfo" />
        <endpoint address="mex" kind="mexEndpoint" />
      </service>
    </services>

  </system.serviceModel>
</configuration>
```

■ **Note** You don't have to specify the binding or contract for `mexEndpoint`.

In addition to the standard `mexEndpoint`, WCF 4.0 comes with a set of predefined standard endpoints that help you pre-configure some default functionality for service discovery. Examples of such standard endpoints are include `discoveryEndpoint`, `announcementEndpoint`, `udpDiscoveryEndpoint`, and `udpAnnouncementEndpoint`. You will learn about WCF 4.0's discovery functionality in the next section of this chapter.

.NET Framework 4.0 also includes a standard endpoint for controlling the execution of workflow instances: `workflowControlEndpoint`. You will learn about this standard endpoint in Chapter 7, in the context of learning about the new changes and functionality in WF 4.0.

The standard endpoints shield you from most of the configuration details, but you might encounter cases where you want to configure the standard endpoint a little bit differently. For example, you might want to change the discovery mode for the standard `DiscoveryEndpoint` endpoint). When you need to do this, you can use the `<standardEndpoints>` section and define a named endpoint configuration for the standard endpoint. Then you can reference that configuration when defining a new `<endpoint>` through the `endpointConfiguration` attribute, as shown in this code:

```
<configuration>
  <system.serviceModel>

    <services>
      <service name="Appraisal.WCF.AppraisalService">
        <endpoint address="" binding="wsHttpBinding"
         contract="Appraisal.WCF.IClaimInfo" />
        <endpoint address="mex" kind="mexEndpoint" />
        <endpoint kind="discoveryEndpoint"
         endpointConfiguration="managedDiscovery" />
</service>
    </services>
```

```
<standardEndpoints>
  <discoveryEndpoint>
    <standardEndpoint name="managedDiscovery" discoveryMode="Managed"/>
  </discoveryEndpoint>
</standardEndpoints>
</system.serviceModel>
</configuration>
```

Enabling Dynamic Service Discovery in WCF 4.0

The next major feature in WCF 4.0 that you'll learn about is *dynamic service discovery*. Some unique service-oriented environments exist for services with a dynamic runtime location. In this case, you need to discover the runtime location dynamically. You can see a great example of such services in the Contoso Insurance service-oriented environment, where the new WCF services create a service façade to *legacy* applications; such applications can be hosted internally (such as Billing application) or externally, on a partner's network (such as **Appraisal Agency** services).

You will add these and other services in subsequent phases. Such services can constantly join and leave the network as part of the overall service-load balancing solution. Dealing with this reality requires clients to discover the runtime location of service endpoints dynamically.

The WS-Discovery[1] specification describes two primary modes of service discovery operation: **ad hoc** mode and **managed** mode. In **ad hoc** mode, clients probe for services by sending multicast messages. Services that match the probe respond directly to the client. To minimize the need for client polling, services can also announce when they join or leave the network by sending a multicast message to any clients that might be listening. Although **ad hoc** discovery is the simplest form, it only works within the context of a local subnet.

When you want to discover services across networks, you will want to turn on the **managed** discovery mode. With **managed** service discovery, you provide a discovery proxy on the network that manages the discoverable service endpoints. Services announce themselves directly to the discovery proxy, and this can even happen across network boundaries when needed. It's the job of the discovery proxy to save the list of known service endpoints and to respond to client discovery requests. Clients talk directly to the discovery proxy to locate services based on probing criteria. This discovery mode is a little more difficult to implement, but it's far more flexible and it greatly reduces multicast traffic. WCF 4.0 provides a complete implementation of the WS-Discovery protocol, and it provides support for both the **ad hoc** and **managed** discovery modes. You will look at both approaches in this in the sections next.

Ad Hoc Service Discovery

ad hoc mode provides the easiest way to enable service discovery. WCF 4.0 makes it easy to enable service discovery within your service host applications by providing some standard discovery endpoints and a service discovery behavior. The service discovery functionality API is a new feature in .NET Framework 4.0; it's provided with the **System.ServiceModel.Discovery** assembly.

You can see this at work in the example by creating a new **Billing** WCF service and make it **discoverable** at runtime.

---

[1] WS-Discovery is an OASIS specification that defines a SOAP-based protocol for dynamically discovering the location of service endpoints at runtime. The protocol allows clients to probe for service endpoints that match certain criteria to retrieve a list of suitable candidates.

Next, you add a new WCF 4.0 web service by right-clicking the **Claims** solution and selecting **Add →
Existing Project...** to navigate to the **Assets** directory and then selecting the existing **Billing.WCF** WCF
service library project. Alternatively, you can create a new WCF 4.0 Service Library project for yourself,
but then you need to implement the service's interface and the service implementation code.

Next, you need to create another host console application to host your new **Billing** WCF service. To
do this, begin by right-clicking the **Claims** solution folder within the solution explorer and selecting the
Add → Existing Project... menu command. This brings up the **Add Existing Project** browse window
from which you can navigate to the **Assets** subfolder under the **Source Code** directory and load the
existing **Billing.ConsoleHost** project.

When you add the provided **Billing.ConsoleHost** project to your solution, you will see this project
has several files (see Figure 6-11).

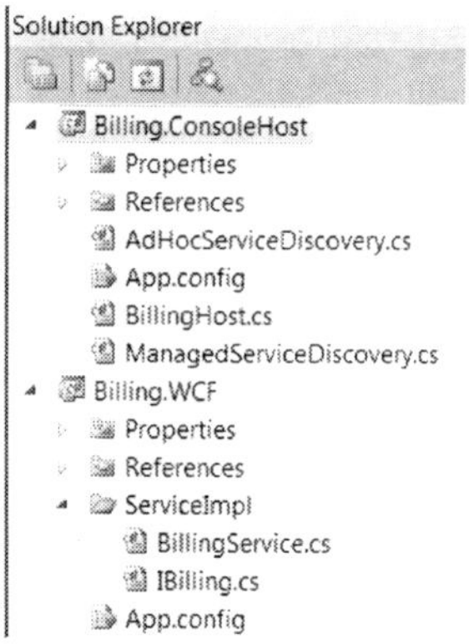

Figure 6-11. *Billing.ConsoleHost Project File Structure*

If you open the **AdHocServiceDiscovery.cs** file and examine its code, you will see that the code
written to host a new **Billing.WCF** web service is the same code you implemented earlier for the
Appraisal Service Host console application. The magic that enables runtime service discovery lies in
configuring the standard **discovery** endpoint for this new WCF service.

To configure your service for discovery, add a new application configuration file to the project and
call it **app.config**. Next, enable the **<serviceDiscovery>** behavior on the service by adding the standard
udpDiscoveryEndpoint endpoint, as shown in the following code excerpt:

```
<configuration>
  <system.serviceModel>
    <services>
      <service name="Billing.WCF.BillingService">
        <endpoint address="" binding="basicHttpBinding"
          contract="Billing.WCF.IBilling" />
        <endpoint name="AdHocDiscovery" kind="udpDiscoveryEndpoint" />
      </service>
    </services>
    <behaviors>
      <serviceBehaviors>
        <behavior>
          <serviceDiscovery />
```

```
        </behavior>
      </serviceBehaviors>
    </behaviors>
  </system.serviceModel>

</configuration>
```

Implementing this code makes a new **Billing.WCF** web service discoverable over **UDP** on the local subnet.

When you run the **Billing.ConsoleHost** application host, you will see two endpoints printed to the console window (see Figure 6-12). You will get one for the **HTTP** base address and one for the **WS-Discovery** custom binding address. Note how the contract name for the **WS-Discovery** enabled service defaults to **TargetService**.

Figure 6-12. Console Output After Running the Service Host Configured for Service Discovery.

At this point, clients can take advantage of **WS-Discovery** at runtime to *discover* the address of the running service. WCF 4.0's new **DiscoveryClient** class makes it easy for clients to accomplish this. The class contains a **Find()** method that performs a blocking synchronous find and a **FindAsync()** method that initiates a non-blocking asynchronous find. Both methods take a **FindCriteria** parameter and provide results to the user through a **FindResponse** object. You initiate a discovery lookup using DiscoveryClient. You can use this to discover one or more services. Performing a **Find** sends a **WS-Discovery Probe** message over the network. Matching services reply with **WS-Discovery ProbeMatch** messages.

Now let's look at how you might implement this in the Contoso scenario. In this case, you'll try to discover Billing service in the runtime rather than by generating a proxy Web service class at design time.

You begin by configuring your **Claims.Web** web site configuration settings with a **udpDiscoveryEndpoint** endpoint:

```
  <client>
    <endpoint name="BillingEndpoint" binding="basicHttpBinding"
     contract="Billing.WCF.IBilling" />
    <endpoint name="adHocDiscovery" kind="udpDiscoveryEndpoint" />
  </client>
```

■ **Note** You don't have to specify the address of **Billing Service**.

Alternatively, you could programmatically add service discovery endpoint and service discovery behavior to accomplish the same thing (see the next code listing). You will learn how to use this technique in your sample scenario to demonstrate various service-discovery implementations:

```
// Announce the availability of the service over UDP multicast
UdpDiscoveryEndpoint adHocDiscovery = new UdpDiscoveryEndpoint();
ServiceDiscoveryBehavior serviceDiscoveryBehavior = new
ServiceDiscoveryBehavior();

// Make the service discoverable over UDP multicast
host.Description.Endpoints.Add(adHocDiscovery);
host.Description.Behaviors.Add(serviceDiscoveryBehavior);
```

Now you can use the DiscoveryClient class in conjunction with this standard discovery endpoint definition to discover service endpoints that match specific criteria. The following client implementation code in ClaimsController.cs's Process() method illustrates how to discover and invoke an IBilling endpoint:

```
public string Process(int id)
{
    //Create DiscoveryClient
    DiscoveryClient discoveryClient = new DiscoveryClient(new
        UdpDiscoveryEndpoint());

    //Create the search criteria for the specified scope
    FindCriteria findCriteria = new FindCriteria(typeof(IBilling));

    //Find BillingService endpoint
    FindResponse findResponse = discoveryClient.Find(findCriteria);

    if (findResponse.Endpoints.Count == 0)
        return View("NotFound");

    //Pick the first discovered endpoint
    EndpointAddress address = findResponse.Endpoints[0].Address;

    //Create the target service client
    ChannelFactory<IBilling> factory = new ChannelFactory<IBilling>(new
        BasicHttpBinding(), address);
            IBilling client = factory.CreateChannel();

    //Call the Billing Service
    string status = client.ProcessClaim(id);

    factory.Close();
    //return  a new status of the processed claim
    return status;
}
```

FindResponse has an Endpoints collection property, which contains any replies sent by matching services on the network. If no services replied, the collection will be empty. If one or more services replied, each reply will be stored in an **EndpointDiscoveryMetadata** object, which will contain the address, contract, and some additional information about the service.

Once the client application retrieves the collection of endpoints, it can use one of the dynamically discovered endpoint addresses to invoke the target service. Figure 6-13 shows the output of running the preceding client code, assuming that the service is also running at the same time. In the preceding example, the **Find** operation on the discovery client is synchronous; discovery also provides support for asynchronous find operations.

Figure 6-13. Console Output After Invoking the Billing Service Configured for Service Discovery

Simply to make the point further, let's review the project file structure of the web client application that invokes **Billing** service using WCF 4.0's **Dynamic Discovery** feature. Figure 6-14 shows Contoso's Claims Web project, which illustrates the scenario this chapter has been discussing.

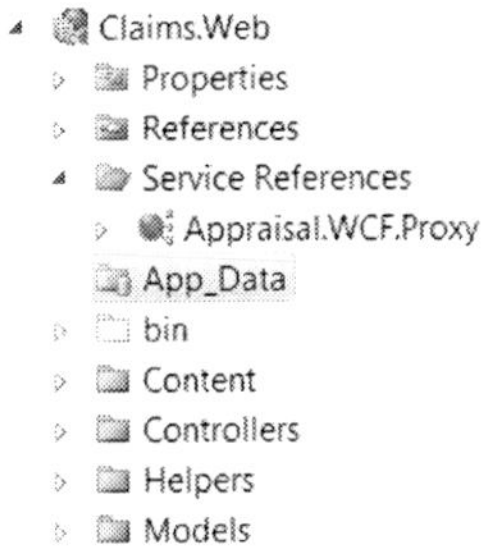

▲ 🌐 Claims.Web
   ▷ 📓 Properties
   ▷ 📓 References
  ▲ 📂 Service References
     ▷ 🌐 Appraisal.WCF.Proxy
     📓 App_Data
   ▷ 🗀 bin
   ▷ 🗀 Content
   ▷ 🗀 Controllers
   ▷ 🗀 Helpers
   ▷ 🗀 Models

Figure 6-14. Claims.Web Application Project File Structure

Note the existence of the **Appraisal.WCF.Proxy** service reference in the project, which uses the traditional direct binding technique to discover the web service endpoint at design time and generate a client proxy stub that the web application calls directly. You don't see the **Billing** WCF service client proxy here because you will discover it later in the process (dynamically at runtime, as explained earlier in this chapter).

Using Scopes When Discovering Endpoints

In the preceding example, you discovered Contoso's **Billing** service by probing for the service's endpoints based on the **IBilling** service-contract type. You can narrow the discovery results by providing additional scoping information when sending the discovery probes. The sample code that follows shows how you can use *scopes* during discovery.

First, the **Billing** WCF service needs to associate one or more scopes with each endpoint that it will publish for discovery. WCF 4.0 comes with an **<endpointDiscovery>** behavior that you can use for defining a set of scopes that you can associate with an endpoint definition. The following code excerpt from **Billing.ConsoleHost**'s **app.config** configuration file illustrates how to associate two scopes with the single endpoint defined on the service:

```
<configuration>
  <system.serviceModel>
    <services>
      <service name="Billing.WCF.BillingService">
        <endpoint address="" binding="basicHttpBinding"
          contract="Billing.WCF.IBilling" />
        <endpoint name="AdHocDiscovery" kind="udpDiscoveryEndpoint"
          behaviorConfiguration="discoveryConfiguration" />
      </service>
    </services>
    <behaviors>
      <serviceBehaviors>
        <behavior>
          <serviceDiscovery />
        </behavior>
      </serviceBehaviors>
      <endpointBehaviors>
        <behavior name="discoveryConfiguration">
          <endpointDiscovery>
            <scopes>
              <add scope="http://www.contoso.com/insurance"/>
              <add scope="ldap:///ou=insurance,o=contoso,c=us"/>
            </scopes>
          </endpointDiscovery>
        </behavior>
      </endpointBehaviors>
    </behaviors>
  </system.serviceModel>
</configuration>
```

Clients can probe for service endpoints based on specific scopes at runtime. They can do so by adding a list of target scopes to the **FindCriteria** instance that you supply to the **Find** operation. The following code from **ClaimsController**'s **Process()** method illustrates how to discover **IBilling** endpoints that match the specific URL and LDAP scopes:

```
...
//Create the search criteria for the specified scope
FindCriteria findCriteria = new FindCriteria(typeof(IBilling));

//Add discovery scopes
findCriteria.Scopes.Add(new Uri("http://www.contoso.com/insurance"));
findCriteria.Scopes.Add(new
    Uri("ldap:///ou=insurance,o=contoso,c=us"));
findCriteria.ScopeMatchBy = FindCriteria.ScopeMatchByExact;
```

```
//Find BillingService endpoint
FindResponse findResponse = discoveryClient.Find(findCriteria);
...
```

Let's look at the preceding code to understand scopes better. Suppose you have multiple printers in different levels of a building. A user in the first level who wants to search for a printer would prefer to find one on his level. If he searches using only the contract, then all the printers will respond back. To fine-tune the responses further, the user can decorate the endpoints of the printers using scopes. The user can then specify the scopes as part of the **FindCriteria**, and only services that have endpoints matching the scopes will respond. In the Contoso Appraisal Agency example, there is one single service with two endpoints. One endpoint is an external-facing **BasicHttpBinding** endpoint and the other is an internal-specific LDAP address.

▪ **Note** If more than one scope is specified, only service endpoints that match *all* scopes reply.

Leveraging scopes makes it possible to fine-tune your discovery implementation so that clients can more easily discover the specific service endpoints of interest to them. Discovery also allows for additional customization. For example, services can add custom XML metadata to an endpoint. This information is sent to the client in response to the client's query.

Service Announcements

Now that you're familiar with some discovery concepts, it's time to learn more about **announcement** endpoints Assume a client needs to find a service. One way to search for it is to poll for available services. Another way is to listen for the **Hello** and **Bye** announcements. WCF 4.0 makes it easy to configure services to announce their endpoints when they start up. This allows clients that are actively *listening* to learn about new service endpoints as they join the network. This reduces the amount of probing (and multicast messaging) clients must perform.

You can configure a service with an **Announcement** endpoint by using the **<serviceDiscovery>** behavior. The **<serviceDiscovery>** behavior allows you to define a collection of **Announcement** endpoints that the service will expose. You can use the standard **udpAnnouncementEndpoint** endpoint for most cases. However, you will still need to configure the service with a standard **udpDiscoveryEndpoint** endpoint if you want it to respond to discovery probes initiated by clients.

WCF 4.0 comes with a class called **AnnouncementService**; this class was designed specifically for this purpose. The **AnnouncementService** class provides two event handlers: **OnlineAnnouncementReceived** and **OfflineAnnouncementReceived**. Client applications can host an instance of the **AnnouncementService** class using **ServiceHost** and register event handlers for these two events.

Whenever a service joins a network and becomes discoverable, it sends a multicast **Hello** message that contains key information about the target service. This message announces the service's availability to listening clients. The client-hosted **AnnouncementService** class will receive the online announcement, and the **OnlineAnnouncementReceived** event handler will fire in the client. Similarly, when a Target service leaves a network, it sends a **Bye** message announcing its departure. The client-hosted **AnnouncementService** class will receive the offline announcement, and the OfflineAnnouncementReceived event handler will fire in the client. This defines the **ad hoc** mode of operation.

In this scenario, you will add yet another WCF service to the Contoso Claims Processing application. This new service will provide a car rental booking service (you can find two existing projects in **Assets** source directory: **CarRental.WCF** and **CarRental.ConsoleHost**). You will take advantage of the **Discovery Announcement** feature to reduce the amount of traffic that you will need to exchange between the Customer Service front-end application and the back-end services to probe on **ICarRental** service's availability.

Configuring both the service and client sides to use discovery announcements requires that you follow a handful of steps.

On the Service Side

To configure the **ICarRental** service to send announcements, you need to add a **ServiceDiscoveryBehavior** behavior with an **Announcement** endpoint.

You can programmatically add the behavior to the **Host()** method of the **ServiceAnnouncementHost.cs** class of the **CarRental.ConsoleHost** application:

```
public void Host()
{
    ServiceHost host = new ServiceHost(typeof(CarRentalService),
        baseAddress);

    // Announce the availability of the service over UDP multicast
    ServiceDiscoveryBehavior serviceDiscoveryBehavior = new
    ServiceDiscoveryBehavior();
    serviceDiscoveryBehavior.AnnouncementEndpoints.Add(new
    UdpAnnouncementEndpoint());

    // Make the service discoverable over UDP multicast
    host.Description.Behaviors.Add(serviceDiscoveryBehavior);

    host.Open();

    foreach (var item in host.Description.Endpoints)
    {
        Console.WriteLine("Address: {0}\nBinding Name: {1}\nContract
            Name: {2}", item.Address, item.Binding.Name, item.Contract.Name);
    }

    Console.WriteLine("Press <Enter> to stop the service.");
    Console.ReadLine();
    host.Close();
}
```

As an alternative to those steps, you could instead add the behavior to the **app.config** configuration file in the **CarRental.ConsoleHost** project:

```
<configuration>
  <system.serviceModel>
    <services>
```

```xml
    <service name="CarRental.WCF.CarRentalService"
     behaviorConfiguration="DiscoveryBehavior">
      <endpoint address="" binding="basicHttpBinding"
       contract="CarRental.WCF.ICarRental" />
      <endpoint name="adHocDiscovery" kind="udpDiscoveryEndpoint" />
    </service>
  </services>
  <standardEndpoints>
    <udpDiscoveryEndpoint>
      <standardEndpoint name="adHocDiscovery"
       multicastAddress="http://localhost:8088/CarRentalService" />
    </udpDiscoveryEndpoint>
  </standardEndpoints>
  <behaviors>
    <serviceBehaviors>
      <!--Add Discovery Endpoint-->
      <behavior name="DiscoveryBehavior">
        <serviceDiscovery>
          <announcementEndpoints>
            <endpoint kind="udpAnnouncementEndpoint" />
          </announcementEndpoints>
        </serviceDiscovery>
      </behavior>
    </serviceBehaviors>
  </behaviors>
 </system.serviceModel>
</configuration>
```

With this configuration in place, the service will announce itself when it comes online; it will also announce when it is about to go offline. To take advantage of these announcements, you need to design your clients so they listen for them at runtime. You do this by hosting an announcement service within the client application that implements the **WS-Discovery** announcement protocol.

On the Client Side

You need to host an **AnnouncementService** class and subscribe to the **OnlineAnnouncementReceived** and **OfflineAnnouncementReceived** events. You host the **AnnouncementService** service in the Claims web site, so the trick is to start an **AnnouncementService** host listener on a separate thread to prevent deadlocking of the main Claims Web application thread. You can do this by modifying the Claims Web site **global.asax** module as follows:

```
protected void Application_Start()
{
    RegisterRoutes(RouteTable.Routes);

    Thread rentalcarThread = new Thread(HostServiceAnnouncements);
    rentalcarThread.Start();
}
```

Note how the preceding code creates a new thread to host the **AnnouncementService** class for the **RentalCar** web service.

To implement the **AnnouncementService** host, you should create two event handlers that respond to the **Announcement** event when a service comes online or goes offline. Let's review the code you can find in the **global.asax** module that implements **AnnouncementService**:

```
public static void HostServiceAnnouncements()
{
    // Create an AnnouncementService instance
    AnnouncementService announcementService = new AnnouncementService();

    // Subscribe the announcement events
    announcementService.OnlineAnnouncementReceived +=
        OnlineAnnouncementReceived;
            announcementService.OfflineAnnouncementReceived +=
                OfflineAnnouncementReceived;

    // Create ServiceHost for the AnnouncementService
    using (ServiceHost announcementServiceHost = new
        ServiceHost(announcementService))
    {
        // Listen for the announcements sent over UDP multicast
        announcementServiceHost.AddServiceEndpoint(new
            UdpAnnouncementEndpoint());
        announcementServiceHost.Open();
        Console.WriteLine("Listening for the announcements sent over UDP
            multicast network...");
        Thread.Sleep(1000000);
    }

    Console.WriteLine("The service announcement host is closed.");
}

static void OfflineAnnouncementReceived(object sender,
    AnnouncementEventArgs e)
{
    CarRentalEndpoint = "";
}

static void OnlineAnnouncementReceived(object sender,
    AnnouncementEventArgs e)
{
    CarRentalEndpoint =
        e.EndpointDiscoveryMetadata.Address.Uri.AbsoluteUri;
}
```

Now assume you want to start the Claims Web site client application in a debug mode and set breakpoints in both the **OnlineAnnouncementReceived()** and **OfflineAnnouncementReceived()** event handlers. Later, you will run an instance of the **CarRental** WCF service host application. When the **CarRental** host application starts up, you will see a **Debug** window stopped at the breakpoint set on the **OnlineAnnouncementReceived()** handler. This event handler takes care of the online announcement message. At the handler, you extract the current WCF endpoint address of the **CarRental** WCF service that you will use in the workflow when submitting claims for processing. When you close the **CarRental** service host application, you will see a breakpoint hit on the **OfflineAnnouncementReceived()** handler, which takes care of the offline announcement message.

The **CarRental** service implementation returns the message back to the Claims web application that confirms the rental-car reservation. You can verify whether the **CarRental** service worked properly by checking the status of the rental car when the claim was processed. Figure 6-15 shows the resulting claim's details window after performing the task just described. Specifically, you can see that the claim's rental-car status changed when you used WCF Discovery Announcement.

Claim '112' Details

Created On: 1/4/2010 @ 5:37 PM

Where: Walt Disney World Resort, Orlando, FL, 32830

Claimer: Garber, Danny

Contact phone: 407-123-9876

Description: Walt Disney World Resort is the best place for family vacation!

Status: Complete

Rental Car: A rental car has been reserved.

IsValid: True

Edit Claim | Back to List

Figure 6-15. *The Resulting Claim's Details After It Has Been Processed*

This approach is slightly faster than when you used the WCF Discovery Lookup for your **Billing** WCF service. This is because the WCF Discovery Announcement responds to the event as the service became available, whereas the Discovery Lookup searches for the particular service it needs to find on the network.

The **ad hoc** discovery mode you have been using so far only works on a local subnet. If you want to use WS-Discovery beyond the boundaries of your local network, you need to turn your attention to the **managed** discovery mode. Fortunately, WCF 4.0 also provides support for **managed** discovery.

Managed Service Discovery

Implementing **managed** service discovery is a little more involved than the **ad hoc** mode because it requires you to implement a discovery proxy service. As Figure 6-16 illustrates, **managed** service discovery involves a client, a service, and a discovery proxy.

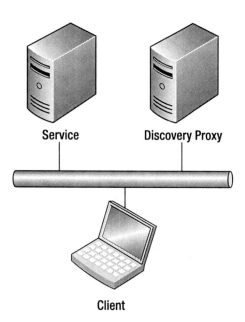

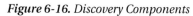

Figure 6-16. *Discovery Components*

What follows aren't strict definitions, but these short descriptions might help you understand these components and their capabilities:

- *A client:* This entity looks for services and utilizes the **DiscoveryClient** class to search for them. A client can also host an **Announcement** service if it wants to listen for announcements from services.

- *A service:* This WCF service has endpoints that you can discover. A Service adds a **ServiceDiscoveryBehavior** behavior in the service host description, which enables it to respond to find requests from clients. A service can also host an announcement client if it wants to announce itself.

- *A discovery proxy:* This centralized repository knows about services. This is a not a required component, and its necessity is completely dependent on your use case. The framework does not include an implementation of a proxy; however, it does provide the building blocks for you to create one easily. There are several uses for a discovery proxy, and you will learn more about this component in the Contoso Insurance scenario that follows.

The discovery proxy service is the component that will keep track of all the online and offline service endpoints. It is essentially an Announcement service and a Discovery endpoint. It is an Announcement service because it has to listen for all the announcement messages and keep track of which endpoints are online or offline. It also knows how to respond to discovery probe requests from clients.

So how do you implement a discovery proxy service in your Contoso environment?

Begin by adding an existing project **Contoso.DiscoveryProxy** to your solution. This project contains **CRMDiscoveryProxy** public class that implements the discovery proxy logic while inheriting the discovery proxy's basic functionality from the new **DiscoveryProxyBase** class that comes with WCF 4.0. The code

excerpt that follows shows a custom discovery proxy service implementation in the
Contoso.DiscoveryProxy project:

```
[ServiceBehavior(InstanceContextMode = InstanceContextMode.Single,
    ConcurrencyMode = ConcurrencyMode.Multiple)]
public class CRMDiscoveryProxy : DiscoveryProxy
{
    Dictionary<EndpointAddress, EndpointDiscoveryMetadata> onlineServices =
        new Dictionary<EndpointAddress,EndpointDiscoveryMetadata>();
    DiscoveryResponse response = new DiscoveryResponse();

    protected override IAsyncResult OnBeginFind(FindRequestContext
        findRequestContext, AsyncCallback callback, object state)
    {
        return response;
    }

    protected override IAsyncResult
        OnBeginOfflineAnnouncement(DiscoveryMessageSequence messageSequence,
        EndpointDiscoveryMetadata endpointDiscoveryMetadata, AsyncCallback
        callback, object state)
    {
        if (this.onlineServices.Count > 0)
        {
            lock (this.onlineServices)
            {
                this.onlineServices.Remove(endpointDiscoveryMetadata.
                    Address);
                PrintTrace(endpointDiscoveryMetadata, "Removing");
            }
        }

        return response;

    }

    protected override IAsyncResult
        OnBeginOnlineAnnouncement(DiscoveryMessageSequence messageSequence,
            EndpointDiscoveryMetadata endpointDiscoveryMetadata,
            AsyncCallback callback, object state)
    {
        lock (this.onlineServices)
        {
            this.onlineServices[endpointDiscoveryMetadata.Address] =
                endpointDiscoveryMetadata;
            PrintTrace(endpointDiscoveryMetadata, "Adding");
        }

        return response;
    }
```

```
    protected override IAsyncResult OnBeginResolve(ResolveCriteria
        resolveCriteria, AsyncCallback callback, object state)
    {
        return response;
    }

    protected override EndpointDiscoveryMetadata
        OnEndResolve(IAsyncResult result)
    {
        if (onlineServices.Count > 0)
        {
            return onlineServices.GetEnumerator().Current.Value;
        }
        return null;
    }

    private void PrintTrace(EndpointDiscoveryMetadata
        endpointDiscoveryMetadata, string message)
    {
        Console.WriteLine("{0} {1}", message,
            endpointDiscoveryMetadata.Address.Uri.AbsoluteUri);
        System.Diagnostics.Debug.WriteLine("{0} {1}", message,
            endpointDiscoveryMetadata.Address.Uri.AbsoluteUri);
    }

...

}
```

Once you finish implementing the discovery proxy service, you need to host it somewhere. In the Contoso scenario, you host the **DiscoveryProxy** service in the main Claims Web application, leveraging the threading technique you used earlier in the **CarRental** WCF service host.

You configure the host with two endpoints: a **Discovery** endpoint and an **Announcement** endpoint. You can find the following code excerpt at the end of the **global.asax** module; it illustrates how to host the **DiscoveryProxy** service with both of these endpoints:

```
Uri probeEndpointAddress = new Uri("net.tcp://localhost:9001/Probe");
Uri announcementEndpointAddress = new
    Uri("net.tcp://localhost:9011/Announcement");
ServiceHost proxyServiceHost = new ServiceHost(new CRMDiscoveryProxy());
DiscoveryEndpoint discoveryEndpoint = new DiscoveryEndpoint(new
    NetTcpBinding(), new EndpointAddress(probeEndpointAddress));
discoveryEndpoint.IsSystemEndpoint = false;
AnnouncementEndpoint announcementEndpoint = new AnnouncementEndpoint(new
    NetTcpBinding(), new EndpointAddress(announcementEndpointAddress));
proxyServiceHost.AddServiceEndpoint(discoveryEndpoint);
proxyServiceHost.AddServiceEndpoint(announcementEndpoint);
proxyServiceHost.Open();
...
```

Next, you store the **Discovery** proxy endpoints in the **DiscoveryProxyStatus** global application variable, which you define as a public static string variable at the top of the **MvcApplication** class. You can use this variable to show the discovery proxy addresses each time the Claims Web application starts. Modifying the **Site.Master** module by adding a status message into the footer enables you to see the discovery proxy message at the startup page of the application (see Figure 6-17).

Welcome to Contoso Insurance Claims Processing Application!

The Claims Queue

Discovery Proxy is listening on: net.tcp://localhost:9001/Probe (Probe) and on: net.tcp://localhost:9011/Announcement (Announcement)

Figure 6-17. Discovery Proxy Status Message

Once you have a discovery proxy service up and running, you can configure your **Billing** service to announce itself directly to the discovery proxy service. Likewise, you can configure your client Claims web application to probe the discovery proxy service directly (no more multicast messaging!).

You configure the **Billing** service to announce itself directly to the discovery proxy service by specifying the discovery proxy's announcement address when creating the **AnnouncementEndpoint** endpoint within the service host application. The following code in **Billing.ConsoleHost**'s **ManagedServiceDiscovery.cs** module lets you accomplish this:

```
ServiceHost host = new ServiceHost(typeof(BillingService), baseAddress);

ServiceEndpoint netTcpEndpoint = host.AddServiceEndpoint(typeof(IBilling),
    new NetTcpBinding(), string.Empty);

// Create an announcement endpoint pointing to the hosted proxy service
AnnouncementEndpoint announcementEndpoint = new AnnouncementEndpoint( new
    NetTcpBinding(), new EndpointAddress(announcementEndpointAddress));
ServiceDiscoveryBehavior serviceDiscoveryBehavior = new
    ServiceDiscoveryBehavior();

    serviceDiscoveryBehavior.AnnouncementEndpoints.Add(
        announcementEndpoint);
host.Description.Behaviors.Add(serviceDiscoveryBehavior);

host.Open();

foreach (var item in host.Description.Endpoints)
{
    Console.WriteLine("Address: {0}\nBinding Name: {1}\nContract Name: {2}",
            item.Address, item.Binding.Name, item.Contract.Name);
}
```

```
Console.WriteLine("Press <Enter> to stop the service.");
Console.ReadLine();
host.Close();
```

Next, you can configure the Claim web application to communicate directly with the discovery proxy service by specifying the discovery proxy's probe address when creating the **DiscoveryEndpoint** endpoint within the client application. You can find the following code fragment in the **ClaimsController** class of the Claims web application; it executes when the claim is submitted for processing:

```
// Create a Discovery Endpoint that points to the proxy service.
Uri probeEndpointAddress = new Uri("net.tcp://localhost:9001/Probe");
    DiscoveryEndpoint discoveryEndpoint = new DiscoveryEndpoint(
        new NetTcpBinding(), new EndpointAddress(probeEndpointAddress));

// Create DiscoveryClient using the previously created discoveryEndpoint
DiscoveryClient managedDiscoveryClient = new
    DiscoveryClient(discoveryEndpoint);

// Find IChapter6Discovery endpoints
FindResponse findResponse = managedDiscoveryClient.Find(new
    FindCriteria(typeof(IBilling)));

if (findResponse.Endpoints.Count == 0) return "";

// Pick the first discovered endpoint
EndpointAddress address = findResponse.Endpoints[0].Address;

//Create the target service client
ChannelFactory<IBilling> factory = new ChannelFactory<IBilling>(new
    BasicHttpBinding(), address);
IBilling client = factory.CreateChannel();

//Call the Billing Service
string status = client.ProcessClaim(id, findResponse.Endpoints.Count,
    address.Uri.AbsoluteUri);

factory.Close();

//return a new status of the processed claim
return status;
```

The great value **managed** service discovery brings two great benefits: it works across network boundaries (it's based on traditional service calls), and it reduces the need for multicast messaging within your discovery solution. In addition, the clients go through a discovery proxy to look for services, so the services themselves do not need to be up and running all the time to be discovered.

Summary

WCF 4.0 brings numerous improvements and several new features that address some of today's most common communication scenarios. First (and most importantly), WCF becomes easier to use through the simplified configuration model and better support for common defaults. Second, WCF now provides first-class support for service discovery and routing, which are common requirements in most enterprise environments and large SOA initiatives. These features alone set WCF apart from other frameworks.

WCF also provides sophisticated integration with WF to provide a new model for developing declarative workflow services. Workflow services make it possible to develop long-running and asynchronous services that benefit from the WF programming model and underlying runtime. Thanks to the new WCF-based activities and the designer support found within Visual Studio 2010, this new programming model is a first-class option for authoring services. You will learn more about WCF integration with WF in upcoming chapters. With the .NET 4.0 Framework, the worlds of WCF and WF are merging to offer you a single, cohesive programming model that offers the best of both worlds.

CHAPTER 7

■ ■ ■

Developing WF Applications

If you have worked with Windows Workflow Foundation (WF) that shipped in .NET 3.0, you might not recognize what it has become in .NET 4.0. The new version represents a major improvement in developer productivity and performance. This release looks like it will fulfill the goal of declarative application development. This chapter doesn't cover all aspects of WF development—that would be a book in itself—but it does include an overview of the new features found in the 4.0 release and how you can use these features to create an application you host in AppFabric.

What's New in WorkFlow 4.0

WF 4.0 introduced several significant changes. You can see and feel these changes from its core programming model to its runtime to its tooling. Microsoft made these changes to provide the best experience for developers utilizing WF, as well as to continue providing a strong foundational component that you can build your applications on.

All these changes raise questions about the work people have done in previous versions of the tool. One of the primary design goals of WF 4.0 was to achieve backwards compatability with previous versions of WF. For example, the new framework components are in separate assemblies, so you can run them side-by-side with previous WF versions on the same machine. In fact, the .NET 4.0 Framework will ship with both the WF 3.X and WF 4.0 runtimes, which means that any existing WF 3.X applications will continue to run as-is. You can find the new components in the **System.Activities.*** assemblies, while you can find components from previous versions in the **System.Workflow.*** assemblies. WF 4.0 also includes an interop layer, so that WF 4.0 version code can call WF 3.X components. Finally, WF 4.0 will ship with guidance on migrating from WF 3.X to WF 4.0.

There is no better place to start than the programming model if you're examining the new features in WF 4.0. The programming model has been revamped to be more robust, but also easier to use. For example, the confusing code-beside feature no longer exists. Also, you no longer need to create a **WorkflowRuntime** object. Another benefit: It's easier and more intuitive to pass data between workflows. With WF 4.0, **WorkflowElement** is the base type, and it is used by both the activities and the workflow itself. When you want to create a workflow, you can now just create an instance of that type and execute it. WF 3.X tended to favor code-based workflows, and you could implement many of its features only through code. With WF 4.0, XAML reigns supreme. WF 4.0 doesn't include templates to create code-based workflows. WF 3.X utilized data bindings when passing data, and it placed no restrictions on the data flow. By contrast, WF 4.0 utilizes arguments and variables, and data flow is restricted to the parent/child relationship. This protects you from creating code paths that are difficult to maintain.

WF 4.0 also introduces several changes to the types of workflows, both introducing new ones and deleting some existing ones. The new version introduces several new types of workflow types. For example, WF 4.0 introduces a new workflow type called FlowChart. This new type of control flow more closely resembles the outline that analysts and developers create when putting together solutions that model the business processes. This type of workflow represents a common task, and it can provide automation for a static model that is commonly created in Visio. Among the workflows that no longer ship with WF 4.0 is the state machine workflow; however, you can still access it through the compatability layer. This isn't as bad as you might think. By utilizing the FlowChart, along with the Pick activity, you can cover a large set of scenarios people utilize state machines for.

You can't review the workflow types without also looking at changes to the designers. The designers are the face of the workflow model, and they have received the most visible improvement. The new designers are hosted in Visual Studio 2010, and Microsoft has redesigned them for better usability and performance. As with many of the new designers in Visual Studio 2010, the workflow designers are based on Windows Presentation Foundation (WPF), and they take heavy advantage of the general trend towards WPF. In addition to letting you leverage WPF-based designers, WPF 4.0 lets you utilize XAML (which the designers support) to define the designers' activities, as well as the interaction between activities in the workflow. And rehosting the designers within your own applications is now a much easier task, which simplifies things for non-developers who must interact with the workflow.

One of the capabilities added in WF 3.5 was integration with WCF. This feature enabled workflows to call and act as services. WF 4.0 also improves the basic functions around creating and consuming services. For example, Microsoft enhanced the messaging between WCF and WF, adding new messaging activities, the addition of message correlation, and fully declarative service definitions.

Incorporating the Business Scenario

In Chapter 6, you learned about Phase I of the new claims-processing system. In this chapter, you will learn about Phase II, which adds new functionality that helps shields customers from mishandled information errors by implementing a workflow process in the Customer Service application. You will learn how to run and manage this new workflow service, as well as the WCF services for the Appraisal Agents and Billing applications, in an AppFabric hosted environment.

An AppFabric host will enable workflow troubleshooting for finding and fixing problems; automating workflow operations (**start**, **resume**, **stop**, and **suspend**); and implementing workflow persistence and configuration for the WCF services.

Also, you will update the customer contact and policy information validation procedure, which a claims representative had to handle manually in the past. In the updated version, this aspect of the app will now be automated through a new customer portal, front-end application that customers will access directly access (see Figure 7-1).

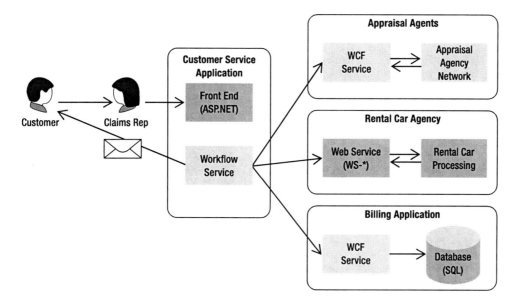

Figure 7-1. Phase II Business Scenario System Architecture

The automation capabilities gained by including a Windows Workflow workflow make it possible to streamline the (previously manual) workflow and interaction required in the Customer Service role. Specifically, you can now handle the customer's policy and claim validation using .NET 4's WF services (see Figure 7-2).

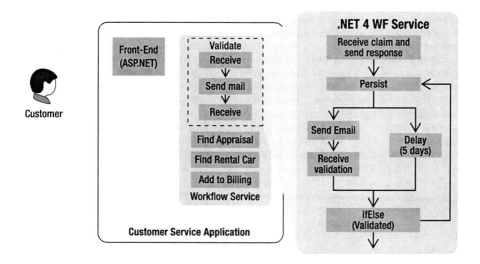

Figure 7-2. Validation Process Workflow

Examining this workflow reveals that you will be receiving a claim, and the workflow will need to send various e-mails back to the customer to confirm that the claim was received, to update the customer with the state of the claim, and to request any additional information that might be needed. The workflow will also call WCF methods exposed by the Appraisal Agent application and the Billing Application. As you might recall from Chapter 6, the services require that you send in parameters such as the `CustomerNumber`, `ClaimID`, `ClientAddress`, and so on. The workflow that is created for the Customer Service Application will need to accept an object that contains the properties just listed, as well as `InsuranceNumber`, `Name`, `Address`, `PhoneNumber`, `EMail`, `DateOfIncident`, and `Description`. This will provide enough information for the workflow to act on, including the information required for the workflow to call the required services.

As you read this chapter, please keep the above description in mind because it will help guide you through the items that you will need to create in the workflow portion of the scenario. This chapter will also show you how to create a workflow, pass data to a workflow, and expose the workflow as a WCF endpoint and how to call a WCF endpoint.

Creating a Workflow

WF 4.0 is more than an upgrade; it is also a faster, sleeker foundation. When working with the workflow, the first thing that you might notice is that the WorkflowRuntime object no longer exists. Instead, you have two new ways to create workflows.

Methods for Creation

Your first method for creating a new workflow is to use the WorkflowInvoker class. This class represents the simplest way to create a workflow, but it doesn't provide fine-grained control over the process. It invokes the workflow as if it were a method. This approach is best used for workflows or activities that don't require the use of any run-time services such as persistence. When using an object of the WorkflowInvoker class, the workflow runs on the calling thread, and the Invoke method will block until the workflow finishes. The default time for the workflow to complete is 60 seconds. If the workflow takes longer than that, a TimeoutException will be thrown. To extend the timeframe, you can pass a TimeSpan object as one of the Invoke method parameters.

The second way to create a workflow is to use the WorkflowInstance class. This class provides events that work against the specific workflow running in this instance. You should use WorkflowInstance rather than WorkflowInvoker if you need greater flexibility and want more control throughout the execution of the workflow. The WorkflowInstance object actually acts as a proxy and provides methods for creating and loading a workflow instance, pausing and resuming that instance, and terminating and raising events. The WorkflowInstance object has several steps in its lifecycle: create the WorkflowInstance, subscribe to whatever events you want to act on, start the workflow and then wait for it to finish. The events that you can act on are `OnCompleted`, `OnUnloaded`, `OnAborted`, `OnIdle`, and `OnUnhandledException`.

An Example

It's time to create your first workflow. Start Visual Studio 2010 and create a new project. Select the workflow node, and you will be presented with four new project types (see Figure 7-3). We are going to select the Workflow Console Application and give it the name, *Chapter7Workflow*. The figure also illustrates how you can create custom activities.

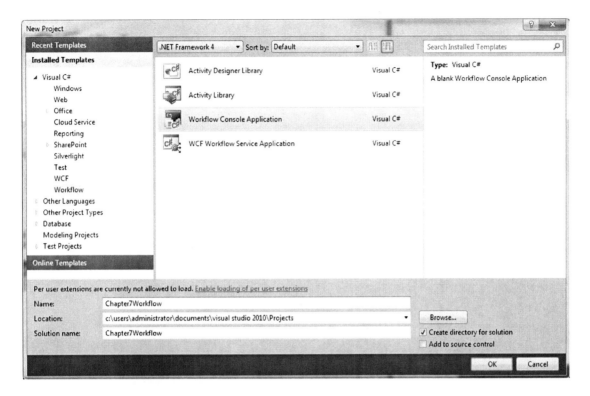

Figure 7-3. New Project Dialog

When our project loads, you will see two files in the project: **program.cs** and **Workflow1.xaml**. The XAML file contains the workflow definition.

■ **Note** You can no longer choose betweeen code or XAML workflows, as you could in .NET 3.x. All workflows in .NET 4 are XAML-based workflows.

Creating an Activity

Before you do anything with the workflow, you need to add a code activity. This code activity will contain the code you will use to diplay your string.

Right-click the **Chapter7Workflow** project node in your solution and select **Add**. When the pop-up menu appears, select New Item… Next, select the **Workflow** node under the Templates section, and then select the **Code Activity**. Name the activity, **PrintString.cs**. It should look like what you see in Figure 7-4.

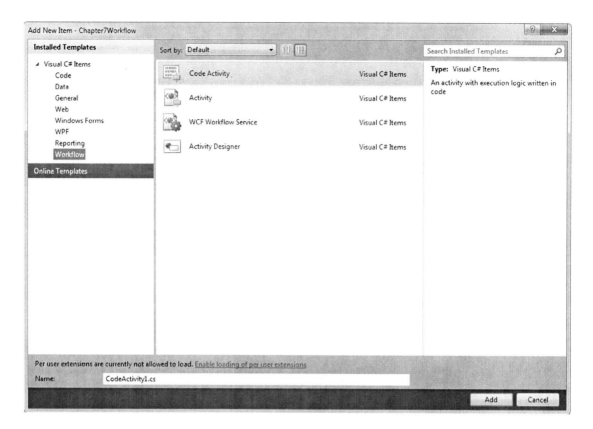

Figure 7-4. Workflow Type Dialog

Open the **PrintString.cs** file, comment out the default code in the **Execute** method, and type the following code into the method:

```
Console.Writeline("Hello Chapter7Worklow");
```

Next, save the **PrintString.cs** file, open the **Program.cs** file, and replace all of the code in the **Main** method with this code:

```
PrintString workflow = new PrintString();
WorkflowInvoker.Invoke(workflow);
```

When this workflow executes, you will see the text in the console window. This code executes the workflow directly and uses less code than if you had used the **WorkflowInstance** object. However, this approach doesn't provide any methods for interacting with the workflow instance.

Gaining Greater Control

Now let's take a look at how your workflow code would change if you used the `WorkflowApplication` object. This approach gives you greater control over the workflow, but it also requires a bit more code.

Open the `Program.cs` file, delete the code in the `Main` method, and type in the following code:

```
PrintString workflowInstance = new PrintString();
AutoResetEvent syncEvent = new AutoResetEvent(false);

WorkflowApplication myInstance = new WorkflowApplication
    (new Workflow1());

myInstance.Completed =
    delegate(WorkflowApplicationCompletedEventArgs e)
{
    Console.WriteLine("The Workflow instance that just
                       completed was: " + e.InstanceId);
    Console.ReadLine();
    syncEvent.Set();
};

myInstance.OnUnhandledException =
    delegate(WorkflowApplicationUnhandledExceptionEventArgs e)
{
    Console.WriteLine(e.UnhandledException.ToString());

    return UnhandledExceptionAction.Terminate;
};

myInstance.Aborted = delegate(WorkflowApplicationAbortedEventArgs e)
{
    Console.WriteLine(e.Reason);
    syncEvent.Set();
};

myInstance.Run();

syncEvent.WaitOne();
```

You will also need to add a using statement for System.Threading and System.Activities.Hosting. Using the previous code ensures that you can catch events you want to handle. The `AutoResetEvent` is a synchronization mechanism to ensure that the workflow completes before the `Main` method finishes. Once the workflow instance is complete, the `Completed` event is raised.

Creating a Sequence Workflow

You know how to invoke a workflow; next, you will learn how to use the Sequence workflow. Open the `Workflow1.xaml` file, and the designer will appear.

The next step is to add an activity to your new workflow. Open the toolbox and drag a Sequence activity onto the designer. Then, expand the Primitives section to find the **WriteLine** activity. Drag the **WriteLine** activity onto the **Sequence** shape in the designer. With the **WriteLine** activity selected, open the property sheet (see Figure 7-5).

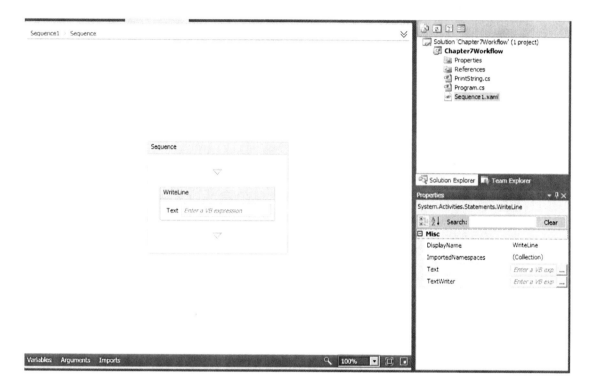

Figure 7-5. Sequence Workflow

You will start with a basic workflow that will illustrate the general steps needed to build a workflow. You can always go back later and add activities. One of things that you might have noticed is that there is a new collection of base activities. All of the activities are completely new and have been rewritten in WF 4.0.

You'll deal with three properties: **DisplayName**, **Text**, and **TextWriter**. The **DisplayName** property can be used only on the design surface, while the **TextWriter** property allows you to provide a **TextStream** object to write the text to. If this is not specified, then the output will go to the console.

The **Text** property is the text that you want to output. This property is an expression editor, and you can place any expression you want into the textbox.

■ **Note** The value that you place in the expression editor must be valid Visual Basic sytax. Even if you are developing using C#, the expressions that you enter must conform to Visual Basic's syntax, and they must include quote marks around text.

Leave the **TextWriter** property blank and enter this text into the **Text** property:

```
"Hello Chapter7Worklow"
```

Leaving the **TextWriter** property blank means that the workflow runtime will send the text to the console window (see Figure 7-6).

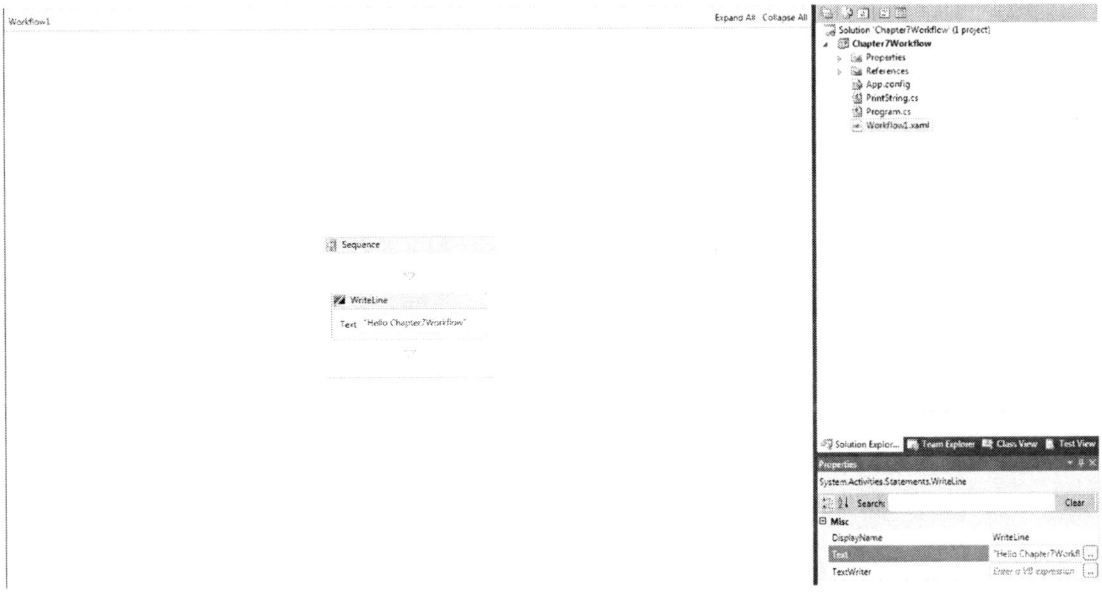

Figure 7-6. Sequence Workflow with WriteLine Activity

You can now press Ctrl + F5 to run the workflow. This will bring up a command prompt, which should contain this text:

```
"Hello Chapter7Workflow"
```

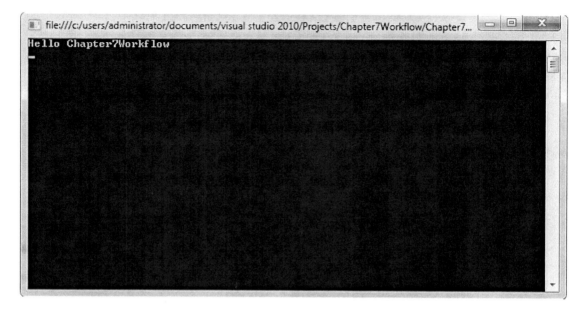

Figure 7-7. Workflow Output

So far, you've learned how to create a simple workflow. Next, let's take it up a notch and look at how you can pass your objects into the workflow.

Passing Data

Earlier, you learned that the way that you work with and pass data has changed in WF 4.0. In WF 3.X, you used properties to store the data. You could use standard .NET properties, but typically you used dependency properties. These dependency properties share only the name when compared to dependency properties in WPF. Dependency properties allowed the workflow runtime to control the way that the data was stored, but the application could use them as though they were regular properties.

How Data Is Stored

WF 4.0 no longer uses properties to store data. Now variables and arguments are the main mechanism when working with data. The **variable** type derives from class **Variable**, and the **argument** type derives from **Argument**. It is interesting that the variables and arguments don't store the data, but instead provide descriptions of the data and point to the underlying data store. To get to the underlying data store, you can use the **LocationEnvironment** class. This class provides an environment that contains arguments and variables. You can also use the **Variable.Get** method and pass in the **LocationEnvironment** object to retrieve the data value. To store data in the workflow, you add a variable to either the workflow or one of the activities. The idea is that the variable should be placed as closely as possible to the activity that will need it.

This brings up another difference introduced in WF 4.0: scoping. In WF 3.X, any activity could get to any piece of data from anywhere in the workflow. In WF 4.0, only the activities from the root activity and lower will be able to get access to the variable. This change makes maintenance easier, but it also to makes persistence easier and faster. Previously, the persistence service needed to persist everything. Now, your variables have a scope, and the persistence service can optimize what is persisted at each point, which results in a faster persistence step.

Despite all these changes, one thing remains the same: you can still utilize a `Dictionary<string, object>` object created outside the workflow and pass data using WF 4.0's `WorkflowApplication` object. The downside of this method is that you don't have compile-time checking. Also, the value will be ignored if you pass in a key that doesn't match an internal argument. This is a big change from the way that WF 3.X treated this situation. In WF 3.X passing in a key that didn't match raised a `System.Reflection.TargetInvocationException` exception with this message: "This operation can not be performed at runtime."

An Example—Passing a Dictionary Object

The code that follows is the same used in the Gaining Greater Control section earlier, but now passes a **dictionary** object to the workflow:

```
PrintString workflowInstance = new PrintString();
AutoResetEvent syncEvent = new AutoResetEvent(false);

WorkflowApplication myInstance = new WorkflowApplication(new
    Workflow1(), new Dictionary<string, object>
    {
        {"Name", "Jonathon"}
    }
);

myInstance.Completed =
    delegate(WorkflowApplicationCompletedEventArgs e)
{
    Console.WriteLine("The Workflow instance that just
                        completed was: " + e.InstanceId);
    Console.ReadLine();
    syncEvent.Set();
};

myInstance.OnUnhandledException =
    delegate(WorkflowApplicationUnhandledExceptionEventArgs e)
{
    Console.WriteLine(e.UnhandledException.ToString());

    return UnhandledExceptionAction.Terminate;
};

myInstance.Aborted = delegate(WorkflowApplicationAbortedEventArgs e)
{
    Console.WriteLine(e.Reason);
    syncEvent.Set();
};
```

```
myInstance.Run();

syncEvent.WaitOne();
```

Once you pass the **dictionary** object passed into the workflow, you will need to set up the arguments. The words used for the argument names must match the names used for the key of the **dictionary** object. The arguments are where you store the data in a workflow. When you open the workflow designer, you will click on the arguments button in the bottom left. You want to create two arguments. The first argument is a name, and you make it an In argument. The second argument is the employee id, which you make an Out argument.

Getting the Result

You can get the result in two ways. First, you can start the workflow using the **WorkflowInvoker** object. This returns a **dictionary** object with the results. The following snippet illustrates how you do this:

```
IDictionary<string, object> outArgs = WorkflowInvoker.Invoke
    (new Workflow1() { Name = "Jonathan" });
string employeeID = (string)outArgs["EmpID"];
```

Your second option is to use the **Completed** delegate. You pass this delegate a **WorkflowApplicationCompletedEventArgs** object, which contains a **dictionary** object with all the Out arguments. When checking the output values you will want to check the workflow completion state and ensure that it is set to closed. In addition, if you access output parameters that are not in the **dictionary** object you may receive either an InvalidCastException or a KeyNotFoundException. In the snippet that follows we have modified the delegate code for the Completed action:

```
myInstance.Completed = delegate(WorkflowApplicationCompletedEventArgs e)
{
    if (e.CompletionState == ActivityInstanceState.Closed)
    {
        try
        {
            EmpID = (string)e.Outputs["EmpID"];
        }
        catch (Exception ex)
        {
            //Catch your exception - Accessing a key that doesn't
            //exist may throw a InvalidCastException or a
            //KeyNotFoundException
        }
        finally
        {
            syncEvent.Set();
        }
    }
    Console.ReadLine();
};
```

If there are many keys that you will be accessing, then utilize the dictionary objects **TryGetValue** method, which is faster and will make it so that no exceptions are thrown. The following code shows this method in use:

```
object objEmpID = null;
string empid = null;
if (!e.Outputs.TryGetValue("EmpID", out objEmpID))
{
    Console.WriteLine("The EmpID value was not found in the output
                       collection");
}
else
{
    empid = objEmpID as string;
    if (empid == null)
        Console.WriteLine("The value in EmpID could not be converted
                           to a string");
    else
        Console.WriteLine("The value of EmpID passed back from the
                           workflow was {0}", objEmpID);
}
```

Using WCF End Points for Workflows

In Chapter 6, you read about the new features of WCF in .NET 4.0. One of the things we covered was how to utilize these features to create WCF endpoints. In the section that follows, you will build on those lessons from Chapter 6 and review the new features in WF 4.0 that enable you to integrate with WCF.

Receive and SendReply Activities

You can use several different approaches to leverage WCF with Windows Workflow Foundation. One approach uses Receive and SendReply activities, while another combines WF and WCF inside a **.xamlx** file.

The Receive and SendReply activites were added with the release of the .NET Framework 3.5, and they have been updated for this release. You use the Receive activity when you want to expose your workflow as a callable WCF service. Using just the Receive activity lets you create a one-way service. If you want to send back a response, you use the SendReply activity.

You get some additional benefits when you implement a web service with a workflow instead of through WCF code. The main benefit is you don't have to worry about the the ABCs of WCF, or the Address, Binding, and Contract that are required to create a WCF service. Using the Receive and SendReply activities lets you ignore those details. Instead, you create a variable of a type that you will be receiving and place it in the Receive shape.

The downside is that this moves you away from a contract-first model. In a contract-first model, you declare the service contract and then select the operation to implement. Also, these workflow endpoints are independent services, and you will not be able to group workflows into operations within a service interface.

■ **Note** When using the Receive and SendReply activities, you won't have a typical WCF contract. Instead, you use a **type** variable and derive a contract from that variable.

When hosting a workflow that will expose a WCF endpoint, you need to utilize the **WorkflowServiceHost** service. This service utilizes a service definition that utilizes **WorkflowServiceImplementation**, which includes the workflow and the WCF endpoint. When setting up EndPoint and Receive, you need to ensure that you configure **Name** and **ServiceContractName** correctly; otherwise, **WorkflowServiceHost** will not be able to start.

Combining WF and WCF Code

A second approach for using WCF and WF together is to combine the WF and WCF code in the .xamlx file.

The sample uses the **Receive** and **Send** shapes from the toolbox (see the workflow in Figure 7-7). When you set these shapes up, all of the properties appear in the **.xamlx** file.

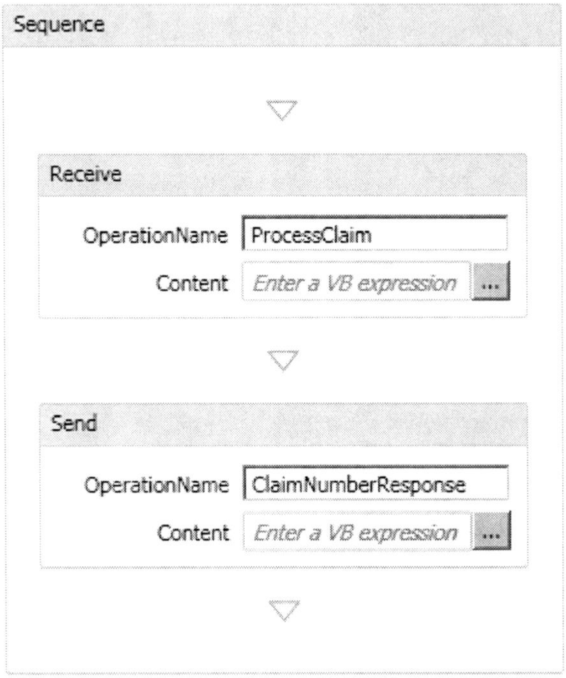

Figure 7-7. Sequence Workflow with WCF End Points

Setting the `OperationName`, `ServiceContractName`, and other properties will present them in the `.xamlx` file; it also enables the new XAMLX handler in IIS to render them. When this handler parses the `.xamlx` file, it will present the standard WCF contract that you're used to seeing with WCF (and which you saw outlined in Chapter 6).

The following snippet shows a .xaml file from the claim service workflow:

```
<Activity mc:Ignorable="sad" x:Class="WorkflowWCFService.Sequence1"
mva:VisualBasic.Settings="Assembly references and imported namespaces serialized as XML
namespaces" xmlns="http://schemas.microsoft.com/netfx/2009/xaml/activities"
xmlns:__Sequence1="clr-namespace:WorkflowWCFService;"
xmlns:mc="http://schemas.openxmlformats.org/markup-compatibility/2006" xmlns:mva="clr-
namespace:Microsoft.VisualBasic.Activities;assembly=System.Activities"
xmlns:p="http://schemas.microsoft.com/netfx/2009/xaml/servicemodel" xmlns:s="clr-
namespace:System;assembly=mscorlib"
xmlns:sad="http://schemas.microsoft.com/netfx/2009/xaml/activities/design" xmlns:sad1="clr-
namespace:System.Activities.Debugger;assembly=System.Activities" xmlns:scg="clr-
namespace:System.Collections.Generic;assembly=mscorlib" xmlns:ssx="clr-
namespace:System.ServiceModel.XamlIntegration;assembly=System.ServiceModel"
xmlns:x="http://schemas.microsoft.com/winfx/2006/xaml">
  <Sequence sad1:XamlDebuggerXmlReader.FileName="C:\Users\Administrator\Documents\Visual
Studio 10\Projects\WorkflowWCFService\WorkflowWCFService\Sequence1.xaml"
sad:VirtualizedContainerService.HintSize="303,348.553333333333">
    <sad:WorkflowViewStateService.ViewState>
      <scg:Dictionary x:TypeArguments="x:String, s:Object">
        <x:Boolean x:Key="IsExpanded">True</x:Boolean>
      </scg:Dictionary>
    </sad:WorkflowViewStateService.ViewState>
    <p:Receive CanCreateInstance="True"
sad:VirtualizedContainerService.HintSize="257,85.2766666666667" OperationName="ProcessClaim"
ServiceContractName="ClaimContract">
      <p:Receive.CorrelatesOn>
        <p:MessageQuerySet>
          <p:XPathMessageQuery x:Key="key1">
            <p:XPathMessageQuery.Namespaces>
              <ssx:XPathMessageContextMarkup>
                <x:String
x:Key="xg0">http://schemas.microsoft.com/2003/10/Serialization/</x:String>
              </ssx:XPathMessageContextMarkup>
            </p:XPathMessageQuery.Namespaces>sm:body()/xg0:string</p:XPathMessageQuery>
        </p:MessageQuerySet>
      </p:Receive.CorrelatesOn>
      <p:Receive.KnownTypes>
        <x:Type Type="x:String" />
      </p:Receive.KnownTypes>
      <p:ReceiveParametersContent>
        <OutArgument x:TypeArguments="x:String" x:Key="ClaimNumber" />
      </p:ReceiveParametersContent>
    </p:Receive>
    <p:Send sad:VirtualizedContainerService.HintSize="257,85.2766666666667"
OperationName="ClaimNumberResponse" ServiceContractName="ClaimService">
      <p:Send.Endpoint>
```

```
<p:Endpoint>
  <p:Endpoint.Binding>
    <p:BasicHttpBinding Name="basicHttpBinding" />
  </p:Endpoint.Binding>
</p:Endpoint>
      </p:Send.Endpoint>
    </p:Send>
  </Sequence>
</Activity>
```

A cursory look at the **.xamlx** file reveals that it differs significantly from the **.svc** service handler that you use for WCF-only services. If you look more closely, however, you will see that this file includes all the necessary parts to construct the WCF endpoint. For example, take a look at the **Receive** element, and you will see that it has **OperationName** and **ServiceContractName** **attributes**. When you create your client in Visual Studio and utilize the functionality of the **SetService** contract to connect to the endpoint, you will see that it picks up **ServiceContractName** as the contract and **OperationName** as the method. You learned earlier that IIS includes a new XAMLX handler in the .NET 4.0 Framework. This new handler provides functionality for IIS to process the **.xaml** file and create the endpoint, as well as the metadata for the service. At this point, you can call this WCF endpoint the same way that you call any WCF service. Integrating WCF and WF makes this process extremely easy.

Consuming an Endpoint

So far, you've only learned how to expose a workflow as a WCF endpoint. What if you want to consume a WCF endpoint within the workflow? You will find this process to be mostly unchanged from WF 3.X. You follow the normal steps of adding a service reference to your workflow project in Visual Studio. The workflow project system will consume the metadata emitted from the service, and it will create a custom activity for each of the service operations in the contract. The custom activity is analogous to the proxy object created in a .NET project.

For example, assume you want to consume the following WCF contract, which returns all of the claims from your business case. The code sample that follows shows the code that the custom activity will be created from:

```
[ServiceContract]
public class AppraisalService
{
    ClaimRepository claimRepository = new ClaimRepository();


    [OperationContract]
    public List<Claim> FindAllClaims()
    {
        return claimRepository.FindAllClaims().ToList<Claim>();
    }
}
```

You can see the activity in Figure 7-8.

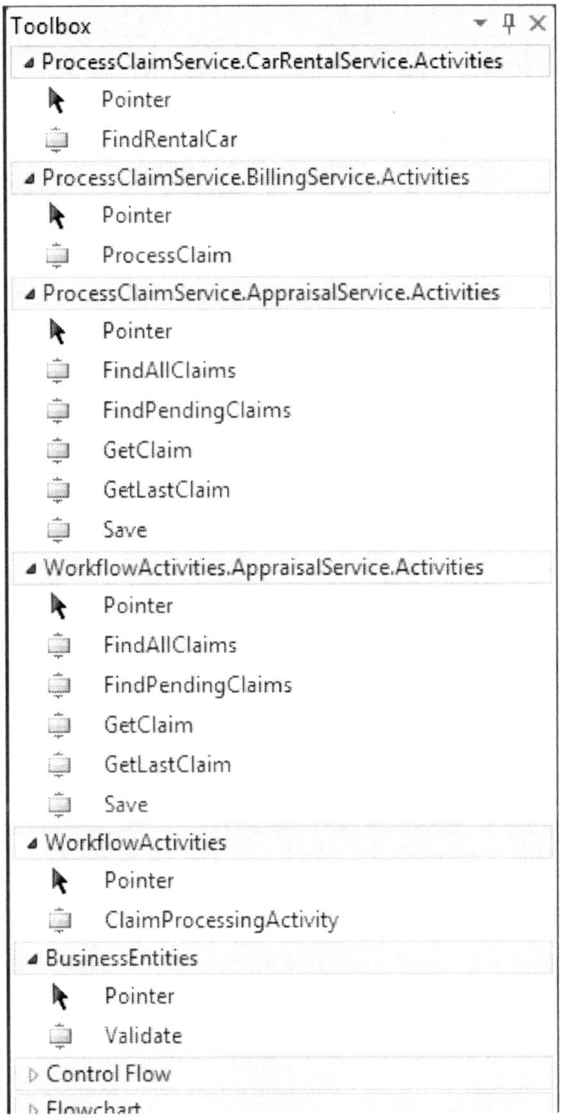

Figure 7-8. Toolbox with WCF End Point Activities

Now that we have added service references to our project, let's see how these services will be utilized in your business scenario. The workflow that is included in the ProcessClaimService project will implement the process flow of validating the claim, finding a rental car, processing the claim, and sending a response. Along the way, the workflow will also set and check status as well as terminate if the claim is not valid. This workflow aggregates five services in order to perform the entire process. You can see the workflow in Figure 7-9.

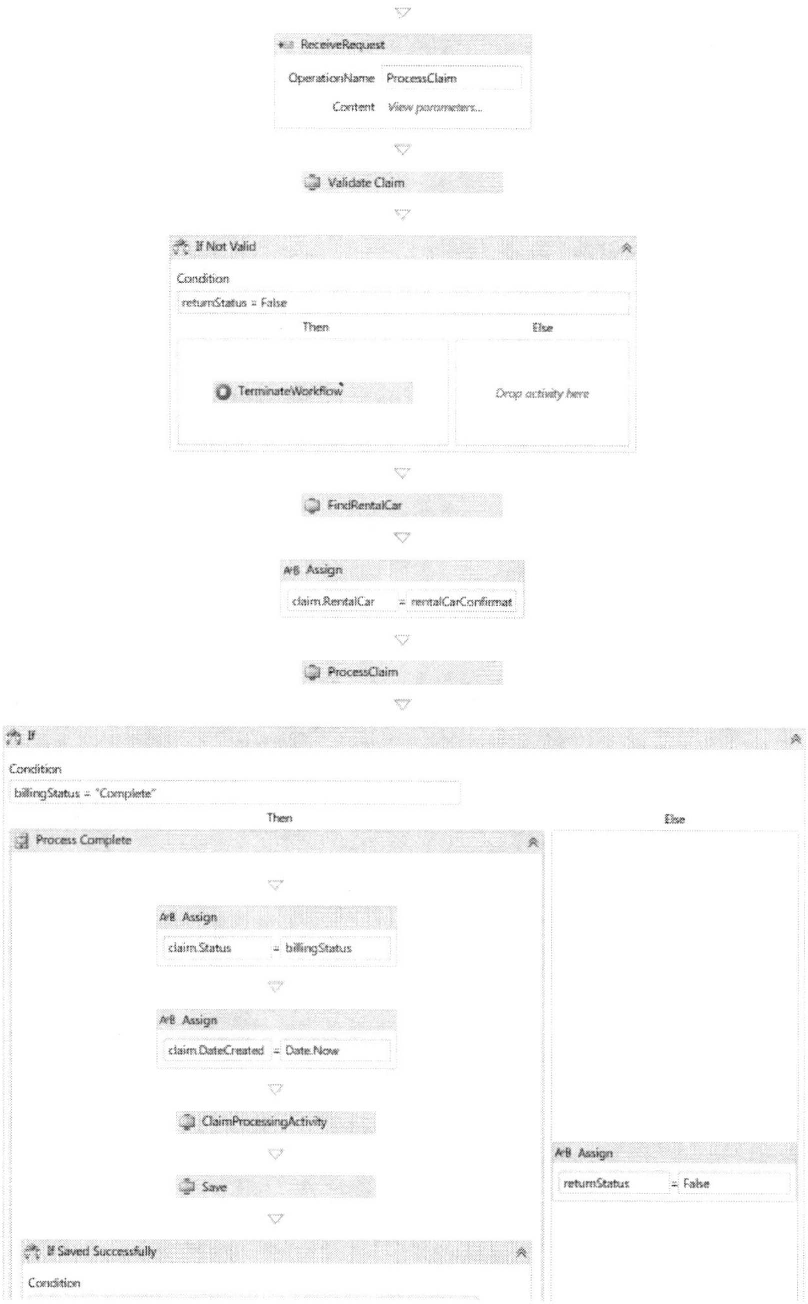

Figure 7-9. Business Case - ProcessClaimService Workflow

We can utilize the activities created for us when we add a service reference to a WCF service, but we can also utilize the service from messaging activities such as the Receive activity. The Receive activity that will start our workflow is the standard activity found under the Messaging section in the toolbox. We can use this activity and configure it to call our ProcessClaim service found under the ProcessClaimService.BillingService.Activities section in the toolbox. This can be done by selecting the Receive activity on the design surface, opening the properties window, and setting specific properties. The first will be to click on the elipses on the **Content** property. This will open the Content Definition dialog box where we will select the Parameters radio button and add a new parameter. Set the name to be Claim, the type to be Claim from the Business Entities project, and, lastly, set the Assign To to the claim object.

Next we need to click the elipses next to the **KnownTypes** properties and set its value to BusinessEntities.Claim. Then we will set the operation name and contract of the WCF service we want to call. Click the **OperationName** property and type in ProcessClaim. Lastly, click on the **ServiceContractName** property and type in IProcessClaimService. All of the information has now been entered to call a WCF service from a standard activity in the workflow.

Adding Extensions

Workflow extensions allow you to add behaviors to the workflow runtime by extending the runtime with custom code. Windows Workflow provides two behavior extensions: **tracking** and **persistence**. The **tracking** extension provides the ability to see what is happening inside your workflow, while the **persistence** extension provides functionality to save the state of the workflow and retrieve it. The **persistence** extension enables you to have long-running processes and provides a mechanism for load balancing across hosts.

Tracking

The **tracking** extension has two components: the *tracking participant* and the *tracking profile*. The profile defines the events and data that you want to track. A profile includes three types of queries: **ActivityQuery**, **WorkflowInstanceQuery**, and **UserTrackingQuery**. Let's jump right into code and see how to use **WorkflowInstanceQuery** and **ActivityQuery**:

```
TrackingProfile profile = new TrackingProfile
{
    Name = "ClaimProfile",
    Queries = {
        new WorkflowInstanceQuery {
            States = { "*" },
            EnvironmentQueries = { "USERNAME" }
        },
        new ActivityQuery {
            ActivityName = "ProcessClaim",
            States={ "*" },
            VariableQueries = {
                new VariableQuery {
                    VariableName = "ClaimID", Name = "Claim ID" }
            }
        }
    }
}
```

};

The preceding code creates a new WorkflowInstanceQuery instance, grabs a machine-level environment variable (USERNAME in this case, but you can access any environment variables), and then creates an ActivityQuery object to grab the value of the ClaimID variable for the specific activity. ActivityQuery allows you to define which activities to collect data from, as well as what data to collect.

The preceding code specified what data to track and where to get the data from, but not what to do with the data. This is where the tracking participant comes in. The tracking participant is an extension that is added to the runtime and acts on the tracking data that is being captured. The TrackingParticipant class that you use to capture the tracked data and write it to a console window includes a Track method. You need to add the code to do this to the entensions collection on the workflow instance. The following code shows you how to create a participant:

```
public class ConsoleOutputTrackingParticipant : TrackingParticipant
{
    public override void Track(TrackingRecord tr, TimeSpan timeout)
    {
        ActivityTrackingRecord atr = tr as ActivityTrackingRecord;
        if (atr != null)
        {
            Console.WriteLine(atr.Name);
            foreach (var item in atr.Variables)
            {
                Console.WriteLine("The variable named {0} equals {1}",
                    item.Key, item.Value);
            }
        }
    }
}
```

This example is interesting, but you're more likely to use the new Event Tracing for Windows (ETW) functionality. This is because Trace data can now be correlated between a WCF service and a WF instance. The ETW is a tracing system that is included in Windows and used by components and services, including kernel-level code and drivers. You can use the data written to the ETW through custom code or through tools in AppFabric. AppFabric will include ETW consumers that collect data and store it in a SQL Server database.

■ **Note** If you're moving your application from WF 3.X, you should be aware WF 4.0 will not include a SQL Tracking Participant. Instead, you will need to utilize the services in AppFabric to provide this functionality. Also, remember that you can write extensions to provide additional services required by your application, such as an ETW consumer or support for other databases.

Persistence

Note that these extensions aren't set up for you when you install the Framework. Instead, you will need to create a database and then run two SQL scripts to set up the database structure and logic. You can find the scripts at this location:

```
%windir%\Microsoft.NET\Framework\v4.0.20506\sql\en
```

This subfolder name will depend on the final version when .NET 4.0 ships. Run the `SqlPersistenceProviderSchema.sql` script to create the tables and then run the `SqlPersistenceProviderLogic.sql` script to create the stored procedures. At this point, you must add the extension to the workflow instance. You can do this by creating an instance of the **persistence** extension and adding it to the **Extensions** collection of the instance. The following code shows you how to add the extension:

```
string cn = "database=WFPersistence;integrated security=SSPI";
WorkflowInstance wf = new WorkflowInstance(new Flowchart1());
SqlPersistenceProviderFactory factory =
    new SqlPersistenceProviderFactory(cn, true);
factory.Open();
wf.Extensions.Add(factory.CreateProvider(wf.Id));
```

The persistence provider provides a factory pattern that lets you create a single factory and create provider instances from the factory. This will come in handy because you need to create a new instance of the provider for each workflow instance.

Now that you have the extension registered, you need to add functionality to the workflow to take advantage of this functionality. You can persist the workflow in one of two ways. First, you can use the **Persist** activity. Second, you can let the host persist the workflow based on certain events.

If you decide to use the **Persist** activity, the workflow will persist its state to the database when the activity executes. This lets the developer control when to save the workflow's state.

If you decide to let the host application persist the workflow, then you need to register for certain events. The most common event will be **OnIdle**. When you hook into the **OnIdle** event, you can specify whether the instance should be persisted, unloaded, or neither. The following line of code shows how to setup the **OnIdle** event.

```
Wf.OnIdle = () => IdleAction.Persist;
```

Once the workflow is persisted, it can continue running, or the workflow runtime can unload the instance from memory, freeing up resources so that other workflow instances can run. If the runtime unloads the workflow, (presumably because it's waiting for an external event to occur), it will need to load it back into memory. To load it back into memory, you must use the **persistence** provider for that specific instance. The **persistence** extension will load the state, whereupon you can call either the **Resume** or **ResumeBookmark** method on the workflow instance.

■ **Note** Persistence has changed in WF4. The workflow no longer serializes the entire set of activities and associated state; instead, it stores only the variables, argument values, and bookmark information. This provides greater flexibility for versioning and better performance because it results in a smaller storage footprint.

Tracking and Tracing Improvements

We, the authors, are strong believers that any piece of code that you write and deploy should provide telemetry. That telemetry should be able to provide monitoring and tracking data to understand what is happening internally when you need to debug and track down issues.

Support for tracking and tracing has changed dramatically in WF4. The improvements both improve performance and provide greater flexibility. In .NET 4, WF and WCF use the same tracking and tracing model, which makes it easier to leverage your existing knowledge. WF 4.0 incorporates the ability to utilize Event Tracing for Windows (ETW). Both WF and WCF utilize the ETW. Incorporating ETW into both technologies provides more control and minimizes the performance overhead when tracking is enabled. This should remove the primary reason developers shy away from tracking. Tracking is important enough that Microsoft has devoted a great deal of attention to improving it for this release of the .NET Framework. The control you now have over tracking and tracing boils down to the ability to specify what to track, when to track it, and what level of verbosity to set.

What follows is a short list of some of the benefits you receive by using the ETW functionality in your code:

- *Improved ETW Integration*: WF 4 includes the **ETWTrackingParticipant**, which allows you to write tracking data to an ETW session.

- *End to End (E2E) Tracing with WCF*: You can now correlate trace data between a WCF service and a WF instance. This provides the ability to have a unified debugging experience.

- *Tracking Profile Config Elements*: The tracking profile in the **.config** file uses the configuration elements instead of XAML. This provides a consistent experience for the way that developers interact with configuration data.

- *OptOut Model*: Variables and arguments are now tracked by default. If you don't want this behavior, then you will need to opt out and specifically suppress tracking for the variable or argument.

- *Tracking Filtering*: WF 4.0 gives you more control in how you configure the runtime logging functionality. In WF 3.X, logging was an all-or-nothing event.

Summary

This chapter looked at the new Windows Workflow functionality available in .NET 4 and outlined how you can take advantage of it in this book's example business scenario.

Specifically, you learned how to create a workflow and pass objects. You also learned about integrating a WCF endpoint with Windows Workflow and the new XAMLX format. Having a deeper understanding of Windows Workflow is important in AppFabric-based applications because many of the services are tightly integrated; Microsoft designed it this way to make the development effort faster and more streamlined.

You also reviewed the runtime extensions, focusing on the **persistence** and **tracking** extensions. Finally, you learned about the ETW service and how that will be incorporated in AppFabric.

What you have not learned about yet is how you can deploy your WCF and WF applications. You'll dive into deployment in Chapter 9, but before you take that plunge, you'll learn about running AppFabric as a host in Chapter 8.

CHAPTER 8

■ ■ ■

Hosting in AppFabric

This chapter picks up right where the previous chapter left off. That is, you will continue to explore your sample business scenario of the Contoso Insurance Claims Processing application. In Chapter 6 and Chapter 7, you learned about some of the more exciting features of the .NET Framework 4.0 as you walked through a practical code listing to implement a fictitious business scenario. You will continue to refer back to that code implementation as you carry on with your journey through the new features of AppFabric.

In the Phase II of the business scenario, you will further shield Contoso's customers from mishandling information errors by running and managing your application in AppFabric hosted environment (see Figure 8-1). Using a combination of IIS and AppFabric as a host enables workflow troubleshooting for finding and fixing problems, automation of workflow operations (start, resume, stop and suspend), as well as workflow and WCF services configuration and persistence.

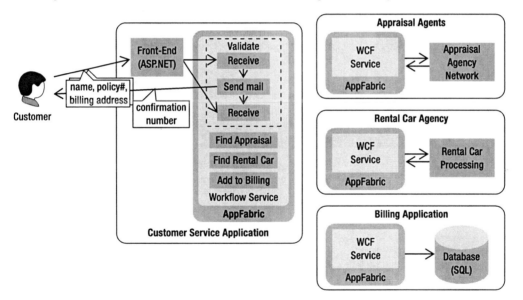

Figure 8-1. Hosting Contoso WCF and WF services in AppFabric

AppFabric takes up where the .NET Framework 4.0 leaves off, providing the server experience for middle-tier applications that include WCF and WF applications. AppFabric leverages the IIS and Windows Process Activation service (WAS) as a host for WCF and WF services. Through IIS extensions,

AppFabric exposes WCF and WF capabilities (service configuration, monitoring, and instance management) in a familiar, centralized management tool.

Using the Contoso Insurance scenario, this chapter will walk you through the experience of using AppFabric for hosting, configuring, monitoring, and troubleshooting WCF and WF services.

Deploying the Application to AppFabric

The Contoso Insurance Claims Processing system consists of five applications: one Claims.Web ASP.NET MVC application, one **ProcessClaimService** WF service, one **Appraisal.WCF** service, one **Billing.WCF** service, and one **CarRental.WCF** service. Instead of deploying all five applications to the default web site, you will create two web sites: one for the ASP.NET application and the other for the four WCF/WF services. You will also create an application pool that the two web sites will share.

Adding a New Application Pool

You can add a new application pool by following these three steps:

1. Click **Start**, click **All Programs**, click **Windows Server AppFabric**, and then click **Internet Information Services (IIS) Manager**.

2. Expand the server node, right-click **Application Pools**, and then click **Add Application Pool** to open the **Add Application Pool** dialog box.

3. Enter or select the following values, and then click OK (see Table 8-1 and Figure 8-2).

Table 8-1. *Entering Values for Your Application Pool*

Property	Value
Name	ContosoAppPool
.NET Framework version	.NET Framework v4.0.21006
Managed pipeline mode	Integrated
Start application pool immediately	(Selected)

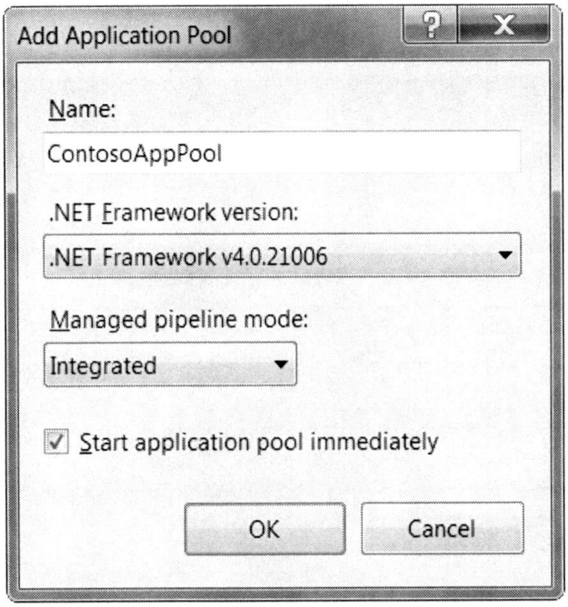

Figure 8-2. Creating a New Application Pool

■ **Note** You must choose the .NET Framework 4.0 for the application pool. AppFabric supports hosting WCF and WF services that you build with .NET Framework 4.0.

Adding a New Web Site

It also requires three steps to add a new web site to host the Contoso Claims Web application:

1. Launch IIS.

2. Expand the server node, right-click **Sites**, and then click **Add Web Site** to open the **Add Web Site** dialog box.

3. Enter or select the following values, and then click **OK** (see Table 8-2 and Figure 8-3).

Table 8-2. Entering Values for a New Web Site

Property	Value
Site Name	Contoso.Claims.Web
Application Pool	ContosoAppPool
Physical Path	`C:\Pro AppFabric Book\Contoso\WebSites\Contoso.Claims.Web`
Port	89
Host	Localhost
Start Web site immediately	(Selected)

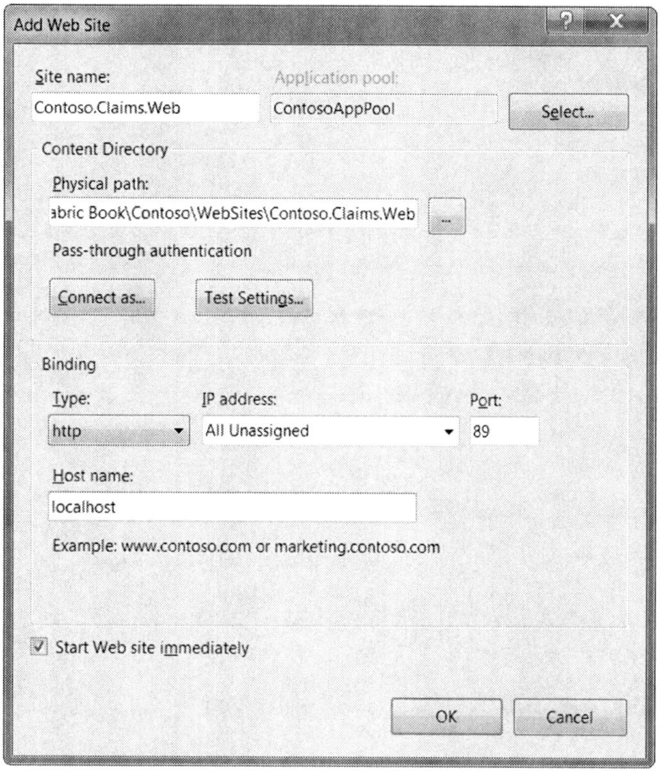

Figure 8-3. Creating a New Web Application

■ **Note** When you create a new Web site, the wizard creates a new application pool with the same name as the Web site by default. Make sure you click **Select** and choose **ContosoAppPool**, which is what you created in the previous step.

Host Contoso WCF and WF Services

You can add a new web site to host Contoso WCF and WF services with an additional three steps:

1. Launch IIS.

2. Expand the server node, right-click **Sites**, and then click **Add Web Site** to open the **Add Web Site** dialog box.

3. Enter or select the following values, and then click OK (see Table 8-3 and Figure 8-4).

Table 8-3. Entering Values for Hosting WCF and WF Services

Property	Value
Site Name	Contoso.Claims.Services
Application Pool	ContosoAppPool
Physical Path	`C:\Pro AppFabric Book\Solution\Claims.Services`
Port	90
Host	Localhost
Start Web site immediately	(Selected)

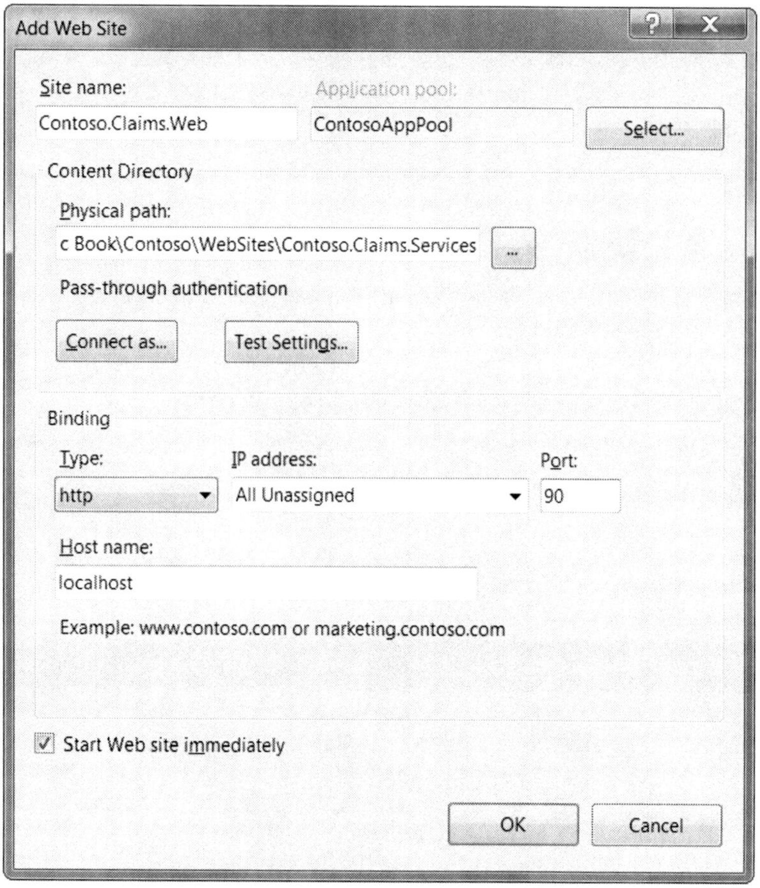

Figure 8-4. *Creating a New Web Application*

Deploying the Contoso WCF Services to AppFabric

These new features for default endpoints, binding configurations, and behavior configurations make hosting in IIS much easier with AppFabric. Developers familiar with ASMX services can now define WCF services that are just as simple in nature. For example, suppose you want to define your Contoso WCF services (from Chapter 6) so they can be hosted directly in AppFabric.

The first step is to migrate each of your WCF services projects from the WCF Service Library to the WCF Service Application. From there, you continue packaging your WCF Service Application projects into web deployment packages using Visual Studio 2010 Package/Publish Wizard. You will use these packages to deploy Contoso WCF services to AppFabric. The final step: After you successfully deploy your WCF services into AppFabric and check that your WCF services are available and are manageable through the AppFabric Dashboard, you need to remove all corresponding console application hosts that you built in Chapter 6.

Migrating to the WCF Service Application Project

The following example uses the Appraisal.WCF service you built in Chapter 6. This example will illustrate the steps are required to migrate an existing WCF Service Library project into a new WCF Service Application project; this is a necessary step for making your application ready to deploy with AppFabric:

- Launch Microsoft Visual Studio 2010.

- Open the solution file you used in the preceding chapters: **Claims.sln**.

- Right-click **Claims** solution node, and then click **Add ➤ New Project...** to open the **Add New Project** dialog box.

- Add a new project of type of **WCF Service Application** (see Figure 8-5). Name it **AppraisalService.WCF**.

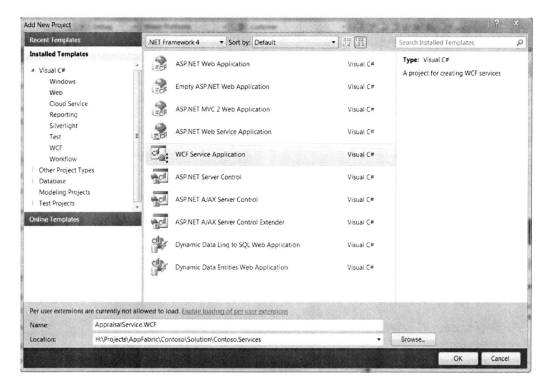

Figure 8-5. *Creating a New WCF Service Application*

1. Add an assembly reference to the **BusinessEntities** project (you will be using the Data model of Contoso entities you created in Chapter 6).

2. Remove **IService1.cs** file from the project.

3. Rename the **Service1.svc** file to **AppraisalService.svc**.

4. Now delete the **AppraisalService.svc.cs** (if it exists) because you will use a single service definition file to describe and implement your WCF service.

5. Right-click the **AppraisalService.svc** module and select the **View Markup** menu option.

6. In the old **Appraisal.WCF** project, open the **AppraisalService.cs** module and copy its content.

7. Paste the clipboard content at the end of the **AppraisalService.svc** file, wrapping it with the **namespace AppraisalService.WCF {}** definition. Also, add the **[ServiceContract]** and **[OperationContract]** attributes, where required.

8. The final **AppraisalService.svc** module should look like this:

```
<%@ ServiceHost Language="C#" Debug="true"
Service="AppraisalService.WCF.AppraisalService" %>

namespace AppraisalService.WCF
{
    using System;
    using System.Collections.Generic;
    using System.Linq;
    using System.Runtime.Serialization;
    using System.ServiceModel;
    using System.Text;
    using BusinessEntities;


    [ServiceContract]
    public class AppraisalService
    {
        ClaimRepository claimRepository = new ClaimRepository();


        [OperationContract]
        public List<Claim> FindAllClaims()
        {
            return claimRepository.FindAllClaims().ToList<Claim>();
        }
```

```
    [OperationContract]
    public List<Claim> FindPendingClaims()
    {
        return claimRepository.FindPendingClaims().ToList<Claim>();
    }

    [OperationContract]
    public Claim GetLastClaim()
    {
        return claimRepository.GetLastClaim();
    }

    [OperationContract]
    public Claim GetClaim(int claimId)
    {
        return claimRepository.GetClaim(claimId);
    }


    [OperationContract]
    public void Save(Claim claim)
    {
        Console.WriteLine("{0}: The claim # {1} is being saved in the backend
            system.", DateTime.Now.ToShortTimeString(), claim.ClaimId);

        Claim originalClaim = claimRepository.GetClaim(claim.ClaimId);

        //Update the claim
        originalClaim.AccidentId = originalClaim.AccidentId;
        originalClaim.Accidents.FName = claim.Accidents.FName;
        originalClaim.Accidents.LName = claim.Accidents.LName;
        originalClaim.Accidents.Address = claim.Accidents.Address;
        originalClaim.Accidents.City = claim.Accidents.City;
        originalClaim.Accidents.ContactPhone = claim.Accidents.ContactPhone;
        originalClaim.Accidents.State = claim.Accidents.State;
        originalClaim.Accidents.Zip = claim.Accidents.Zip;
        originalClaim.Accidents.Latitude = claim.Accidents.Latitude;
        originalClaim.Accidents.Longitude = claim.Accidents.Longitude;
        originalClaim.Description = claim.Description;
        originalClaim.DateCreated = claim.DateCreated;
        originalClaim.Status = claim.Status;
        originalClaim.RentalCar = claim.RentalCar;


        claimRepository.Save();

        Console.WriteLine("{0}: The claim # {1} has been saved.",
            DateTime.Now.ToShortTimeString(), claim.ClaimId);

    }
  }
}
```

This is the simplest form of the WCF service definition because you are not using a separate interface definition to define the service contract, and you define everything in one file: **AppraisalService.svc**. There are simply fewer moving parts. This definition should feel a lot like typical ASMX definitions; the primary difference exists in the attribute names that you use on the service (such as **[WebService]** and **[WebMethod]** rather than **[ServiceContract]** and **[OperationContract]**).

Your new project file structure should now look similar to what you see in Figure 8-6.

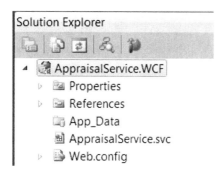

Figure 8-6. *A New AppraisalService.WCF project File Structure*

You use the same procedure to migrate the other two WCF Service Library projects using the information provided in Tables 8-4 and 8-5.

Table 8-4. *Entering Values for the Billing WCF Service*

Property		New Name
Project	Billing.WCF	BillingService.WCF
Namespace	Billing.WCF	BillingService.WCF
Interface	IBilling.cs	N/A
Service Implementation	BillingService.cs	BillingService.svc
Web Package Location	N/A	Package\BillingService.WCF.zip
IIS Web Application name	N/A	Contoso.Claims.Services/BillingService.WCF

Table 8-5. *Entering Values for the CarRental WCF Service*

Property		New Name
Project	CarRental.WCF	CarRentalService.WCF
Namespace	CarRental.WCF	CarRentalService.WCF
Interface	ICarRental.cs	N/A
Service Implementation	CarRentalService.cs	CarRentalService.svc
Web Package Location	N/A	Package\CarRentalService.WCF.zip
IIS Web Application name	N/A	Contoso.Claims.Services/CarRentalService.WCF

Deploying a WCF Service Application

Now let's continue developing the **AppraisalService.WCF** project you started in the last section. In this step, you will demonstrate how to create and publish the WCF package into AppFabric.

1. Launch Microsoft Visual Studio 2010.

2. Open the solution file you used in the previous chapters: **Claims.sln**.

3. Build the solution. Make sure it builds without any errors.

4. Right-click the **AppraisalService.WCF** project, then select **Properties** to open the **AppraisalService.WCF** project properties.

5. Select the **Package/Publish** tab. Go to **Web Deployment Package Settings** and make sure the **Create web package as a ZIP file** check box is selected.

6. Use the details shown in Figure 8-7 to specify the location for creating the package, as well as the IIS Web site to use on the destination server. Save the project settings.

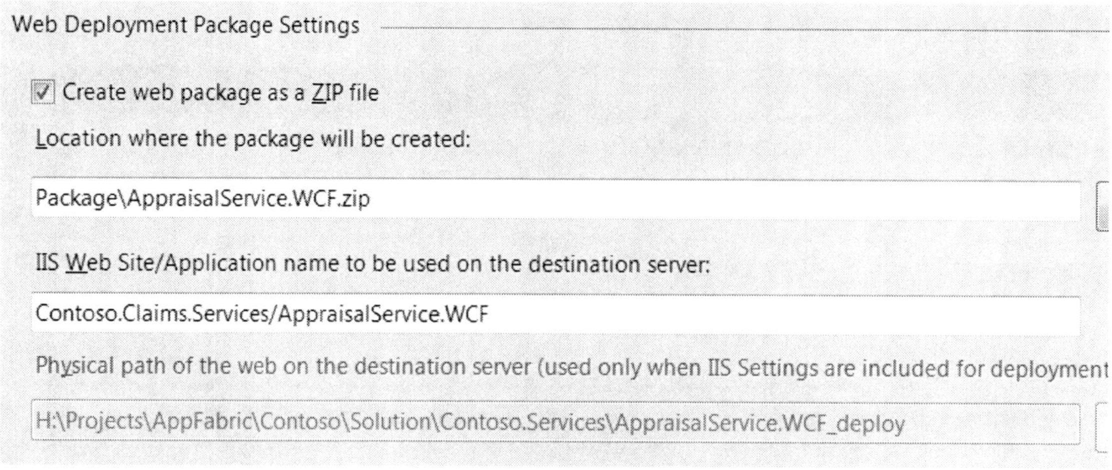

Web Deployment Package Settings ──

☑ Create web package as a ZIP file

Location where the package will be created:

Package\AppraisalService.WCF.zip

IIS Web Site/Application name to be used on the destination server:

Contoso.Claims.Services/AppraisalService.WCF

Physical path of the web on the destination server (used only when IIS Settings are included for deployment

H:\Projects\AppFabric\Contoso\Solution\Contoso.Services\AppraisalService.WCF_deploy

Figure 8-7. Web Deployment Package Settings for AppraisalService.WCF

7. Right-click the **AppraisalService.WCF** project in the Solution Explorer and select **Create Package**. This packages and creates the **AppraisalService.WCF.zip** deployment package in the location specified in the Step 6.

8. Start or switch to IIS.

9. Expand the server node, expand **Sites**, and click **Contoso.Claims.Services**.

10. In the **Actions** pane, click **Import Applications** to open the **Import Application Package** dialog box.

11. Enter the value for the **Package Path** property shown in Table 8-6 and click **Next**.

Table 8-6. Entering Values for Hosting WCF and WF Services

Property	Value
Package path	`C:\Pro AppFabric Book\Contoso\Solution\Contoso.Services\` `AppraisalService.WCF\Package\AppraisalService.WCF.zip`

12. Click **Next** two more times, then click **Finish**. You will now see a new Web application called **AppraisalService.WCF** listed under the **Contoso.Claims.Services** Web site, as shown in Figure 8-8. At this point, you can browse to the **AppraisalService.svc** in your Internet Explorer browser without any additional WCF configuration or activation logic (see Figure 8-9).

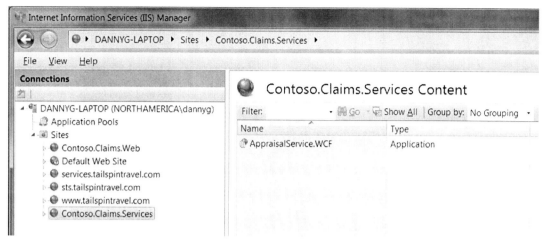

Figure 8-8. A New WCF Service Application Deployed to AppFabric

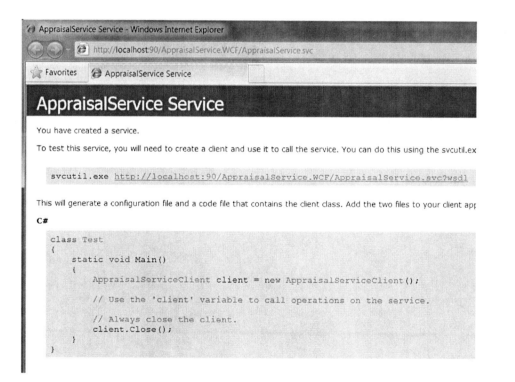

Figure 8-9. Browsing the Contoso AppraisalService WCF Service in a Browser

13. Now, you can safely remove the old **Appraisal.WCF** and **Appraisal.ConsoleHost** projects from your solution.

Use the same procedure to deploy the other two applications using the information provided in Tables 8-7 and 8-8.

Table 8-7. *Entering the Location of the BillingService Deployment*

Property	Value

Import Application Package Location	`C:\Pro AppFabric Book\Contoso\Solution\`
	`Contoso.Services\BillingService.WCF\Package\`
	`BillingService.WCF.zip`

Table 8-8. *Entering the Location of the CarRentalService Deployment*

Property	Values

Import Application Package Location	`C:\Pro AppFabric Book\Contoso\Solution\`
	`Contoso.Services\CarRentalService.WCF\`
	`Package\CarRentalService.WCF.zip`

Once you complete the preceding steps, you can verify that you have correctly deployed all your WCF services by browsing the WCF services in IE and checking the services listed under the Contoso.Claims.Services web site (see Figure 8-10).

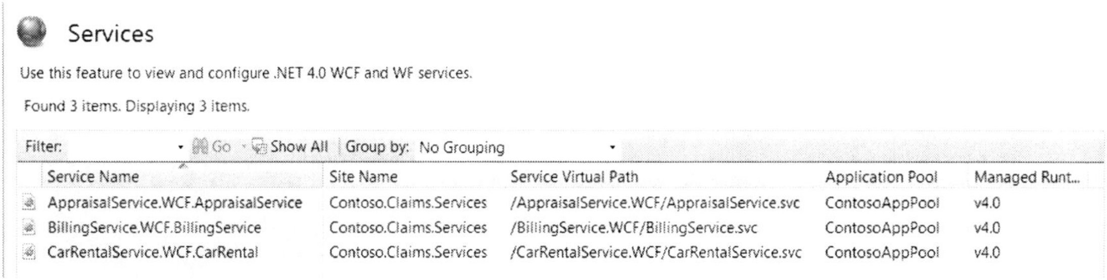

Figure 8-10. *Browsing Contoso WCF services in the AppFabric Services Dashboard*

Making Other Required Modifications

When you replace the existing **Billing** and **CarRental** services with new WCF AppFabric-ready service applications, the older **IBilling** and **ICarRental** interfaces can be removed. Now, in the **WorkflowActivities** project you need to add service references to the **BillingService.WCF** and **CarRental.WCF** projects so you can later use **ChannelFactory** class to create the corresponding WCF service proxies. Do this by using the URL you could obtain after deploying these services to AppFabric.

You will also need to update the **Appraisal.WCF.Proxy** and **ProcessClaimServiceWF** service references in the Claims.Web main project to the **AppraisalService.svc** and **ProcessClaimService.xamlx** WCF and WF services, respectively. Also, for sake of brevity, you need to remove the **DiscoveryHost** dependency from **Claims.Web** application and comment out all references in the **Global.asax** module to the **DiscoveryHost** proxy.

Now, as you move your WCF services from console application hosts to the AppFabric host, you no longer need to find and discover the **Billing** WCF service and obtain the endpoint for the **CarRental** WCF service's UDP announcement (refer back to Chapter 6 for details on this).

With all the WCF services known at design time, you can now use the WF 4.0 messaging toolbox controls to invoke **CarRentalService** and **BillingService** WCF services directly from the **ProcessClaimService** WF workflow (see Figure 8-11).

AppraisalEndpoint	String	Process Claim	"http://localhost:90/AppraisalService.WCF/AppraisalService.svc"
BillingEndpoint	String	Process Claim	"http://localhost:90/BillingService.WCF/BillingService.svc"
CarRentalEndpoint	String	Process Claim	"http://localhost:90/CarRentalService.WCF/CarRentalService.svc"
Create Variable			

Variables	**Imports**		

Figure 8-11. Defining WCF endpoints directly in ProcessClaimService WF Variables list

You can also replace the flowchart workflow design with the WF service sequence to make the **ProcessClaimService** workflow callable from WCF client applications.

You can see the updated workflow for **ProcessClaimService** in Figure 8-12.

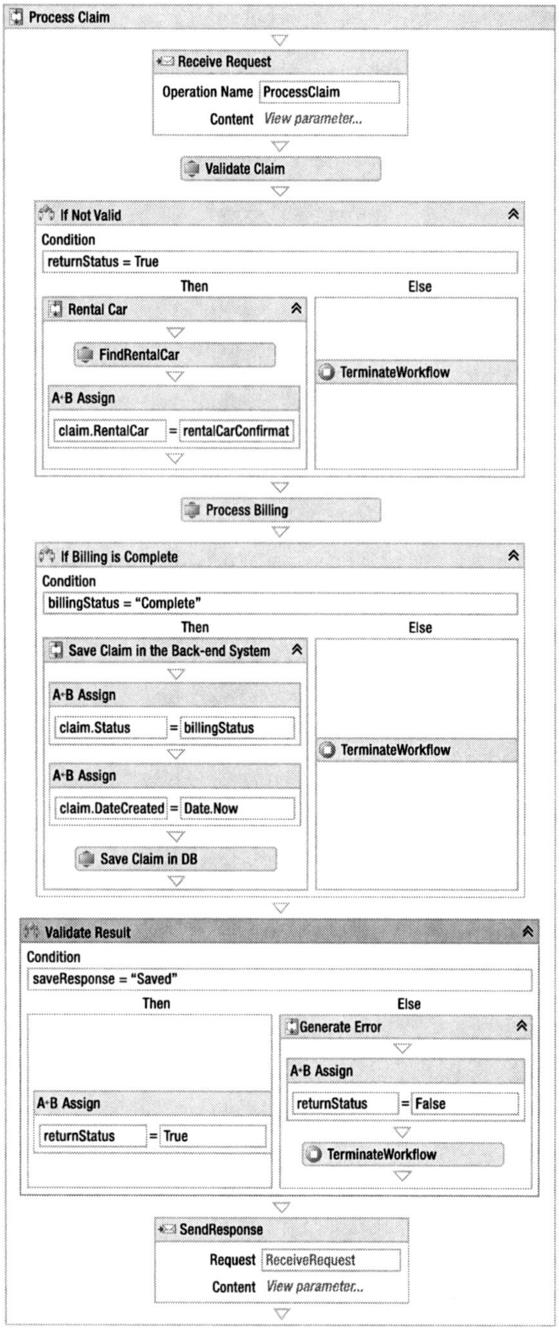

Figure 8-12. *The ProcessClaimService Workflow Design*

Overall, these WCF configuration simplifications should make it much easier for developers to get WCF services up and running with their Web applications. These simplifications also bring the simplest case of using AppFabric much closer to the experience of developers used to developing with ASP.NET Web services.

Deploying a WF Service

The following steps illustrate how to deploy the single workflow service you built in Chapter 7:

1. Launch Microsoft Visual Studio 2010.

2. Open the solution file you used in the preceding chapters: `Claims.sln`.

3. In the `ProcessClaimService` project, find and open the `ProcessClaimService.xamlx` workflow module.

4. In the opening design canvass of the workflow, click anywhere outside of the `Claim Processing` flowchart element. This causes the property window to show the properties for the WorkflowService activity (see Figure 8-13).

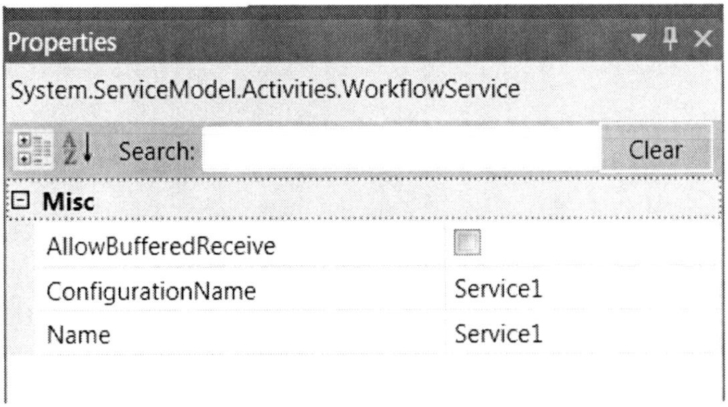

Figure 8-13. Default WorkflowService Properties

5. Change the default name for the `ConfigurationName` and `Name` properties from `Service1` to `ProcessClaimService.WF` (see Figure 8-14).

183

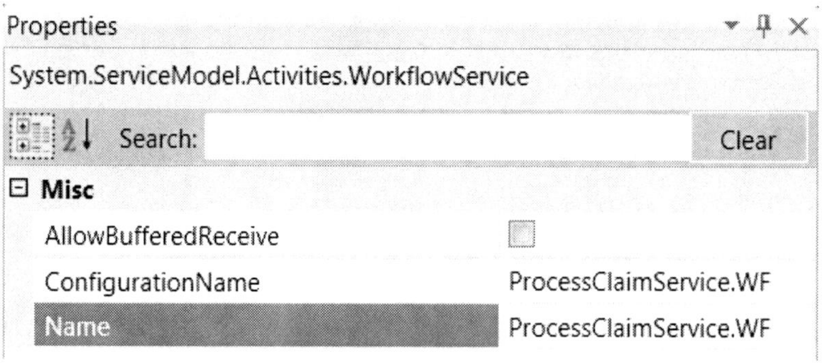

Figure 8-14. Changing the ProcessClaimService WorkflowService Properties

6. Build the solution and make sure it builds without any errors.

7. Right-click the **ProcessClaimService** project and then select **Properties** to open the project properties.

8. Select the **Package/Publish** tab, then go to **Web Deployment Package Settings** and make sure the **Create web package as a ZIP file** check box is selected.

9. Use the details shown in Figure 8-15 to specify where the package will be created, as well as the IIS Web site to use on the destination server.

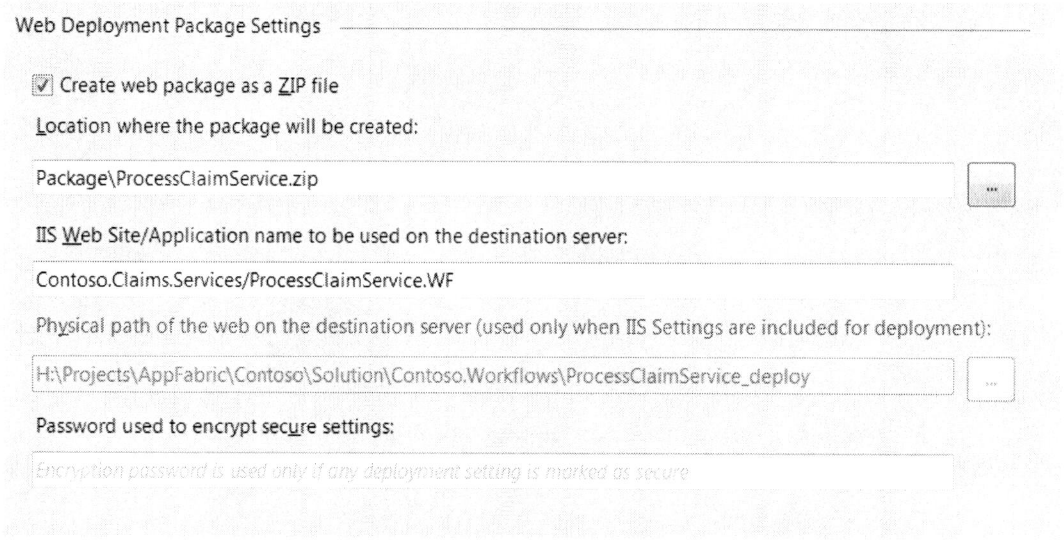

Figure 8-15. Web Deployment Package Settings for the ProcessClaimService WF service

10. Right-click the **ProcessClaimService** project in the Solution Explorer and select **Create Package**. This will package and create the **ProcessClaimService.zip** deployment package in the location you specified in the Step 9.

11. Start or switch to IIS.

12. Expand the server node, expand **Sites**, and then click **Contoso.Claims.Services**.

13. In the **Actions** pane, click **Import Applications** to open the **Import Application Package** dialog box.

14. Enter the value shown in Table 8-9 and click **Next**.

Table 8-9. Entering the Location of ProcessClaimsService.zip

Property	Value
Package path	`C:\Pro AppFabric Book\Contoso\Solution\Contoso.Workflows\` `ProcessClaimService\Package\ProcessClaimService.zip`

15. Click **Next** two more times and then click **Finish**. You can see a new Web application called **ProcessClaimService.WF** listed under the Contoso.Claims.Services Web site (see Figure 8-16):

Services

Use this feature to view and configure .NET 4.0 WCF and WF services.

Found 4 items. Displaying 4 items.

Filter:　　　　　　▾ 🔍 Go ▾ 🔲 Show All | Group by: No Grouping　　　　　▾

Service Name	Site Name	Service Virtual Path	Application Pool
AppraisalService.WCF.AppraisalService	Contoso.Claims.Services	/AppraisalService.WCF/AppraisalService.svc	ContosoAppPool
BillingService.WCF.BillingService	Contoso.Claims.Services	/BillingService.WCF/BillingService.svc	ContosoAppPool
CarRentalService.WCF.CarRentalService	Contoso.Claims.Services	/CarRentalService.WCF/CarRentalService.svc	ContosoAppPool
ProcessClaimService.WF	Contoso.Claims.Services	/ProcessClaimService.WF/ProcessClaimService.xamlx	ContosoAppPool

Figure 8-16. The Final List of All Contoso WCF and WF Services

Configuring the Contoso Claims Processing application in AppFabric

AppFabric's configuration management tools provide the easiest, most straightforward way to configure Web applications and services. Changes you make in the AppFabric GUI are made to the Web.config files that define the configuration for a service or application. Using AppFabric's configuration management tools means you do not have to write code in a series of Web.config files; AppFabric does that for you. In this section, you will perform some basic configurations for the Contoso Claims Processing WCF and WF services.

Deploy a Single Workflow Service

You can follow the steps shown previously for deploying WCF services to AppFabric to deploy the single workflow service you built in Chapter 7:

1. Start or switch to IIS Manager.

2. Expand the server node, expand **Sites**, expand **Contoso.Claims.Web,** and click the **Claims.Web** web application.

3. In the **Actions** pane, click **Configure** under the **.NET 4.0 WF and WCF** section to open the **Configure WF and WCF for Server** dialog box. Note that you can also use the right-click context menu to get to the same configuration dialog box.

4. In the left pane, click **Monitoring** and then select the values shown in Figure 8-17.

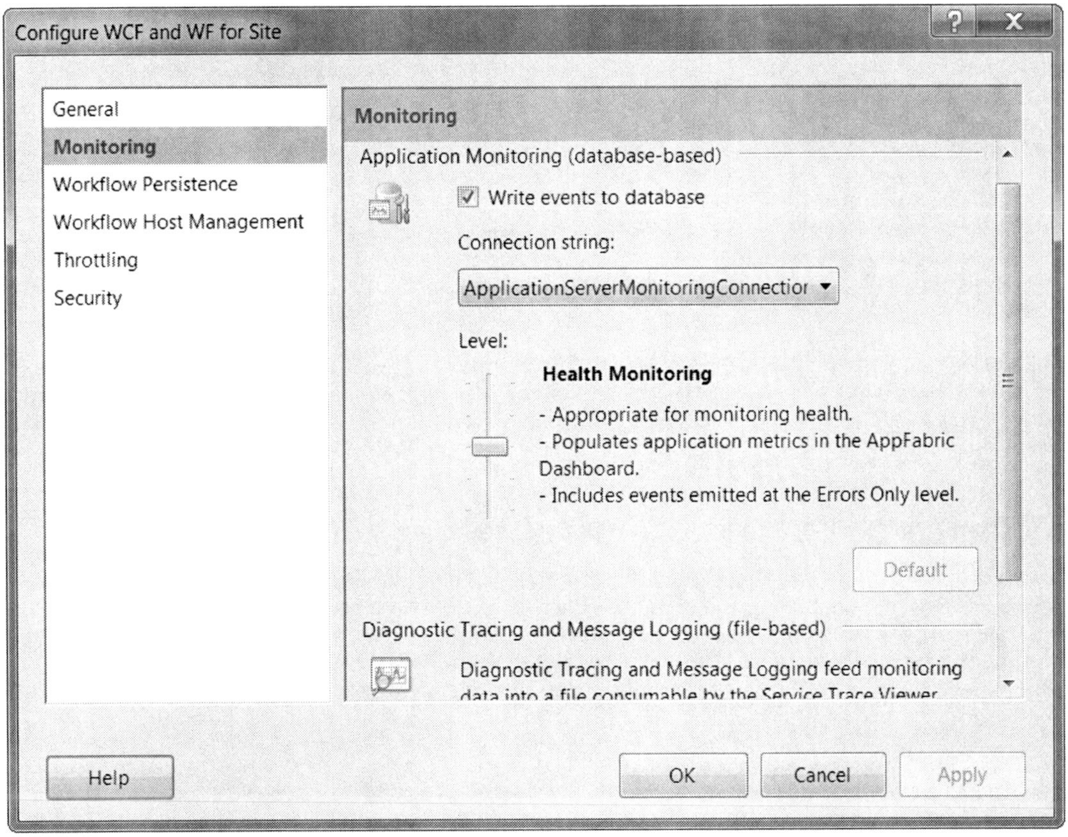

Figure 8-17. Configuring Monitoring Settings for the Contoso Claims Web Application

■ **Note** You should determine the monitoring level by considering the amount of data you want to collect and the performance impact that higher monitoring levels will have on your application. You must set the monitoring level to at least `Health Monitoring` to collect the data required to populate the AppFabric Dashboard's WCF calls and tracked WF instances sections.

5. Click `OK` to close the `Configure WF and WCF for Site` dialog box.

After you complete these steps, a **Web.config** file is generated and dropped into your Web application's physical folder at **C:\Pro AppFabric Book\Contoso\WebSites\Contoso.Claims.Web**. You should see the following lines when you open the file and look for the **<monitoring>** element and its attributes:

```
<microsoft.applicationServer>
    <monitoring>
        <default enabled="true"
connectionStringName="ApplicationServerMonitoringConnectionString"
monitoringLevel="HealthMonitoring" />
    </monitoring>
</microsoft.applicationServer>
```

Whenever you update a **Web.config** file—whether manually or by configuring monitoring settings in the AppFabric Dashboard—the system recycles the associated application domains. For example, if you update a **Web.config** file at the site level, the application domains for all services beneath that site will be recycled.

Configuring the Contoso Claims Processing Workflow Service

You can leverage the AppFabric Persistence Services described in Chapter 4 to configure your workflow service to monitor its health using one of the AppFabric's out-of-the-box Workflow Tracking profiles. These profiles are stored in the persistence database you configured in Chapter 5. You can configure the monitoring level at all scopes in AppFabric: IIS server, the web site, and the web application. You can also configure a tracking profile on a given service by following these steps:

1. Start or switch to IIS Manager.

2. Expand the server node, expand **Sites**, expand **Contoso.Claims.Services**, and then click **ProcessClaimService.WF**.

3. In the center pane, double-click **Services**. You should now see **ProcessClaimService.WF** listed in the services list.

4. Right-click **ProcessClaimService.WF** and click **Configure** to open the **Configure Service** dialog box (see Figure 8-18).

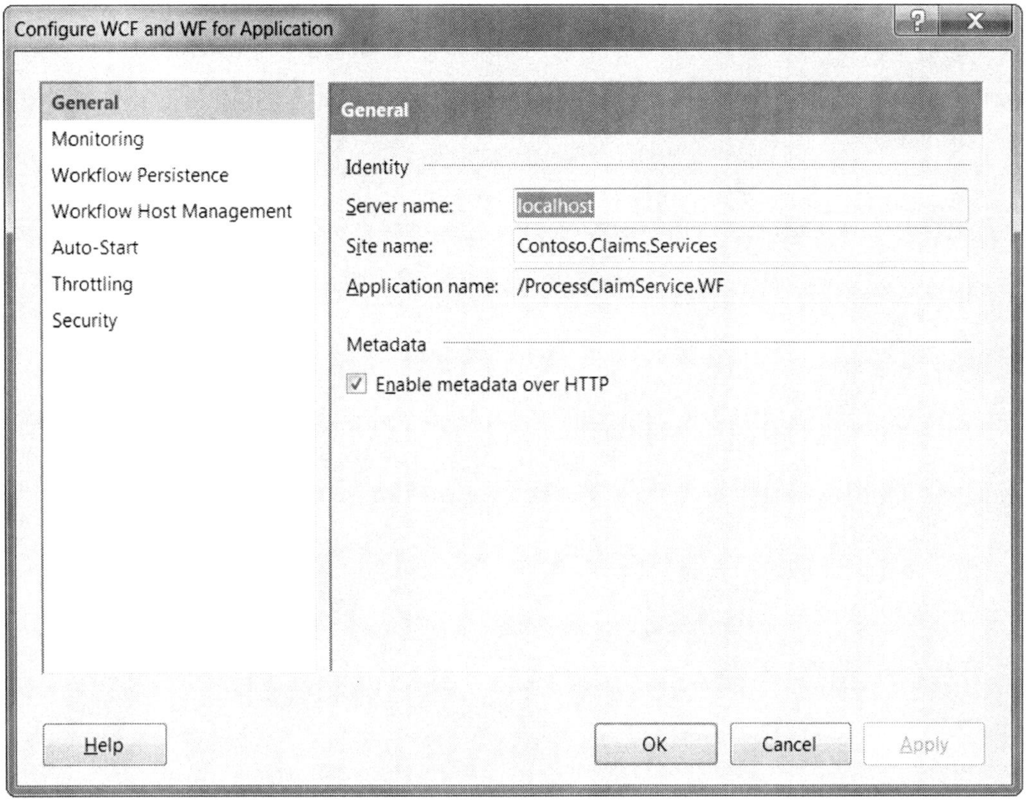

Figure 8-18. Configuring Workflow Service in AppFabric

5. In the left pane, click **Monitoring**.

6. Click **Configure** in the **Workflow Tracking profile** section.

7. In **Tracking Profile**, select **End-to-End Monitoring or Troubleshooting tracking profile**and then click **Apply** (see Figure 8-19). When you change the Monitoring level, the appropriate workflow tracking profile is set automatically. For example, if you want to track workflow variables on the **ProcessClaimService** workflow, you could change the tracking profile by editing the configuration for that service. You will learn more about this part of AppFabric's functionality in Chapter 11.

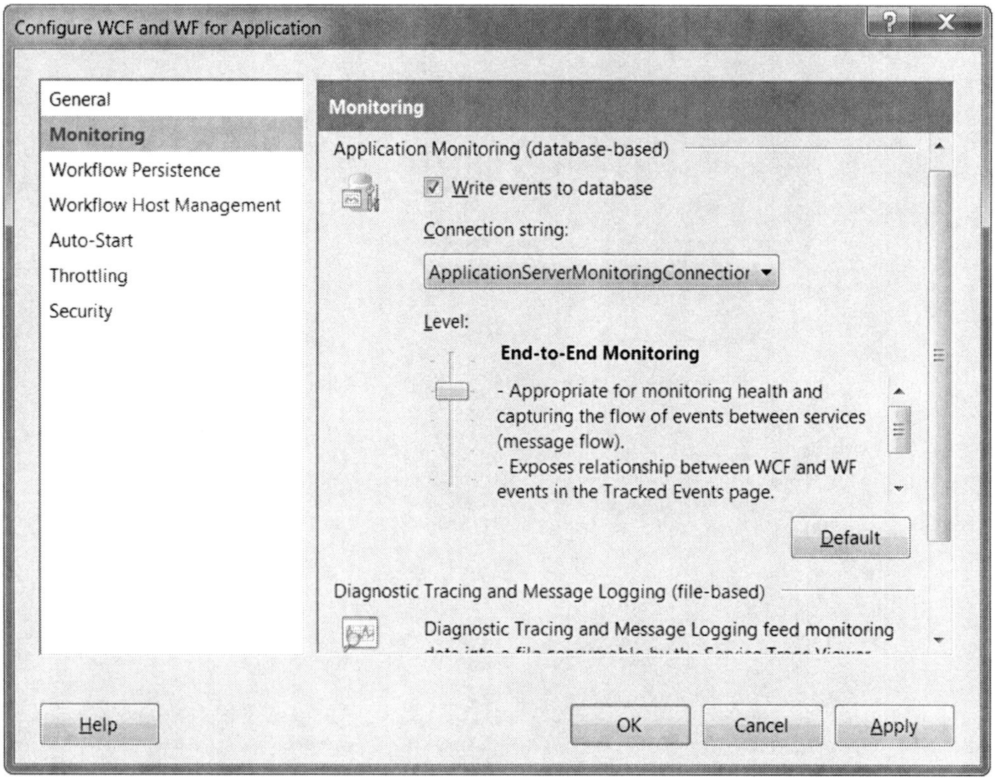

Figure 8-19. The Workflow Tracking Profile Dialog Box

8. In the left pane, click **Workflow Persistence** and then select the values shown in Figure 8-20:

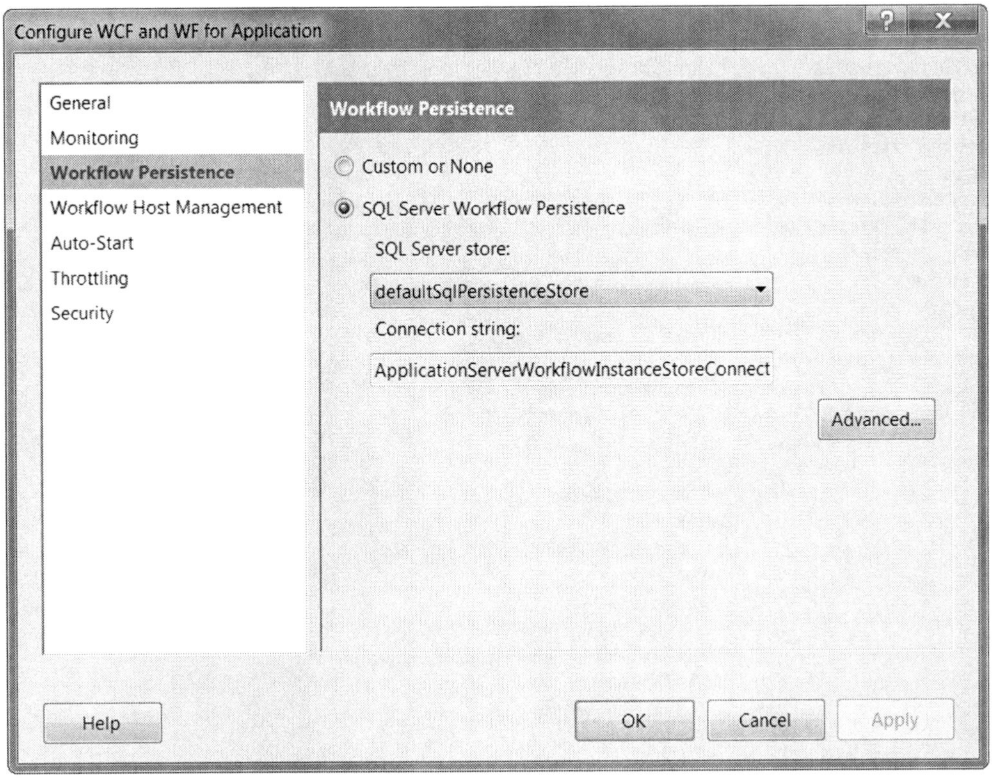

Figure 8-20. Workflow Persistence Setting Values for the Claims Processing Workflow Service

9. Click **OK** to close the **Configure Service** dialog box.

After you complete these steps, a **Web.config** file is generated and dropped into the Web application's physical folder at **C:\Pro AppFabric Book\Contoso\WebSites\Contoso.Claims.Web**. You should see the following lines when you open the file:

```
<?xml version="1.0" encoding="utf-8"?>
<configuration>
  <system.web>
    <compilation debug="true" targetFramework="4.0" />
  </system.web>
  <system.serviceModel>
  <behaviors>
    <serviceBehaviors>
      <behavior>
        <serviceMetadata httpGetEnabled="true" />
        <serviceDebug includeExceptionDetailInFaults="true" />
            <etwTracking profileName="Troubleshooting Tracking Profile" />
            <sqlWorkflowInstanceStore
```

```
        connectionStringName="ApplicationServerWorkflowInstanceStoreConnectionString"
        hostLockRenewalPeriod="00:00:30" runnableInstancesDetectionPeriod="00:00:05"
        instanceEncodingOption="None" instanceCompletionAction="DeleteAll"
        instanceLockedExceptionAction="NoRetry" />
          </behavior>
        </serviceBehaviors>
      </behaviors>
        <diagnostics etwProviderId="4678ca55-f9bd-4f5e-bb78-8da3ef40e6a8">
         <endToEndTracing propagateActivity="true" messageFlowTracing="true" />
        </diagnostics>
        <tracking>
            <profiles>
                <trackingProfile name="ClaimProfile">
                    <workflow>
                        <workflowInstanceQueries>
                            <workflowInstanceQuery />
                        </workflowInstanceQueries>
                        <activityStateQueries>
                            <activityStateQuery>
                                <states>
                                    <state name="Closed" />
                                </states>
                                <variables>
                                    <variable name="saveResponse" />
                                    <variable name="AppraisalEndpoint" />
                                </variables>
                            </activityStateQuery>
                        </activityStateQueries>
                    </workflow>
                </trackingProfile>
            </profiles>
        </tracking>
  </system.serviceModel>
  <system.webServer>
    <modules runAllManagedModulesForAllRequests="true" />
  </system.webServer>
    <microsoft.applicationServer>
        <monitoring>
            <default enabled="true"
            connectionStringName="ApplicationServerMonitoringConnectionString"
            monitoringLevel="Troubleshooting" />
        </monitoring>
    </microsoft.applicationServer>
</configuration>
```

Note that sometimes as you execute configuration settings for monitoring and persistence of your WF services, you may encounter two configuration warnings (as shown in Figure 8-21).

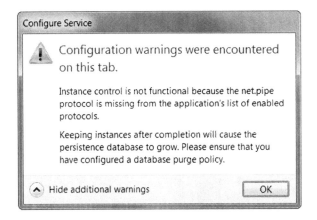

Figure 8-21. ***Workflow Persistence Configuration Warnings***

As the first warning message states, the workflow instance control is not functional until you enable the **net.pipe** protocol. The reason for this: AppFabric's Workflow Management Service (WMS) requires the **net.pipe** protocol to control the workflow instances.

Adding the net.pipe Protocol

The following steps show you how to add the **net.pipe** binding for the **Contoso.Claims.Services** Web site, as well as how to enable the **net.pipe** protocol for the **ProcessClaimService** workflow:

1. Start or switch to IIS Manager.

2. Expand the server node, expand **Sites**, and then click **Contoso.Claims.Services**.

3. From the **Actions** pane, click **Bindings** to open the **Site Bindings** dialog box (see Figure 8-22).

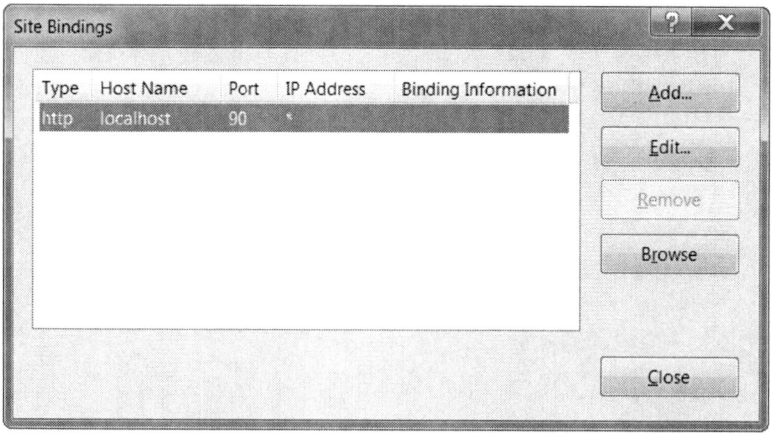

Figure 8-22. Site Bindings Dialog Box

4. Click **Add** to open the **Add Site Binding** dialog box, select the **net.pipe** type of binding from the dropdown list box, and enter ***** in the **Binding information** box, as shown in Figure 8-23.

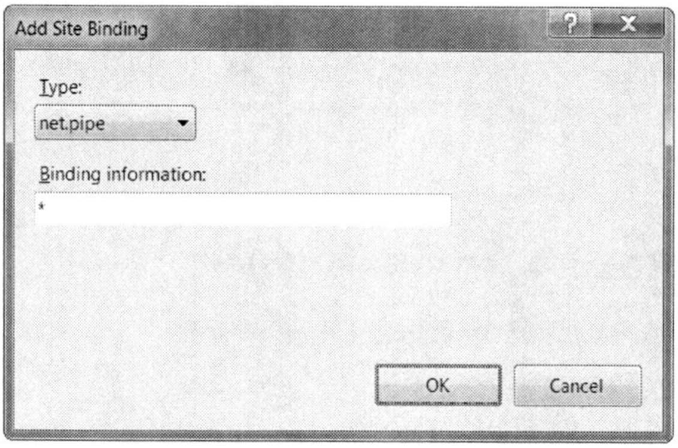

Figure 8-23. net.pipe Protocol Binding Values

■ **Note** Each protocol has associated protocol-specific configuration settings in the **Binding Information** attribute. The ***** specifies that all host names are valid.

5. Click **Close** to close the **Site Bindings** dialog box.

Enabling the net.pipe Protocol

You can follow these steps to enable the **net.pipe** protocol for the ProcessClaimService workflow:

1. Start or switch to IIS Manager.

2. Expand the server node, expand **Sites**, expand **Contoso.Claims.Services**, and then click **ProcessClaimService.WF**.

3. From the **Actions** pane, click **Advanced Settings** to open the **Advanced Settings** dialog box.

4. Enter **http,net.pipe** in the **Enabled Protocols** box, as shown in Figure 8-24.

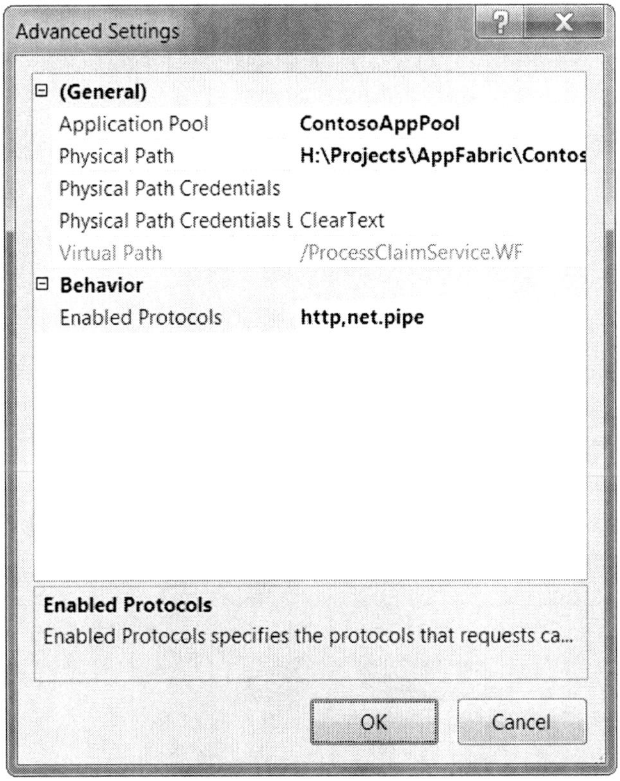

Figure 8-24. Enabling net.pipe Protocol Binding for the ProcessClaimService.WF Workflow

5. Click **OK** to close the **Advanced Settings** dialog box.

Running the Application in AppFabric

So far you have deployed and configured your Contoso Claims Processing application in AppFabric. The next step is to run it and validate that all your WCF and WF services are indeed hosted by AppFabric. You also want to make sure that the AppFabric Monitoring and Persistence services collect the health tracking information you have asked it to collect. Validating the Contoso Claims Processing application requires three steps:

1. Navigate to the AppFabric Dashboard.

2. Invoke the Contoso Claims WCF and WF services.

3. Monitor the Process Claims workflow instance.

Navigating to the AppFabric Dashboard

The AppFabric Management Services allow you to manage monitoring databases, set the monitoring level, and query and analyze tracked events. Using the AppFabric Dashboard, you can view selected metrics from the monitoring and persistence databases. The following steps will show you how to navigate to the AppFabric Dashboard to view the key performance counters and metrics:

1. Start or switch to IIS Manager.

2. Expand the server node, expand **Sites**, and then click **Contoso.Claims.Services**.

■ **Note** You deployed the Contoso Claims WCF and WF services to the **Contoso.Claims.Services** Web site earlier in the chapter. You choose the **Contoso.Claims.Services** scope because you deploy all the WCF and WF services to this Web site. You can also choose the server scope.

---

3. Double-click **Dashboard** in the **AppFabric** section. If you don't see the Dashboard, switch to the **Features View** from the bottom of the screen first (see Figure 8-25). After a few seconds, the screen will refresh, displaying the latest metrics for all WCF and WF services deployed in the **Contoso.Claims.Services** web site. The AppFabric Dashboard shows the WCF calls and WF Instance activities in the past 24 hours by default. The length of this time period is controlled by the **Time Period** drop-down list at the top of the Dashboard.

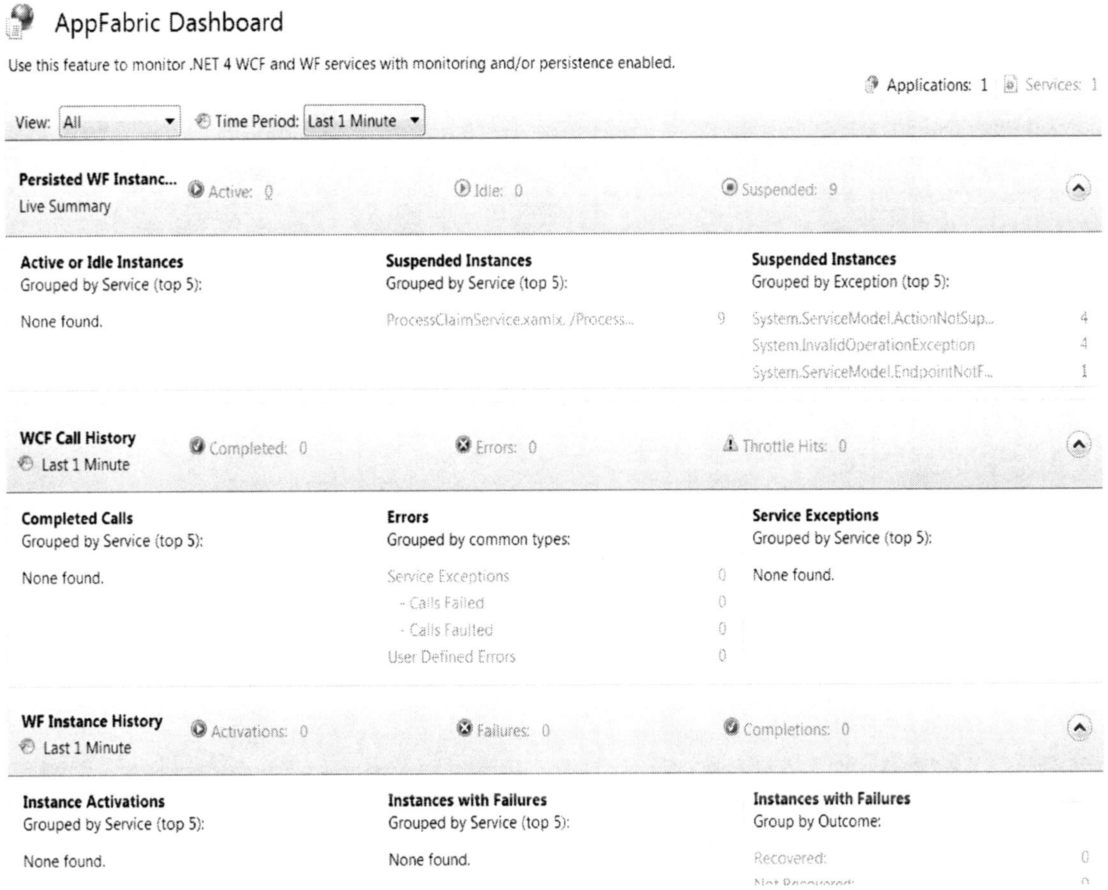

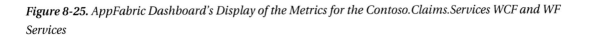

AppFabric Dashboard

Use this feature to monitor .NET 4 WCF and WF services with monitoring and/or persistence enabled.

Applications: 1 Services: 1

View: All ▼ Time Period: Last 1 Minute ▼

Persisted WF Instanc... Active: 0   Idle: 0   Suspended: 9 ▲
Live Summary

Active or Idle Instances Grouped by Service (top 5):	**Suspended Instances** Grouped by Service (top 5):	**Suspended Instances** Grouped by Exception (top 5):	
None found.	ProcessClaimService.xamlx, /Process... 9	System.ServiceModel.ActionNotSup...	4
		System.InvalidOperationException	4
		System.ServiceModel.EndpointNotF...	1

WCF Call History Completed: 0   Errors: 0   Throttle Hits: 0 ▲
Last 1 Minute

Completed Calls Grouped by Service (top 5):	**Errors** Grouped by common types:	**Service Exceptions** Grouped by Service (top 5):	
None found.	Service Exceptions 0	None found.	
	- Calls Failed 0		
	- Calls Faulted 0		
	User Defined Errors 0		

WF Instance History Activations: 0   Failures: 0   Completions: 0 ▲
Last 1 Minute

Instance Activations Grouped by Service (top 5):	**Instances with Failures** Grouped by Service (top 5):	**Instances with Failures** Group by Outcome:	
None found.	None found.	Recovered:	0
		Not Recovered:	0

Figure 8-25. AppFabric Dashboard's Display of the Metrics for the Contoso.Claims.Services WCF and WF Services

■ **Note** If you have not yet invoked any Contoso WCF or WF services, all counts in the dashboard should be zero.

4. Look at the **Persisted WF Instances** group (see Figure 8-26). This section shows the count of persisted workflow instances grouped by their status (see Table 8-10).

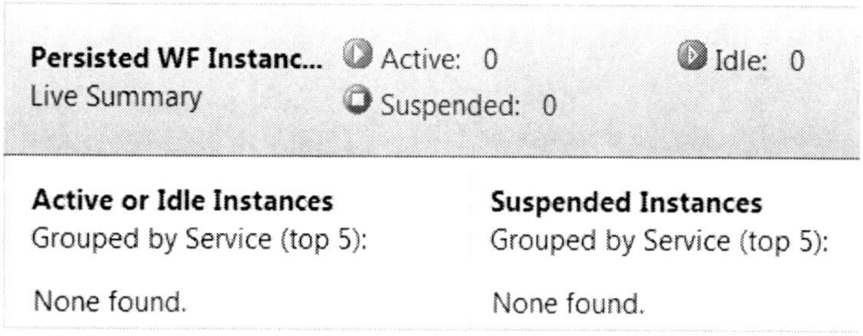

Persisted WF Instanc... ● Active: 0 ● Idle: 0
Live Summary ● Suspended: 0

Active or Idle Instances **Suspended Instances**
Grouped by Service (top 5): Grouped by Service (top 5):

None found. None found.

Figure 8-26. Persisted WF Instances Group

Table 8-10. Persisted WF States

State	Description
Active	A WF instance is *Active* when it is loaded in memory for work.
Idle	A WF instance is *Idle* when it is not yet complete but has no work to do and has been unloaded from memory.
Suspended	A WF instance is *Suspended* when its operation has been halted, either programmatically or by human intervention. The workflow instance can be resumed from the suspended state.

5. Look at the `WCF Call History` group (see Figure 8-27). This section shows the count of WCF calls received in the past 24 hours, grouped by the status of the call (see Table 8-11):

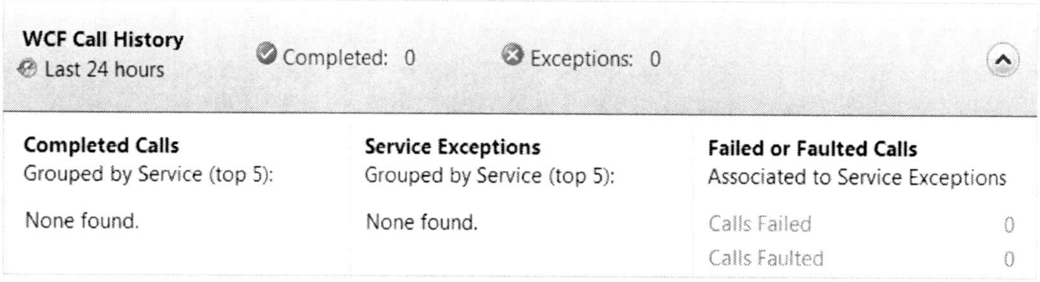

WCF Call History
● Last 24 hours ● Completed: 0 ● Exceptions: 0 ⌃

Completed Calls **Service Exceptions** **Failed or Faulted Calls**
Grouped by Service (top 5): Grouped by Service (top 5): Associated to Service Exceptions

None found. None found. Calls Failed 0
Calls Faulted 0

Figure 8-27. WCF Call History group

Table 8-11. WF Call Results

Status	Description
Completed	Most calls are *Completed*. This is the successful state for a WCF service call.
Failed	A call is *Failed* when a WCF service experiences an unhandled exception.
Faulted	A call is *Faulted* when a WCF service returns a fault.

6. Now look at the `WF Instance History` group (see Figure 8-28). This section shows the count of the tracked workflow instances, grouped by the instance activity (see Table 8-12).

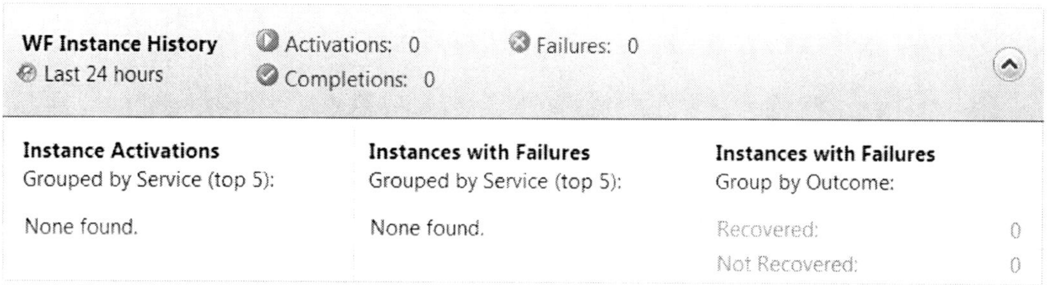

WF Instance History ◐ Activations: 0   ⊗ Failures: 0
🜂 Last 24 hours   ◉ Completions: 0   ⌃

Instance Activations Grouped by Service (top 5):	Instances with Failures Grouped by Service (top 5):	Instances with Failures Group by Outcome:	
None found.	None found.	Recovered:	0
		Not Recovered:	0

Figure 8-28. The WF Instance History Group

Table 8-12. Tracked WF Activities

Activity	Description
Activations	A WF instance is counted in the *Activations* section if it has been activated in the past 24 hours.
Failures	A WF instance is counted in the *Failures* section if it has experienced a failure in the past 24 hours.
Completions	An instance is counted in the *Completions* section if it has completed in the past 24 hours.

Invoking the Contoso Claims WCF and WF Services

The next step is to validate that you have successfully deployed and hosted the Contoso Claims application into the local AppFabric. Begin this process by launching the front-end Contoso Claims ASP.NET Web application and then start a new claim processing workflow. The Contoso Claims Web application invokes three WCF services (**Appraisal**, **Billing**, and **CarRental**) and one WF service (**ProcessClaim**). The following steps show you how to process a new pending car insurance claim in the Contoso Claims Web application:

1. Open Internet Explorer, and browse to this location: **http://localhost:89/Claims.Web**. This opens the Contoso Claims Processing Web application's default home page.

2. Click **The Claims Queue** hyperlink to be redirected to the page containing the list of all pending and completed (if any) claims. After you click **The Claims Queue** hyperlink, the ASP.NET page makes a request to the AppraisalService.WCF service, which queries the ContosoDb database and brings back the list of pending and completed claims, with a summary for each claim.

3. From the list of **Pending Claims,** pick up any pending claim and click the **date @ time** hyperlink to get all the claim's details, including the location of the accident shown on the Bing Map image at the right side of the page. You obtain this detailed information about the claim using a call to the **AppraisalService**.WCF service.

4. Now click **Edit Claim** hyperlink at the bottom of the page to open the claim for editing. Now take note of the current **Status** value (**Pending**)_and the value (empty) for the **RentalCar** property.

■ **Note** When you try to enter the editing mode on the **Claim's Details** page, you might be presented with a **Log On** page. You need to enter the proper username (**Reader**) and password (**pass@word1**) before the site will grant you the authorization to edit the claim.

---

5. Change the default text for **Description** from **New Claim** to some other text, and then click the **Process Claim** button. After you click the **Process Claim** button, the ASP.NET page makes a request to the **ProcessClaimService.WF** workflow service. A new workflow instance is created to manage this request. The workflow service validates the claim, invokes the, simulating the reservation of the rental car. Next, the **CarRentalService** WCF service invokes the **BillingService** WCF service and obtains the result. If the returned result is **Complete**, then **CarRentalService** invokes the **AppraisalService** WCF service to save the claim into **ContosoDb** database. At the end of this process, the workflow engine persists the workflow instance into the persistence database.

6. Switch to the IIS Manager window.

7. From the **Actions** pane on the right, click **Refresh**, and compare the new Dashboard (see Figure 8-29) to the one you saw earlier.

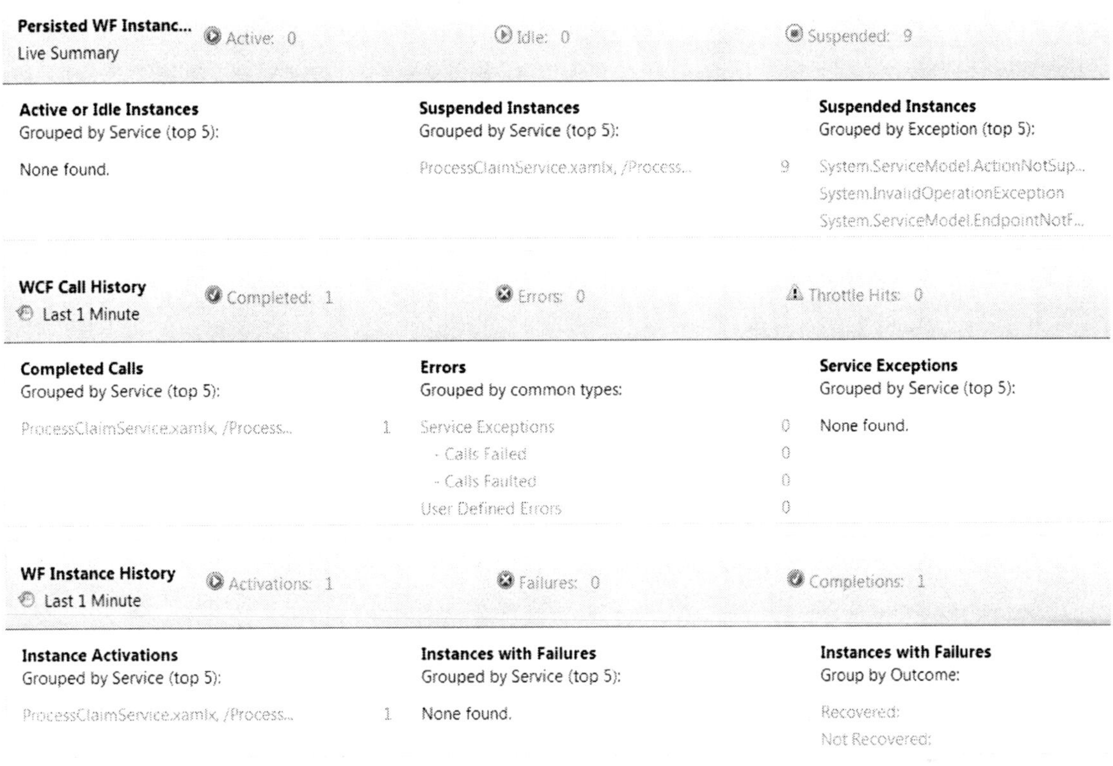

Persisted WF Instanc... Live Summary	Active: 0	Idle: 0	Suspended: 9
Active or Idle Instances Grouped by Service (top 5):	**Suspended Instances** Grouped by Service (top 5):		**Suspended Instances** Grouped by Exception (top 5):
None found.	ProcessClaimService.xamlx, /Process...		9 System.ServiceModel.ActionNotSup... System.InvalidOperationException System.ServiceModel.EndpointNotF...

WCF Call History Last 1 Minute	Completed: 1	Errors: 0	Throttle Hits: 0
Completed Calls Grouped by Service (top 5):	**Errors** Grouped by common types:		**Service Exceptions** Grouped by Service (top 5):
ProcessClaimService.xamlx, /Process...	1 Service Exceptions - Calls Failed - Calls Faulted User Defined Errors	0 0 0 0	None found.

WF Instance History Last 1 Minute	Activations: 1	Failures: 0	Completions: 1
Instance Activations Grouped by Service (top 5):	**Instances with Failures** Grouped by Service (top 5):		**Instances with Failures** Group by Outcome:
ProcessClaimService.xamlx, /Process...	1 None found.		Recovered: Not Recovered:

Figure 8-29. AppFabric Dashboard AfterProcessing the Claim

■ **Note** AppFabric uses an import job that periodically runs to process monitoring data. If you don't see the changes, wait another 10 seconds and then refresh the Dashboard again. If your AppFabric Dashboard continues to show zeroes in all counters, you might need to check that both the **Application Server Event Collector** and **Windows Event Collector** Windows Services are up and running. Also, if you use Microsoft SQL Server and not SQL Express, make sure that the **SQL Agent** service is up and running.

By default, the workflow engine persists a workflow instance after the workflow instance has been activated for one minute. You can see that the workflow instance for the **ProcessClaimService** workflow has been activated once as it is shown in the **WF Instance History** window.

Now, click the **Tracked Events** menu item from the Actions section on the IIS panel. After query is ran, you should be able to review the list of all tracked events occurred during the workflow instance activity (see Figure 8-30).

Level	Event Type	Emit Time	WF Activity Name
Informati...	ActivityStateRecord	3/9/2010 1:10:23.578 AM	Find Rental Car
Informati...	ActivityScheduledRecord	3/9/2010 1:10:23.578 AM	Rental Car
Informati...	ActivityScheduledRecord	3/9/2010 1:10:23.580 AM	Process Claim
Informati...	ActivityStateRecord	3/9/2010 1:10:23.580 AM	If Not Valid
Informati...	ActivityStateRecord	3/9/2010 1:10:23.580 AM	Assign
Informati...	ActivityStateRecord	3/9/2010 1:10:23.580 AM	Assign
Informati...	ActivityStateRecord	3/9/2010 1:10:23.580 AM	Rental Car
Informati...	ActivityStateRecord	3/9/2010 1:10:23.582 AM	Process Billing
Informati...	MessageSentByTransport	3/9/2010 1:10:23.585 AM	
Informati...	MessageSentToTransport	3/9/2010 1:10:23.585 AM	
Informati...	ClientOperationPrepared	3/9/2010 1:10:23.585 AM	

Figure 8-30. Tracked Events

Configuring the AppFabric Host for Troubleshooting

To make sure you get the information you need for troubleshooting, you must configure monitoring and persistence for the workflow service.

AppFabric defines five monitoring levels. The top level is called **Troubleshooting**. Typically, you don't want to use this level because it slows down the overall server performance. However, for purposes of troubleshooting the workflow service, you want to enable it, so you can get enough information to identify the problem.

You can configure the monitoring level to the web site scope or the web application scope. The web application inherits the web site configurations unless you set the properties explicitly. The authors of this book recommend that you generally configure the monitoring level to the web application scope; this will help you minimize the impact on performance.

Enabling the Troubleshooting Tracking Level

This section will show you how to enable the Troubleshooting tracking level in AppFabric. You'll use the Contoso Claims application's `ProcessClaimService` workflow, for which you'll increase the event tracking level from `Health Monitoring` to `Troubleshooting Monitoring`:

1. Start or switch to the IIS Manager window.

2. Expand the server node, expand `Sites`, expand `Contoso.Claims.Services`, and then click `ProcessClaimService.WF` to select it.

3. From the `Actions` pane, click `Configure` to open the `Configure WF and WCF for Site` dialog box.

4. In the left pane, click `Monitoring`.

5. In the details pane, drag the `Level` slider to the top (or `Troubleshooting`), as shown in Figure 8-31.

6. Click `OK` to close the dialog box.

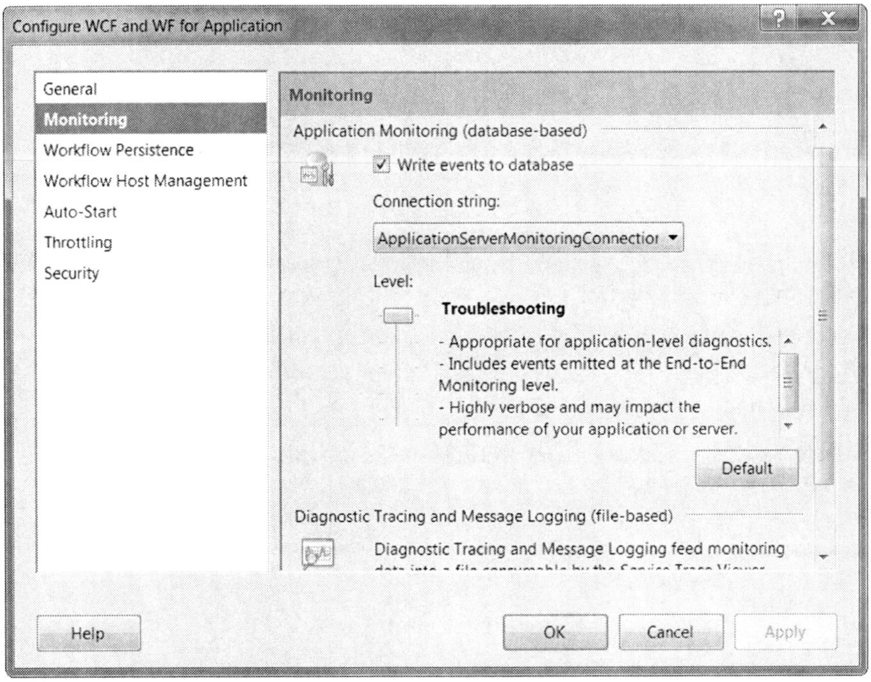

Figure 8-31. Configuring AppFabric for Troubleshooting

203

You can also configure how AppFabric reacts to unhandled exceptions. The default setting is
Abandon. Table 8-13 shows the list of possible actions.

Table 8-13. Acting on Unhandled Unexceptions

Possible Action	Description
Abandon	The workflow engine aborts the workflow instance and unloads it from memory. The status of the workflow instance remains unchanged, and the Workflow Management Service will retry the instance based on the settings in the `WorkflowManagementService.exe.config` file.
AbandonAndSuspend	The workflow engine aborts the workflow instance and unloads it from memory. The status of the workflow instance status is changed to **suspended**. Users can resume the workflow instance manually.
Terminate	The workflow engine aborts the workflow instance and unloads it from memory. The workflow instance status is changed to `Completed (Terminated)`.
Cancel	The workflow engine invokes any cancellation handlers that are defined in the workflow.

Configuring the Action for an Unhandled Exception

Follow these steps to configure the desired action when an application hosted in AppFabric throws an
unhandled exception:

1. Start or switch to the IIS Manager window.

2. Expand the server node, expand `Sites`, expand `Contoso.Claims.Services`, and then
   click `ProcessClaimService.WF` to select it.

3. From the `Actions` pane, click `Configure` to open the `Configure WF` and `WCF for Site`
   dialog box.

4. In the left pane, click `Workflow Host Management`.

5. In the `Workflow Host Management` section, select the desired action on an
   unhandled exception (see Figure 8-32).

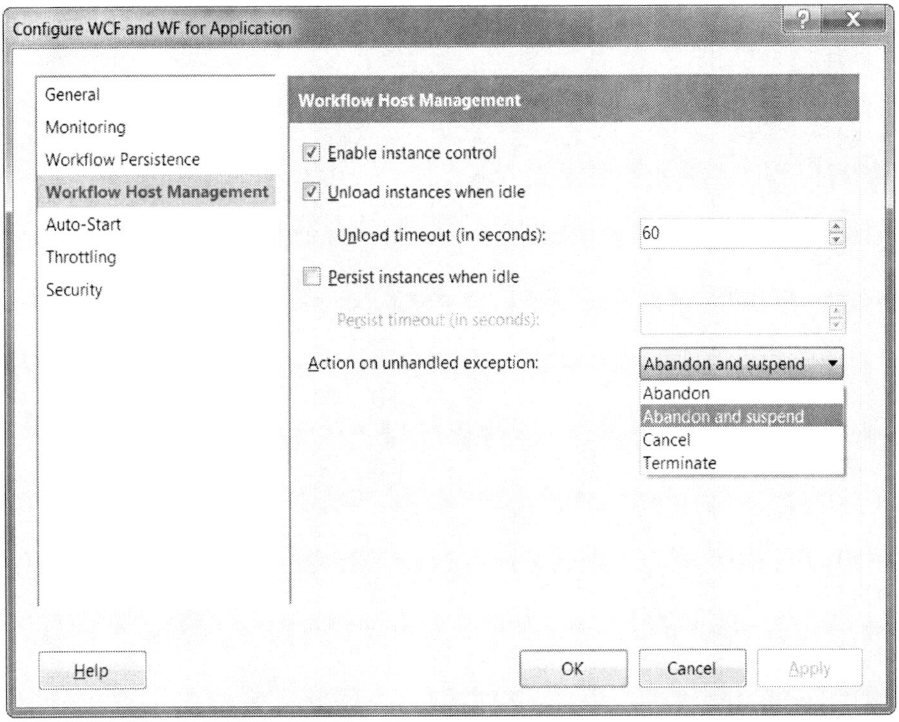

Figure 8-32. *Configuring an Action on an Unhandled Exception*

Summary

The .NET Framework 4.0 makes it simple to develop long-running services. But once you finish developing the service, you need to address several questions around its life cycle:

- How do you deliver the application for testing?
- How do you deploy the application to production?
- How does the operations team monitor the health of the application?
- How does the application scale to handle demand?

AppFabric takes up where the .NET Framework leaves off and provides the server experience for middle-tier applications, including WCF and WF applications. AppFabric leverages the Windows Process Activation (WAS) service as a host for WCF and WF services. AppFabric also extends the IIS Manager Management interface. These extensions expose WCF and WF capabilities (service configuration, monitoring, and instance management) in a familiar, centralized management tool.

Using a sample Contoso Claims Processing service scenario, which we use throughout this book, this chapter guided you through how to host applications in AppFabric, including how to deploy, configure, monitor, and troubleshoot your WCF and WF services.

■ ■ ■

CHAPTER 9

Deploying AppFabric Applications

So far you've built your application and hosted it in AppFabric; next, you need to deploy it to the AppFabric instances in your other environments. You do this in AppFabric by leveraging the Web Deployment Tool functionality in IIS 7 with `msdeploy.exe`.

Understanding the Tool

The Web Deployment Tool (this, combined with AppFabric's functionality, will be referred to as the AppFabric Deployment Tool) can move artifacts into and out of the web server. It can also perform synchronization of content across web servers and replicate content with fine-grained control at a server content scope, as well as at a site or application scope. You can accomplish this using either of two models: push or pull.

When discussing deployment with AppFabric, the deployment scope is always the application. However, the boundary of the application can be a bit ambiguous. The application, and therefore the deployment package, can encompass all of the AppFabric artifacts for an entire machine, web site, or an individual application contained in a site. For this reason, this chapter will refer to all the artifacts you deploy (whether importing or exporting them), no matter the scope, as an *application package*. This use of application package is consistent with Microsoft's documentation, as well.

■ **Note** An application package can contain the artifacts for either an application under a specific part of a web site, a whole web site, or all the web sites on the server.

What You Get

Let's begin by taking a closer look at what AppFabric provides with its deployment functionality. Then you will dive more deeply into the underlying technology of the Web Deployment Tool.

The AppFabric Deployment Tool provides the ability to export or import an application:

Export an application: This allows you to package the artifacts and move the application from one AppFabric server to another. You can accomplish this using the Manage Packages option in the IIS Manager. You can also accomplish this by selecting Project Menu ➤ Create Package in Visual Studio 2010. When you package the artifacts, the deployment tool creates a package that contains all configuration data including configuration data, registry settings, associated web content, scripts, and SQL Server database scripts. The package will contain all of the information and artifacts

207

required to run the application on another server running AppFabric. AppFabric also provides support for server farms by letting you first export the application and then import it on all the servers in a load balanced farm.

Import an application: This allows you to import a package that has been exported from an AppFabric server by selecting Manage packages ➤ Import Application. It also allows you to import a package created from Visual Studio 2010 that has not been previously imported.

■ **Note** It should go without saying, but you should back up your system and its configuration before importing an application.

The Underlying Foundation

Now that you know what you can do, it's time to take a deeper look into the underlying technology. The Web Deployment Tool ships with IIS 7 and provides additional functionality beyond what you need in AppFabric. You can use the Web Deployment Tool to synchronize web servers, migrate IIS6 servers to IIS7, and deploy ASP.NET and PHP applications.

The Web Deployment Tool integrates with both the IIS7 Manager and Visual Studio 2010 to create packages and deploy them either locally or remotely. This provides the same experience for both developers and administrators, as well as the same process for deployment whether you're targeting a local server or a set of remote servers. You can also perform these tasks using PowerShell cmdlets or through the command line.

■ **Note** The Web Deployment Tool does not utilize the Microsoft Sync Framework. The Microsoft Sync Framework was created to implement the multimaster sync pattern; however, AppFabric utilizes a single-master system, so it relies on a different tool to implement this functionality.

Exporting an Application

To export an application, you begin by starting Internet Information Services (IIS) Manager. You can start IIS Manager in one of two ways. First, you can click **Start**, point to **Programs**, then `ApplicationServer Extensions` for .NET, and finally, select Internet Information Services (IIS) Manager. Second, you can click Start, then Run, and finally, type this: `inetmgr`.

Once you load the IIS Manager, select the item (scope) that you wish to deploy. If you want to deploy your application to all your sites, then start at the sites scope; if you want to deploy a single application, then start at the scope of that specific application. In the **Actions** pane on the right-hand side, click `Export Application` (see Figure 9-1). This launches the `Export Application Package` wizard.

■ **Note** You can also right-click an application, and then select `Deploy` ➤ `Export Application` to launch the wizard (see Figure 9-1).

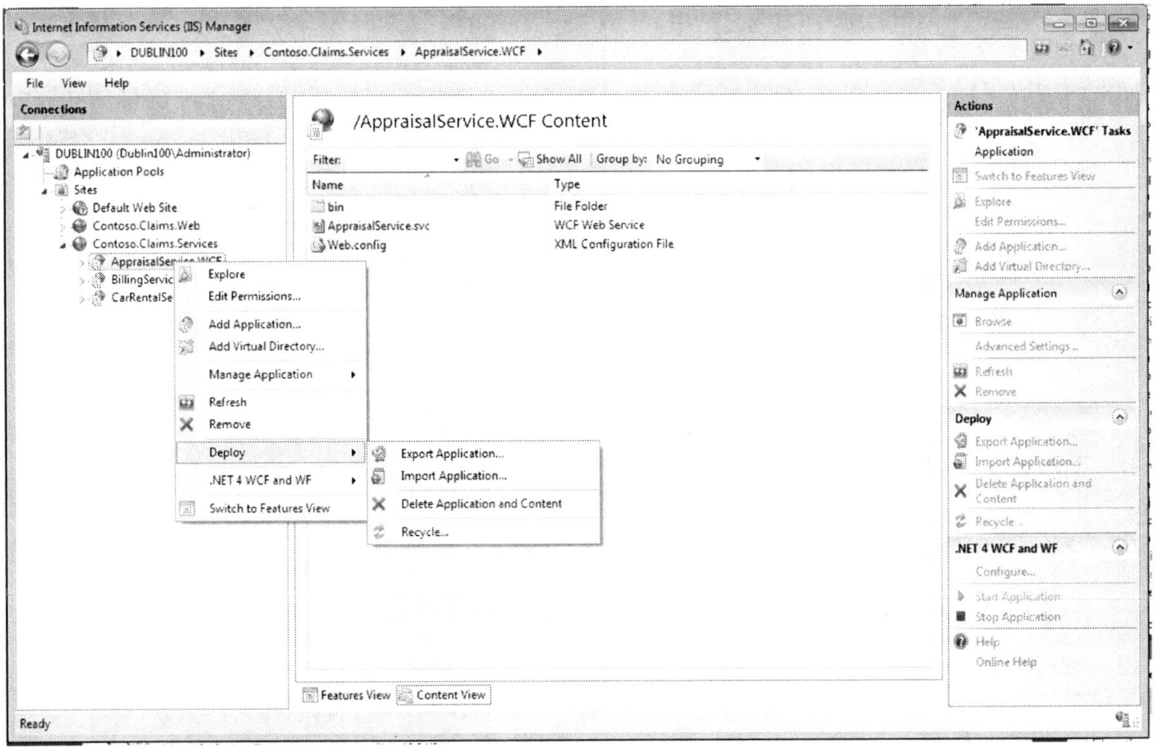

Figure 9-1. Export Application

When the wizard appears (see Figure 9-2), its package contains the scope (site, application, and so on) that you have selected, along with its content folders. If you see items that you don't want included in the package, then uncheck the associated checkbox. However, make sure that the **Create an application** checkbox is selected.

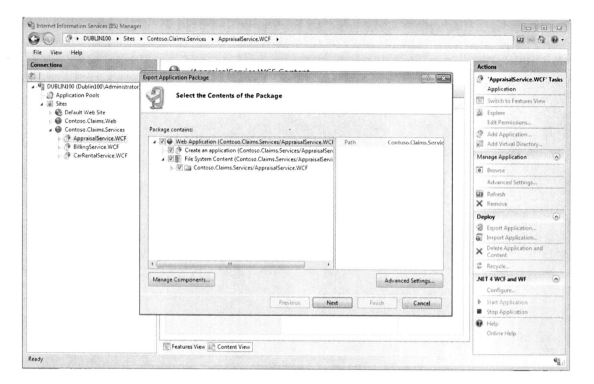

Figure 9-2. Export Package Wizard

Click the **Manage Components** button to bring up the **Manage Components** dialog box. The first row shows the **iisApp** provider entry, which represents your application. You will add an additional provider that will point to your database. In the second row, select the **dbFullSql** item. Make sure that you take a moment to look at the other options available; hovering over any of these items brings up a description and an example (see Figure 9-3).

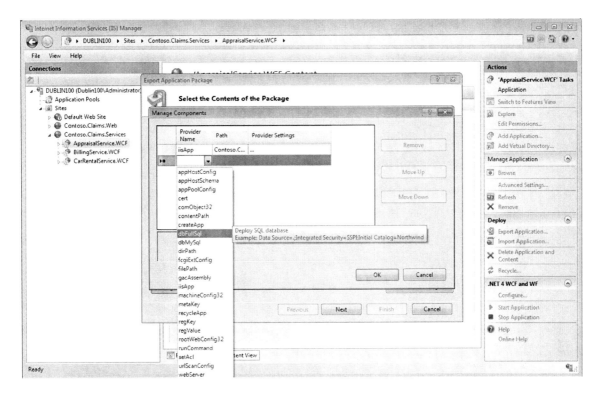

Figure 9-3. Export Package Wizard-Manage Components

Select the **dbFullSql** provider and enter the database connection string in the **Path** field. Once the validation occurs, hit the **OK** button. This brings up the database entry that you can see in the Package in Figure 9-4. Click **Next** to continue.

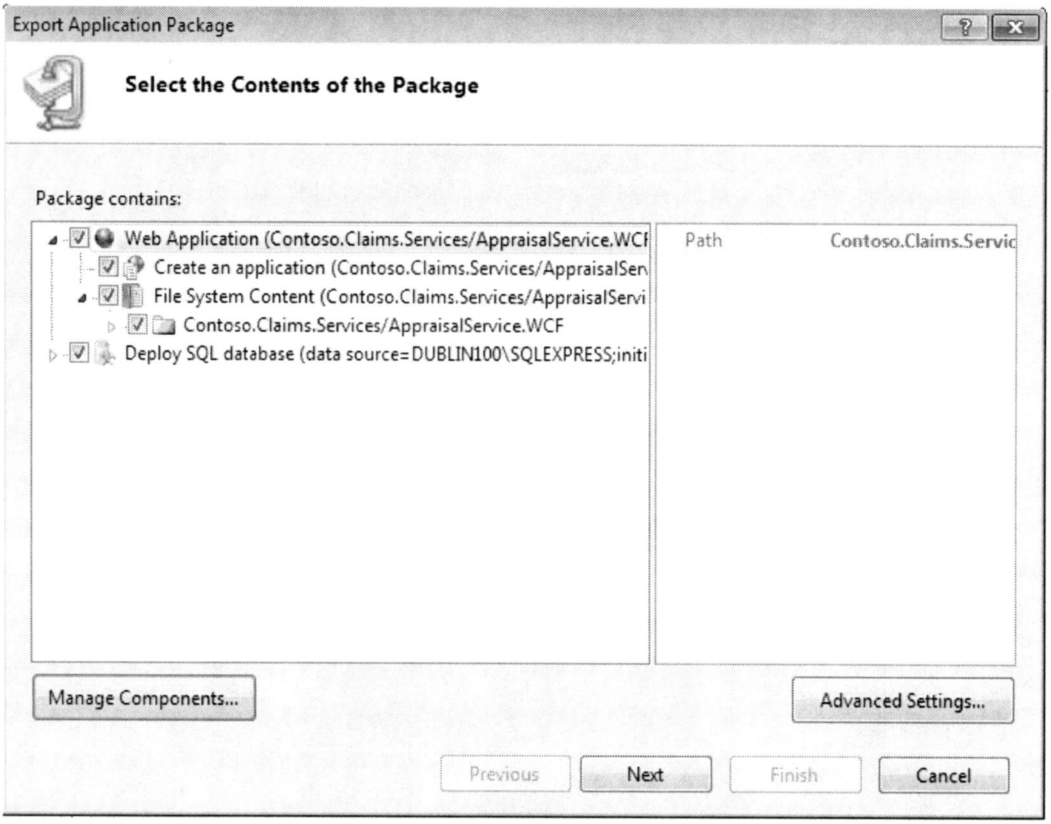

Figure 9-4. Export Package Wizard—Export Application Package Dialog

This brings up a list of parameters that have been generated for the two providers that you included in the **Manage Components** dialog. **Parameter1** and **Parameter2** aren't the friendliest names, so let's give them better names. Select the second parameter and click the **Add Parameter Entry** button (see Figure 9-5).

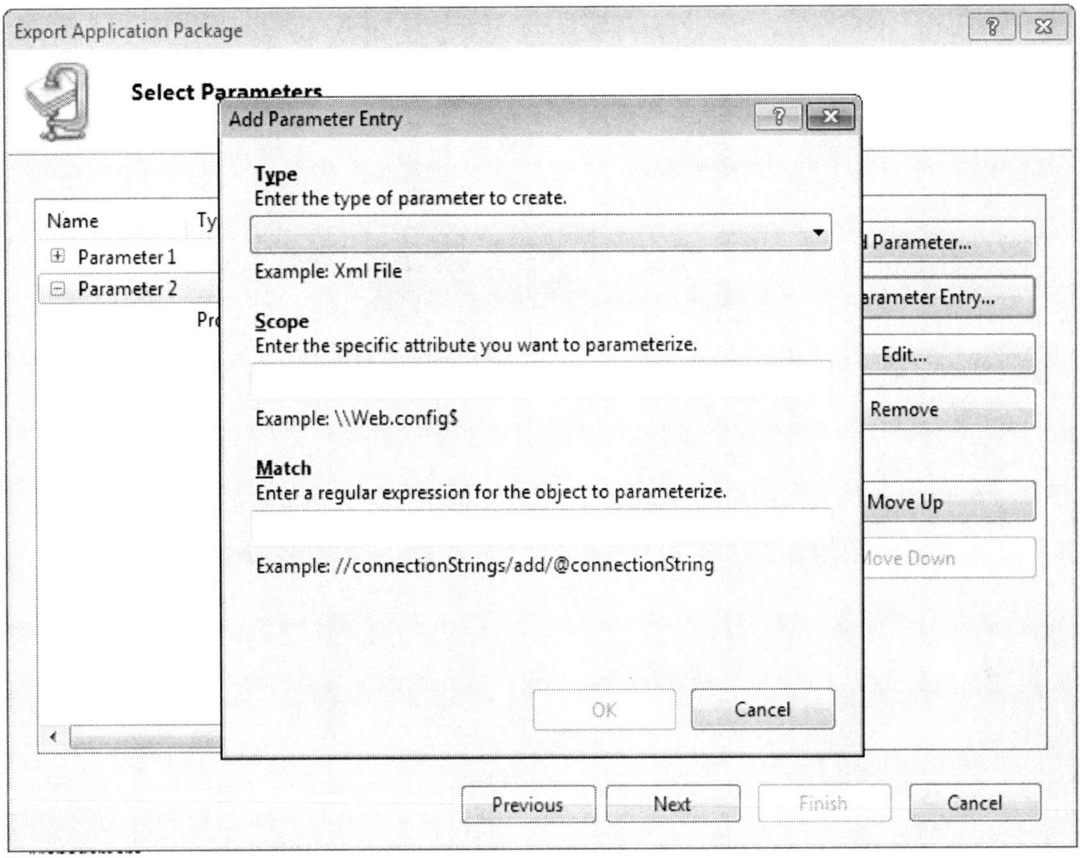

Figure 9-5. Export Package Wizard—Add Parameter Entry Dialog

You also need to modify the parameter so that it points to a connection string contained in the application's **web.config** file. In the **Type** dropdown select **Xml file**. As you did before, take a moment to observe all the available options. In the **Scope** text box, enter this: **\\Web.config$**. The **\\** designates the start of the file, and the **$** designates the end of the file name. You add the **$** so that **Web.config.bak** won't be included in any updates.

Finally, you need to enter an xpath expression in the **Match** text box to point to the element in the **web.config** XML document. In the **Match** text box, enter this path: **//connectionStrings/add/@connectionString**. This allows the connection string to be updated in two places: when running the SQL script and in the deployed **web.config** file. Click **OK** to return to the wizard.

While still highlighting the **Parameter2** entry, click the **Edit** button to bring up the **Edit Parameters dialog** (see Figure 9-6).

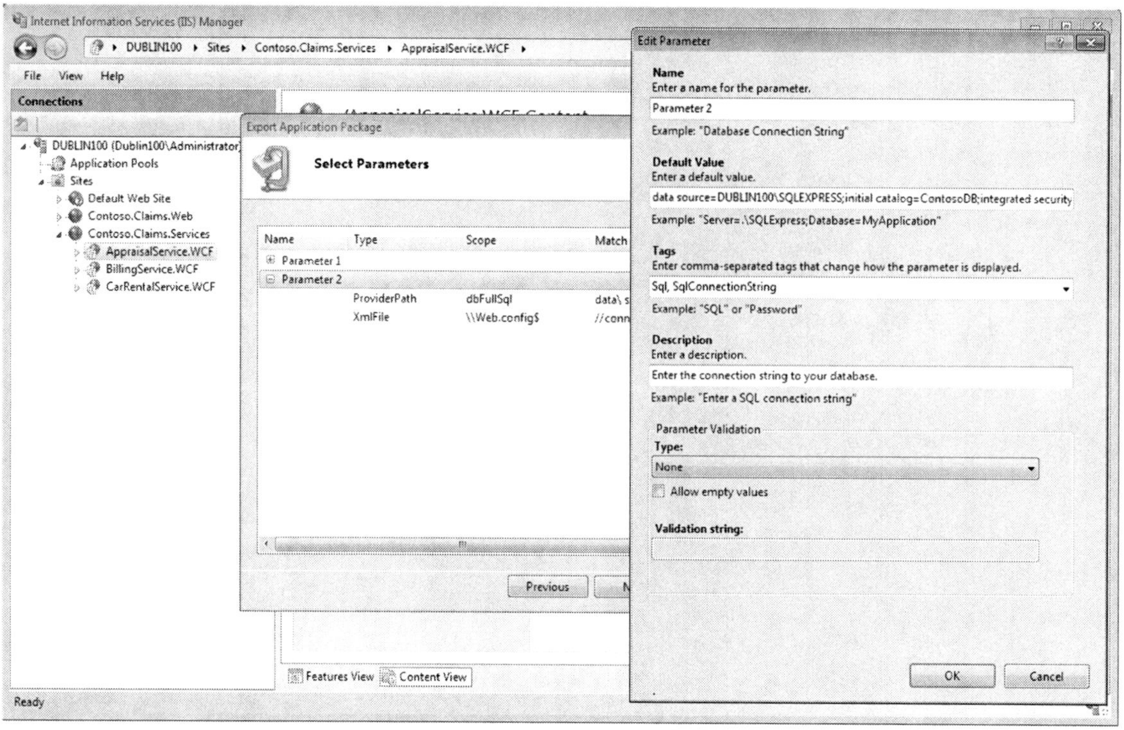

*Figure 9-6. **Export Package Wizard—Select ParametersDialog***

The dialog shown in Figure 9-6 lets you edit the name of the parameter to give it a friendlier name. You can also provide a different description. Let's rename the **Parameter2** to this: **Database Connection String**. You can also rename the **Parameter1** if you wish. Remember that **Parameter1** represents the application name.

At this point, you can click **Next** to bring up the **Save Package** page of the wizard. Select a location and a name for the **.zip** file, then click **Next**. You've now completed the wizard and created a package. You can now copy this package and import it into either another server in the farm or into another server in the next environment.

Importing an Application

To import an application, start up Internet Information Services (IIS) Manager. Remember, you can open this in one of two ways. You can click **Start**, point to **Programs**, point to **ApplicationServer Extensions** for .NET, and finally, select **Internet Information Services (IIS) Manager**. Or, you can click **Start**, select **Run**, and type this: **inetmgr**.

Once IIS Manager loads, you can expand the **Server** node, expand the **Sites** node, and then select **Default Web Site**. In the **Actions** pane on the right-hand side, click **Import Application** (see Figure 9-7). This launches the **Import Application Package** wizard.

■ **Note** You can also right-click `Default Web Site` and select `Deploy` ➤ `Import Application` to launch the wizard (see Figure 9-7).

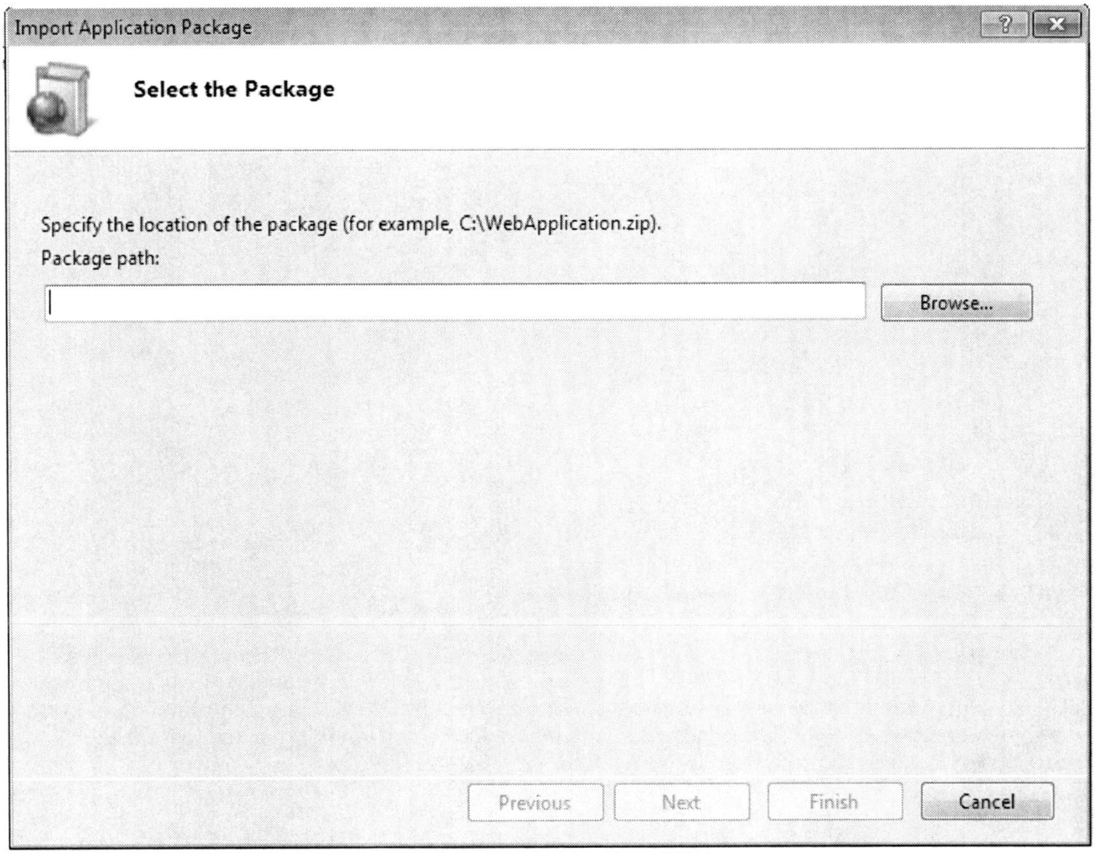

Figure 9-7. Import Package Wizard

Now select the `.zip` package you created through the export process. When the **Select the Contents of the Package** dialog appears, you will see the application, any file contents, and the name of the database. If you see parts that you do not wish to install, then uncheck the checkbox alongside the entry in the tree node. When you click **Next**, the **Enter Application Package Information** dialog appears (see Figure 9-8). In this dialog, you will be able to enter a new application name (if you wish), as well as a SQL connection string.

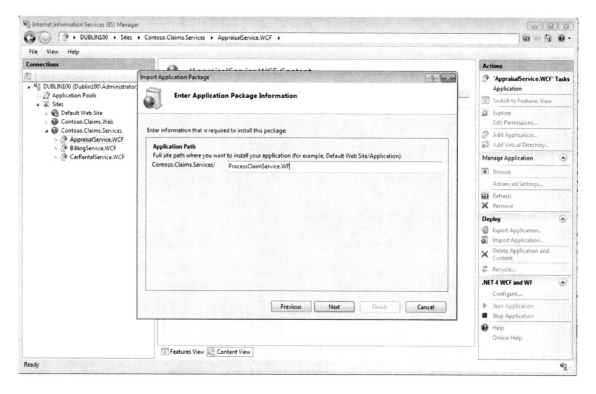

Figure 9-8. Import Package Wizard—Package Information

When you click **Next**, one of two things will happen, depending on whether the application already exists or you're importing a new application. If you're importing an application that already exists, you will be presented with two options: the first option is to append the files to the existing application, and the second option is to delete all the extra files and folders on the destination that are not in the application package. You can see the overwrite option at work in Figure 9-9.

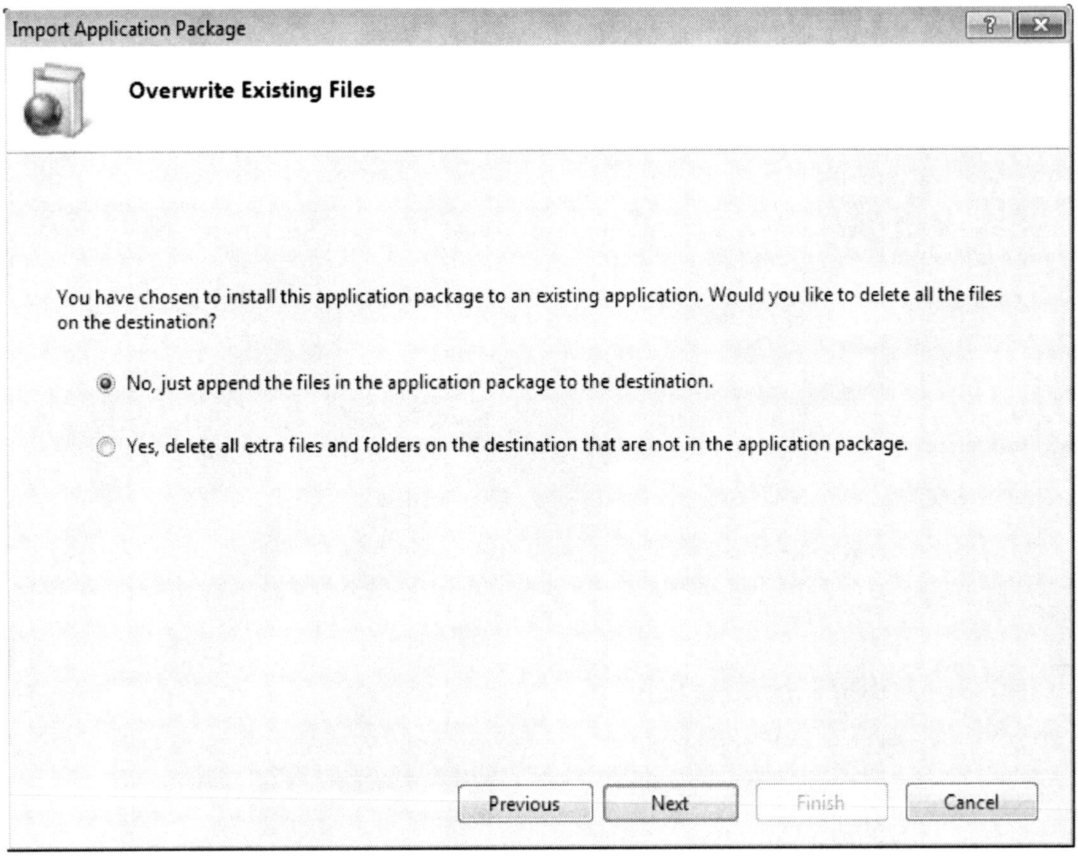

Figure 9-9. Overwrite Existing Files

If you're importing a new application, then the installation will take place, and you will be presented with a summary of the actions taken, as well as a tab that shows the details of what occurred.

■ **Note** The imported application will utilize the application pool of the site that you deploy the application to. If you need to, you can change the application pool to any application pool running under .NET 4.0 once you import the application.

Click **Finish** to end the import process.

Managing and Deploying with PowerShell

PowerShell 2.0 is now available, and it includes a number of improvements and added functionality. As you look at how to use PowerShell with AppFabric, you will want to take advantage of this new version. One of its new features is its Integrated Scripting Environment (ISE). This is a hosting application for PowerShell, and it provides an environment where you can run commands, as well as write, test, and debug scripts. To run the ISE, click **Start ➤ All Programs ➤ Windows PowerShell V2**, and then click **Windows PowerShell ISE** or enter this either at the Visual Studio Command Prompt or in the PowerShell console window: `powershell_ise.exe`.

Enable Execution

Before you start creating and running scripts, you need to enable execution of scripts and change the execution policy from the default of **Restricted** to **RemoteSigned**. To do this, type in the following command in the bottom window, at the > prompt in the ISE:

```
Set-ExecutionPolicy -ExecutionPolicy RemoteSigned –Scope Process
```

When the Execution Policy Change dialog appears, click the **Yes** button. To verify that the setting was changed, or to see what the ExecutionPolicy is set to, type this in: **Get-ExecutionPolicy**. You should see that it now says **RemoteSigned**.

Review Available Commands

At this point, you can run scripts without getting permissions errors. Now let's look at what commands are available. Back in the ISE, type in this: **Import-Module ApplicationServer**. This imports the AppFabric module. Now type this line into the ISE:

```
Get-Command –module ApplicationServer.
```

This provides a list of the available AppFabric cmdlets:

```
Clear-ASAppAnalyticTracing
Clear-ASAppServiceCertificate
Clear-ASAppServicePersistence
Clear-ASAppServiceThrottling
Clear-ASAppServiceTracking
Clear-ASInstanceExceptionPolicy
Clear-ASInstanceUnloadPolicy
Clear-ASMonitoringDatabase
Disable-ASAppDebugTracing
Disable-ASAppMessageLogging
Disable-ASAppServiceAutoStart
Enable-ASAppDebugTracing
Enable-ASAppMessageLogging
Enable-ASAppServiceAutoStart
Get-ASAppAnalyticTracing
Get-ASAppDebugTracing
```

```
Get-ASApplication
Get-ASAppMessageLogging
Get-ASAppMonitoring
Get-ASAppPerformanceCounter
Get-ASAppService
Get-ASAppServiceAutoStart
Get-ASAppServiceBehaviorName
Get-ASAppServiceCertificate
Get-ASAppServiceEndpoint
Get-ASAppServiceEndpointAuthentication
Get-ASAppServiceEndpointTransportQuota
Get-ASAppServiceInstance
Get-ASAppServicePersistence
Get-ASAppServiceThrottling
Get-ASAppServiceTracking
Get-ASAppServiceTrackingProfile
Get-ASInstanceExceptionPolicy
Get-ASInstanceUnloadPolicy
Get-ASMonitoringDatabaseArchiveConfiguration
Import-ASAppServiceTrackingProfile
Initialize-ASMonitoringDatabase
Initialize-ASPersistenceDatabase
Remove-ASAppServiceInstance
Remove-ASAppServiceTrackingProfile
Remove-ASMonitoringDatabase
Remove-ASMonitoringDatabaseArchiveConfiguration
Remove-ASPersistenceDatabase
Resume-ASAppServiceInstance
Set-ASAppAnalyticTracing
Set-ASAppDebugTracing
Set-ASApplication
Set-ASAppMessageLogging
Set-ASAppMonitoring
Set-ASAppPerformanceCounter
Set-ASAppServiceBehaviorName
Set-ASAppServiceCertificate
Set-ASAppServiceEndpoint
Set-ASAppServiceEndpointTransportQuota
Set-ASAppServicePersistence
Set-ASAppServiceThrottling
Set-ASAppServiceTracking
Set-ASInstanceExceptionPolicy
Set-ASInstanceUnloadPolicy
Set-ASMonitoringDatabaseArchiveConfiguration
Start-ASApplication
Start-ASAppMonitoring
Stop-ASApplication
Stop-ASAppMonitoring
Stop-ASAppServiceInstance
Suspend-ASAppServiceInstance
```

Learn to Pipe

The AppFabric PowerShell cmdlets support *cmdlet piping*. Cmdlet piping allows you to combine cmdlets and chain their functionality together, so that the object returned by the first cmdlet becomes the input for the next cmdlet in the chain. You use the pipe character (|) to do this.

Table 9-1 shows the AppFabric cmdlets that you can pipe together. The column headings refer to producers and consumers. A *producer* is a cmdlet that generates output that you might want to pipe into another cmdlet as input. The other cmdlet becomes the *consumer*.

Note that only certain combinations of consumer and producer are possible. The reason for that boils down to the specific datatypes produced and consumed. You cannot pipe data to a consumer that is of some other type than what that consumer is designed to accept.

Table 9-1 shows possible producers in the leftmost column. The data type of the result for each producer is shown beneath the producer's name. The table lists compatible consumers in the right-hand column.

Table 9-1. Valid cmdlet producer / consumer combinations

Cmdlet Producer / Output Data Type	Cmdlet Consumer

`Get-ASApplication`
`ApplicationInfo`
	Common with `ServiceInfo`:
	`Get-ASInstanceUnloadPolicy`
	`Set-ASInstanceUnloadPolicy`
	`Get-ASAppServicePersistence`
	`Set-ASAppServicePersistence`
	`Get-ASInstanceExceptionPolicy`
	`Get-ASAppServiceTracking` Profile
	`Get-ASAppServiceTracking`
	`Import-ASAppServiceTrackingProfile`
	`Remove-ASAppServiceTracking` Profile
	`Get-ASAppServiceCertificate`
	`Set-ASAppServiceCertificate`
	`Get-ASAppServiceThrottling`
	`Set-ASAppServiceThrottling`
	Only `ApplicationInfo`:
	`Enable-ASAppDebugTracing`
	`Disable-ASAppDebugTracing`
	`Get-ASAppDebugTracing`
	`Set-ASAppDebugTracing`

	Get-ASApplication
	Enable-ASAppMessageLogging
	Disable-ASAppMessageLogging
	Get-ASAppMessageLogging
	Set-ASAppMessageLogging
	Get-ASAppPerformanceCounter
	Set-ASAppPerformanceCounter
	Get-ASAppService

Get-ASAppService
ServiceInfo
	Common with ApplicationInfo:
	Get-ASInstanceUnloadPolicy
	Set-ASInstanceUnloadPolicy
	Get-ASAppServicePersistence
	Set-ASAppServicePersistence
	Get-ASInstanceExceptionPolicy
	
	    Get-ASAppServiceTrackingProfile
	    Import-ASAppServiceTrackingProfile
	    Remove-ASAppServiceTrackingProfile
	    Get-ASAppServiceCertificate
	    Set-ASAppServiceCertificate
	    Get-ASAppServiceThrottling
	    Set-ASAppServiceThrottling
	
	Only ServiceInfo:
	    Enable-ASAppServiceAutoStart
	    Disable-ASAppServiceAutoStart
	    Get-ASAppServiceAutoStart
	    Get-ASAppServiceTracking
	    Get-ASAppServiceEndpoint
	    Set-ASAppServiceEndpoint

	Get-ASAppServiceEndpointAuthentication
	Get-ASAppServiceEndpointTransportQuota
	Set-ASAppServiceEndpointTransportQuota
	Get-ASAppServiceInstance
Get-ASAppServiceEndpoint ServiceEndpointInfo	Get-ASAppServiceEndpointAuthentication
	Get-ASAppServiceEndpointTransportQuota
Get-ASAppServiceInstance ServiceInstanceInfo	Stop-ASAppServiceInstance
	Suspend-ASAppServiceInstance
	Resume-ASAppServiceInstance

Create Packages

Now that you know what cmdlets are available and which ones you can use in conjunction with each other, you're ready to see how you can use PowerShell to create packages from Visual Studio solutions, as well as how you can use PowerShell to deploy those packages.

Begin by taking the solution that you've been creating in Visual Studio and build an AppFabric package. You will use PowerShell in conjunction with MSBuild and the web deployment functionality. You use MSBuild because it's the build platform Visual Studio uses. It also has the benefit of not requiring Visual Studio to be installed to build a deployment package. You can issue the commands that you will use line-by-line or build them into a broader script that you can reuse, as needed.

To use MSBuild with PowerShell, you need to assign a variable to the path of **MSBuild.exe** that is included with the .NET Framework 4.0. Type the following command into the ISE editor:

```
$MSBuildPath = "$($(gp -Path HKLM:\Software\Microsoft ↵
\'NET Framework Setup'\NDP\v4\Full).InstallPath)MSBuild.exe"
```

This assigns **MSBuild.exe** to the **$MSBuildPath** variable. At this point, you can start to issue MSBuild commands. When you build a Visual Studio solution using MSBuild, you can typically type MSBuild, followed by the name of the solution, to create the artifacts for that solution type (such as a **.dll** or **.exe**. In this case, you need to create a Web Deploy Package. You can do this by providing a **/T:Package** parameter like this one:

```
MSBuild "YourProject.csproj" /T:Package
```

The **/T:Package** parameter refers to the Package target that is specified as a Web Package. If you do not specify this target, then MSBuild will build the solution instead of creating the package.

Visual Studio also includes an option to specify properties for Web Packaging on the **Package/Publish** tab of the project properties windows. The values that you enter on the tab shown in Figure 9-10 are used by MSBuild when you select **Project ➤ Create Package** or when you select Create

Package on the popup menu when you right-click the project in the Solution Explorer window. The values that you enter on this tab are saved in the **csproj** file. You can also specify different property values for different build environments.

■ **Note** You can override all values entered on the **Package/Publish** tab by specifying new values through the MSBuild command line. This allows you to store common values in the project file while providing override values through MSBuild scripts.

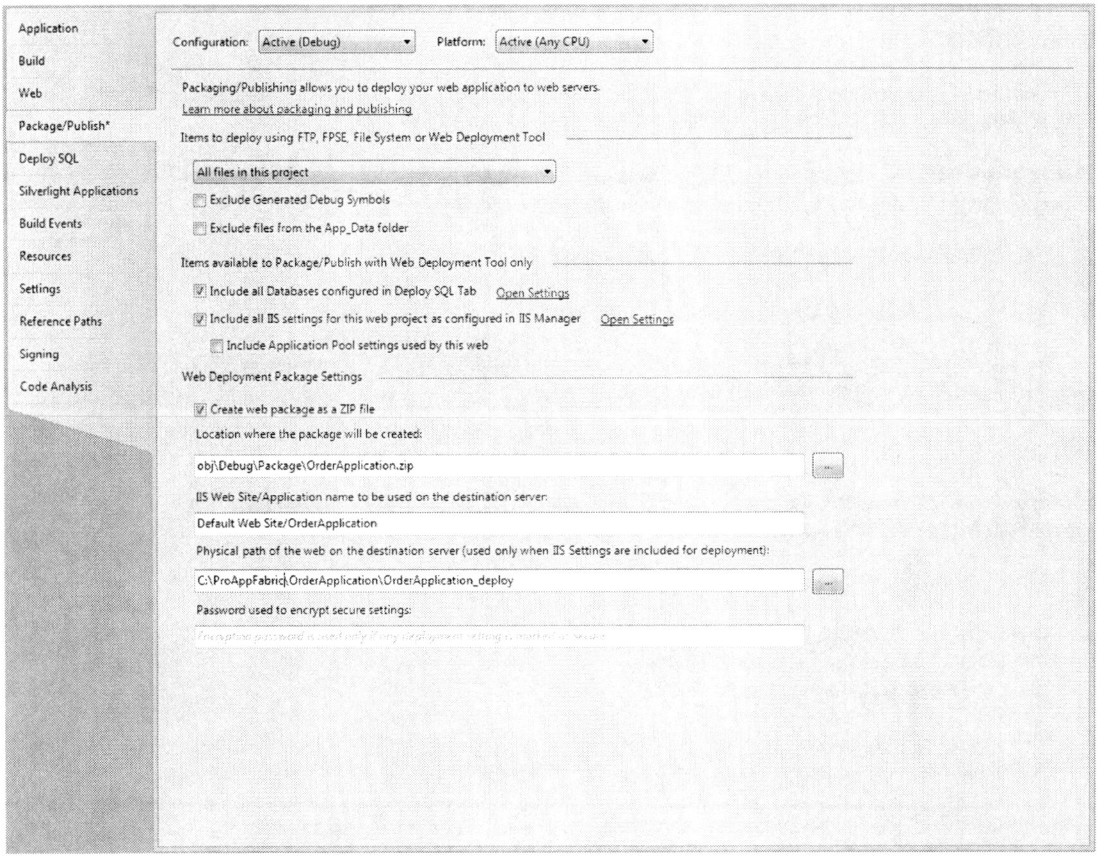

Figure 9-10. **Visual Studio Package/Publish**

You can build your package by typing the following MSBuild script into the ISE:

```
.$MSBuildPath 'C:\ProAppFabric\OrderApplication\ ↵
```

```
OrderApplication.csproj' /T:Package /P:PackageLocation= ↵
'C:\ProAppFabric\OrderApplication\ ↵
OrderApplicationDeployPackage.zip'
```

Check the output location to ensure that the package has been successfully created. If the package is there, then you're ready to take the package and deploy it to your AppFabric server.

Deploy Packages

As part of your deployment, you need to create a web site, a web application, and an application pool. You will then need to assign the application pool and configure the site. You will utilize the **appcmd.exe** tool for all of these tasks.

In the PowerShell ISE, type the following command to reference the path to the **appcmd.exe**:

```
$env:SYSTEMROOT
```

The first thing you do is create the **Application Pool**. Next, you ensure that it uses the .NET Framework 4.0. To do this, you enter this information into the ISE:

```
.$env:SystemRoot\System32\inetsrv\appcmd.exe add apppool ↵
 /Name:OrderApplicationAppPool -managedRuntimeVersion:v4.0
```

This command should return the following result:

```
APPPOOL object "OrderApplicationAppPool" added
```

If you do not see this preceding line returned, then take a moment to fix the error, reissue the command, and move on to the next command.

Next, you will create the new web site and configure it to use port 8089. Type this command into the ISE:

```
.$env:SystemRoot\System32\inetsrv\appcmd.exe add site /name:OrderApplication ↵
 /bindings:http/*:8089: /physicalPath:C:\ProAppFabric\OrderApplication
```

The preceding command should return the following result:

```
SITE object "OrderApplication" added
APP object "OrderApplication" added
VDIR object "OrderApplication" added
```

If this is not what you see, please take a moment to fix the errors before continuing.

You're now ready to assign the app pool to the web site. Type the following command:

```
.$env:SystemRoot\System32\inetsrv\appcmd.exe set site OrderApplication ↵
/applicationDefaults.applicationPool:OrderApplicationAppPool
```

The preceding command should return this result:

```
SITE object "OrderApplication" changed
```

At this point, you're ready to take the package you created in Visual Studio and deploy it to your new OrderApplication site. You will use the WebDeploy utility and issue WebDeploy commands within your PowerShell session. As when using MSBuild previously, you need to assign a variable that points to **msdeploy.exe**. You need to execute the following command to create the variable:

```
$MSDeployPath = "$env:ProgramFiles\IIS\Microsoft Web Deploy\msdeploy.exe"
```

Before you issue **msdeploy** commands, you should look at the differences between running this command-line tool in the command window as opposed to running it in PowerShell. On the command line, the Web Deploy utility uses the following syntax:

```
msdeploy -verb:sync -source:metakey=/lm/w3svc/1 -dest:metakey= ↵
/lm/w3svc/2 -verbose
```

However, when you use this in PowerShell, you need to change the colons to equal signs. The syntax for the Web Deploy now looks like this:

```
.\msdeploy.exe -verb=sync -source=metakey=/lm/w3svc/1 -dest= ↵
metakey=/lm/w3svc/2 -verbose
```

You can use the preceding syntax to create the PowerShell command-line syntax for your deployment. Type in the following command to deploy the **OrderApplication.zip** package to the OrderApplication web site:

```
.$MSDeployPath -verb:sync -source:package='C:\ProAppFabric\OrderApplication\ ↵
OrderApplicationDeployPackage.zip -dest:auto -setParam:Name=`"IIS Web ↵
Application Name`"`,value=OrderApplication/OrderApplication
```

The output from this command should let you know that it is updating the application and adding all of the artifacts that are present in package.

Configure Application

At this point, you have a deployed application; however, you haven't configured the application yet, nor have you set up montoring or tracking. The next section will walk you through the PowerShell commands to configure and implement these services. It's easy to see why you should save all of these commands in a PowerShell script file; however, it's also important to walk through each command and understand what it is doing and what steps you must take to automate the deployment of your application.

Create Databases

When configuring your application, your first step is to create and initialize the monitoring and persistence databases. You will use the **Initialize-ASMonitoringDatabase** cmdlet and piping to send the results to the **Format-List** PowerShell cmdlet. The **Format-List** cmdlet is handy because it formats the results better than the default handler (the default handler truncates the results). Before you issue the **Initialize-ASMonitoringDatabase** cmdlet, be aware that these instructions assume that you have used the default AppFabric permissions and principal names. Type the following command into the ISE to initialize the monitoring database:

```
Initialize-ASMonitoringDatabase -Database "OrderApplication" -Admins ↵
"AS_Administrators","NT AUTHORITY\LOCAL SERVICE" -Readers "AS_Observers" ↵
-Writers "BUILTIN\IIS_IUSRS" | fl *
```

You should see the following results:

```
Server          : DUBLIN100
Database        : OrderApplication
ConnectionString : Data Source=DUBLIN100;Initial Catalog= ↵
OrderApplication;Integrated Security=True
```

You can verify that the database has been created by opening SQL Server Management Studio and browsing the list of databases.

Now return to the ISE and create the persistence database. You will use the **Initialize-ASPersistenceDatabase** cmdlet. This cmdlet requires three parameters: **Admins**, **Readers**, and **Users**. You use the **COMPUTERNAME** environment variable to prefix your security groups. If you have created domain groups instead, then you need to adjust the command to fit your fully qualified security group names. Also, you use the **Confirm:$false** parameter to bypass the prompts and confirm the database changes. Type in the following command to create the persistence database:

```
$env:COMPUTERNAME
```

```
Initialize-ASPersistenceDatabase -Database "OrderService_PS" -Admins ↵
"$($env:COMPUTERNAME)\AS_Administrators" -Readers ↵
"$($env:COMPUTERNAME)\AS_Observers" -Users "BUILTIN\IIS_IUSRS" ↵
-Confirm:$false | fl *
```

You should see the following results:

```
Server          : DUBLIN100
Database        : OrderApplication
ConnectionString : Data Source=DUBLIN100;Initial Catalog=OrderApplication
```

Connection String

So far you've created the two databases. Next, you need to add connection strings to the **config** file, so that you can connect to those databases. You will use a function contained in the **scriptedConfigurationofAppFabric.ps1** file.

The preceding file ships with AppFabric, and you can find it at this location:

```
<AppFabricInstallLocation>\Samples\scriptedConfigurationOfAppFabric\code
```

You don't need any of the other functions in the file, and you might want to reuse this function with other deployments. To do this, you'll pull this function out of the file and place it into its own **.PS1** file. Open your favorite text editor and create a PowerShell script called **Utilities.PS1**. Copy the following code from the AppFabric file into your own **Utilities.PS1** file:

```
#==============================================================================#
#===                                                                        ===#
#=== Adds or updates the specified connection string setting               ===#
#=== in the specified .NET configuration file.                             ===#
#=== This utility is from the scriptedConfigurationOfAppFabric.ps1         ===#
#==============================================================================#

function UpdateConnectionString([string]$name, [string]$connectionString)
{
    $providerName = "System.Data.SqlClient"

    $NETFramework4Path = gp -Path HKLM:\Software\Microsoft\'NET Framework↵
        Setup'\NDP\v4\Full
    $ConfigPath = "$($NETFramework4Path.InstallPath)Config\Web.config"

    Write-Output ("ConfigPath : " + $ConfigPath)

    $xml = [xml](Get-Content $ConfigPath)
    $root = $xml.get_DocumentElement()


    $connectionStrings = $root.SelectSingleNode("connectionStrings")
    if ($connectionStrings -eq $null)
    {
        $locations = $root.SelectNodes("location")

        foreach ($locationNode in $locations)
        {
            $locStrings = $locationNode.SelectSingleNode("connectionStrings")

            if ($locStrings -ne $null)
            {
                $connectionStrings = $locStrings
            }
        }

        if ($connectionStrings -eq $null)
        {
            $connectionStrings = $xml.CreateElement("connectionStrings")
            $root.AppendChild($connectionStrings) | Out-Null
        }
    }

    $xpath = "add[@name='" + $name + "']"
    $add = $connectionStrings.SelectSingleNode($xpath)
    if ($add -eq $null)
    {
        Write-Output "Adding new connection string setting..."
        $add = $xml.CreateElement("add")
        $connectionStrings.AppendChild($add) | Out-Null
    }
    else
```

```
{
    Write-Output "Updating existing connection string setting..."
}

$add.SetAttribute("name", $name)
$add.SetAttribute("connectionString", $connectionString)
$add.SetAttribute("providerName", $providerName)
Write-Output $add | Format-List

$xml.Save($ConfigPath)
}
```

Type this command into the ISE:

```
import-module .\Utilities.ps1
```

This will add the function and allow you to call it from within PowerShell. You will also utilize the UpdateConnectionString function to add the connection string.

If you're running AppFabric with SQL Express, then run the following command:

```
UpdateConnectionString "OrderApplication" "Data Source= ↵
    .\SQLEXPRESS;Initial Catalog=OrderApplication;Integrated Security=True"
```

If you're using SQL Server, then run the following command instead:

```
UpdateConnectionString "OrderApplication" "Data Source=(local);
    Initial Catalog=OrderApplication;Integrated Security=True"
```

You can verify that the connection string has been configured by opening Internet IIS Manager and double-clicking the **Monitoring Database Configuration** applet. You should see a connection string named **OrderApplication**, and you should also see that the status is set to **Initialized**.

Reconfigure the Web Site

You're almost there. You now need to reconfigure the OrderApplication web site to use the database for monitoring. Run the following command to set the monitoring functionality:

```
Set-ASAppMonitoring -SiteName OrderApplication -MonitoringLevel ↵
    HealthMonitoring -ConnectionStringName OrderApplication
```

The output from the command should list **ConnectionStringName**, **ConnectionString**, **MonitoringLevel**, and other properties.

Your next step is to run the following command, which lets you use the new database for persistence:

```
Set-ASAppServicePersistence -SiteName OrderApplication ↵
    -ConnectionStringName OrderApplication
```

The output from this command should list the following properties:

```
ConnectionString           :
ConnectionStringName        : OrderService_PS
HostLockRenewalPeriod       : 00:00:20
InstanceCompletionAction    : DeleteNothing
InstanceEncodingOption      : GZip
InstanceLockedExceptionAction : BasicRetry
AuthorizedWindowsGroup      : AS_Administrators
IsLocal                     : True
BehaviorName                :
```

You're finally done with your deployment tasks, and you have an application installed in your new environment. To automate the deployment, you can take the commands that you have issued throughout this chapter and put them in a script. You can also look at the sample code for the book, which includes a completed script. You can also find a script that is included with the AppFabric install called **MultiMachineConfiguration**; this file is located in the **samples** subdirectory. This PowerShell script provides the functionality to configure throttling on multiple machines when your AppFabric application is installed in an IIS farm.

Consider Other Tasks

Once you complete the deployment and configuration, you will want to write scripts for a couple of other tasks. For example, you will want to write scripts to control monitoring and tracking once you have your application up and running.

You can control monitoring using the **Get-ASAppServiceInstance** cmdlet. You can use this cmdlet to retrieve all the instances of the workflow. This cmdlset can also be used with a workflow instance id to **suspend**, **resume**, and **stop** the specified instance. You can accomplish this by piping the output of the **Get-ASAppServiceInstance** cmdlet into the **Suspend-ASAppServiceInstance**, **Resume-ASAppServiceInstance,** or **Stop-ASAppServiceInstance** cmdlet. You can learn more about monitoring and tracking in Chapter 11.

Summary

This chapter walked you through the packaging and deployment of AppFabric applications. You also learned how to import an application into an AppFabric Web Site through the IIS Manager, as well as how to export an AppFabric application. This chapter also looked at how you can accomplish these tasks through PowerShell scripts. The PowerShell scripts represent an interesting area because they let you automate the steps required to deploy an AppFabric application. You can then reuse this script for all of your AppFabric applications.

CHAPTER 10

Advanced Concepts

So far you have built and deployed an application. Now let's go back and look at some of the advanced concepts that you can utilize in your applications. These advanced concepts revolve around message handling. As you create more complex and more advanced applications, you will find that you require these services. The advanced concepts that you will learn about in this chapter include content-based routing, message correlation, long-running workflows, and compensation.

Content-Based Routing

The purpose of content-based routing is to route messages based on the content of the messages or the message headers, as opposed to a destination address. Traditionally, content-based routing is performed by opening a message and applying rules that act on the contents of the message to determine who is interested in receiving the message. The benefit to this approach is that it frees the sending application from needing to know anything about where the message is going.

Background and Motivation

You can encounter several scenarios where a content-based routing pattern can prove especially handy. Assume that a company has installed a new version of a service. How does the message get routed to the correct version? Also, what if the company wants to have more than one service receive the same message?

Content-based routing can also handle error situations. The error handler can detect whether the endpoint address is no longer valid or if the service has been removed. It can also respond appropriately if a message is received, and there is no endpoint specified. This error-handling functionality can automatically resend the message to another endpoint.

You build content-based routers using two parts. The first is the router and the second is the service. You can have only one router service; you can have many services (and typically do). This means you need a mapping or set of rules that you register with the routing service to direct the incoming messages. The router service examines the content of a message, applies the rules, and forwards a message as designated. The router service included with WCF and AppFabric contains the following services: content-based routing with service aggregation, service versioning, and priority routing. It also provides protocol bridging, as well as robust error handling. The ability to utilize these services to perform endpoint virtualization and composition has traditionally been difficult to implement. Also, they have typically required a lot of infrastructure logic, and they haven't been readily available outside of more expensive server-based software. However, AppFabric gives you the ability to implement this functionality, while helping you avoid all the difficulties you faced when implementing this functionality in the past. Let's look at what each of the services provides.

The content-based routing functionality included contains everything that you've learned about so far, plus the ability to configure the routing logic at run time.

The service aggregation scenarios let you expose a single service to a client application and then route each message to the appropriate internal service endpoint based on a value in the message. This allows you to aggregate several internal services, which you can design to look like a single external service by exposing a single endpoint.

The service versioning capabilities allow you to maintain older versions side-by-side with newer versions. This also lets you expose a single endpoint address and then route the incoming message to the appropriate internal version of the service, as long as there is a version-specific identifier in the message body or header.

The priority-routing capabilities allow you to route based on specific client messages, so that you can meet specific service-level agreements. You can create a routing rule that filters specific client messages and routes the message to a specific endpoint that you can dedicate to processing messages for particular clients.

The protocol bridging capabilities allow you to separate and segment communications protocols used internally between services from the protocols that are used between clients and the service. In this scenario, you might decide to use the SOAP protocol between the client and service, but use Net TCP between the internal services.

The dynamic configuration allows you to modify the routing configuration at run time. This means you can change the configuration without having any endpoint downtime.

Finally, the error handling capabilities gives you an exceptional amount of functionality. The routing service lets you define a secondary endpoint as a backup endpoint to route a message to when an error occurs while submitting the message to the primary endpoint.

Implementation

You know the theory, and you've walked through what it includes; the next step is to create some code that shows content-based routing in action. Let's extend the scenario from the previous chapters by saying that if you submit a claim where the status is pending, you want it to be routed to a claims adjuster before it can be submitted for processing. If you submit a claim where the status is active, then it can be submitted without any intervention.

Determining What You Need

Let's begin by looking at what you need to do to implement this with configuration and code. First, you need to implement content-based routing as a WCF service that you define within the `System.ServiceModel.Routing` namespace. You implement this WCF service through the `RoutingService` class. This routing service works hand-in-hand with the `MessageFilter` class implementations. `MessageFilter` is a base class, and there are five implementations:

- `XPathMessageFilter`: This implementation allows you to specify an XPath expression to define the value to match on.

- `MatchAllMessageFilter`: This implementation allows you to match (filter) all the messages.

- `MatchNonMessageFilter`: This implementation allows you to match none of the messages.

- **ActionMessageFilter**: This implementation allows you to determine whether the action of the message matches a specific set of actions.

- **EndpointAddressMessageFilter**: This implementation allows you to determine whether the messages endpoint address matches a specified endpoint address.

You can group all of these **MessageFilters** together into a filter table to create a set of composite-routing rules. This allows you to create a filter table that contains **MessageFilters** that would allow you to route an incoming message to a specific internal destination.

Defining Elements

Next, you will start by defining the elements that you need in the **web.config** file. Within the **<system.serviceModel>** element, you will set up your routing service using the **<services>** element. When you set up your router, you need to set the contract of the endpoint element to **System.ServiceModel.Routing.IRequestReplyRouter**. In addition to setting up the endpoint, you also need to associate a behavior with it. When using a configuration file to configure the routing service, you need to specify a **RoutingBehavior** that will specify the filter table that to contain the routing rules. If you set this up in code, then you use the **RoutingConfiguration** object. The first part of the **web.config** file appears follows; it outlines the configuration setting to create the routing service and associate a behavior with it:

```xml
<?xml version="1.0"?>

<configuration>

    <system.web>
        <compilation debug="true"
            targetFramework="4.0"/>
    </system.web>

  <system.serviceModel>

    <client>
     <endpoint name="AutoSubmitClaimService"
               address="http://localhost/SubmitClaim/AutoSubmitClaim.svc"
               binding="wsHttpBinding" contract="*" />
     <endpoint name="AdjusterSubmitClaimService"
               address="http://localhost/SubmitClaim/AdjusterSubmitClaim.svc"
               binding="wsHttpBinding" contract="*" />    </client>

   <services>
    <service behaviorConfiguration="RoutingServiceBehavior"
       name="System.ServiceModel.Routing.RoutingService">
       <endpoint address="" binding="wsHttpBinding"
                name="RoutingServiceEndpoint"
                contract="System.ServiceModel.Routing.IRequestReplyRouter" />
    </service>
   </services>
```

```
<behaviors>
  <serviceBehaviors>
    <behavior name="RoutingServiceBehavior">
      <serviceMetadata httpGetEnabled="true"/>
      <serviceDebug includeExceptionDetailInFaults="false" />
      <routing routingTableName="routingRules"
              routeOnHeadersOnly="false" />
    </behavior>
  </serviceBehaviors>
</behaviors>
...
```

You will continue to add to the `web.config` to specify the routing logic. Before you do this, you need to determine what data within the message you will use to identify uniquely which endpoint to route the message to.

■ **Note** If the endpoints that you route to all share the same SOAP action, then you shouldn't use that action as an indicator in your routing rules because the message will be delivered to all of the services.

Creating Filters and a Routing Table

Implementing the next section of your `web.config` file requires building on the previous snippet. The `<routing>` element contains the filters that you will use, as well as the filter table. The filter must return **true** for the routing service to route the message. The next snippet checks whether the status is equal to either **active** or **pending**. Either of these will return a **true** or **false** from the evaluation of the XPath expression. If multiple filters return **true**, then the message will be routed to multiple endpoints:

```
...
<routing>
  <filters>
    <filter name="ActiveFilter" filterType="XPath"
            filterData="boolean(//*[local-name()= 'Status']
            /text() = 'Active')"/>
    <filter name="PendingFilter" filterType="XPath"
            filterData="boolean(//*[local-name()= 'Status']
            /text() ='Pending')"/>
  </filters>
  <filterTables>
    <filterTable name="routingRules">
      <!--<entries>-->
        <add filterName="ActiveFilter"
            endpointName="AutoSubmitClaimService"/>
        <add filterName="PendingFilter"
            endpointName="AdjusterSubmitClaimService"/>
      <!--</entries>-->
    </filterTable>
```

```
        </filterTables>
    </routing>

  </system.serviceModel>
</configuration>
```

You now have a complete **web.config** file, with the routing configured. You will need some knowledge of XPath to put together the filter expressions. In this case, the status element is directly off the root, which means you can use the **//** along with the name of your element. In some cases, you will want to include the namespace prefix in the XPath query. Namespaces can get quite long, and it becomes difficult to type such a string repeatedly. It also becomes difficult to read such a string when you include it in each query. Instead, you can modify the configuration file, add a **namespaceTable** element, and define the namespace in one place, as follows:

```
...
    <routing>
        <namespaceTable>
          <add prefix="ns" namespace=http://mynamespace/>
        </namespaceTable>
         <filter name="ActiveFilter" filterType="XPath"
                filterData="//ns:Status = 'Active'"/>
...
```

You learned previously that if multiple filters return **true**, then the message will be routed to multiple endpoints. This pattern is called the multicast pattern, and you can utilize it when a client submits one message, but there are many services that need to consume the message. To implement this, multiple filters need to return **true** and the routing contract cannot be **request-reply** because only one reply can (or should) be sent back to the client. However, you can utilize one-way or duplex contracts.

Consuming the Configuration File

Finally, let's dive into the code and see what you need to do to consume the configuration file and route between your services.

Your solution will have three projects. One project will contain the code for the router, the service, and a client. You implement the router and the service projects as WCF Service Applications, and you implement the client as a console application. Let's tackle the router first. The sample code that is included with this chapter contains the full code for the router. The **RouterService** project contains the configuration file mentioned previously, as well as a **.svc** file. You will modify the default **.svc** file that is created when you create the project. First, you need to delete the code behind file, and then you need to delete the default code in the **.svc** file and replace it with the following snippet:

```
<%@ ServiceHost Language="C#" Debug="true"
Service="System.ServiceModel.Routing.RoutingService, System.ServiceModel.Routing,
Version=4.0.0.0, Culture=neutral, PublicKeyToken=31bf3856ad364e35" %>
```

All messages received will be routed to the **System.ServiceModel.Routing.RoutingService** class. This class reads the configuration file information and routes according to the filters and the service endpoints they point to. At this point, you've completed the RouterService; the next step is to create the service project.

The service project, **ClaimServices**, will contain an **.svc** file for each of the endpoints that you point to in **RouterService**. This means you need to add a new item to your project. When you navigate to Add New Item for your project, you will add the WCF Service, which will add a new **.svc** file. You can delete the interface file that gets added. Before you work on the **.svc** file, you need to add a class file, along with an interface, that you will use in your services.

The service exposes a set of operations that process a claim. The claim object is based on the class that follows. Add a new **Claim** class file to the project and then add the following code to the class file:

```
[DataContract]
public class Claim
{
    [DataMember]
    public string ClaimID { get; set; }
    [DataMember]
    public string AccidentID { get; set; }
    [DataMember]
    public string Description { get; set; }
    [DataMember]
    public string Status { get; set; }
    [DataMember]
    public string DateCreated { get; set; }
    [DataMember]
    public string RentalCar { get; set; }
}
```

You use this class in the interface that you will reference for each of your services. Add a new **IClaim** class file to the project and then add the following interface code to the class file:

```
namespace Chapter10Routing
{
    [ServiceContract(Namespace = "http://Chapter10Routing")]
    public interface IClaim
    {
        [OperationContract]
        string SubmitClaim(Claim claim);
        [OperationContract]
        string RentalHold(Claim claim);
        [OperationContract]
        string RemoveRentalHold(Claim claim);
    }
}
```

The **Claim** class is passed to the operations on the service. Now let's go back and implement the code for your service endpoints. Open the first **.svc** you added and rename it to **AutoSubmitClaim**. Your service class will inherit from the **IClaim** interface and will implement the three methods in the **.svc** code behind:

```
namespace Chapter10Routing
{
    public class AutoSubmitClaim : IClaim
    {
        public string SubmitClaim(Claim claim)
```

```
    {
        claim.Description = "AutoSubmitClaimService:SubmitClaim
                            Method Called";
        return claim.Description;
    }

    public string RentalHold(Claim claim)
    {
        claim.Description = "AutoSubmitClaimService:RentalHold
                            Method Called";
        return claim.Description;
    }

    public string RemoveRentalHold(Claim claim)
    {
        claim.Description = "AutoSubmitClaimService:RemoveRentalHold
                            Method Called";
        return claim.Description;
    }
  }
}
```

This code accepts a **Claim** object from the client and modifies the description field to pass back both the method that was called and the service the method was on. Remember that the client won't know what service is being called, so you want to let the user know which service was invoked.

Next, right-click the **.svc** file and select **View Markup**. This will open the **.svc** file. Modify the code in this file so that it points to the service class, as well as the code behind:

```
<%@ ServiceHost Language="C#" Debug="true"
Service="Chapter10Routing.AutoSubmitClaim"
CodeBehind="AutoSubmitClaim.svc.cs" %>
```

You need to do this for each of the two remaining **.svc** files. Next, you need to rename it to AdjusterSubmitClaim, and finally, you will rename the other ClaimErrorService. The code to implement the service will be the same; however, each method will return the name of the correct service in the **claim.description** field.

Before you can run the service, you need to look at the configuration file. The configuration file contains the service endpoints for **AutoSubmitClaim** and **AdjusterSubmitClaim**, as well as their associated behaviors. This .config file is a standard WCF configuration file and looks like this:

```
<system.serviceModel>
  <services>
    <service behaviorConfiguration="ClaimServiceBehavior"
            name="Chapter10Routing.AutoSubmitClaim">
      <endpoint address="" binding="wsHttpBinding"
              contract="Chapter10Routing.IClaim" />
      <endpoint address="mex" binding="mexHttpBinding"
              contract="IMetadataExchange" />
    </service>

    <service behaviorConfiguration="ClaimAdjusterServiceBehavior"
```

```
                 name="Chapter10Routing.AdjusterSubmitClaim">
        <endpoint address="" binding="wsHttpBinding"
                 contract="Chapter10Routing.IClaim"/>
        <endpoint address="mex" binding="mexHttpBinding"
                 contract="IMetadataExchange" />
    </service>
  </services>

  <behaviors>
    <serviceBehaviors>
      <behavior name="ClaimServiceBehavior">
        <serviceMetadata httpGetEnabled="true" />
        <serviceDebug includeExceptionDetailInFaults="false" />
      </behavior>
      <behavior name="ClaimAdjusterServiceBehavior">
        <serviceMetadata httpGetEnabled="true" />
        <serviceDebug includeExceptionDetailInFaults="false" />
      </behavior>
    </serviceBehaviors>
  </behaviors>

</system.serviceModel>
```

You now have both of the WCF Service Applications coded. Next, you need to configure them in IIS. Open the IIS Manager and drill down to the Default Web Site. Right-click and select **Add Application**. Add **SubmitClaim** to the **Alias** textbox and browse to the location of the **ClaimServices** project. Do not browse to the **bin** folder. You need to be at the project level, so that IIS can see the **.svc** files. Do the same steps and add an application for the **RouterService**. Once you set up these two applications, click each one and switch the view to **Content View**. Next, right-click each of the **.svc** files and click **browse**. Make sure that the services appear in the browser window. You might be tempted to launch the WCF Service Application from within Visual Studio by right-clicking the project and selecting **Debug ➤ Start new instance**. This will let you check whether the **.svc** service files launch correctly, but you will find, when you need to add the service reference to your client project, that the selection will be grayed out. This means you need to set up your projects in IIS, so that you can set the service reference on the client without any issues.

You're now at a point where you can create the client. The client calls the service through the router service. You connect to the router service based on settings in the config file. However, you need to create a proxy. You do this by setting a service reference and pointing it at one of your **.svc** files in the **ClaimServices** application. This adds items to the **app.config** that you will modify so that you can point to the **RouterService, rather than** directly to the service. You should configure your **app.config** file first. As with any other WCF-based **app.config** file, you will have a **binding** element, as well as a **client** element. The **binding** element is standard, and it contains all the elements you would expect to see. What is interesting here is that the client node will point directly to the **.svc** file contained in the **RouterService** application:

```
<client>
    <endpoint address=http://localhost/RouterService/RouterService.svc
             binding="wsHttpBinding"
             bindingConfiguration="WSHttpBinding_IClaim"
             contract="ClaimServices.IClaim"
             name="WSHttpBinding_IClaim">
```

```
        </endpoint>
</client>
```

The code in your client calls the claim service through the **ClaimClient** method on your proxy. You need to create a claim and call the **SubmitClaim** method. You do this twice, but change the status value so that you can see the routing in action. The first time, you set the status field to **Active**; the second time, you set it to **Pending**. Your service object is the same, as is your method, but behind the scenes you call two different services. You can learn which service was called by looking at the returned description field:

```
namespace Chapter10Routing
{
    class client
    {
        static void Main()
        {
            Console.WriteLine();
            Console.WriteLine("Make sure that the ClaimServices project &
                              RouterService project started");
            Console.WriteLine("Press <ENTER> to run the client code.");

            while (Console.ReadLine() != "quit")
            {
                string ReturnedClaimDesc = string.Empty;

                ClaimServices.ClaimClient cs = new
                    ClaimServices.ClaimClient();

                ClaimServices.Claim claim = new ClaimServices.Claim();
                claim.AccidentID = "1190";
                claim.ClaimID = "A8493";
                claim.Status = "Active";
                claim.Description = "";
                claim.DateCreated = DateTime.Now.ToString();

                ReturnedClaimDesc = cs.SubmitClaim(claim);

                Console.WriteLine("Claim Submitted: The service called was "
                                  + ReturnedClaimDesc);

                cs.Close();

                ClaimServices.ClaimClient csPending = new
                    ClaimServices.ClaimClient();

                ClaimServices.Claim claimPending = new ClaimServices.Claim();
                claim.AccidentID = "1191";
                claim.ClaimID = "A8494";
                claim.Status = "Pending";
                claim.Description = "";
                claim.DateCreated = DateTime.Now.ToString();
```

239

```
                    ReturnedClaimDesc = csPending.SubmitClaim(claim);

                    Console.WriteLine("Claim Submitted: The service called was "
                                        + ReturnedClaimDesc);

                    csPending.Close();

                    Console.WriteLine();
                    Console.WriteLine("Press <ENTER> to run the client again or
                                        type 'quit' to quit.");
                }
            }
        }
    }
```

At this point, you have done everything required for all three of your projects. Build the solution and get ready to test. Right-click the **Client** project and select **Debug ➤ Start new instance**. The console application should start and hit the Enter key to start the calls to the services. You will see that the call is made to the service through the router and that both service endpoints were invoked. You should see the output shown in Figure 10-1 in your client window.

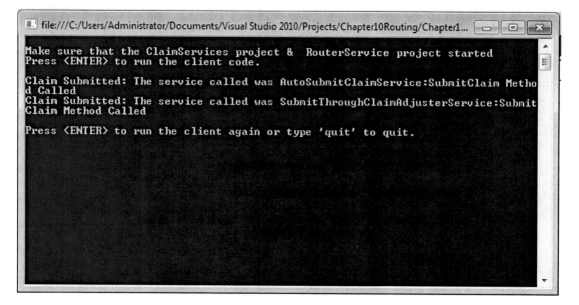

Figure 10-1. Routing Client Output

You have now setup a basic routing service, but you still need to review and address several issues.

Dynamic Configuration

Let's begin by exploring how you implement the rest of the functionality mentioned earlier in this chapter. For example, I stated that the routing service has the ability to support dynamic configuration. This means you can change the filters at run time, without having to recycle the application. In certain situations, you want to be able to modify the routing rules for future messages, but still process the messages that have already been submitted and ensure that no messages get lost. If you didn't have this functionality, then you would need to modify the configuration file and that would recycle the service.

You need to keep in mind a couple of rules when utilizing this functionality. First, you can only change the routing filter programmatically. You will still start the services utilizing the data contained in the **web.config** file; any changes will require that you create a new **RoutingConfiguration** object and pass it as a parameter to the **ApplyConfiguration** method on the **RoutingExtension** service extension. Second, when you update the routing service, you need to pass a new complete configuration; you cannot modify only certain elements or append new elements to the configuration. Third, any sessions already in process will continue with the original configuration, but new sessions will utilize the new configuration.

Now let's look at how you would use the **RoutingConfiguration** object to implement the dynamic configuration functionality.

You begin by instantiating the **RoutingConfiguration** object. Next, set some properties and then pass it to an instance of the **RoutingBehavior** object. You then create a new ServiceEndPoint; you will use this in the **RoutingConfigurations** FilterTable. After you configure RoutingConfiguration, you call ApplyConfiguration on the host:

```
void UpdateConfiguration()
{

    RoutingConfiguration rc = new RoutingConfiguration();

    //first service endpoint configuration
    ServiceEndpoint submitClaim = new ServiceEndpoint(
    ContractDescription.GetContract(typeof(IRequestReplyRouter)),
    new BasicHttpBinding(),
    new EndpointAddress("http://localhost:2010/"));
    rc.FilterTable.Add(new MatchAllMessageFilter(), new
        List<ServiceEndpoint> { submitClaim });

    //second service endpoint configuration
    ServiceEndpoint submitToAdjuster = new ServiceEndpoint(
    ContractDescription.GetContract(typeof(IRequestReplyRouter)),
    new BasicHttpBinding(),
    new EndpointAddress("http://localhost:2011/"));
    rc.FilterTable.Add(new MatchAllMessageFilter(), new
        List<ServiceEndpoint> { submitToAdjuster });

    rc.RouteOnHeadersOnly = false;

    //Apply the configuration to the service host
    routerHost.routerHost.Extensions.Find<RoutingExtension>()
            .ApplyConfiguration(rc);
}
```

Error Handling

It's also important that you understand how error handling works. When you implement a distributed system, you are subject to a host of different things that can go wrong. Many of these things center on communication errors. Three types of communications errors that you are likely to encounter include an inability to communicate with the service, finding the network protocol is blocked, or learning that the service that you want to connect to isn't available. AppFabric's error-handling capabilities provide the ability to address all of these error situations.

When the routing service detects that a CommunicationException has been thrown, the error handling process is initiated. You can derive many exception types from this exception type; these derived types cover situations such as not being able to find the endpoint (EndpointNotFoundException), the server being busy (ServerTooBusyException), the message filter not being correctly set to route messages (MessageFilterException), and a communication object having faulted (CommunicatedObjectFaultedException). You will also another want to consider another important exception: when a timeout exception occurs. The error-handling functionality will also catch when a System.TimeoutException occurs and will retry to send the message. This chapter lists only some of the most common exceptions, but you can catch many others, as well.

Now let's look at how to modify the config file that you created earlier to route a message to a backup service if the primary service isn't available or throws an exception.

You need to modify three sections of the config file and add additional elements to the <client>, the <routing>, and the <routingTables> sections. At this point, you have a choice regarding your backup endpoint. You can either create a different endpoint for each backup service, or you can route all errors to a single backup service. In this example, you will route all errors to a single backup service. To set this up, you modify your client section by adding an additional endpoint element, as shown in bold sections below:

```
<client>
 <endpoint name="AutoSubmitClaimService"
           address="http://localhost/SubmitClaim/AutoSubmitClaim.svc"
           binding="wsHttpBinding" contract="*" />
 <endpoint name="AdjusterSubmitClaimService"
           address="http://localhost/SubmitClaim/AdjusterSubmitClaim.svc"
           binding="wsHttpBinding" contract="*" />
 <endpoint name="ClaimErrorService"
           address="http://localhost/SubmitClaim/ClaimErrorService.svc"
           binding="wsHttpBinding" contract="*" />
</client>
```

Next, you will modify the routing element by adding a <backupLists> node; that remains is to change in your config file to add a backupList attribute to the <add> node under the <routingTables> node. You can see these changes to the config file in the parts highlighted in bold:

```
<routing>
    <backupLists>
      <backupList name="errorService">
        <add endpointName="ClaimErrorService"/>
      </backupList>
    </backupLists>
    <filters>
      <filter name="ActiveFilter" filterType="XPath"
```

```
                filterData="boolean(//*[local-name()= 'Status']
                /text() = 'Active')"/>
        <filter name="PendingFilter" filterType="XPath"
                filterData="boolean(//*[local-name()= 'Status']
                /text() ='Pending')"/>
    </filters>
    <filterTables>
      <filterTable name="routingRules">
        <!--<entries>-->
          <add filterName="ActiveFilter"
               endpointName="AutoSubmitClaimService"
               backupList="errorService"/>
          <add filterName="PendingFilter"
               endpointName="AdjusterSubmitClaimService"
               backupList="errorService"/>
        <!--</entries>-->
      </filterTable>
    </filterTables>
  </routing>

  </system.serviceModel>
</configuration>
```

If you run your application at this point, but turn off the service, submitting a message to your service causes the error handling to reroute the message automatically to the backup service you defined.

Message Correlation

At its core, correlation is the ability to route a message to an instance of a workflow that already exists. The need for this arises because workflows have state, and you wouldn't want workflow instance A to receive a response to a message that workflow instance B sent out. When you set up correlation, you are providing the means for the `WorkflowServiceHost` to locate the correct instance of a running workflow. If correlation is not set up, then you will get different default behavior: a new instance of the workflow will be started each time a new message is received.

Types of Correlation

Traditionally, there are two types of correlation: content based and protocol based. Content-based correlation relates messages based on a unique piece of data contained in the message, such as a `ClaimID`. Protocol-based correlation takes data from the protocol infrastructure, then uses it to provide a token to map messages together.

Content-based correlation requires the developer to identify a data element and where it exists in the message. You implement this in the activities that understand correlation using CorrelationQuery.

Protocol-based correlation relies on the transport mechanism to associate messages. Protocol correlation covers both context correlation and request-reply correlation. You use request-reply to group a pair of activities together; for example, you might use it to tie a `Receive` shape tied to a `SendReply` shape, or *vice versa*. With protocol correlation, you need to utilize a context-based binding, such as WSHTTPContextBinding, BasicHTTPContext Binding, or the NetTcpContextBinding.

When implementing correlation in Windows Workflow, you use the **CorrelationHandle** property to join the activities that can be bound together. The times that you will utilize this is when you have a Send shape and then have a Receive shape waiting for a incoming message that needs to find the correct running instance. These two shapes will use the same **CorrelationHandle**. You would also use the **CorrelationHandle** property when you have two **Receive** shapes within a **Parallel** shape waiting for messages, as well as when you have two **Send** shapes and then two **Receive** shapes associated with the **Send** shapes. Examples of these scenarios might occur when you need to receive two incoming messages before the workflow can proceed; or when you will be calling two separate web services at the same time, and you need to receive a response back from each of them before the workflow can proceed.

Scope

Windows Workflow also provides the **CorrelationScope** shape as a container for other activities. You do not need to set the CorrelationScope for activities that reside in the **CorrelationScope;** instead, you look to the **CorrelationHandle** contained in the CorrelationScope.

Embedded Correlation

You can encounter several scenarios in which Windows Workflow knows that there will be correlation, and where the activities have been designed to embed that functionality. For example, you can see this clearly when setting up a request/response pattern. There are two shapes that provide the implementation for this pattern: the **ReceiveAndSendReply** shape (which you use on the service) and the **SendAndReceiveReply** shape (which you use on the client). When you drag the **ReceiveAndSendReply** shape onto the workflow surface, you get a **Sequence** shape with a Receive shape with a **SendReply** shape directly underneath it. The latter's **Request** property is set to the **Receive** shape. Likewise, when you drag the **SendAndReceiveReply** shape onto the workflow surface, you get a **Sequence** shape, but this time you will have a **Send** shape with a **ReceiveReply** shape directly underneath it. The latter's Request property is set to the **Send** shape (see Figure 10-2).

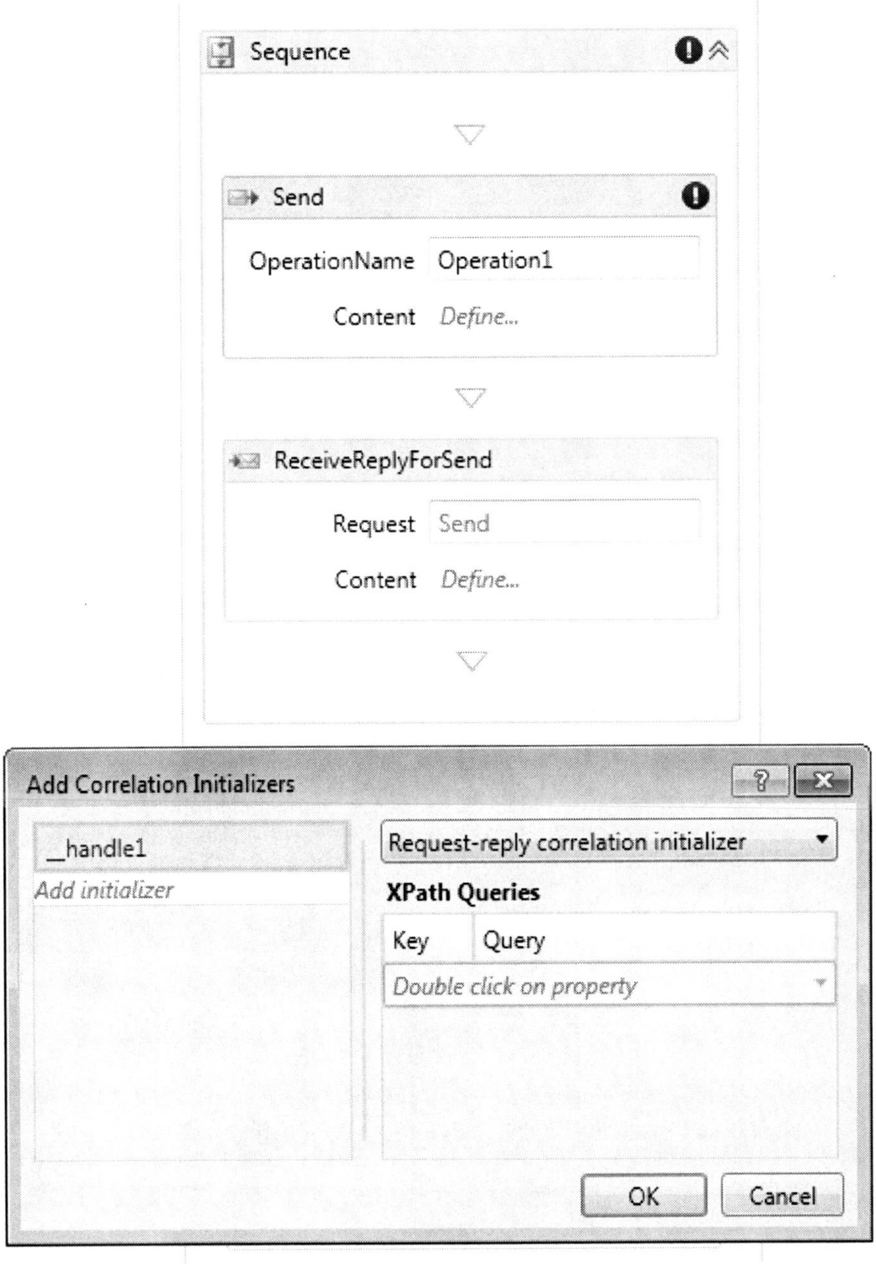

Figure 10-2. SendAndReceiveReply Correlation

When you have a **Receive** shape after a **SendReply** shape, and the correlation was initialized by the **SendReply** shape, then both activities need to share the same **CorrelationHandle**. The interesting thing is that each shape will need to have its own XPath query to specify the location to the data element that you use for correlation from within the message (see Figure 10-3).

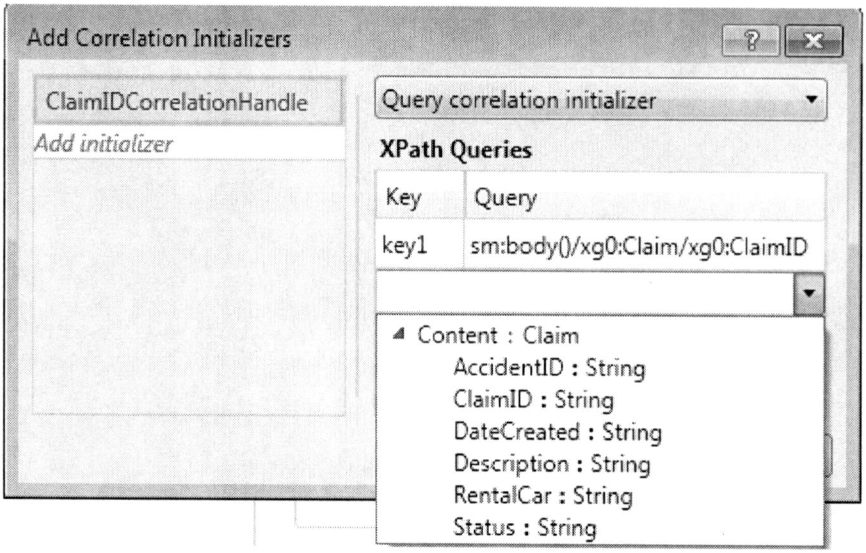

Figure 10-3. *Message Query Correlation*

Let's look more closely at the preceding case. When you have a **SendReply** shape and a **Receive** shape, the **SendReply** shape will have its **CorrelationInitializer** property set because that will be the shape that initializes the correlation set. The associated **Receive** shape that will participate in this correlation set must have the **CorrelatesOn** property set. Note that it is possible to initialize the correlation through either a **Receive** shape or a **ReceiveReply** shape. You initialize the correlation in the **Receive** shape if the client is able to provide the identifying piece of data. If you initialize the correlation set from the **ReceiveReply** shape, then another service based on a call to that service would need to provide the identifying piece of data.

An Example

So let's create a workflow that utilizes correlation. First, create a new Sequential Workflow Console Application. Next, add a C# Class Library project to the solution. The Class Library project will contain your message type, as shown here:

```
[DataContract]
public class Claim
{
    [DataMember]
    public string ClaimID { get; set; }
    [DataMember]
```

```
      public string AccidentID { get; set; }
      [DataMember]
      public string Description { get; set; }
      [DataMember]
      public string Status { get; set; }
      [DataMember]
      public string DateCreated { get; set; }
      [DataMember]
      public string RentalCar { get; set; }
}
```

Remember to add a reference to **System.Runtime.Serialization**, or the **DataContract** and **DataMember** attributes won't resolve. You need to compile this project and add a reference to your workflow project before you continue. Back in your **Workflow1.xaml** workflow, drag a **Sequence** shape from the Control Flow section in the Toolbar onto the workflow surface. Next, drag a **Send** shape from the Messaging section into the **Sequence** shape. Finally, drag a **Receive** shape and place it in the Sequence shape, underneath the **Send** shape.

You now need to allow your workflow to accept your **Claim** message. To do this, select the **Sequence** shape and click the **Variable** button on the bottom left of the workflow designer. This brings up the **Variables** window. Create a variable named **ClaimRequest** and set the **Variable** type to the **Claim** object in your referenced assembly. Next, create another variable, name it **ClaimResponse**, set the **Variable** type to your **Claim** object, and then type **New Claim()** in the default window.

■ **Note** Rules and expressions in WF 4 must conform to Visual Basic syntax. Even if all the projects in your solution are written in C#, you will still need to enter the rules and expressions using Visual Basic syntax.

You need to create one more variable: the correlation variable. So, create a variable and name it **ClaimIDCorrelationHandle**. Next, set its type to **CorrelationHandle** (which will be located at **System.ServiceModel.Activities.CorrelationHandle**). Your **Variable** list should look like the one shown in Figure 10-4.

Name	Variable type	Scope	Default
_handle1	CorrelationHandle	Sequence	*Handle cannot be initialized*
ClaimRequest	Claim	Sequence	*Enter a VB expression*
ClaimResponse	Claim	Sequence	New Claim()
ClaimIDCorrelationHandle	CorrelationHandle	Sequence	*Handle cannot be initialized*
Create Variable			

Figure 10-4. Variable List

With this done, it's time to select your **Send** shape. In the properties window, start off by clicking the ellipsis next to the **Content** property. This opens the Content Definition window. Under the Message section, type in **ClaimResponse** in the **Message data** text box. Leave the **Message type** text box set to null, as shown in Figure 10-5.

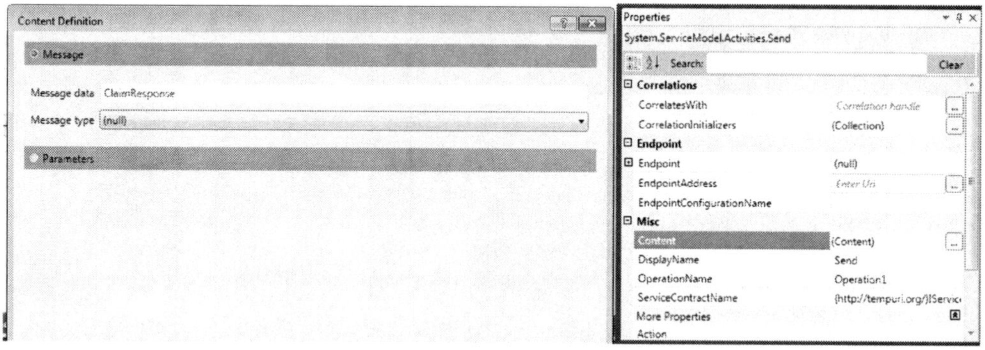

Figure 10-5. Content Property

This sets the message type that this shape will operate on. It also sets the message object that you will use when setting up your **CorrelationInitializer**. Your next step is to set up the correlation. Your **Send** shape initializes the correlation in this scenario. To do this, click on the ellipsis next to the **CorrelationInitializers** property. This opens the **Add Correlation Initializers** dialog window. On the left side on the first text box, type in the name of the **CorrelationHandle** variable you created: **ClaimIDCorrelationHandle**. Next, in the drop down in the top right of this dialog, select the **Query correlation initializer** option. At this point, you can use the drop down under the XPath Queries section, as shown in Figure 10-6. Select the **ClaimID** value.

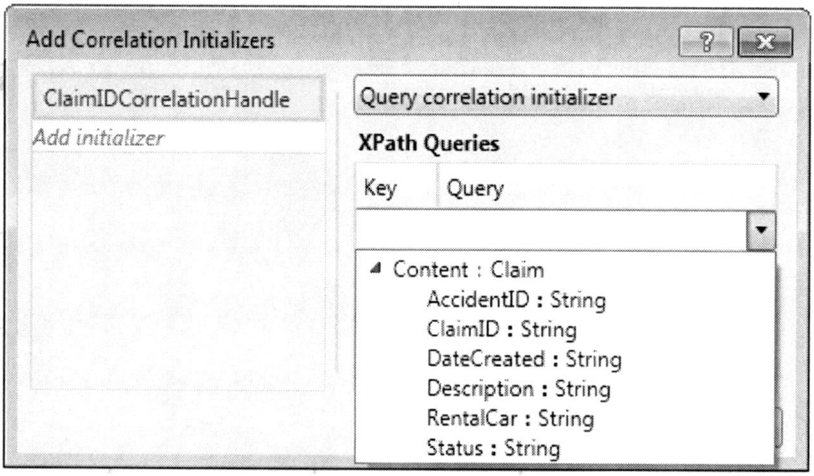

Figure 10-6. Correlation Initializer

You're now finished configuring your **Send** Shape, so select the **Receive** shape, and you can configure that next. Select the ellipsis next to the **Content** property and type **ClaimRequest** into the **Message data** text box; leave the **Message type** text box set to null, just as you did for the **Send** shape. Next, click on the ellipsis next to the **CorrelatedOn** property to open the CorrelatesOn Definition windows. Type **ClaimIDCorrelationHandle** into the **CorrrelatesWith** text box at the top and click the drop down list box. You will see a **Claim** object similar to the one shown in Figure 10-6. Select **ClaimID** and click **OK**. When this window closes, the **CorrelatesWith** property is populated. You have now setup correlation in your workflow.

Long-Running Workflows

Windows Workflow provides the capability for both short- and long-running processes. Short-running processes are those that complete in seconds or less; long-running processes are those that take longer, which can mean hours, days, or months. By default, workflows execute entirely in memory. With long-running workflows, you don't want idle workflows taking up resources and occupying valuable memory while waiting for an incoming message to start the process. To free up idle workflow instances, WF provides the ability to persist the workflow instances to a database. When an incoming message is received, it can wake up the workflow instance, and WF will load into memory and continue running from the last persistence point. The wake-up call is handled automatically by AppFabric, and it's efficient.

The persistence mechanism (including persistence points) provides recovery in case the server fails. It also provides scalability by paging out the state memory within idle workflow instances. Persistence also provides scalability because it's akin to having multiple servers hosting your application, perhaps with a load balancer in front of both servers. Persistence also provides the ability for a workflow to be running on one machine, persist, and then instantiate on the other server to process the rest of the activities.

The persistence model follows three steps: establishing the persistence point, collecting the data to persist, and delegating the persistence work to the persistence provider.

The code that follows shows you how to create a persistence provider:

```
private PersistenceProvider CreatePersistenceProvider(Guid instanceId)
    {
        string Conn = "Data Source=localhost;Initial
                       Catalog=InstanceStore;Integrated
                       Security=True;Asynchronous Processing=True";

        //Create the provider factory object
        SqlPersistenceProviderFactory factory = new
           SqlPersistenceProviderFactory(Conn, true, false,
           new TimeSpan(0, 1, 0));
        factory.Open();

        // Create the provider
        PersistenceProvider persistenceProvider =
           factory.CreateProvider(instanceId);

        return persistenceProvider;
    }
```

Once you create the persistence provider, you can associate it with your workflow instance when you load the workflow, as shown in this code snippet:

```
public void LoadWFInstance(Request request)
  {
    ...

      // Load the instance specifying the workflow ID
      WorkflowInstance instance = new WorkflowInstance(wf,
          input, instanceId);

      // On Idle perform the persistence
      instance.OnIdle = () => IdleAction.Unload;

      // Register the provider
      PersistenceProvider persistenceProvider =
          this.CreatePersistanceProvider(instanceId);

      instance.Extensions.Add(persistenceProvider);

      // execute the workflow instance
      instance.Run();
  }
```

Now you can force persistence points in two ways. First, you can drag the **Peristence** shape and place it at the location on the workflow surface where you want to create a persistence point. Second, you can specify that you want a persistence point on the **SendReply** shape in the **ReceiveAndSendReply** composite shape. The **SendReply** shape exposes a **PersistBeforeSend** property that you can checked to ensure that a persistence point occurs (see Figure 10-7).

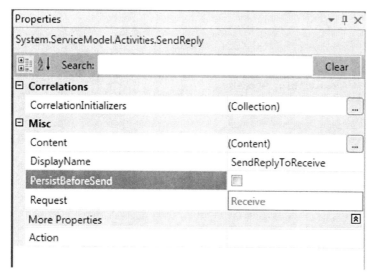

Figure 10-7. Persistence Point Property

Finally, let's talk about persistence and correlation. Correlation comes into play when you need to implement a long-running conversation with a client, utilizing the duplex communication pattern. The client must provide a means for the service to call the client back at another time. To implement this pattern, you use a **Send** and a **Receive** shape. On the **Receive** shape, you initialize a correlation and specify the key value as **ClaimIDCorrelationHandle**. Next, you configure the **Send** shape to specify the correlation name in the **CorrelatesWith** property (see Figure 10-8).

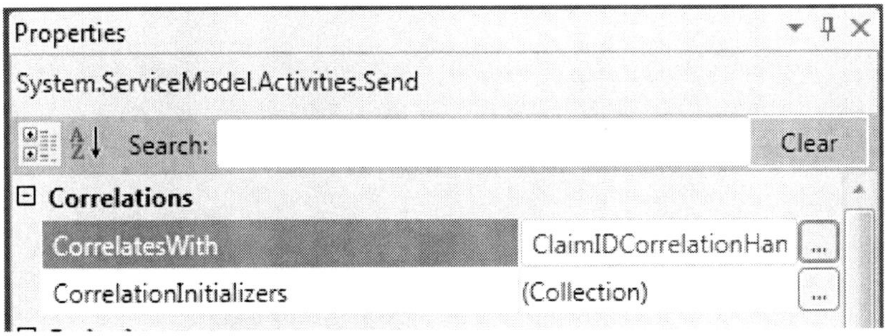

Figure 10-8. Persistence Point Property

You can see an example of this pattern in use when you send a claim to an adjuster for approval. The adjuster might not process this claim immediately if he is on vacation or out off the office for the day. When the adjuster approves the claim, the workflow must be able to correlate with the correct persisted instance, resume from the last processing point, and finish the workflow.

Compensation

An offshoot of long-running workflows is the need to provide functionality that allows you to back out of a unit of work. When working with atomic transactions, you have the ability to abort the transaction, and everything reverts back to the state immediately before the transaction was initiated.

With a long-running workflow, you don't have that ability. Therefore, you need to take advantage of compensation. *Compensation* is the ability to define a long-running unit of work where, if an exception occurs, you provide a set of activities that clean up the activities that were invoked, returning the system back to a consistent state. For example, assume you want to submit a claim and rent a car. The claim submission was sent asynchronously, and you make another call to the car rental service to put a hold on a car. If the submit claim resulted in an exception, but the car rental was successful, you need a way to clean this up, so that you are not left with a partial rental hold, but no claim.

You can accomplish this by using a **CompensableActivity** shape. This shape has a **Body** and a **CompensationHandler**. In this example, you place the call to the claim service and a call to the **Rental** service in the Body section. In the CompensationHandler section, you add a service call to a **Cancel** method on the car rental service. The CompensationHandler section is called automatically when an exception occurs, and you can place any logic necessary for cleaning up or undoing the work that was done in the Body section (see Figure 10-9).

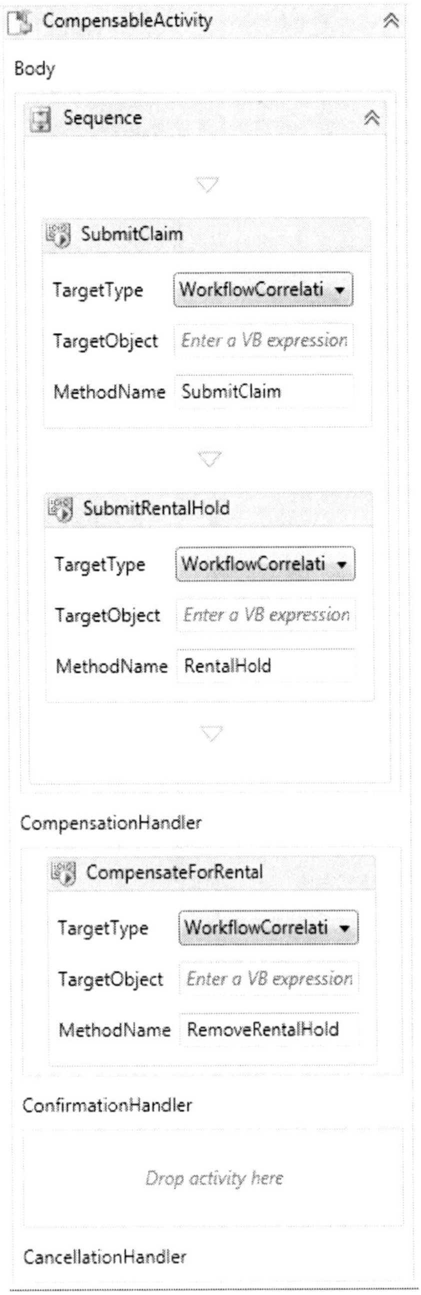

Figure 10-9. *CompensableActivity*

Summary

In this chapter, you learned many advanced concepts; specifically you tackled content-based routing, message correlation, long-running workflows, and compensation. You also learned how to implement these patterns, as well as your options when doing so. You also learned about correlation options and their implementation. Finally, you walked through several practical examples that demonstrated how to use these patterns.

CHAPTER 11

■ ■ ■

Monitoring and Tracking

An application is like an automobile: you can't just deploy it and forget about it. You need to monitor it, just as you need to you monitor your vehicle's speed to ensure that you don't go too fast. Your vehicle also has warning devices built into its dashboard to tell you if your engine stops or if you lose oil pressure. In a similar vein, AppFabric includes monitoring features that enable you to view the status of your current applications.

Monitoring produces a good deal of data. AppFabric lets you retain that data in a database for reporting purposes. You can purge data when it's old. AppFabric even includes support for archiving older data, in case you decide that you need that older data again.

Finally, AppFabric includes a built-in tracking capability. You might think of tracking as what a mechanic does when he troubleshoots a problem in your automobile. AppFabric's tracking gives you visibility into AppFabric workflows. You can view events, and you can look at data in a currently executing workflow. Tracking gives you the ability to troubleshoot and resolve problems that might occur in your production environment.

Monitoring

Taking a look at the whole application development lifecycle reinforces why developers and system administrators need the ability to monitor an application, see the state of its service instances and workflows, and view workflow instances with problems. AppFabric provides a dashboard that allows both developers and systems administrators to peer into the running system and see what is going on.

The AppFabric Dashboard

You can access this dashboard by clicking the **Dashboard** icon under the Application Server Extension for .NET 4 section in the Internet Information Services (IIS) Manager at the desired scope in the IIS hierarchy. Figure 11-1 shows the icon to click.

Figure 11-1. Launching the AppFabric Dashboard

You probably remember from previous chapters that the different scope levels are server, site, and application. The metrics displayed in each section at each scope are the same, but the values change based on what is included at the specific scope. Depending on what scope level you select, you might see metrics from the instances of all services on the server or site, or you might be able to select an application and see only the metrics for those instances.

■ **Note** The amount of monitoring data displayed for a specific view corresponds to the values that you configure on the `Monitoring` tab in the `Configure WCF and WCF` dialog box for that scope.

The dashboard will display categories for `Persisted WF Instances`, `WCF Call History`, and `WF Instance History` (see Figure 11-2). The dashboard will also show you the pertinent statistics for each of these three categories.

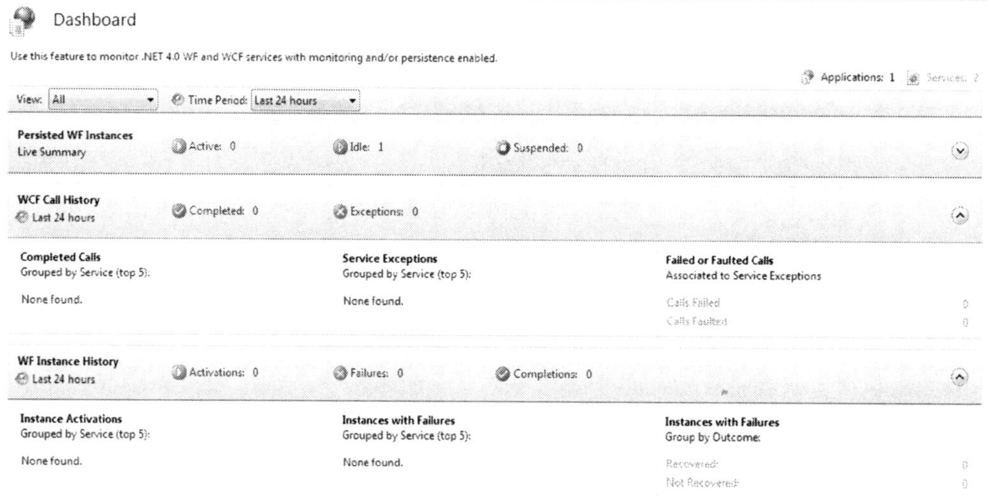

Figure 11-2. AppFabric Dashboard

The `Persisted WF Instances` section of the dashboard displays a live summary. It also shows the active instances, idle instances, and suspended instances. The idle and suspended instances are important because they point to Workflow instances that are blocked or that have encountered an error. These are the states that require human intervention, so you can right-click on any of the instances that appear to see a dropdown menu that lets you drill down on and look at either `Tracked WF Instances` or `Tracked Events`. When you click the `Tracked Events` menu item, AppFabric takes you to the `Tracked Events` page, were you can see the Event Level, Event Type, WF Activity Name, Time, Service Name and the Service Virtual Path (see Figure 11-3).

≡ **Note** AppFabric doesn't support the persistence of WCF instances; it supports only the persistence of Workflow instances.

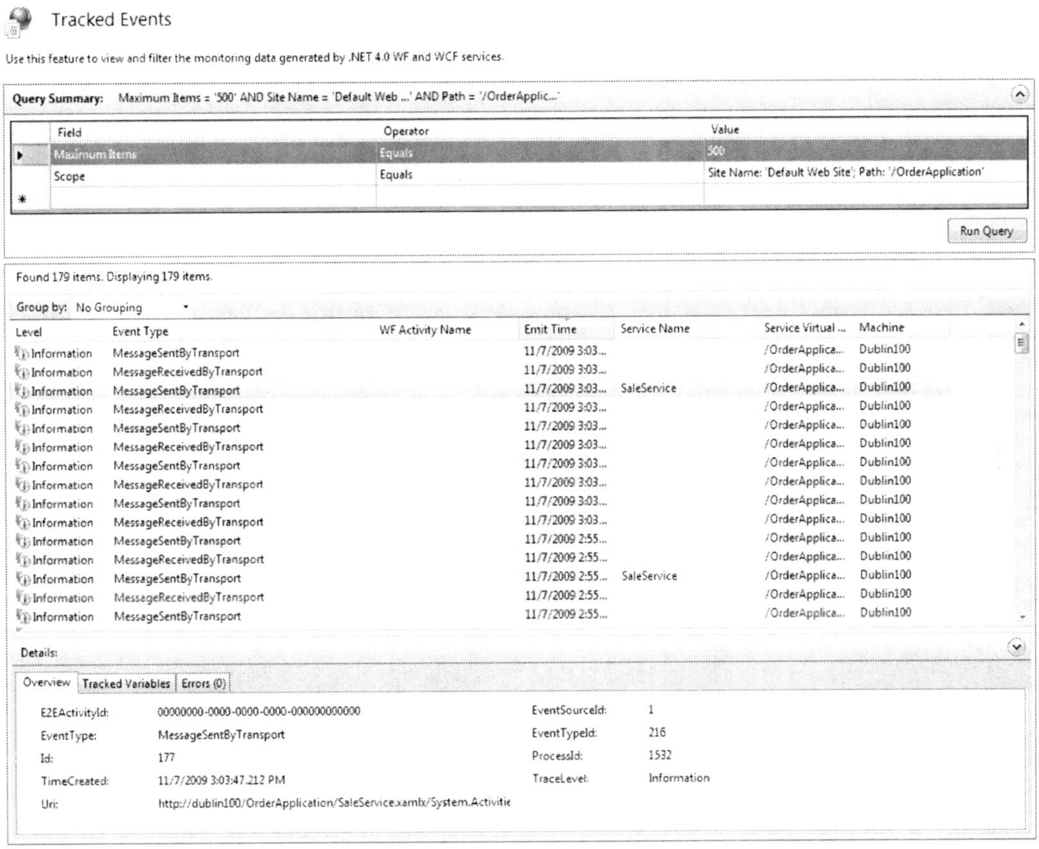

Figure 11-3. Tracked Events Page

Clicking any of the events listed in the search results pane in the middle of the screen brings up the details of the tracked event. You will also be able to see any of the tracked variables, as well as any errors that might have occurred. Right-clicking any of the events listed in the search results pane brings up a menu item that lets you drill into Tracked WF Instances or All Related Events.

If you go back to the dashboard and select an idle instance, you can drill into the **Persisted WF Instances** page. This page displays your idle instances. It also lets you query for instances based on specific criteria, including the status field (see Figure 11-4).

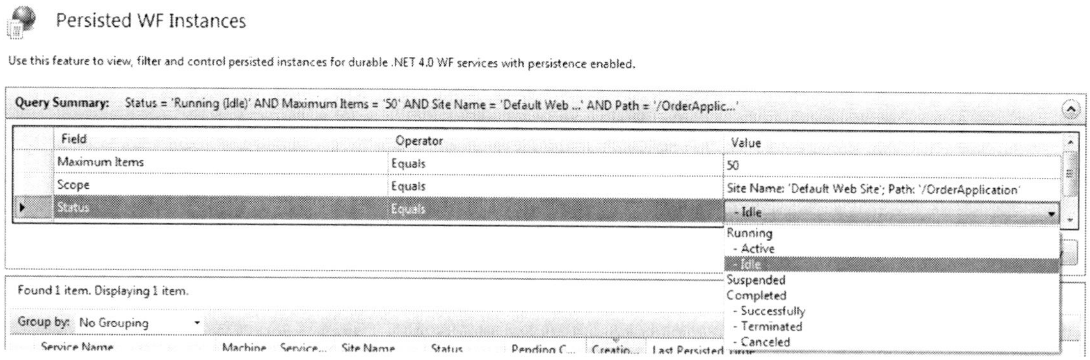

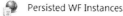

Use this feature to view, filter and control persisted instances for durable .NET 4.0 WF services with persistence enabled.

Query Summary:	Status = 'Running (Idle)' AND Maximum Items = '50' AND Site Name = 'Default Web ...' AND Path = '/OrderApplic...'		
Field	**Operator**		**Value**
Maximum Items	Equals		50
Scope	Equals		Site Name: 'Default Web Site'; Path: '/OrderApplication'
Status	Equals		- Idle

Running
 - Active
 - Idle
Suspended
Completed
 - Successfully
 - Terminated
 - Canceled

Found 1 item. Displaying 1 item.

Group by: No Grouping

| Service Name | Machine | Service... | Site Name | Status | Pending C... | Creatio... | Last Persisted |

Figure 11-4. WF Instance Status Options

Once you have the workflow instance that interests you, you can resume, suspend, cancel, terminate, or delete the instance (depending on the current state of the instance), as shown in Figure 11-5. Suspending an instance stops the execution of that instance and prevents it from continuing or receiving new messages. You can resume a suspended instance later point and then continue processing and receiving new messages. Terminating an instance stops its execution and removes the instance from the persistence store. A terminated instance cannot be resumed. Cancelling an instance clears the current memory state held for the instance and reverts the instance to the last persistence point stored in the persistence database.

 Persisted WF Instances

Use this feature to view, filter and control persisted instances for durable .NET 4.0 WF services with persistence enabled.

Query Summary: Status = 'Running (Idle)' AND Maximum Items = '50' AND Site Name = 'Default Web ...' AND Path = '/OrderApplic...'

	Field	Operator	Value
▶	Maximum Items	Equals	50
	Scope	Equals	Site Name: 'Default Web Site'; Path: '/OrderApplication'
	Status	Equals	- Idle

Run Query

Found 1 item. Displaying 1 item.

Group by: No Grouping

Service Name	Machine	Service...	Site Name	Status	Pending C...	Creatio...	Last Persisted Time
	DUBLI...	/Order...	Default Web...	Running (I...		11/7/2...	11/7/2009 3:04:47.163 PM

Refresh
Resume
Suspend
Cancel
Terminate
Delete
View Tracked Instance
View Tracked Events
Help
Online Help

Details:

Overview | Errors (0)

Service Name:	SaleService	Site Name:	Default Web Site
Service Virtual Path:	/OrderApplication/SaleService.xamlx	Workflow Instance ID:	a94bd797-f161-4386-bf06-c6ac2da113be
Creation Time:	11/7/2009 2:51:38.543 PM	Last Persisted Time:	11/7/2009 3:04:47.163 PM
Active Bookmarks:	[GetStatus{http://tempuri.org/}ISaleService: InternalReceiveMessage]	Tracked Events:	0

Figure 11-5. WF Instance View

You can access all of the capabilities provided through the user interface through PowerShell cmdlets. The `Get-ASAppServiceInstance` and the `Stop-ASAppServiceInstance` cmdlets provide the same functionality that you see in the menu item in Figure 11-5. The arguments of the cmdlets let you specify the service instance, as well as what you want to do with that service instance.

Let's go back to the dashboard again and look at the `WCF Call History` category. It includes three summary sections: `Completed Calls`, `Service Exceptions`, and `Failed or Faulted Calls`. When you click the Completed Calls or the Exceptions sections, the dashboard takes you to the `Tracked Events` page. Many of these links will take you to the Tracked Events page, but the data displayed will be different because each event has its own query to find the specified data in the monitoring database.

The last section on the dashboard is the `WF Instance History` category. Its three summary statistics show the number of `Activations`, `Failures`, and `Completions` of the services that have monitoring enabled. When you expand a section, you will see data for `Instance Activations` (grouped by the top five), `Instances with Failures` (also grouped by the top five), and `Instances with Failures` broken out by `Recovered` and `Not Recovered`.

Items that Affect Metric Counts

When looking at the data that appears in the dashboard, you can find differences between the various scope views. For example, you might find differences in certain counters depending on the scope level you select. When viewing the information in the dashboard at the server scope, the summary counters display a total of all the data provided from all of the monitoring databases. This doesn't occur when you view the dashboard from the application scope because you have only one database per application. However, when you view the dashboard from the server scope, you see all of the included databases, and this view can contain data that might not be current. You might also see two applications once shared a database, but that one of those applications no longer is configured to use that database; regardless, the old data is still included in the dashboard counts. If you encounter this scenario, then you must purge your old data, so don't receive inconsistent metrics. You must ensure that you only purge the data from the old application and not the application currently using the database. The purging process isn't performed automatically when the application is no longer tied to the database.

Setting the Monitoring Configuration Parameters

At this point, you know what the dashboard is and some of the capabilities it provides. Next, you need to look at how you get data to appear in the dashboard. When you install your application in AppFabric, you will see two monitoring settings that are configured automatically: **Monitoring Level** and **Diagnostic Tracing and Message Logging**. You can view and modify these settings by right-clicking the desired scope in the IIS hierarchy and then selecting the **.NET 4 WCF and WF** menu item. Next, select **Configure** from the submenu (see the **Configuration** dialog box in Figure 11-6).

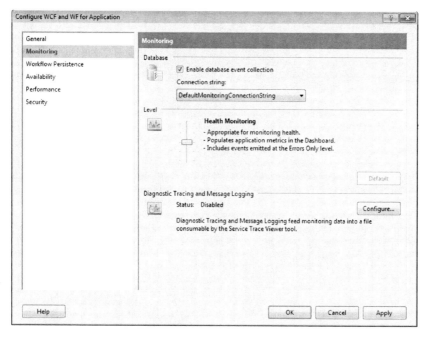

Figure 11-6. *Monitoring Configuration*

Choosing a Health Monitoring Level

The monitoring level shown in Figure 11-6 is enabled for all services by default, and it's currently set to **Health Monitoring**. This is the middle setting, and it's considered to be the best performance choice for normal health monitoring. This setting also represents the minimum setting to ensure that you can use all metrics on the dashboard. This setting includes a rollup from all of the lesser settings.

The other setting selections are **Off**, **Errors Only**, **Health Monitoring**, **End-To-End Monitoring**, and **Troubleshooting**. Changing the setting to **End-To-End** enables you to expose the relationship between WCF and WF events in the **Tracked Events** page. This enables you to correlate the events and provide a better, more complete picture of what is happening inside each part of your AppFabric application. After you perform your troubleshooting exercise, you should set the monitoring level back to the **Health Monitoring** level.

The **Troubleshooting** level provides you with the most tracking data. Use this level when you need to see the most information emitted from the monitoring functionality provided by AppFabric. Again, once you finish troubleshooting the issue, you should set the monitoring level back to **Health Monitoring**.

⬛ **Note** When you select a monitoring level, it corresponds to a default tracking profile for that level. A tracking profile is a declarative definition that provides filters against event types from the workflow instance. You can also write your own custom tracking profiles if the defaults don't meet your monitoring needs. You will learn how to create custom tracking profiles in the later in this chapter.

When you set the monitoring level, the monitoring data is collected by the **Event Collector** service and written to the monitoring database using the connection string listed in the dropdown list box under the **Database** section. The default setting is **DefaultMonitoringConnectionString**. Every new application that is installed into AppFabric will now have the **Enable database event collection** checkbox will be selected by default. If you disable database event collection, no new events will be tracked. However, if you already have tracked events before deselecting the checkbox, you will still see those events in the **Tracked Events** page.

Enabling Diagnostic Tracing and Message Logging

Finally, AppFabric's dashboard includes the Diagnostic Tracing and Message Logging setting. This setting is disabled by default because this setting provides the ability to send the data to a file that can be viewed by the Service Trace Viewer utility. Enabling this function doesn't change the options available in the dashboard. Instead, it provides an additional mechanism to aid you in troubleshooting your AppFabric apps, augmenting the basic functionality of the dashboard.

The use of the **Configure Diagnostic Tracing and Message Logging** setting allows you to configure legacy **System.Diagnostics** monitoring at the server, site, or application level. This functionality provides additional integration between AppFabric troubleshooting and the .NET Framework's features. Setting this functionality creates a **svclog** file that you can use through the SvcTraceViewer tool. To enable this functionality, you set both the WCF tracing-level and the Workflow tracing-level dropdown boxes. The values for the both of these options are **Off**, **Critical**, **Error**, **Warning**, **Information**, and **Verbose**. Once you select a level, you need to enter a trace file name.

You can set **Message Logging** level. Once you check the Enable checkbox, you will have the option to select whether you want to log at the transport level and whether you want to log malformed messages. You will also need to specify a log file name for **Message Logging**.

The data that the tracing functionality emits is meant to be used by the Service Trace Viewer Tool (**SvcTraceViewer.exe**) to help you analyze the generated trace data. Configuring AppFabric's message logging functionality causes AppFabric to perform some behind-the-scenes work for you. Specifically, it configures trace listeners and implements the configuration that corresponds to the functionality found in the following configuration file:

```
<system.diagnostics>
  <sources>
    <source name="System.ServiceModel"
            switchValue="Information, ActivityTracing"
            propagateActivity="true">
      <listeners>
        <add name="xml" />
      </listeners>
    </source>
    <source name="System.Activities"
            switchValue="Information, ActivityTracing">
      <listeners>
        <add name="xml" />
      </listeners>
    </source>
    <source name="System.ServiceModel.MessageLogging">
      <listeners>
        <add name="messages"
             type="System.Diagnostics.XmlWriterTraceListener"
             initializeData="c:\AppFabric\messagelog.svclog" />
      </listeners>
    </source>
  </sources>
  <sharedListeners>
    <add name="xml"
         type="System.Diagnostics.XmlWriterTraceListener"
         initializeData="c:\AppFabric\Tracelog.svclog" />
  </sharedListeners>
</system.diagnostics>
<system.serviceModel>
  <diagnostics>
    <messageLogging
         logEntireMessage="true"
         logMalformedMessages="false"
         logMessagesAtServiceLevel="true"
         logMessagesAtTransportLevel="false"
         maxMessagesToLog="3000"
         maxSizeOfMessageToLog="2000"/>
  </diagnostics>
</system.serviceModel>
```

Archiving and Purging

Once you get a good amount of data in the monitoring database, you will sometimes need to archive it and purge it. You can use either two methods for this. The first method performs these tasks for you automatically; the second method requires that you handle these tasks manually.

The Automatic Method

The automatic method is meant to ensure that the size of the monitoring database does not grow out of control; it essentially deletes the oldest events to make room for new events. This method purges the database automatically based on either of two criteria: when your monitoring database reaches a specific size or when events reach a certain age.

To configure automatic purging, you need to modify a table in the `ApplicationServerExtensions` database that was created when you installed AppFabric. More specifically, you need to modify a row in `dbo.ConfigurationPropertiesTable`. This table contains six columns and includes the ability to specify an `ArchiveServer` and `ArchiveDatabase` value. The automatic method doesn't use these two columns. For archiving capabilities, you need to use the PowerShell cmdlets described later in this chapter.

■ **Note** The automatic method only purges the data and does not provide any archiving capability.

The next column determines whether the automatic purging is enabled or disabled. If the column contains a value of **1** (the default), then it purges the data based on the values in the next three columns: `APThreshold`, `APMaxEventAge`, and `APTrimPercentage`.

The APThreshold column is set by default to a value of **1500**. When the database size exceeds this number of megabytes, the data is deleted based on the percentage amount in the `APTrimPercentage` column. The `APMaxEventAge` column specifies that events older than the number of days entered will be deleted. This column is set to **NULL** by default. Finally, the `APTrimPercentage` column specifies the percentage of database space to purge. This column is set to **10%** by default.

The `AutoPurge` stored procedure runs when the size of the database exceeds the specified threshold. This prompts the stored procedure to overwrite the specified percentage of the database's oldest rows with newer entries. If the stored procedure finds events older than the value entered into the `APMaxEventAge`, then it will also delete those events.

■ **Note** This database purge functionality can only be used for AppFabric based applications where the monitoring store utilizes Microsoft SQL Server. Also, you can only use this functionality for the monitoring database and you cannot configure them for use with the `Persistence` database.

The Manual Method

The manual method provides the ability to archive the **Monitoring** database and to purge the **Monitoring** and/or the **Persistence** databases. The archive and purge functionality is provided through a set of five PowerShell cmdlets, which you will learn about in the upcoming sections.

Associate a Destination Archive

The `Set-ASMonitoringDatabaseArchiveConfiguration` cmdlet associates a monitoring database with a destination archive database; note that this destination database must be an existing and initialized monitoring database.

This cmdlet has two different command-line syntaxes:

```
// First command-line syntax
Set-ASMonitoringDatabaseArchiveConfiguration -ArchiveDatabase ↵
<String> -Database <String> [-Confirm] [-LinkedArchiveServer <String>] ↵
[-Server <String>] [-WhatIf] [<CommonParameters>]

// Second command-line syntax
Set-ASMonitoringDatabaseArchiveConfiguration -ArchiveDatabase ↵
<String> -ConnectionString <String> [-Confirm] [-LinkedArchiveServer ↵
<String>] [-WhatIf] [<CommonParameters>]
```

The parameters for both of these commands contain the following information:

- *ArchiveDatabase*: Specifies the destination archive database name

- *Database*: Specifies the name of the primary database to be archived

- *ConnectionString*: Specifies a standard SQL Server connection string for the primary monitoring database

- *LinkedArchiveServer*: Specifies the name of the SQL Server that contains the destination archive database

- *Server*: Specifies the name of the SQL Server server that contains the primary monitoring database

- *WhatIf* (optional): Connects to the databases, but does not configure archiving

Set the Archive Database Connection String

The `Get-ASMonitoringDatabaseArchiveConfiguration` cmdlet returns the connection string that represents the archive destination database setup in the specified monitoring database.

This cmdlet has two different command-line syntaxes:

```
// First command-line syntax
Get-ASMonitoringDatabaseArchiveConfiguration -Database <String> ↵
[-Server <String>] [<CommonParameters>]
```

```
// Second command-line syntax
Get-ASMonitoringDatabaseArchiveConfiguration -ConnectionString ↵
<String> [<CommonParameters>]
```

The parameters for both of these commands contain the following information:

- *Database*: This parameter is optional only when a connection string is used, and it is the name of the primary database for the archive information you want to retrieve.

- *Server*: This parameter specifies the name of the SQL Server server that contains the primary monitoring database. This parameter is optional, and it will default to the local computer you don't specify a primary monitoring database.

- *ConnectionString*: This parameter represents a standard SQL Server connection string for the primary monitoring database. This parameter is optional; you don't need it if you use the **Database** parameter.

Purge from Monitoring Database

The **Clear-ASMonitoringDatabase** cmdlet purges data from a monitoring database and allows the purged data to be moved to an archive database.

This cmdlet has two different command-line syntaxes:

```
// First command-line syntax
Clear-ASMonitoringDatabase -Database <String> [-Archive] [-CutoffTime ↵
<DateTime>] [-MaxAge <TimeSpan>] [-PurgeMode {<EventAgeMode | None | ↵
WFInstanceCompletedMode}] [-Server <String>] [<CommonParameters> [-WhatIf]]
```

```
// Second command-line syntax
Clear-ASMonitoringDatabase -ConnectionString <String> [-Archive] ↵
[-CutoffTime <DateTime>] [-MaxAge <TimeSpan>] [-PurgeMode {<EventAgeMode ↵
| None | WFInstanceCompletedMode>}] [-WhatIf] [<CommonParameters>]
```

The parameters for both of these commands contain the following information:

- *Database*: This parameter represents the name of the database to purge. This parameter is optional when you use a connection string.

- *ConnectionString*: This parameter represents a standard SQL Server connection string for the database. This parameter is optional; you don't need it if you use the **Database** and **Server** parameters.

- *Archive*: This optional parameter archives the data to the archive database specified through the **Set-ASMonitoringDatabaseArchiveConfiguration** cmdlet before the purge occurs.

- *CutOffTime*: This parameter specifies the time interval you want to elapse before you purge event data. This parameter is optional; however, if you don't specify a value for it, the cmdlet uses the current time and subtracts the value from the **MaxAge** parameter to use as the **CustOffTime** value. This parameter respects the value entered in **PurgeMode** when flagging events to purge.

- *MaxAge*: This parameter represents the time that an event can be in the monitoring database before it will be flagged to be purged. The default is 0.

- *PurgeMode*: This parameter specifies how the purge will occur and provides three options for how you want this to happen: `None,` `EventAgeMode`, and `WFInstanceCompletedMode`. The default option is `EventAgeMode`.

    - *EventAgeMode*: This option deletes all WCF and WF events based on the age of the event. This includes deleting WF instance monitoring data for incomplete instances.

    - *WFInstanceCompletedMode*: This option deletes events based on age, but only those events for Workflow instances that aren't associated with active instances.

- *Server*: This parameter specifies the name of the SQL Server server that contains the database you want to purge. This parameter is optional, and it defaults to the local computer if you don't use specify one.

Remove Configuration Information

The `Remove-ASMonitoringDatabaseArchiveConfiguration` cmdlet removes the configuration information that you set using the `Set-ASMonitoringDatabaseArchiveConfiguration` cmdlet.

This cmdlet only has one command line:

```
Remove-MonitoringDatabaseArchiveConfiguration [-Database <String>] ↵
[-Server <String>] [-Confirm <Switch>][-ConnectionString<String>]
```

The parameters for this command contain the following information:

- *Database*: This parameter is optional only when a connection string is used and is the name of the primary database for the archive information you are trying to retrieve.

- *Server*: This parameter specifies the name of the SQL Server server that contains the primary monitoring database. This parameter is optional, and it defaults to the local computer if you don't specify one.

- *Confirm*: This parameter specifies whether the user needs to confirm removing the configuration data.

- *ConnectionString*: This parameter represents a standard SQL Server connection string for the primary monitoring database. This parameter is optional; you don't need it if you use the **Database** parameter.

Remove Old Data

The `Remove-ASAppServiceInstance` cmdlet removes old data from the **Persistence** database. This cmdlet provides no archiving capability. The `Remove-ASAppServiceInstance` cmdlet differs from the `Clear-ASMonitoringDatabase` cmdlet in that it purges only the Persistence database; the `Clear-ASMonitoringDatabase` cmdlet acts only on the Monitoring database.

You use the `Remove-ASAppServiceInstance` cmdlet to clean up *stale instance data*. Stale instance data can occur when persistence data is collected from servers set up in a web farm, and one of the computers is removed from the farm. Persisted instances linked to the removed machine can still remain and skew the data returned from persistence store queries.

This cmdlet has three different command-line syntaxes:

```
// First command-line syntax
Remove-ASAppServiceInstance -Database <String> -InstanceId <Guid> ↵
[-Confirm] [-Force] [-Server <String>] [-WhatIf] [<CommonParameters>]

// Second command-line syntax
Remove-ASAppServiceInstance -ConnectionString <String> [-Confirm] ↵
[-Force] [-WhatIf] [<CommonParameters>]

// Third command-line syntax
Remove-ASAppServiceInstance -ServiceInstanceInfo <InstanceInfo> ↵
[-Confirm] [-Force] [-WhatIf] [<CommonParameters>]
```

The parameters for this command contain the following information:

- *Database*: This parameter is optional only when you use a connection string; this parameter specifies the name of the primary database you want to purge.

- *InstanceID*: This parameter is the GUID that represents the persisted instance.

- *Confirm*: This parameter specifies whether the user needs to confirm removing the configuration data. You shouldn't use this parameter if you specify a value for the **Force** parameter.

- *Force*: This parameter performs an action without user confirmation. You shouldn't us this parameter if you specify a value for the **Confirm** parameter.

- *Server*: This parameter specifies the name of the SQL Server server that contains the database. This parameter is optional and defaults to the local computer if you don't specify a server.

- *WhatIf*: This optional parameter connects to the databases, but it doesn't purge data.

- *ConnectionString*: This optional parameter represents a standard SQL Server connection string for the **Persistence** database. You don't need this parameter if you use the **Database** and **Server** parameters.

Another key scenario you must keep in mind when you need to clean up your persistence database occurs when you have instances that have started, but haven't yet been persisted. You need to run a SQL command to find the non-persisted instances. When you delete the non-persisted instance, you also delete instances that have started, but not yet persisted.

For example, run the following command to return instance IDs of non-persisted instances:

```
select instanceId from [System.Activities.DurableInstancing].[Instances]
where IsInitialized = 0 and IsLocked = 0;
```

Once you have the IDs, you can delete them either through the `Remove-ASAppServiceInstance` cmdlet or by using the `[System.Activities.DurableInstancing].DeleteInstance` stored procedure.

Tracking

Monitoring lets you see the health of the application. It also aids you in troubleshooting, but you need visibility into the execution of your code to achieve that. Tracking provides you with this visibility. The tracking features give you the ability to capture event data from the execution of the workflows. This event data includes standard events such as instance start time and finish time; it also provides the ability to extract data from the variables within the executing workflow instance. This provides useful data for IT staff and business analysts, helping you to ensure that you can perform diagnostics and measure business trends.

Tracking Architecture

The tracking architecture consists of three components: the **tracking records**, the **tracking profile**, and the **tracking participants**. You issue tracking records from the workflow runtime during the lifetime of the workflow instance. You use a tracking profile to filter the tracking records, while the tracking participants subscribe to the filtered records. The tracking participants encompass the logic you use to process the filtered tracking records and send them on to their storage location.

The tracking architecture utilizes *the observer pattern* where records are published, whether anything exists to subscribe to or not. The subscriber, the tracking participant, must register as an extension to the workflow to receive the tracking data.

■ **Note** The observer pattern is used to notify registered objects when state changes. This is a one-to-many relationship between the workflow runtime and the tracking participants, where all registered tracking participants are notified when the state changes.

There are four types of tracking records published during the life of the workflow instance:

- A workflow-instance tracking record

- An activity-tracking record

- A bookmark-resumption tracking record

- A user-tracking record

The workflow instance tracking records are generated for lifecycle events, such as instance start and completion. The activity-tracking records are generated when each activity within the workflow executes and specifies the state of the activity. The bookmark-resumption tracking record is generated whenever a workflow is resumed at that bookmark. Finally, the user-tracking records are generated from custom activities; these can also contain data from the variables in the workflow instance.

AppFabric utilizes the Event Tracing for Windows (ETW) tracking participant that ships with .NET 4.0. This tracking participant subscribes to the tracking records. It also writes them to the ETW session, so they can be viewed in Windows Event Viewer. It is also possible to create your own tracking participant and store the records in a place of your choosing.

■ **Note** The ETW tracking participant replaces the SQL Server Tracking Provider included in the previous version of the .NET Framework.

The SQL Server Tracking Provider that shipped in previous versions of the .NET Framework is no longer included, but that doesn't mean you can't achieve similar functionality. AppFabric ships with the **Application Server Event Collector** windows service. This Windows service starts an ETW session and listens for **WCF Tracing** and **WF Tracking** events published by your WCF and WF services. The Event Collector stores these events in the **Monitoring** database. The volume of the events collected from applications and stored in the monitoring database is controlled by the application's monitoring level.

Tracking Profiles

As stated in the preceding section on architecture, you use the tracking profile to filter the tracking records. You can create these tracking profiles in either of two ways. First, you can create them in the .NET configuration file in the **system.serviceModel** section; second, you can them through code.

Implementation Through Configuration

When you create a tracking profile, you should take a moment to think about the granularity you require. You might decide to create a profile that filters a small subset of changes on the workflow, or you might decide that you need to create a granular profile that captures a large amount of event data, so you can recreate the steps that were executed. The beauty of tracking profiles is that you can associate them with one or more tracking participants from within a single configuration file. Also, you can define multiple tracking profiles. This allows you to apply different tracking profiles to different tracking participants. You can also create different profiles for different environments, such as development and production; this enables you to switch them in and out easily.

When creating a profile in the .NET configuration file, you give it the following structure, starting with the **<tracking>** node inside the **<system.serviceModel>** node:

```
<tracking>
    <trackingProfile name="JustTheBasicsTrackingProfile">
      <workflow>
        <workflowInstanceQuery>
          <states>
            <state name="Started"/>
            <state name="Completed"/>
          </states>
        </workflowInstanceQuery>
      </workflow>
    </trackingProfile>
  </profiles>
</tracking>
```

Take a careful look at this configuration snippet, which shows a **workflowInstanceQuery** node. Tracking profiles define the subscription filter for events. You have six tracking queries that let you define the filter level for capturing specific event records. Of these six queries, you'll probably find yourself using four of them frequently:

- *ActivityQuery.* This query tracks the events for each individual activity.

- *FaultPropagationQuery.* This query tracks the handling of faults that occur within an activity.

- *UserTrackingQuery.* This query tracks events that you define in your code activities.

- *WorkflowInstanceQuery.* This query tracks the workflow instance lifecycle state changes.

The preceding configuration snippet uses **WorkflowInstanceQuery.** It was able to capture the **Started** and **Completed** states, but it's more likely that you will want to capture variable values. You can capture variable values from any activity in the workflow. To create a tracking profile that captures a variable value from an activity, you need to use the **activityName** property on the **activityQuery** node, provide the state of the activity that you want to capture, and finally, utilize a **variableQuery** query to specify the name of the variable. The configuration snippet looks like this:

```
<workflow>
...
<activityQueries>
  <activityQuery activityName="GetOrderNumber">
    <states>
      <state name="Closed"/>
    </states>
    <variableQueries>
      <variableQuery name="OrderNumberVariableValue" variable="OrderNumber"/>
    </variableQueries>
  </activityQuery>
</activityQueries>
...
</workflow>
```

The preceding snippet uses the **name** property on the **variableQuery** query. You don't have to do it this way, but it's strongly recommended that you do so because this name is what you see in the ETW traces. Also, the ability to extract variable values is not limited to the **ActivityQuery query**. You can also accomplish this task using the **ActivityInitialized**, **ActivityScheduled**, **CancelRequested**, and **FaultPropagatation** queries.

It's useful to know the value of these variables, but it can also be useful to know the order that the activities executed in, as well as what activity might execute next. The workflow runtime scheduler queues up the activities, and you can query the queue through the **activityScheduledQuery** attribute. This query operation has two attributes and identifies the parent activity, as well as the child activity. This record is published only when the child activity is being scheduled. This code configures **activityScheduledQuery**:

```
<workflow>
...
<activityScheduledQueries>
    <activityScheduledQuery activityName="*" childActivityName="*"/>
</activityScheduledQueries>
...
</workflow>
```

Finally, you will find it helpful to learn how to set up the configuration file to filter for exceptions. You do this using the `faultPropagationQuery` node. This query node allows you to specify an `activityName` attribute, a `faultHandlerActivityName` attribute, and an `extractFaultData` attribute. The `extractFaultData` attribute lets you capture the exception as a payload of the record. This code configures the attribute:

```
<workflow>
...
<faultPropagationQueries>
    <faultPropagationQuery activityName="*" extractFaultData="true"
faultHandlerActivityName="*"/>
</faultPropagationQueries>
...
</workflow>
```

The preceding code lets you filter for handled exceptions, but it also includes a mechanism that you can use to track unhandled exceptions. All that you need to do is insert the following inside the workflow node:

```
<workflowInstanceUnhandledExceptionQuery includeException="true"/>
```

You will want to make sure that you set the `includeException` attribute to `true`, so you can include the details of the exception in the tracked data.

The sample code includes a full sample configuration file; you can download this file from this book's page at **www.apress.com**.

Implementation Through Code

In the previous section, you implemented the tracking profiles through a configuration file. Now let's take a look at how you would create tracking profiles through code. In the preceding examples, you created a class library and a class that instantiated a `TrackingProfile` object. You can find the `TrackingProfile` object in the `System.Activities` namespace; set a reference to that namespace in your project and include a **using** statement that points to `System.Activities.Tracking`.

You need to set three properties when you create the `TrackingProfile` object: `Name`, `ActivityDefinitionId`, and `Queries`. The `Name` property is self explanatory; the `ActivityDefinitionId` property sets the activity definition id of the profile (the snippet below sets it to the name of the workflow in that snippet); and the `Queries` property lets you specify the `TrackingQuery` object that specifies the subscription definition, such as `WorkflowInstanceQuery`. You can then specify the `WorkflowInstanceStates` properties that you want to subscribe to, as in the following example:

```
TrackingProfile tp = new TrackingProfile()
{
    Name = "JustTheBasicsTrackingProfile",
    ActivityDefinitionId = "ProcessClaimService",
    Queries =
        {
            new WorkflowInstanceQuery()
            {
                States =
                {
                        WorkflowInstanceStates.Started, ↩
WorkflowInstanceStates.Completed
                }
            }
        }
};
```

As you follow the configuration file examples from the preceding section, you can also create a profile that will capture the order that the activities executed in. You can do this with the **ActivityScheduledQuery** object. Similar to the configuration file elements, this class has properties that let you specify the parent and child activity names:

```
TrackingProfile tp = new TrackingProfile()
{
    Name = "JustTheBasicsTrackingProfile",
    ActivityDefinitionId = "ProcessClaimService",
    Queries =
        {
            new ActivityScheduledQuery()
            {
                ActivityName = "*",
                ChildActivityName = "*"
            }
        }
};
```

Finally, you can use the **ActivityStateQuery** query to capture the state of the variable and argument values from any activity in the workflow. **ActivityStateQuery** has five properties and lets you specify the ActivityName property and the states you want to monitor; it also returns a collection of the arguments and variables. You can get a collection containing **QueryAnnotations**, as well.

Tracking Participants

As outlined in the preceding section on tracking architecture, a tracking participant listens to the tracking records being published and contains the logic to process the filtered tracking records and send them on to their storage location. Multiple tracking participants can consume the tracking records at the same time, and you can associate each tracking participant with different tracking profiles.

AppFabric ships with a tracking participant that writes tracking records to the ETW. As noted previously, the SQL Server tracking provider that was included in previous versions of the .NET framework has been replaced by the ETW provider. Microsoft made this change for several reasons.

Moving to the ETW provider allows Microsoft to provide developers with a unified tracking and tracing model for WF and WCF, while also leveraging the same model that Windows uses. It also provides the flexibility for administrators to manage the verbosity of the tracing level at runtime.

If you still need a SQL Server tracking provider, the .NET Framework 4 includes a sample that illustrates how to do this; however, the sample writes to its own schema, so it isn't incorporated with the AppFabric monitoring databases.

To use the ETW tracking participant, you need to configure it in **web.config** under the **System.ServiceModel** node:

```
<tracking>
  <participants>
    <add name="EtwTrackingParticipant"
         type="System.Activities.Tracking.EtwTrackingParticipant,
         System.Activities,
         Version=4.0.0.0,
         Culture=neutral,
         PublicKeyToken=31bf3856ad364e35"
         profileName="EtwTrackingProfile"/>
  </participants>
```

In addition to setting up the ETW participant, the ETW provider has the ability to specify a unique ID. If you do not provide one, then the default ETW provider ID will be used. However, if you want to segregate your events from other applications, then you should specify an application-specific provider ID in the configuration file. You do this by adding a diagnostics node before the tracking node illustrated moments earlier. The syntax to do this looks like this:

```
<diagnostics etwProviderId="CE006FB7-5319-400E-B45C-A1AB099DFD5B"/>
```

After you enter the participants into the configuration file, you can add the participants to the service behavior. Adding a participant to the **<serviceBehaviors>** node adds it to the workflow instances extension and sets it up so it can begin receiving tracking records. The behaviors syntax looks like this:

```
<behaviors>
    <serviceBehaviors>
      <behavior name="OrderServiceBehavior">
        <trackingComponents>
          <add name="EtwTrackingParticipant"/>
        </trackingComponents>
      </behavior>
    </serviceBehaviors>
</behaviors>
```

When the tracking records start flowing through the tracking participant, they will be delivered to the ETW session, and you can see them in Event Viewer. You can see the records by opening **Windows Event Viewer** and then navigating to the following folder: **Application and Services Logs\Microsoft\WCF\WF-Development**. Right-click and select **Enable View**; next, click **Show Analytic and Debug** logs. Your navigation screen in Event Viewer should look similar to what you see in Figure 11-7.

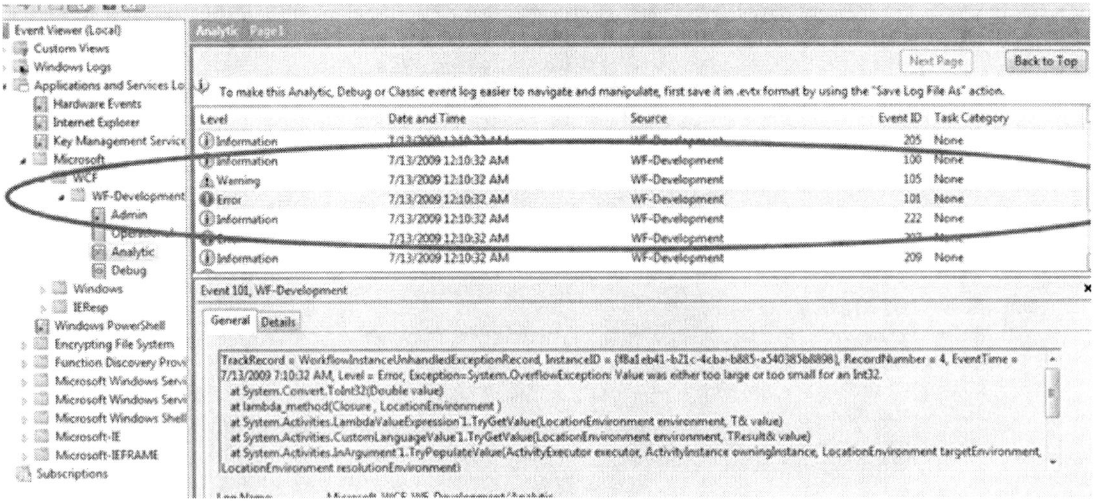

Figure 11-7. Event Viewer

Creating Your Own Tracking Participant

There might be times when you need additional or different functionality than that provided by the included ETW tracking participant. The tracking architecture helps you create your own custom tracking participants—just inherit from the **TrackingParticipant** base class. This base class provides a **TrackingProfile** property, as well as a **Track** method. The code snippet that follows outlines a simple tracking participant that receives a tracking record and writes it to the console window. You can include this class in any kind of .NET application (such as WinForms, WPF, ASP.NET, or console) and display the subscribed events as you wish by changing the **Debug.WriteLine** statement:

```
using System;
using System.Activities.Tracking;
using System.Collections.Generic;
using System.Diagnostics;
using System.Linq;
using System.Web;

public class DebugTrackingParticipant : TrackingParticipant
{
    public override void Track(TrackingRecord record, TimeSpan timeout)
    {
        if (record != null)
        {
            Debug.WriteLine(record.ToString());
            var userRecord = record as UserTrackingRecord;
            if (userRecord != null)
            {
                Debug.Indent();
```

```
            foreach (var item in userRecord.Data)
            {
                Debug.WriteLine("{0}: {1}", item.Key, item.Value);
            }

            Debug.Unindent();
        }
      }
    }
}
```

This code ships with the Visual Studio 2010 and .NET Framework 4 Training Kit found at **www.microsoft.com/downloads**.

To use this code, you need to link it with a tracking profile and register it with the workflow runtime extensions collection. You can accomplish this through configuration entries in the **tracking** and **trackingProfile** nodes. You probably recall setting up the ETW Tracking Participant from the configuration settings earlier in this chapter; you can take that configuration section and add another participant, as follows:

```
<tracking>
  <participants>
    <add name="EtwTrackingParticipant"
         type="System.Activities.Tracking.EtwTrackingParticipant,
         System.Activities,
         Version=4.0.0.0,
         Culture=neutral,
         PublicKeyToken=31bf3856ad364e35"
         profileName="EtwTrackingProfile"/>
    <add name="DebugTrackingParticipant"
         type="ProAppFabric.Chapter11.DebugTrackingParticipant,
             ProAppFabric.Chapter11,
             Version=1.0.0.0,
             Culture=neutral,
             PublicKeyToken=null"
         profileName="DebugTrackingProfile"/>
  </participants>
...
```

After you add the participant, you need to add the tracking profile. The **profileName** property needs to match the **name** attribute under the **profiles** node. Also, you will need to configure the queries under the **profiles** node to filter the types of records that you want to see output to the console window. In the configuration snippet that follows, you pull out the **OrderNumber** value using a **variableQuery** and specify the states that you want to pull out of the variable.

```
<profiles>
 <trackingProfile name="DebugTrackingProfile">
    <workflow>
      <activityInitializedQueries>
        <activityInitializedQuery activityName="GetOrderNumber">
          <variableQueries>
```

```
            <variableQuery name="OrderNumberVariableValue"
                variable="OrderNumber"/>
          </variableQueries>
        </activityInitializedQuery >
      </activityInitializedQueries >

      <workflowInstanceQuery>
        <states>
          <state name="Started"/>
          <state name="Completed"/>
        </states>
      </workflowInstanceQuery>
      <workflowInstanceUnhandledExceptionQuery includeException="true"/>
      <workflowInstanceAbortedQuery includeReasonAborted="true"/>
      <faultPropagationQueries>
        <faultPropagationQuery activityName="*"
            extractFaultData="true" faultHandlerActivityName="*"/>
      </faultPropagationQueries>
      <userTrackingQueries>
        <userTrackingQuery name="*" activityName="*"/>
      </userTrackingQueries>
    </workflow>
  </trackingProfile>
</profiles>
```

Summary

This chapter walked you through AppFabric monitoring and tracking. You looked at the dashboard and drilled into tracked events, as well as AppFabric's ability to query events, persisted instances, and instance status.

You also learned about monitoring configuration levels, as well as how to configure diagnostic tracing and message logging functionality. After you captured the monitoring data, you looked at ways to manage the monitoring data. You learned about both automated and manual methods of accomplishing this, including a number of PowerShell cmdlets for configuring, archiving, and purging the database.

Finally, the chapter walked you through the AppFabric's tracking functionality. You learned how to configure and create tracking profiles through configuration and explicitly through code; you also learned how to configure and create tracking participants.

CHAPTER 12

Implementing High Availability

Having both AppFabric and SQL Server installed on a single computer is sufficient for a development environment; however, a production environment will often consist of multiple computers in a server farm, as well as one or more dedicated SQL Server machines. Scaling-out allows you to implement load-balancing solutions, so that the processing of incoming messages is spread across multiple servers. This also enables you to provide increased fault tolerance for workflows that use persistence. Such an environment might also use queues to manage incoming messages destined for your application and SQL Server clustering for high availability.

In this chapter, you will learn the best practices for installing, configuring, and implementing AppFabric in a server farm to achieve high availability. You will learn about the important differences between a small-scale deployment of AppFabric, where you install everything on a single machine; and a server farm, where you deploy your applications across multiple servers to create a highly distributed application.

Planning for Scale-Out

When dealing with a long-running process, it is vital that your application be able to survive system reboots, hardware failures, and other unforeseen server outages. AppFabric provides a default persistence provider that your workflow applications can take advantage of to provide persistence for long-running applications.

In a single server deployment, persistence provides the ability for a workflow instance to resume execution when the server that hosts it returns to a healthy state; however, in a server farm deployment, the application can be resumed on any eligible machine in the server farm. Also, if a workflow instance is executing on one server and a message destined for that instance arrives on another, persistence can move the executing instance to the machine that has the pending message, enabling the workflow to process the message.

Figure 12-1 shows a typical AppFabric deployment configuration for a development environment. In this example, all AppFabric-hosted applications and services are deployed on a single server, and all AppFabric persistence and monitoring information is stored in one database.

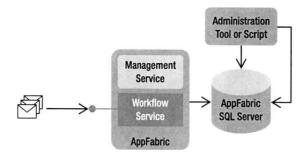

Figure 12-1. *A typical AppFabric deployment configuration for a development environment*

The configuration shown in Figure 12-1 is sufficient for a development environment; however, a production environment usually requires a more robust set of resources for high availability, scalability, and data storage. Figure 12-2 illustrates how you might deploy AppFabric components and services on multiple servers, forming a server farm with shared resources on a separate SQL Server machine.

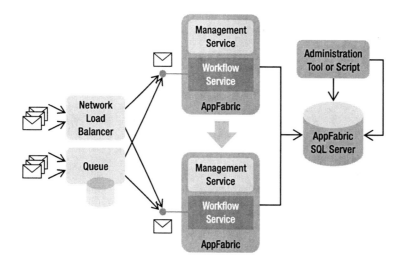

Figure 12-2. *AppFabric deployment Configuration in a Small Server Farm*

WCF and WF services deployed in AppFabric typically reside physically in IIS virtual directories, and you can virtualize them further behind a load balancer. The load balancer pushes HTTP or TCP requests to the services using one or more algorithms implemented by the specific software or hardware load balancer. For example, the load balancer might use a round robin algorithm.

■ **Note** AppFabric does not have a notion of a cluster; nevertheless, AppFabric makes it possible to put WCF and WF services behind a load balancer by providing a persistence lock retry mechanism. You create a "cluster" by configuring machines behind a load balancer and then configuring them to use a shared persistence database.

WCF and WF services can also get requests coming through queues (MSMQ, for instance), thus allowing for hybrid configurations where, for example, some services receive their requests from a load balancer, while others get their feeds from a queue.

You replicate AppFabric configuration on all servers using the MSDeploy tool. You first learned about this tool in Chapter 9, when you used it to deploy your Contoso Insurance services. (*MSDeploy* is the Microsoft Web Deployment Tool). MSDeploy allows you to synchronize sites, applications, and servers efficiently across your AppFabric server farm by detecting differences between the source and destination content, then transferring only those changes that need synchronization. The tool simplifies the synchronization process by automatically determining the configuration, content, and certificates to be synchronized for a specific site. You also have the option to specify additional providers for the synchronization, including databases, COM objects, GAC assemblies, and registry settings. Later in this chapter, you will learn how to synchronize AppFabric servers to keep all AppFabric configuration settings in sync between server nodes in an AppFabric server farm.

On each machine in your server farm, you can bring up an IIS Manager or PowerShell command utility to manage any assets and configuration settings on that farm. For example, you can access any workflow service instances or event data from any servers of the farm from within an IIS Manager running on any given machine of that farm. When you look at the AppFabric Dashboard in IIS Manager on any of the machines that belong to your server farm, you will see monitoring data from all the machines, not just the local machine. Likewise, you will see WF persisted instance information for instances that have been active on any of the machines in your farm, not just the local machine. You can control persisted WF instances running on any machine from the centralized point.

■ **Note** the initial, 1.0 version of AppFabric contains no central configuration database per a server farm; however, this could be introduced in a future release of AppFabric.

Let's take a closer look at this concept by walking through a practical example. For example, assume you have a WF service is running on machine A and a message for it arrives at machine B? Will the message be lost, or will it turn into a zombie message[1]?

To answer to this question, you should look at the mechanics of the AppFabric Workflow Management Service (WMS). Whenever a workflow service host takes ownership of a persisted instance (when the host loads the instance to do work), it acquires a *lock* on the instance, and the lock has an expiration time. The host must continue to update the expiration time as long as it is doing work. If the

---

[1] A *zombie message* is a message that a workflow did not process. It is in neither a suspended queue, nor anywhere else where you can retry it.

instance's expiration time expires and the instance is still locked, WMS assumes that the host has crashed. It then unlocks the instance to make it available for another host to own. WMS does not ping each host machine. Instead, each host continually updates the expiration time for its locked instances. WMS repeatedly queries the persistence database for *orphaned* locked instances that should be unlocked, and it unlocks them.

Now let's get back to the original scenario. If AppFabric host A owns a persisted WF instance and a message for this instance arrives on an AppFabric host B, this creates an instance lock exception. AppFabric Host B cannot take ownership of the instance because host A already owns it. The persistence provider includes a *lock retry* feature that lets you specify a time interval for retrying the lock. The idea here is that, in many workflow scenarios, an AppFabric host will have a lock on an instance for a short amount of time; it will load the instance, do a burst of work, and then unload it again. The lock retry takes advantage of this typical pattern; if an AppFabric host gets a lock exception, it waits for a specific time interval and then tries again.

For scenarios like the preceding example, you should consider having the messages delivered to a queue, so they can be consumed when the AppFabric host is ready for them.

Scaling Your AppFabric Persistence and Monitoring Databases

By default, AppFabric lets you configure a shared database for persistence and monitoring (see Figure 12-2). However, AppFabric enables even more scalability and flexibility by letting you create multiple and separate persistence and monitoring databases to support data isolation over multiple SQL Server machines (see Figure 12-3).

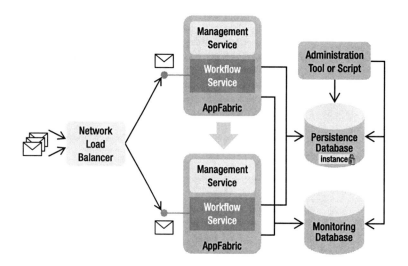

Figure 12-3. Multiple Persistence and Monitoring Databases in an AppFabric Deployment Configuration

AppFabric also supports the creation of multiple databases. This means you can do more than just separate data by function (persistence and monitoring); you can also separate it by application. If you have an application that has robust data storage requirements, you can create persistence and monitoring databases that are specifically associated with only this application or service (see Figure 12-4).

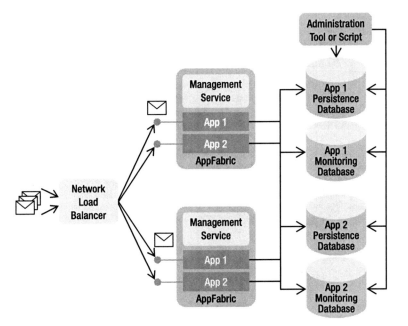

Figure 12-4. Separating Persistence and Monitoring Databases per Application

Expanding an AppFabric Server Farm

Now, suppose your applications and services load has grown to the point that you want to add another AppFabric server to the farm. The good news: It's easy to extend your farm with another AppFabric server. All you have to do is follow these steps:

1. Prepare a sysprep2 of a new AppFabric server or VM (virtual machine) image.

2. Synchronize (using MSDeploy) one of the existing AppFabric servers with the new server.

3. Configure a load balancer by adding an IP address of the new server to the load balancer's configuration metadata to start fanning out requests to the new server.

You're done!

---

[2] **Sysprep** is the name of Microsoft's System Preparation Utility for the Microsoft Windows operating system deployment.

Failover Capabilities in AppFabric

Now assume something goes wrong with one of the servers in the farm and that server shuts down. Obviously, the bad news is that you must recover from the crash on that machine and possibly rebuild it or replace it with another server. The good news, however, is that your server farm has never stopped working. It continues to process messages and deliver data in and out to all the services and workflows deployed into this farm, as long as you have at least one AppFabric server and one SQL Server database node running your workflow service instances and other monitoring data. This highly available scenario becomes possible thanks to the AppFabric Instance Recovery and Durable Timer services provided to you out-of-the-box as part of the AppFabric Runtime Service components, which were described in detail in Chapter 4. If one of your servers goes down, these built-in services make sure that your workflow continues from the last known persisted point on another available server in the farm.

Now consider the scenario where a WF service instance is prematurely terminated. AppFabric's WMS will detect that the instance should be running, and it will restart it on another machine in the farm. AppFabric also deals with orphan messages in a graceful manner. An orphan message is one that cannot be consumed by its correlated WF instance because the message was routed into a different machine in a server farm. Instead of throwing an exception, AppFabric will retry for a configurable timeout period to obtain a lock on the instance, load it on the local machine, and then pass the "orphan" message to the correct instance.

Synchronizing AppFabric Servers

This section demonstrates how to synchronize the content and the configuration on all computers in an AppFabric server farm to a single model computer. You can easily modify the procedure to synchronize only parts of the IIS content and configuration. For example, you might choose to synchronize only a single application.

Applying multiple changes to an AppFabric server farm requires that you apply all changes to all computers in exactly the same way. If you write scripts for all the needed changes, then applying them all in the same way is an easy task. Otherwise, you need to deal with the problem of recording and reproducing all the changes on all computers in your farm. One possible solution is to apply all your changes to a single computer and then replicate this computer across the AppFabric server farm.

Prepare your Server Farm

For synchronization of AppFabric servers to work, you need at least two servers that meet the following requirements:

- The Web Deployment Tool's Remote Agent Service is installed and running on all computers participating in the server farm. By default, AppFabric installs the Web Deployment Tool, but its Remote Agent Service is not part of the default installation.

- All the accounts that you use to synchronize the farm have administrative privileges on all computers in the farm. Alternatively, you can modify the sample script to run in a non-domain environment. To do this, you use the WMsvc provider setting, where you specify the computerName, username, and password settings. You'll see a sample that shows you how to do this later in this chapter.

You might be able to install the Remote Agent Service only on the source server if you want to *pull* the data from a remote source; or you might be able to install it on the destination server only if you want to *push* the data to a remote destination. However, the authors recommend that you install the Remote Agent Service on all servers; obviously, the approach you adopt will depend on your organization's policies and procedures.

Install Web Deployment Tool's Remote Agent Service

Follow these steps to install Remote Agent Service:

1. Open the Programs and Features control panel.

2. Select Web Deployment Tool and click Change.

3. When prompted, click Next; on the following screen, click Change.

4. When the list of features is displayed, make sure that Remote Agent Service is marked Entire feature will **be installed on the local hard disk** (see Figure 12-5).

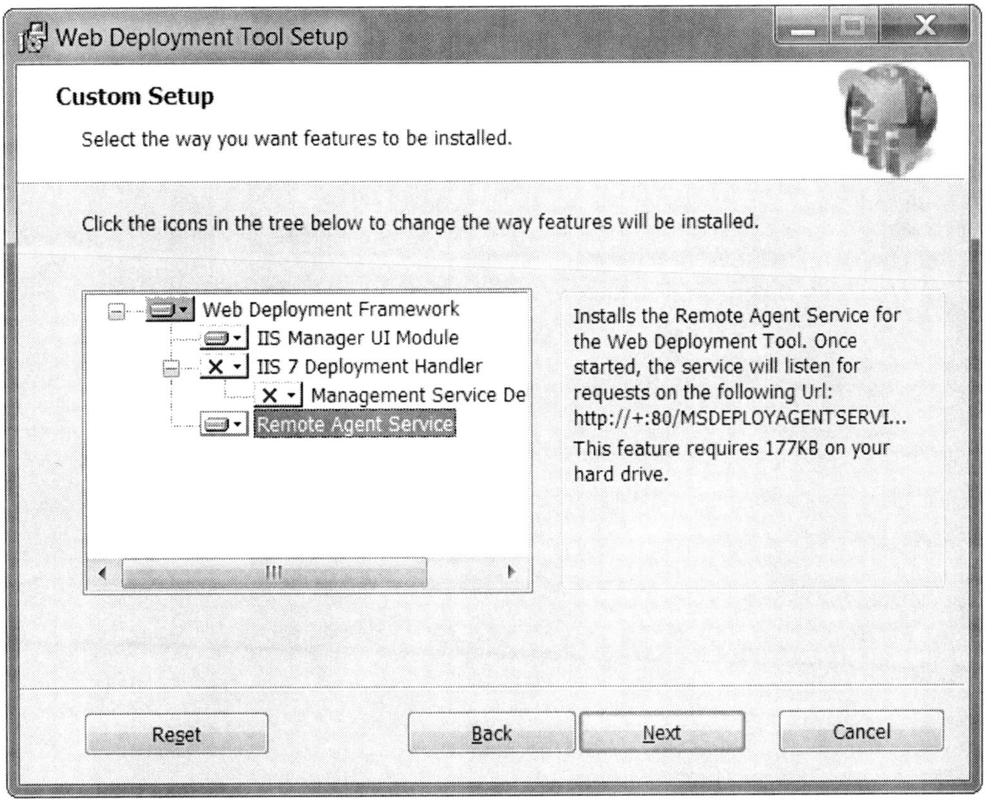

Figure 12-5. Installing Remote Agent Service for Web Deployment Tool

4. Complete the setup wizard.

5. After the wizard completes, start the service by typing the **net start msdepsvc** command into a command window, like this:

```
C:\>net start msdepsvc
The Web Deployment Agent service is starting.
The Web Deployment Agent service was started successfully.
```

6. If you want the service start automatically every time Windows starts, type the command shown in this example:

```
C:\>sc config msdepsvc start= auto
[SC] ChangeServiceConfig SUCCESS
```

Now that you've installed the Remote Agent Service—and assuming you have the proper administrative privileges—you can start making your application or site configuration changes to one of the computers in your farm.

View Your AppFabric Hosted Application Dependencies

This section will show you how to call **getDependencies**, how to analyze and verify the output, and how to determine the actions to take based on the output. All servers and sites differ, so your output will look different, depending on what you have installed and configured.

In this next step, you obtain the dependencies of the Contoso Insurance sample application that you hosted in AppFabric, and then compile the list of all components needed on all other servers. You should start by getting the dependencies of the Contoso.Claims.Services web site; you can do so by running the following command:

```
msdeploy -verb:getDependencies
-source:apphostconfig="Contoso.Claims.Services"
```

■ **Note** If your site inherits any script maps, you will not see these listed in the dependencies; instead, you should review the script maps for your site manually.

The listing that follows illustrates the sample dependencies output for an application with various dependency types:

```
<dependencyInfo>
   <dependencies>
      <dependency name="AnonymousAuthentication">
         <trigger absolutePath="/lm/w3svc/1/ROOT/AuthFlags" />
      </dependency>
```

```
        <dependency name="WindowsAuthentication">
            <trigger absolutePath="/lm/w3svc/1/ROOT/AuthFlags" />
        </dependency>
        <dependency name="ServerSideIncludeDisabled">
            <trigger absolutePath="systemInfo scriptmaps" />
        </dependency>
    </dependencies>
    <apppoolsInUse>
        <apppoolInUse name="DefaultAppPool" definitionIncluded="False">
            <trigger absolutePath="/lm/w3svc/1/AppPoolId" />
            <trigger absolutePath="/lm/w3svc/1/ROOT/AppPoolId" />
        </apppoolInUse>
        <apppoolInUse name="MSSharePointAppPool" definitionIncluded="False">
            <trigger absolutePath="/lm/w3svc/1/ROOT/_vti_bin/AppPoolId" />
        </apppoolInUse>
    </apppoolsInUse>
    <isapis>
        <isapi dll="C:\WINDOWS\system32\inetsrv\httpodbc.dll" enabled="False">
            <trigger absolutePath="systemInfo scriptmaps" />
        </isapi>
    </isapis>
</dependencyInfo>
```

The **<dependencies>** section contains built-in IIS components that are identified as *in use*. The **<trigger>** elements identify the locations where the dependencies were detected. The sample output shows that Anonymous authentication and Windows authentication are being used, while server-side includes (SSI) are disabled.

The **<apppoolsInUse>** section identifies the application pools that the site is using. A separate **<apppoolInUse>** element appears for each application pool. For the default application pool, the **definitionIncluded="False"** attribute indicates that the application pool will not be included in the synchronization.

If a **<cgis>** element is present in the dependencies, it will contain the CGI script maps that are on the source computer. The attribute value **Restricted="Unknown"** means that the tool could not check the Web Service Restriction List, and you will have to check it manually.

The **<isapis>** element contains other script maps that are not recognized as built-in IIS components (such as **Fcgiext.dll**, the FastCGI **DLL**). You will also see custom ISAPI or CGI script maps listed here.

After running the **msdeploy** command for your Contoso.Claims.Services site, you should get output showing that this web site has dependency on an application pool named **ContosoAppPool**; this application pool will not be included in the synchronization, so you should create this application pool on all servers manually, as in the following example:

```
C:\>msdeploy -verb:getDependencies
-source:apphostconfig="Contoso.Claims.Services"
<output>
  <dependencyInfo>
    <apppoolsInUse>
      <apppoolInUse name="ContosoAppPool" definitionIncluded="False" />
    <apppoolsInUse>
  </dependencyInfo>
</output>
C:\>
```

Next, you should run the dependencies check for the main web client application, Contoso.Claims.Web, issuing a command similar to the one you used for Contoso WCF and WF Services:

```
msdeploy -verb:getDependencies -source:apphostconfig="Contoso.Claims.Web"
```

The output for the Contoso.Claims.Web web site dependencies is identical to that of Contoso.Claims.Services:

```
C:\>msdeploy -verb:getDependencies -
source:apphostconfig="Contoso.Claims.Web"
<output>
  <dependencyInfo>
    <apppoolsInUse>
      <apppoolInUse name="ContosoAppPool" definitionIncluded="False" />
    <apppoolsInUse>
  </dependencyInfo>
</output>
C:\>
```

Configure the Destination Server

Based on the output from both web sites you're about to synchronize, you should pre-install an application pool: ContosoAppPool. The <apppoolsInUse> section shows that both sites are using the ContosoAppPool application pool. Its definitionIncluded attribute is set to false, so the application pool will not be synchronized.

By default, application pools are not included in site-level synchronization. To include the ContosoAppPool application pool, you can add the following syntax to the msdeploy command shown in the preceding section (you will learn more about the synchronization commands later in this chapter):

```
 -enableLink:AppPoolExtension
).
```

Alternatively, you can synchronize the ContosoAppPool application pool first in a separate operation with this snippet:

```
metakey=lm/w3svc/apppools/ContosoAppPool
```

Alternatively, you can manually create the application pool on the destination server prior to the synchronization.

Sync to the Destination Server

Note that you should always make a backup of the servers' configuration files and server components before you make any changes to your destination and source servers. Even if you are just testing, proper and regularly scheduled backups allow you to restore the state of your servers easily.

Backing up Your Server

To issue the backup command to your AppFabric server, run this command to backup an IIS 7.0 server:

```
%windir%\system32\inetsrv\appcmd add backup "Contoso.PreDeploy"
```

Running the preceding command creates a backup with an auto-generated name that represents the date and time of backup:

```
%windir%\system32\inetsrv\appcmd add backup "Contoso.PreDeploy"
BACKUP object "Contoso.PreDeploy" added
```

Appcmd.exe is the command-line tool for managing IIS 7.0. It exposes all key server management functionality through a set of intuitive management objects that you can manipulate from the command line or from scripts.

Simulating the Synchronization Process

Another recommended prerequisite before starting the synchronization process is to simulate the synchronization and see what would have happened if you had actually run the sync. You do that by specifying the **–whatif** option when executing the command to synchronize. The **whatif** option specifies that you want to run the command without making any changes.

Now run the following commands on the source AppFabric server (you will be pushing the data out) to validate what would happen if you were to run the sync. Output from the **-whatif** option will not show every change; rather, it will show an optimistic view of what might change if everything succeeds:

```
msdeploy -verb:sync -source:apphostconfig="Contoso.Claims.Web"
-dest:apphostconfig="Contoso.Claims.Web",computername
={your destination server name} -whatif > contosowebsync.log

msdeploy -verb:sync -source:apphostconfig="Contoso.Claims.Services"
-dest:apphostconfig="Contoso.Claims.Services",computername
={your destination server name} -whatif > contososervicessync.log
```

■ **Note** A command that appears successful when run with the **whatif** operation setting might fail when you run the command without it because there are errors that the **whatif** operation cannot foresee. For example, write permission errors will not be detected because no data is written during a **whatif** operation. The **whatif** setting shows only what will happen if all operations in the command succeed.

As you learned earlier in the chapter, you can use the Web Management Service (WMSvc) when you're using Basic authentication. To do this, you should add the **WMsvc** provider settings to the **msdeploy** commands you issued earlier:

```
msdeploy -verb:sync -source:apphostconfig="Contoso.Claims.Web",wmsvc
={your source server name},username={username1},password={password1},
```

```
authtype=basic -dest:apphostconfig="Contoso.Claims.Web",
computername={your destination server name},wmsvc
={your destination server name},username={username2},password={password2},
authtype=basic -whatif > contosowebsync.log

msdeploy -verb:sync -source:apphostconfig="Contoso.Claims.Services",wmsvc
={your source server name},username={username1},password={password1},
authtype=basic -dest:apphostconfig="Contoso.Claims.Services",computername
={your destination server name},wmsvc={your destination server name},
username={username2},password={password2},authtype=basic
-whatif > contososervicessync.log
```

If you decide you want to pull data from a remote AppFabric server, you need to run a slightly different command on the destination machine. Specifically, you need to edit the command syntax like this:

```
msdeploy -verb:sync -source:apphostconfig="Contoso.Claims.Web",computername
={your source server name} -dest:apphostconfig="Contoso.Claims.Web"
-whatif > contosowebsync.log
```

Synchronizing for Real

When you are satisfied with the test runs, you can drop the **whatif** flag and run the synchronize commands. Take care that you verify the output from the test runs, then run the same commands again, this time without the **whatif** flag:

```
msdeploy -verb:sync -source:apphostconfig="Contoso.Claims.Web"
-dest:apphostconfig="Contoso.Claims.Web",computername
={your destination server name}  > contosowebsync.log

msdeploy -verb:sync -source:apphostconfig="Contoso.Claims.Services"
-dest:apphostconfig="Contoso.Claims.Services",computername
={your destination server name}  > contososervicessync.log
```

The resulting synchronization commands look like this when you use Basic authentication:

```
msdeploy -verb:sync -source:apphostconfig="Contoso.Claims.Web",wmsvc
={your source server name},username={username1},password={password1},
authtype=basic  -dest:apphostconfig="Contoso.Claims.Web",computername
={your destination server name},wmsvc={your destination server name},
username={username2},password={password2},authtype
=basic > contosowebsync.log

msdeploy -verb:sync -source:apphostconfig="Contoso.Claims.Services",wmsvc
={your source server name},username={username1},password={password1},
authtype=basic -dest:apphostconfig="Contoso.Claims.Services",
computername={your destination server name},wmsvc
={your destination server name},username={username2},password={password2},
authtype=basic > contososervicessync.log
```

You are now done synchronizing the Contoso.Claims.Web and Contoso.Claims.Services sites. You can verify this by browsing to the Contoso.Claims.Web web site on the destination server.

Future Roadmap for AppFabric High Availability

Now imagine yourself implementing a complex business scenario with .NET 4.0 WCF and WF services that you have deployed successfully into a Windows Server AppFabric server farm. Also, imagine that everything has been working well until one day, high business demands for scalability and availability in your organization became so unmanageable in your current production environment that you are compelled to make a swift and effective decision to migrate to ... *something*.

The previous sentence is intentionally incomplete because the scalability and high availability of AppFabric can only go so far. In this section, you will learn what you can do if you need to cross that line and exceed what AppFabric can do. The good news is that you have at least two strong solutions if you find yourself in that position: BizTalk Server and Windows Azure.

BizTalk Server

Microsoft has announced that BizTalk Server will support WF 4.0 with the upcoming release of BizTalk Server 2009 R2 (and beyond); this makes BizTalk a crucial and effective solution to manage large-scale AppFabric deployments.

BizTalk adds durable and reliable messaging, as well as performance and high availability capabilities for mission critical workloads. Like AppFabric, BizTalk Server 2009 R2 runs on .NET 4.0 and is well integrated with familiar developer tools like Visual Studio and Team Foundation Server.

By migrating your AppFabric solutions to BizTalk, you gain many other features, including Enterprise Service Bus, Business Activity Monitoring, dozens of adapters for line-of-business applications, network protocols, mainframe and host systems, and EDI (without VAN costs). You also gain a complete RFID system. These features are some of the reasons why BizTalk Server has become the most popular integration server in the industry.

In addition to adding WF 4.0 to BizTalk, Microsoft is also committed to supporting the investments of many customers who have existing BizTalk deployments, and it will continue to support BizTalk Server's XLANG orchestration technology, along with other artifacts in BizTalk Server.

BizTalk Server provides great flexibility for addressing high availability because you can strategically dedicate logical hosts to run specific areas of functionality, such as receiving messages, sending messages, or processing orchestrations. After you create a logical container (host), you can configure instances of the host to run on physical BizTalk Server computers in the BizTalk Server group. A host instance runs as a Windows Service on the designated BizTalk Server computer(s). To provide high availability for BizTalk hosts, you must have two or more host instances for each host in your multi-server environment. Having more than one host instance for each host helps you ensure that if one host instance becomes unavailable, the other computers that are running instances of that host can resume the functions of the problematic or failed host instance. It also helps you ensure that the overall system can continue performing with minimal disruption. The bottom line is that the added support for WF 4.0 workflow services in BizTalk Server lets you take advantage of the flexible and highly scalable BizTalk environment.

Windows Azure

Relying on a multi-server AppFabric server farm with multiple servers distributed across your physical network or hosted for you by third parties might serve your needs for a given time interval; however, you might reach a point where extending your AppFabric server farm might not provide you with an adequate return on your investments. During the last couple of years, organizations have begun leveraging cloud computing for building and migrating existing applications to add scalability, reduce capital expenditure, and improve reliability.

A cloud-computing platform enables applications to be hosted in an Internet-accessible virtual environment that supplies the necessary hardware, software, network, and storage capacities. Such a platform also provides for security and reliability, removing much of the burden of purchasing and maintaining hardware and software in-house. You can find many vendors that compete with each other in the cloud computing market these days, including Microsoft's Windows Azure platform. The Azure platform offers developers the most familiar development platform in the cloud, which helps you quickly develop, deploy, and manage applications as you have in the past. It also simplifies integrating these services into your on-premise applications. With Azure, You pay only for the time, resources, and capacity you use while scaling up to accommodate your changing business needs.

Microsoft first unveiled its cloud services platform at the Professional Development Conference (PDC) 2008. At PDC 2009, Microsoft announced the release of other core elements of its cloud services platform, such as Windows Azure and SQL Azure. Microsoft also announced beta availability of Windows Server AppFabric, a set of integrated, high-level app services that enable developers to deploy and manage apps spanning both server and cloud. AppFabric technology combines hosting and caching technologies (formerly known by their codenames, *Dublin* and *Velocity*) with the Windows Azure Platform AppFabric Service Bus and AppFabric Access Control (formerly known as .NET Services). You can see the most recent services stack of the Microsoft Windows Azure platform in Figure 12-6.

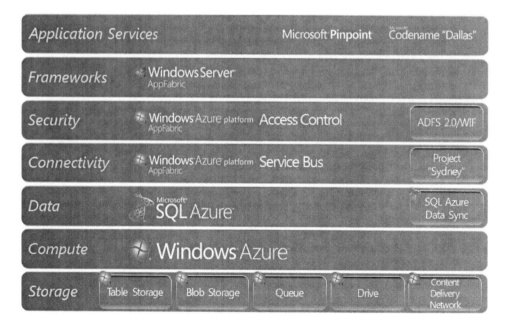

Figure 12-6. The Windows Azure Platform Services Stack

The Windows Azure Platform AppFabric Service Bus makes it possible to integrate your on-premises workflow services with your services running in the cloud. It also lets you integrate with a variety of third-party services provided by Microsoft or other vendors, as well as with a variety of desktop, handheld devices, and web applications that might be running in satellite locations outside of your enterprise firewall. To make this possible, the implementation needs to provide federated solutions based on open Internet standards and a robust messaging fabric capable of bidirectional communication at Internet scope. The Windows Azure Platform AppFabric Service Bus provides a federated identity and access control mechanism (through the Windows Azure Platform AppFabric Access Control Service), a federated naming system, a dynamic service registry, and a robust messaging fabric. The Service Bus's messaging fabric is a central component of the Windows Azure Platform AppFabric's architecture, which is a highly load-balanced relay service that supports a variety of different transport protocols and Web services standards, including SOAP, WS-*, and REST. This combination makes it possible for any SOAP or REST-capable programming environment to integrate with these Azure services.

As these new technologies mature over time, developers will be able to design and implement scalable and highly available AppFabric environments by combining both on-premises Windows Server AppFabric hosting and hosting in the clouds. You will also be able to leverage the Azure AppFabric Service Bus and the Azure AppFabric Access Control (for authentication). You can use Windows Azure's flexible and interoperable platform to build new applications to run from the cloud or enhance existing applications with cloud-based capabilities. Its open architecture lets developers build web applications, workflow services running on Windows Server AppFabric servers, or hybrid solutions that feature the best of online and on-premises approaches.

Now let's get back to the scenario described in the beginning of this section. If you were to decide to take the cloud-computing path, you could migrate your AppFabric server farm to the clouds. Combining several clicks in your Visual Studio development environment with a few more configuration and UI settings in your Windows Azure AppFabric virtual environment enables you to deploy your existing AppFabric server farm to the cloud by leveraging Windows Azure AppFabric Service Bus and AppFabric Access Control Services. And you won't spend any time writing or modifying lines of code to accommodate this scenario. The only caveat you need to be aware of is that Windows Azure, as of early 2010, does not support WF 4.0; however, Microsoft has stated it will be adding that functionality to the platform in the future.

Adopting this approach means you would not have to worry about authentication while modeling; you would also be able deploy the same application in staging and production that you run in your on-premises environment. You would also effectively increase your server farm's scalability and high availability without any capital expenditures and additional operational cost. But the greatest value of hosting your application in the cloud is that it allows your developers (and IT department generally) to focus on the business requirements of your application, rather than on what hardware and software updates and patches you need to install to keep your production environment up and running.

Summary

This chapter illustrated various deployment scenarios that can help you achieve high availability and scalability in your AppFabric applications and services. You learned how to synchronize a Contoso web application from a source AppFabric server to a destination AppFabric server; you also learned how to view the dependencies, configure the destination server, and perform the synchronization between servers in a server farm.

You also examined your options for a high availability strategy using AppFabric. This chapter outlined the steps required to build highly available hybrid online and on-premises solutions based on BizTalk Server, Windows Server, and Azure AppFabric technologies.

It was not the goal of this chapter to give you prescriptive guidance on which high availability strategy you should elect for your business or organization, especially when a potential solution involves the hot topic of cloud computing. However, you should be aware that BizTalk Server is a key component of Microsoft's Software plus Services (S+S) initiative. Cloud computing is ideal for certain workloads, but Microsoft knows that most organizations are not going to run their IT functions 100% in the cloud. This is especially true for proprietary processes that touch the core competency of a given business.

The reality is that many applications and services will remain on-premises, and some will move to the cloud. What developers need now is an intelligent hybrid solution that gives them choices; it is in this vein that S+S is an extension of SaaS. You can think of BizTalk Server, with its numerous adapters, Enterprise Service Bus, and Business Activity Monitoring, as an excellent interface and manageability gateway for connecting your on-premises applications with cloud services.

Of course, moving to the cloud requires careful planning. If you begin adopting cloud services without planning, you could end up with a spider web of inbound and outbound cloud traffic that defies governance. So consider using a powerful integration server like BizTalk Server to compose and aggregate on-premises applications with cloud services; that's the power of S+S.

CHAPTER 13

■ ■ ■

Upgrading to AppFabric

So far you have built an AppFabric application and deployed it; however, you might wonder how you take existing .NET applications and upgrade them to AppFabric. You need to keep many things in mind when looking to upgrade your existing applications. AppFabric only hosts applications that are written in .NET 4, so this chapter will focus this chapter on upgrading and migrating to .NET 4.0. The one area where this is not the case centers on AppFabric's caching capabilities. AppFabric's caching capabilities can host and deal with .NET components created with previous versions of the framework, but the rest of the hosting functionality uses .NET 4.

One of the more significant benefits of .NET 4 is that Windows Workflow is designed so that WF 3.X and WF 4 can run side-by-side. The assemblies for both versions of WF are in different namespaces (WF 3.X in System.Workflow and WF 4 in System.Activities), both of which are included in .NET 4. This allows you to install only the .NET 4 Framework and still have the functionality of WF 3.X. You also have the ability to take your .NET 3.X workflows and edit them in Visual Studio 2010.

The reason that both versions of the namespaces are included is that WF 4 is a breaking change from WF 3.X. If you want to utilize WF 3.X artifacts in WF 4, then you will need to utilize the Interop activity. The Interop activity allows you to execute a WF 3.X workflow or activity from within a WF 4 workflow. This activity surfaces the properties as arguments to provide a consistent model with the rest of WF 4.

The idea of using the Interop activity might be intriguing, but it is only an intermediate solution because applications that you want to host in AppFabric should be upgraded to .NET 4. As part of this upgrade, you can find many best practices that have been identified to make the process easier.

Workflows

When you look at your existing application, you should identify areas where you use the CodeActivity. There is no equivalent to the CodeActivity in .NET 4, and code contained in this activity should be identified as code that should be placed in a WF 4 custom activity.

The next area to identify in your existing workflows is the use of *code beside* for event handlers for activity events, which include the InitializeTimeoutDuration or the DelayActivity events. WF4 doesn't have code beside, so you either need to handle all custom logic in custom activities or create custom activities that utilize activity delegates to handle these events.

Finally, you need to identify areas where you have used ActivityBind to bind a property from an activity to the property of another activity. This model has changed in WF 4, where you should create variables, which are now part of the activity model, and bind these variables to the input or output arguments.

Activities

You will need to rewrite custom activities in .NET 4 because it includes a new base class for custom activities. If your code overrides the `Activity.Initialize` or the `Activity.Uninitialize` methods, you will need to change it because .NET 4 no longer contains the initialization and uninitialization phases.

Next, you need to identify areas where you utilized custom events that were handled in code beside. The lack of code beside in WF4 means that you need to utilize activity delegates to handle events to interact with activities.

Workflow Host

You need to keep several differences in mind when dealing with the changes in Workflow Hosting. In WF 3, hosting was provided through the WorkflowServiceHost when hosting workflows or through the WorkflowRuntime when hosting .NET components. In WF 4, you can accomplish the hosting through any of four different host containers: WorkflowInvoker, WorkflowApplication, WorkflowServiceHost, and WorkflowInstance. You should use WorkflowInvoker for short-running workflows where you won't need persistence. You should use WorkflowApplication for cases where you only need to host a single instance. You should use WorkflowServiceHost when you need to hose multiple instances or for workflows that are not exposed as services. This host also provides integration with AppFabric and can utilize the deployment, configuration, management, and monitoring—all of which you've learned about previously in this book. Finally, you should use WorkflowInstance when you need to create a custom host.

In addition to the hosting types, you can find several other differences in the hosting code that you must take into account. When creating a workflow instance in WF 3, you would provide either a Type or an XmlReader; in WF 4, the workflow definition is an activity object. You also need to keep this fact in mind when using the WF 4 WorkflowApplication host: it hosts a single instance of a workflow. This was not true in WF 3 because WorkflowRuntime was a container of many workflow instances. Finally, WF 3 utilized the `WorkflowInstance.Start` method, while WF 4 uses the `WorkflowApplication.Run` method.

Passing Data

WF 3 let you pass a `Dictionary<string, object>` object where the string represented the name of the property contained on the workflow type. The workflow matched the key name to the property name and set the value contained in the object parameter. WF 4 behaves similarly; however, you must pass an IDictionary<string, object> (note the interface) instead. The string now represents the name of an `InArgument` or an `InOutArgument` on the root activity.

When passing data back from workflows in WF 3, the output values were available from the `WorkflowCompletedEventArgs.WorkflowCompleted` event. In WF 4, these values are available through the `WorkflowApplicationCompletedEventArge.Output` collection. As with the inputs, the outputs match the `OutArguments` or the `InOutArguments` on the root activity.

In addition to passing data, you can also receive and send data through the WF 4 `Receive` and `SendReply` activities. These two activities replace the WF3 `Receive` activity. You also have the ability to receive event information through the `Pick` activity, which replaces WF 3's `Listen` activity. You use the `Pick` activity along with the `EventDriven` activity.

Rules

Rules in WF 4 are not entirely contained in the rules engine. You can find rules capabilities spread throughout different activities in the workflow. If you focus on the capabilities of the rules engine itself, then you won't find an equivalent out-of-the box feature in WF 4. However, .NET 4 contains both the assemblies for WF 3 and WF 4, so you can utilize the capabilities in the WF 3 rules engine. You will encounter several areas where it will make sense to use the rules engine functionality in your new code, and a few areas where it doesn't.

Let's begin by looking at two areas where it doesn't make sense. If you use sequential rules or declarative expressions, then the new activities in WF 4 will cover these. The ability to create sequential rules is provided through the use of the **Sequence** and **If** activities.

The area where you would want to utilize the WF 3 rules engine is when you require forward-chaining functionality. WF 4 contains a **Policy40** custom activity, provided in the SDK, that wraps the WF 3 rules engine. The **Policy40** activity accepts a **TargetObject** in the form of an **InOutArgument** and allows you to specify a RuleSet. The Policy40 activity also includes a re-hosted WF 3 RuleSet editor.

One option in the WF3 rules engine is the ability to select whether you want sequential- or forward-chaining functionality. You learned earlier that it doesn't make sense to use the rules engine for sequential-rule processing, but that was because there is overlap functionality provided by the new technology. You might decide to use the rules engine for sequential processing if you are already using rule sets; or because you have experience doing this in the rules engine, and you find it a more natural design experience.

You need to keep one more item in mind: where the rule definitions are stored. In WF 4, rule definitions are serialized with the policy activity in the XAML, and they are no longer stored in separate **.rules** files. The nice part of this is that you only have one file that contains both the workflow and rules. The downside is that you will not be able to use the ruleset across multiple workflows. If you want to store the rules in a separate file and utilize them across multiple workflows, the recommended approach is to create a custom activity and provide the ability to accept a path to the rules file.

Workflow Types

You can find several out-of-the box workflow types that ship with WF 4, and many of the workflow types and activities are the same as what WF 3 included. However, you will find one workflow type has disappeared, and another has been added. The missing workflow type is the **StateMachine**. The new workflow type is the **Flowchart**. Microsoft received feedback stating that, while the StateMachine workflow was helpful, most of the functionality that it modeled was sequential, with the ability to flow state back to a previous step. Microsoft decided that the **StateMachine** model didn't fit the needs of most of the implementations, and it needed to provide a new model. This new model is the **FlowChart** model. The **FlowChart** model provides the ability to model the paths of execution (arcs) between related activities; it also provides the ability to have multiple arc flows to different activities. This gives developers the simplicity of the sequence model, yet also the flexibility of the **StateMachine**. This also means that the **FlowChart** model, along with the **Pick** activity, should give you similar functionality to what the **StateMachine** model provided previously.

Summary

This chapter discussed many of the changes that you should keep in mind when upgrading your existing WF applications. It described how WF 4 represents a breaking change from WF 3, but also how both versions can run side-by-side.

You also learned about many of the best practices that you should follow throughout your design and development effort. And you learned about replacement/updated objects in WF 4 for workflows, activities, workflow host, passing data, rules, and workflow model types.

Most importantly, you learned that using your WF 3 code in AppFabric requires that you upgrade and migrate your code to WF 4. The best practices found in this chapter should help ensure that you have a smooth migration path, enabling you to take advantage of the new capabilities in AppFabric.

Index

■ E

■ F

■ G

49 99

14+

RECEIVED APR 2 6 2010

Breinigsville, PA USA
08 April 2010

2BV00004B/3/P